9780670233991

THE COMPLETE BOOK
OF KNITTING

Also by Barbara Abbey

101 Ways to Improve Your Knitting

Barbara Abbey

THE COMPLETE BOOK OF KNITTING

A Studio Book

THE VIKING PRESS · New York

*To my husband, without whose patience and encouragement
this book could not have been written.*

Copyright © 1971 by The Viking Press, Inc.
All rights reserved
First published in 1971 by The Viking Press, Inc.
625 Madison Avenue, New York, N.Y. 10022
Published simultaneously in Canada by
The Macmillan Company of Canada Limited
SBN 670-23399-4
Library of Congress catalog card number: 79-168526
Printed in U.S.A.

Acknowledgments

To the uninitiated, knitting often seems a complicated procedure, but once the individual steps are understood and the final results are seen, it all becomes quite easy and well worth the effort. For this reason, illustrations are an important part of any guide to knitting, for they help to show the reader what should be done, and how it should be done, in a way that would otherwise be possible only if the knitter had a teacher sitting beside her, going through each of the motions with needles and yarn in hand as they were being explained. My thanks to Vilma A. Hellstern, of Lake Geneva, Wisconsin, who has patiently sat beside me for many hours working out the beautifully detailed drawings of the procedures explained in this book, and to Virgil Wuttke, also of Lake Geneva, for his excellent photographs of the finished examples of Pattern Stitches and Ribbon Knitting.

I am also indebted to the following for their kind help in providing me with the materials used in preparation of the actual knitted swatches shown in the photographs: to the Bucilla Yarn Company for yarns; to C. J. Bates & Son, Incorporated, for knitting equipment and for photographs used in the Equipment section; to Reynolds Yarns, Inc., for ribbons, and to Elizabeth Zimmerman of Babcock, Wisconsin, for steel needles.

Contents

INTRODUCTION	13
1. EQUIPMENT	15
CHOOSING YOUR NEEDLES	15
nickel-plated (steel) / aluminum (aluminum alloy) / plastic / wood / bone	
TYPES AND SIZES OF NEEDLES FOR SPECIAL USES	18
Single-pointed or Straight Needles: steel / aluminum / plastic / wood	
Double-pointed Needles: steel / aluminum / plastic / wood	
Circular Needles: circular steel needles / Jumper needles / choosing a circular needle	
CROCHET HOOKS	22
Materials and Sizes: nickel-plated metal / bone / plastic and aluminum / wood	
GIANT OR JIFFY KNITTING	23
needles / crochet hooks	
EXTRA EQUIPMENT	24
stitch holders / knitting counters / ring markers / point protectors / tape measures / gauge counters / rulers / needles for sewing / yarn bobbins / cable stitch holders / scissors / case to hold small items / notebooks / graph paper / gauge cards / nail file and emery board / knitting bags	
CARE OF EQUIPMENT	29

2. KNITTING YARNS   31
Wool Yarns   31
Hair Yarns   32
mohair / cashmere / alpaca / vicuña / angora
Manufacture: the History, Structure, and Processes of Making Worsted and Woolen Yarns   34
Choosing Yarns: Selecting the Correct Type for the Article to be Made   37
Weights and Thicknesses (two-ply two-fold / three-ply three-fold / four-ply)
Very Light-Weight Yarns
Medium-Weight Yarns
Sports-Weight Yarns
Heavy-Weight Yarns: four-ply worsted and Germantown
Super-Weight or Bulky Yarns
Mohair Yarn
Man-Made Fibers: Rayon, Nylon, Orlon, Dacron   41
Summary   42

3. ABBREVIATIONS AND TERMS   45
United States   46
British   47
French   47
German   50
Spanish   52
Swedish   52

4. BASIC KNITTING PROCEDURES   54
Casting On: Methods and Uses   55
I through V with one needle: simple / less simple / using one needle and two lengths of yarn / using one needle and two lengths of yarn — the German or Continental method / English method
VI and VII with two needles
VIII with three needles or a circular needle
Knitting and Purling   59
"English" method / "German" or "Continental" method
Left-Handed Knitting   61
Uneven Knitting   62

Variations: How to Use Knitting and Purling to Form Patterns 62
cross knit (Italian or Twist stitch) / cross purl / plaited Stockinette Stitch / combined cross and plain / double throw / knitting a loop from below

Binding Off 64
plain bind-off, Knit Side / plain bind-off, Purl Side / ribbing bind-off / crocheted bind-off / pattern stitch bind-off / binding off two pieces together / miscellaneous notes / binding off in lace patterns

Decreasing 67
Knit Decreases:
knit two together (K2tog) / slip, knit, and pass (Sl 1, K 1, and psso—or SKP) / knit two together from the back (K2togb) / knit three together (K3tog) / knit three together from the back (K3togb) / right-cross double decrease / left-cross double decrease / slip, knit two together, and pass (SK2togP) / double slip decrease (Sl 1, K 1, pnso)

Purl Decreases:
purl two together (P2tog) / purl two together from the back (P2togb) / purl three together (P3tog) / taking a large number of sts together / double slip decrease, purled (P2tog pnso)

Increasing 71
Knit Increases:
plain yarn-over / yarn-over when changing from knit to purl / yarn-over before working the first stitch: knit; purl / reverse yarn-over / yarn-over, cross right / yarn-over, cross left / plain increase / knit and purl the same stitch / lifted increase, right (M1R) / lifted increase, left (M1L) / invisible increase, right / invisible increase, left

Purled Increases:
plain yarn-over / yarn-over when changing from purl to knit / reverse yarn-over when changing from purl to purl / reverse yarn-over when changing from purl to knit / yarn-over, cross right / yarn-over, cross left / plain increase / invisible increase, left / invisible increase, right / lifted increase, right (M1P) / lifted increase, left (M1P)

Miscellaneous Increases:
pick up one stitch / KP—PK—KPK—and variations

Cross-Over Stitches: Cables 79
cross-over on two stitches, right—knit / cross-over on two stitches, left—knit / cross-over on two stitches, right—purl / cross-over on two stitches, left—purl / cross through two stitches, right / cross through two stitches, left

Multiple Stitch Cross-Overs 80
cable cross, right / cable cross, left / making a rib cable / cable braid / double cable / right and left (braid cable) / crossing on an uneven number of stitches / crossing on three stitches, cross right, cross left

MISCELLANEOUS MULTIPLE STITCHES   85
    tie stitch / knot stitch / tuft stitch / bowknot or butterfly stitch / rosebud / popcorn or bubble stitch / leaf stitch

SLIPPED STITCHES   87
PICKING UP STITCHES   88
KNITTED HEMS   89
    Alternate Method I / Alternate Method II

GRAFTING   90
    grafting from two needles (Kitchener Stitch) / garter stitch grafting / horizontal grafting / vertical grafting

TURNING AND SHAPING   92
KNITTING WITH MORE THAN ONE COLOR: ARGYLE, FAIR ISLE, AND SCANDINAVIAN KNITTING   93
PICKING UP STITCHES FROM WOVEN MATERIAL   96
DUPLICATE STITCHING   96
DETERMINING YOUR GAUGE   99
KNITTING WITH RIBBONS   102
    fourteen ways of forming ribbon stitches / knitting with silk organdy ribbon

CROCHETED FINISHES   111
    chain stitch (ch) / slip stitch (sl st) / single crochet (sc) / crocheted buttonhole band / double crochet (dc) / waistband

5. TAKING CORRECT MEASUREMENTS   115
    "average" knitting measurements / how to take measurements / how to use these measurements

6. ASSEMBLING AND FINISHING   119

SWEATERS   119
FRONT BORDERS FOR CARDIGANS   120
    knitted ribbing, vertical / knitted ribbing, horizontal / crocheted borders

INSERTING ZIPPERS   122
DRY BLOCKING   123
    dry blocking a sweater / dry blocking a skirt

WET BLOCKING: MAKING A BLOCKING SCREEN   125
TAILORED FINISHING   126
LININGS AND LINING MATERIALS: HOW TO MAKE LININGS FOR JACKETS, COATS, DRESSES, SWEATERS, BLOUSES, SKIRTS   127

7. KNITTING STITCH PATTERNS: HOW TO SELECT AND USE THEM   *131*

8. 200 PATTERN STITCHES: ILLUSTRATIONS AND INSTRUCTIONS   *138*
    LIST OF PATTERN STITCHES   *138*
    REVERSIBLE STITCHES I   *141*
    REVERSIBLE STITCHES II   *150*
    RIBBING STITCHES   *159*
    FABRIC STITCHES   *170*
    NON-REVERSIBLE STITCHES   *198*
    "SMALL" STITCHES   *205*
    CABLE STITCHES   *211*
    LACE STITCHES   *219*

9. INDEX   *231*

Introduction

More than anything else, I would wish this book to be one of *interpretation*, a key to better knitting. I have made no attempt to tell the knitter what to make or how to make specific garments or articles. Every knitting magazine, periodical, or manual, each month and year, gives such designs and instructions. This book is more akin to a knitting thesaurus or dictionary, a permanent guide and reference, if you will, rather than a book of current fashions. It has been written to inform the knitter about the various techniques used in knitting, offering as wide a choice as possible of ways to perform all the twists and turns used in the making of stitches and stitch patterns. The explanations of basic knitting procedures, of methods of taking measurements, and of assembling and finishing should become the knitter's constant companion, a source of help and advice that will enable the knitter to work more speedily and easily, with greater confidence, obtaining better results, no matter what project may be undertaken. The characteristics of a wide choice of materials are described in the chapter on Knitting Yarns, to help in choosing the correct one for the item to be made. The instructions for Pattern Stitches also indicate, wherever practical, the most suitable yarns for the many patterns pictured and described.

Pattern Stitches have been informally grouped in separate categories for convenience, although the elements of one frequently intermingle with those of another, and they can be combined and used in so many different ways. Just looking at the pictures will tell you as much about the possibilities of a particular pattern as the text— the instructions tell you how to make your knitting look like the photographs, but the photographs themselves will suggest the uses to which these patterns can or should be put.

Helpful cross references relate the Basic Knitting Procedures to the Pattern Stitches in which they are used. I earnestly hope that you will master all the Basic Procedures so that when the need arises you will be fully prepared to use the correct method for the stitch you have chosen. Too many of us tend to use the one-and-only cast-on, bind-off, and stitch-making methods we were first taught, or the ways of knit-

← *Photograph: Charles Holme*

ting we figured out for ourselves by consulting a "know-how" book. I have often stressed, and will always continue to do so, that there is no *right* or *wrong* way to knit. There is only a right or wrong *result*. I have heard of a paraplegic who knits with his toes, with astonishing success.

Throughout the book many words are capitalized and italicized. The reader will find that many words and phrases are frequently repeated. This emphasis and re-emphasis is deliberate, the repetition intentional, and is there for only one reason: Developing good knitting habits and knowledge at the start results in easier performance and a better product, and there is nothing in the world that can take the place of accomplishment, of pride in a job well done!

1. Equipment

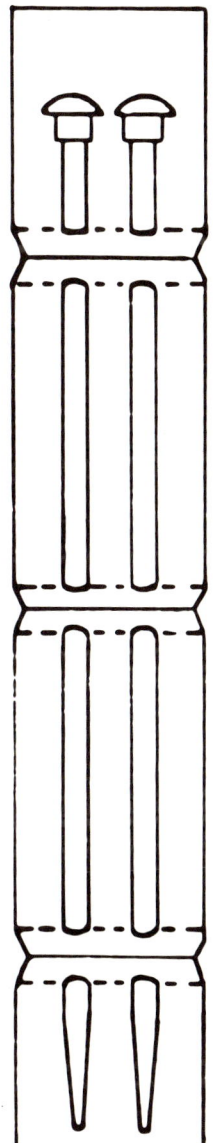

CHOOSING YOUR NEEDLES

For ease and speed in knitting, needles should be chosen carefully, with special attention being given to the task they will perform and the article to be made. Some knitters prefer to use a long needle, no matter how few stitches are to be worked; others just can't manage to knit with any but the shorter lengths. The customary procedure, however, is to choose a length of needle suitable to the article to be made, bearing in mind the total number of stitches it will have to accommodate.

It is unfortunate that there is no strict adherence by *all* manufacturers and production sources to an accurate *standard* measurement of gauge of knitting needles and crochet hooks. The leading name brands, however, hew closely to the same line, and it is wise to ask for them by name.

As the size of the needle or hook is simply a means to an end, it is important only that the proper *gauge* of the stitch (st) or stitches (sts) is achieved, and the exact size of the needle or hook is therefore relatively unimportant (see page 99 on Determining Your Gauge).

The selection of the number size—i.e., the diametric size—depends entirely upon the stitch gauge which must be attained. It must be understood, of course, that the smaller the needle, the finer and tighter the knitting. It follows naturally that the larger the needle, the coarser and looser the work will be.

In many instances more than one size of needle is called for in the same garment in order to achieve more than one size of gauge. For example, the ribbing at the bottom of a sweater or sleeve is usually a tighter stitch (smaller gauge) than the body of the sweater or sleeve. This tighter portion could, of course, be worked on the same needle which is used for the body of the sweater, using fewer stitches to attain the correct measurement and abruptly increasing the number of stitches when the ribbing is completed. The final result, however, is better when a smaller-size needle is used in these and similar instances.

The point or tip of the needle, which is the working end, should be well tapered to allow the needle to slip easily into the stitch and draw the stitch back onto the shaft, but the tip must not be sharp. It should be slightly rounded at the very point, but not so rounded that it will split the yarn or thread of the stitch when inserted. It should be evenly and gradually tapered back to the shaft to insure the uniform delivery and size of each loop in the entire piece of work. The shaft as well as the tip should be very smooth, with no nicks or slivers (in the case of wooden needles).

Needles are listed here according to the materials they are made of, not by any system of historical significance or preference.

NICKEL-PLATED *(Steel)*

So-called steel needles nowadays are difficult to obtain, as knitted laces are considered old-fashioned (temporarily, we hope), with no proper place in the modern scheme of living. An art as beautiful as knitted lacemaking, however, will never be totally neglected, and there is a steadily increasing number of enthusiasts whose requirements must be met. A few decades ago, when knitting for the men in the Armed Services and the vogue for knitted dresses and other garments pushed knitted lacemaking into the background, the demand for steel needles became so slight that manufacture of them was curtailed almost to the vanishing point, and they are now stocked by very few shops.

As a general rule, the really fine gauges of steel needles are not stocked at all in even the best-equipped needlework departments. The reason for this lack of supply is only lack of *demand* on the part of the customer, and this, in turn, is brought about by the extremely small number of patterns for knitted laces available in books and leaflets. It must be stressed, however, that these patterns would be furnished by the thread manufacturers to the general public if enough interested people were to express their desire for them emphatically enough to warrant the expense of printing and distribution. Obviously, where there is enough *demand*, the *supply* is sure to follow.

Because of their shiny hard nickel plating, steel needles are very slippery when used and are too heavy to be used regularly in any but the smallest sizes. Other materials have successfully supplanted steel in all sizes from #0 and larger gauges, and these materials are much easier to use for general knitting. There is no substitute for steel, however, in the smallest sizes. It is rigid enough to keep its shape and flexible enough to be used in making very fine thread stitches.

ALUMINUM *(Aluminum Alloy)*

Aluminum is one of the lightest-weight metals in common use for needles today, but without the addition of certain other metals (therefore making it an aluminum alloy) it would be too soft, without the property of elasticity, too easily bent out of shape. When choosing a needle of this material, flex it slightly to determine its ability to return immediately to its proper straight line. Aluminum needles are made in a number of attractive colors which are applied in various ways as a coating or plating. These colors are important, as it is desirable to have needles in a contrasting color to that of the yarn being used.

Make certain that the color or the metal itself will not rub off onto the yarn, causing discoloration. This may wash out of the finished article in some instances, but the stain could prove to be permanent.

PLASTIC

Different companies make varying grades and types of plastic needles, merchandising them under their own trade names. These needles, too, are made in colors.

Choose any plastic needle carefully, keeping in mind that the smaller sizes will of necessity be quite flexible and, when cold, will break easily. When plastic needles have been exposed to cold temperatures, take care that they are sufficiently warmed to room temperature before you use them.

WOOD

This was probably the first kind of material used in the making of knitting needles: small straight sticks peeled, polished, and fined down by hand to form a point. Nowadays, however, wooden needles are made by exacting machine methods from well-cured hardwoods, carefully pointed and polished to prevent roughness. As newer and better materials have replaced wood for needles in smaller sizes, it is now used for the larger sizes only.

Test any wooden needle before purchase for smoothness, examining especially carefully the tapering of the point for any defect.

BONE

Bone needles have not been manufactured in this country for more than fifty years. Bone was probably the best material used until the development of plastics with similar and, in some cases, better characteristics. If you have a set of genuine bone needles, they should be cherished; they could well be a collector's item.

TYPES AND SIZES OF NEEDLES FOR SPECIAL USES

SINGLE-POINTED or STRAIGHT NEEDLES

So designated because they have only one tapered point, with a permanently attached head at the opposite end.

STEEL

English needles, running from size 16, the smallest, to size 9, the largest. All the larger sizes are made in aluminum or plastic.

The American sizes run from size 0000, the smallest, to size 0, the largest.

ALUMINUM

#0 through #15 in 10″ length.
Uses: Two-needle socks, gloves, and mittens, or any small pieces for working with heavy yarns.
#0 through #15 in 14″ lengths.
Uses: Any two-needle work holding up to 30″ of stitches.
#5 through #15 Jumper needles.
Uses: Any two-needle work holding up to 52″ of sts.

PLASTIC *(Not made in #0 size — see Plastic on page 17.)*

#1 through #15 in 10″ and 14″ lengths.
Uses: Same as similar sizes in aluminum. The larger sizes are excellent for ribbon knitting.

WOOD

Sizes 7, 9, 11, 13, 14, and 15 in 14″ length.
Uses: Articles and garments in loose lacy stitches of lightweight materials or heavy yarns; ribbon knitting.

DOUBLE-POINTED NEEDLES

So designated because both ends are tapered to a point. They are sold in sets of four except in the case of steel or real bone needles. These may come in sets of five in some cases, but mostly in sets of four.

STEEL

American sizes 0 — 00 — 000 — 0000.

English or European sizes 13, 14, 15, and 16 — 9″ lengths and, if you can get them, on up to size 21, the very finest needle obtainable anywhere.

ALUMINUM

#0 through #8 in 7" length.
> *Uses:* Any small round-and-round knitting, such as socks, stockings, gloves, sleeves.

#0 through #8 in 10" length.
> *Uses:* Same as 7" length, but especially good for round or V-neck finishes.

PLASTIC

#1 through #8 in 7" length.
> *Uses:* Same as similar sizes in aluminum.

#1 through #15 in 10" length.
> *Uses:* Same as similar sizes in aluminum. These are also used in sets of eight or more for larger-size garments, but mostly in foreign countries. With the advent of the circular needle, this practice has generally been discarded.

WOOD

Double-pointed wooden needles are not manufactured in this country, but they have been made and used extensively in European countries for centuries. They have been gradually supplanted, however, by plastic and aluminum needles.

CIRCULAR NEEDLES

#0 through #10½ in 11" length.
#0 through #10½ in 16" length.
#0 through #10½ in 24" length.
#0 through #15 in 29" length.
#0 through #15 in 36" length.

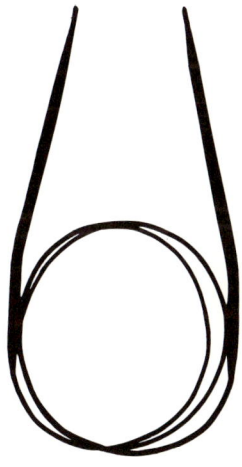

CIRCULAR STEEL NEEDLES

Sizes 15, 14, and 13 (or 2mm) in 16", 20", and 48" lengths.

Circular needles have been designed and manufactured comparatively recently and are used in place of a number of double-pointed needles for fashioning the tubular or round-and-round knitting required for skirts, sweaters, large centerpieces or doilies. There are recorded instances, in fifteenth- and sixteenth-century instructions, where sixteen or more double-pointed needles were called for in the making of a petticoat! They were still used in this manner through the first few years of the twentieth century.

When plastics were introduced, experiments were successfully carried out with the shaping and drawing of this material into a hooplike pattern, retaining a sufficient amount of rigidity to keep its shape. It had definite drawbacks as a circular needle, however; breakage was high and there was not enough flexibility in the needle to allow rolling up the work in the knitting bag when the worker was ready to lay it aside. After much trial and error to improve design and construction, the metal cable finally came into general use for the connecting portion of the circular needle, with nickel-plated metal for the tips or working points. This, again, was not considered to be entirely satisfactory as the constant movement of the knitting manipulation set up a condition of metal fatigue in the cable threads. This caused breakage of the wire strands at the juncture of cable and point, interrupting the knitting until the needle could be replaced. However, nylon has proved to be highly satisfactory for the connecting flexible portion, with tips or points made of various materials, nickel-plated metal and aluminum predominating. In the largest sizes the entire needle is made of nylon and breakage is almost impossible.

JUMPER NEEDLES

With the advent of bulky knits, Jumper needles have acquired a decidedly important place in knitting equipment. They employ the principles of the circular needle but are actually straight single-point knitting needles with a firm portion for stitch forming and a super-flexible nylon shaft which allows the weight of the work to lie in the lap. Jumper needles are used in pairs, each with a point at one end and a cap at the other to keep the stitches from falling off. If ordinary straight needles were required to accommodate the same number of stitches of bulky yarn, they would have to be made in much longer lengths than those in ordinary use, and this might be very clumsy indeed, especially if your favorite knitting place is a wing chair or an armchair or some other confined area such as a bus or car seat. These flexible needles can also be more easily stored in a knitting bag than long straight needles.

Jumper needles are 18″ long and come in sizes 4 through 15.

CHOOSING A CIRCULAR NEEDLE

When selecting a circular needle, consider the circumference of the article to be worked and judge the number of stitches the needle will be required to hold. If there are few stitches in your piece of work, the points will not meet properly if your needle is too long. For instance, if you are working to a gauge of 8 stitches to the inch and you have only 200 stitches, your needle points will not meet if the length of the needle is 24″ or over; 200 divided by 8 is 25, so your needle must not exceed 16″ in length. You would have to overlap the points of the needle to bring the ends of the knitted row together, an obviously impossible situation. On the other hand, if your article requires a great number of stitches, any needle shorter than 24″ or 29″ will prove very awkward because the work will bunch up.

The 11″ and 16″ lengths have recently been used very successfully in lacework, because these will easily accommodate a large number of fine thread stitches. Recently a very large (92″ × 120″) dinner cloth was shown at a needlecraft exhibition. It was made on *eight* 29" circular needles!

As mentioned previously, steel needles are rigid and slippery, even in the smallest sizes to some extent, and the fine threads used in lacework, because they are mercerized and tightly twisted, have no clinging quality. Therefore, it is difficult to retain a large number of stitches on double-pointed needles; they are apt to slip off the ends. Anyone who has experienced this in lacework knows the tragedy of ripping back many rows or rounds and hundreds of stitches to regain the pattern. Of course, the small center rounds, at the beginning of the centerpiece or doily, *must* be started on double-pointed needles. No circular needle is short enough for this part of the work.

The 16" length of circular needle is also convenient when the finishing of a garment necessitates a round-and-round portion of knitting with too many stitches involved for double-pointed needles to hold them comfortably. This needle is invaluable for finishing a V neck or a deep U neckline, and it is absolutely necessary for making a deep round yoke. If the stitches are picked up on straight needles and worked back and forth, a seam must be made, which, no matter how it is done, never has the professional, finished look for which every conscientious needleworker strives.

The 11" circular needle is the shortest length made and may be hard to find. The demand for it is slight because the small circumference makes it awkward to use. It brings the hands close together without enough bulk of yarn for a firm grasp. Some knitters, however, prefer working on a circular needle whenever possible to using double-pointed needles and choose the 11" circular needle whenever the number of stitches permits its use (providing, of course, such a needle can be found).

A circular needle is especially valuable when more than one color is to be worked in horizontal stripes, and particularly when an odd number of rows is involved. When using two needles, the procedure would necessarily mean that the stitches in the second color would have to be slipped back onto a third needle in order to pick up the thread of the first color at the opposite end of the row. On a circular needle the work is simply pushed to the other end and the next row worked with no time lost.

It must be pointed out, too, that any back-and-forth knitting can be done on a circular needle. It is unexcelled for making a skirt which is to be fastened at the side or down the front or back, and for any large article which requires holding a great number of stitches, such as a one-piece afghan or blanket.

Raglan-sleeved pullovers are started at the neckline and worked without joined seams, with increases usually made at eight points every second round. It is easily seen that this speedy accumulation of stitches requires a needle long enough and flexible enough to hold them comfortably. The circular needle is virtually indispensable for this use.

Examine any circular needle carefully to be sure that the tip and center portions are smoothly joined. Run the back of your thumbnail lightly over this spot. If you hear a decided click, you can tell that the stitches might catch on this rough spot.

Because of its soft finish, the aluminum-tipped needle is an especially good choice when you are following a pattern stitch that requires close attention. The glare reflected by steel-tipped needles is apt to cause eyestrain in any prolonged knitting operation.

CROCHET HOOKS

Your knitting equipment will not be complete without a fairly extensive assortment of crochet hooks. They are used in many ways, such as joining seams, finishing edges, working a trimming edge, binding off, and they are the ideal implement for picking up dropped stitches. The size of the hook must be determined by the use to which it will be put, and it should be one that will produce a stitch gauge comparable to that of the knitting on which it will be used.

The very smallest sizes, #9 to #15 inclusive, are usually too fine for wool and other yarns, but many laces, made of fine cotton and linen threads and worked on fine needles, require the use of a small-size crochet hook for finishing. Knitted centerpieces or collars are often finished with one or several rows of crocheting.

Select crochet hooks as carefully as you choose knitting needles. If the point of a crochet hook is too sharp, it will split the yarn or thread and also irritate the fingers. However, if it is too blunt, you will find it difficult to insert it in the work.

The hook itself, at the cut, should not be too sharply notched or pointed, as this may prevent the hook from pulling the yarn or thread back through the stitch or edge into which it has been inserted. It should not taper too abruptly back to the spot where it will be held by the thumb and forefinger, as this is apt to cause a loosening of long or retained stitches and the result will be uneven or untidy work.

MATERIALS AND SIZES

NICKEL-PLATED METAL — *the so-called steel hook*
#00, the largest, to #15, the smallest.

Steel hooks also come with a clip at the top end to allow the worker to slip the stitch under it when work is interrupted; thus no time or stitches are lost.

BONE

These are no longer being made in the United States. #1, the smallest, to #6, the largest.

PLASTIC and ALUMINUM

#B/1, the smallest, to #K/10½, the largest.

Besides being numbered, the plastic and aluminum hooks are given a letter designation, the better to distinguish the size as compared to steel hooks which have only a *number* size. In other words, these follow the sizes of knitting needles; for instance, #B/1 is the same as the #1 knitting needle. (Strangely enough, the #7 hook has no letter designation.) A crochet hook that has been matched in size to the knitting needle is unsurpassed when used for picking up a dropped stitch (see page 111).

WOOD

#7 and #9, the smallest, and then in sizes 11, 13, and 15, the largest.

GIANT OR JIFFY KNITTING

A fashion for loosely knit garments made of heavy yarns has brought about the manufacture of knitting needles and crochet hooks in much larger sizes than the traditional ones. The speed with which sweaters and scarves can be knitted or crocheted with these heavy yarns on big needles has made them popular with busy people, and many instruction booklets are devoted entirely to this style of knitting and crocheting. The necessary equipment, once hard to find, is now available everywhere.

NEEDLES

These may be found in various materials and in sizes as follows:
- #17 — ½" diameter, in aluminum and in solid wood.
- #19 — ⅝" diameter, in aluminum.
- #35 — ¾" diameter, in aluminum.
- #50 — 1" diameter, in aluminum and in hollow core wood.
- #Q — ⅝" diameter, in aluminum and in hollow core wood.

CROCHET HOOKS

These are made of hollow plastic in the following sizes:
- #35 — ¾" diameter.
- #50 — 1" diameter.

These needles and hooks are used to make afghans, dresses, sweaters, hats, and tote bags. Several strands of yarn are used together, to form a single strand. Clothing made on such large needles is figured to a *definite size,* and directions must be followed exactly. Changing so much as a single stitch may be disastrous (see page 102).

A newcomer to the market is a combination crochet hook and knitting needle. It is constructed like a double-pointed knitting needle, but with a crochet hook at one end, and it is made of aluminum. It is especially convenient for picking up a large number of stitches which may be hooked up through the work at one end and then either worked off or slipped onto a knitting needle at the other end (see page 89 on Picking Up Stitches). This new tool comes in knitting-needle sizes of 1, 2, and 3.

EXTRA EQUIPMENT

STITCH HOLDERS

Made of small-gauge knitting-needle material, stitch holders are much like safety pins, but have no hampering extra twist at the bend and are closed by a simple catch. They come in various lengths, from the midget size to the largest 10″ size, in steel, plastic, and/or aluminum, and are designed to hold securely stitches that have been set aside. Thread or yarn run through these stitches will secure them but may leave a pronounced line in the knitting. Moreover, stitches can be much more easily worked off a holder than off a thread, sometimes directly, without being transferred to a needle.

KNITTING COUNTERS

These are small, light-weight devices slipped over the point and back to the head of the needle to keep count of the rows. Each type of counter (there are several good types and makes) has a dial arrangement with two sets of numbers which, when reset at the beginning of each row, will record a count of from 1 to 99.

These counters relieve the knitter of the uncertainty of counting rows, especially difficult when a pattern requires several rows for completion. Counting visually the number of rows made when working a cable can be baffling when the work has been put aside for any reason. If the counting device is kept on the needle and set to the number of the row being worked, there is no confusion, and the pattern can be continued without fear of having miscounted.

In some instances it is advisable to use *two* counters, one on each needle. For example, in making an article (a tie, for instance, which is shaped differently on each side and requires increasing or decreasing on varying numbers of rows), one counter is used for one side of shaping and the other for the opposite side.

On a circular needle the counter, of course, cannot be affixed to either end, but it can still be used to advantage, by running a stitch holder through the counter *and* then through the knitted material itself, advancing the numbers as each new round is begun.

RING MARKERS

These are sold in packages or in small plastic boxes containing twenty or more small- or medium-size colored plastic rings. The rings are slipped onto the needle to designate separate sections of work, where patterns begin and end, or where increases and/or decreases are to be made. They are invaluable in making skirts or sweaters where the number of stitches in every round or row would be difficult to determine visually.

King-size markers are also available and usually come twelve to a box.

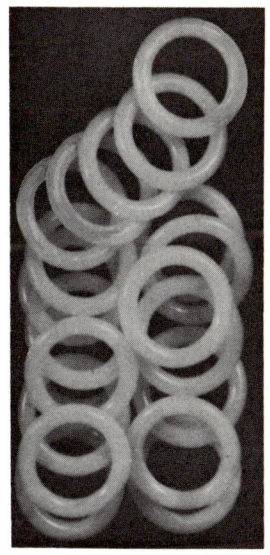

POINT PROTECTORS

Made of rubber and slipped over the points of the needles when the work is not in use, these point protectors guard both the knitting and the knitter. They come in small, medium, and giant sizes.

TAPE MEASURES

A good tape measure is one of the most important knitting accessories and should be chosen carefully. It is unfortunate that some are inaccurately marked to begin with. Others are likely to stretch or shrink because of weather conditions. It is, therefore, no economy to buy an inexpensive one of poor quality.

Paper, cotton, and plastic tape measures are all apt to shrink or stretch. Plastic tape measures in particular shrink in cold weather and stretch in hot weather. If possible, try to find a tape measure made of linen. Do *not* use a carpenter's steel tape. Also, make sure always to use the *same* tape measure during the making of any one garment. This simple precaution is always worthwhile.

GAUGE COUNTERS

An aluminum counter, made especially for the purpose, is helpful in determining gauge. This device has a 6″ measure down one side, a measure device for determining the size of knitting needles (and *some* crochet hooks) down the opposite side, and a 2″ open square in the middle for determining stitch and row gauge. If metal ones are not available, however, you can make a very dependable gauge counter from heavy cardboard or any similar tough but thin material. Cut a 4″ square of cardboard. Then *inside* of this square mark a 2″ square. Cut out this inner square very carefully and mark it off in ¼″ distances all around the four inside edges. Counting the number of rows and stitches to the inch is very much simplified when this handy gadget is laid over a sample swatch of the knitting.

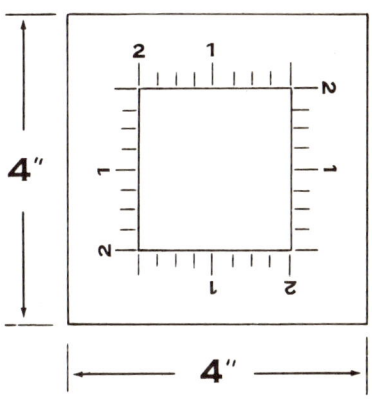

25

RULERS

A flat 6″ ruler, preferably of transparent plastic, is handy for the knitter to have, although not an absolute necessity. It is easier to use than a soft tape measure for measuring short distances on the knitting, and it will keep the work flat.

NEEDLES FOR SEWING

For sewing seams, grafting, weaving two pieces together (see page 91 on Kitchener Stitch) and working Duplicate Stitching (see page 96), a needle with a blunt point, often called a tapestry needle, is best.

If the type of yarn allows it, a more sharply pointed crewel needle should be used for finishing off ends at seams or on the wrong side of the work, and for hemming and finishing where the stitches must not show on the right side. Both types of needles should have a large enough eye to allow the free passage of the yarn.

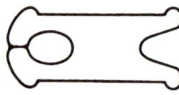

YARN BOBBINS

Many types are available, usually in sets of ten, for multicolor knitting, such as Argyle or Fair Isle patterns. Bobbins in extra-large sizes may be bought separately or in sets of two.

Bear in mind that bobbins should be very light in weight, should hold a considerable amount of yarn without crowding, should not release the yarn too readily, and should be exceptionally smooth at all points, free of projections that might catch into the work or hook the bobbins together.

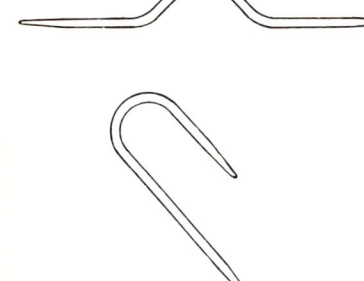

CABLE STITCH HOLDERS

In the knitting of cable patterns (page 211), some stitches must be held on a separate device, while others are worked from the left-hand needle. A crochet hook, toothpick, bobby pin, or some such small article will serve, but these awkward tools can be replaced with much better ones.

There are several types and sizes to choose from. Some are made of #1 knitting-needle material, with a point at either end and a bend in the middle. Another is U-shaped, and is made for the express purpose of holding bulky yarns. Both types hold the reserved stitches out of the way of the work area. (See page 80 on Cabling).

SCISSORS

Scissors are an absolute requisite and are useful in the finishing off of threads. They are most necessary for nylon yarn, which is usually too tough to break with the hands. Scissors should have sharp points and should be kept in a case so that no harm will come to other items in the knitting bag.

CASE TO HOLD SMALL ITEMS

Since small items are easily misplaced or lost, it is wise to keep them all together and readily available in a small box or case. An envelope or box, at least 6½" × 4", with some way of fastening it securely, will do. Keep your tape measure, ruler, gauge counter, scissors, and sewing needles in it. If a case of transparent plastic is used, each item can be easily located.

NOTEBOOKS

The wise and meticulous knitter will find it worth-while to keep a notebook in the knitting bag. Memory is not altogether dependable when there are so many little points that come up during conversations with other knitters. Short cuts, a better method of doing something, a new material to experiment with, tips received at the instruction table or in practice, can be jotted down just as easily as they can be forgotten (or remembered incorrectly) if not put in writing.

A large loose-leaf notebook should be kept at home for permanent records. It can be used as a scrapbook of useful information, tabulated by subject. Only a few items in any of the great number of pattern books on the market have special significance to any one knitter. Instead of saving large stacks of magazines, clip out items of interest and keep them in your record book. Include illustrations of dresses or suits, new necklines, sleeve treatments, or other fashion details that suggest new knitting ideas. You may not use them for some time, or even at all, but they will keep the creative instinct active and lively and may help you design and knit something original.

If a certain stitch pattern appeals to you, work up a swatch (a four-inch square will do nicely) and clip it into the book with the directions. Squares made to the same dimensions may be joined to form a sampler afghan when they have served their purpose as a reference.

GRAPH PAPER

Graph paper is sold under the name of Cross Section Paper in sheets of many different sizes and number of squares to the inch. It is used largely by architects and engineers and at times may be difficult to find in some rural areas. However, almost any office-supply firm in any large city will fill small mail orders. Graph paper comes in 8½" × 11" pads and in sheets up to 17" × 22".

For working out the *shape* of a large article, graph paper is almost indispensible. Each square on the paper represents one single stitch or row, and the outline of the work can be drawn on the paper, square by square. The knitter will then be able to see at a glance the form the piece of knitting under consideration will take. Colored pencils can be used to plot multicolor designs. Each stitch will stand out clearly and the graph will be easy to follow.

Perplexing pattern stitches can be marked on the paper, one stitch to a square, with horizontal lines or x's indicating the Purled stitches and blank spaces the Knit stitches.

It is very simple to work out designs from sketches or illustrations by tracing the outline on the paper and then squaring it off, but BEWARE—consult page 96 on Duplicate Stitching before attempting this procedure.

The graph paper most useful for the knitter is marked in eight or ten squares to the inch, with a slightly lighter line marking each half-inch, as shown in the illustrations. This makes it easy to count numbers of stitches and rows.

GAUGE CARDS

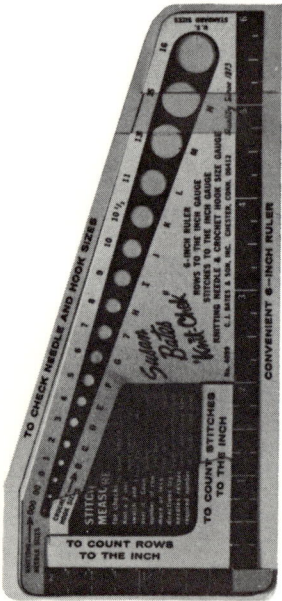

Needle sizes today are usually so plainly indicated that there is very little common use for a gauge card. Sometimes, however, number indications are missing, and the gauge card is then needed to establish the size of unwrapped needles before putting them to work (see page 29 on Care of Equipment).

There are many types of gauge cards. Better ones give both the U.S. Standard and millimeter sizes. The best gauge card is one made of plastic or metal, *not* paper or cardboard, so that the hole will not be enlarged by frequent use. The needle should slip easily through the hole. If it sticks, it is probably a larger size than you thought. Try the next larger hole.

NAIL FILE and EMERY BOARD

Yarn is easily caught by even the slightest fingernail roughness, so keep a nail file and emery board handy with your knitting equipment.

An emery board is also useful to file out any roughness on the tips of plastic or wooden needles or on any other piece of equipment.

KNITTING BAGS

Two major points should be considered when choosing a knitting bag: *size* and *proper shape*. Beautiful materials and attractive styles should *not* be the first concern.

First: The bag should be constructed so that any small items of equipment can easily be found.

Tall standing boxes, round or rectangular, are convenient only while you are working. Standing on the floor, close to your chair, they keep yarn from rolling away and are good receptacles. They are most *inconvenient,* however, when something must be found at the bottom of the box. Everything must be dumped out first. If a container is needed just to keep yarn from rolling around the floor, a round pint or quart food container is just as good or better.

Second: The bag should be small enough for easy carrying but large enough to hold large pieces of knitting—a skirt or raglan sweater, for instance. You should be able to fold it up without damaging the work. The best ones collapse vertically, have a loop or handle, and unfold and sit on the floor on four legs. If small items are carried in a separate envelope, everything is handy and work may be continued immediately after unfolding the bag.

CARE OF EQUIPMENT

Double-pointed needles are usually sold in packages of some sort, slipped through a piece of cardboard or wrapped in a plastic tube. Keep these containers and slip the needles back into them when you are not using them.

Single-pointed needles can be stored by cutting a strip of cardboard a little longer than the needles and folding it in three or four places with the needles run through, and the cardboard marked with the size. This insures easy identification and keeps the needles from being bent. Pairs of straight needles can be held together with rubber bands, but these are apt to disintegrate over a period of time and become sticky and adhere to the needles.

Properly plated steel needles or hooks should not rust. We all favor articles that have given many years of good service, and old steel needles are particularly treasured as family heirlooms. The constant friction of the thread or yarn usually keeps the needles smooth and polished, but if needles do become a little rusty through disuse or improper care, they can be reconditioned with a piece of wool flannel, dipped first in kerosene or machine oil and then in kitchen cleanser, rubbed vigorously over the needle until it is smooth and shiny. Wash the needle, dry it thoroughly, and store it in a long stoppered bottle with a small piece of camphor wrapped in cloth to check further rusting. This same treatment can be applied to steel crochet hooks. A light film may appear but can easily be buffed off with silver polish.

If wooden needles become rough and catchy, dip a slightly dampened cloth in a fine-grain kitchen cleanser and rub the needle with it. Let it dry thoroughly, then rub off all the dry cleanser with a rough cloth and polish the needle by rubbing hard with a thick fold of heavy wax paper.

Circular needles should be loosely rewound and stored flat. These, too, may be put back on their original cards in most instances, or a piece of cardboard can be used.

All needles and hooks can be refurbished for better wear and easier operation with heavy wax paper; plastic needles respond especially well to this treatment. Fold a piece of wax paper several times and crush it. Then rub the whole shaft of the needle vigorously and smooth around the point.

Large collections of knitting needles and crochet hooks may be stored in tubes saved from paper toweling and aluminum foil. Paper-towel tubes are large enough to carry several pairs of 10″ needles and/or crochet hooks. The long tubes for heavy-duty aluminum will carry 14″ needles. When shopping for new projects you seldom know which size of needles you will need. If you have several sizes to choose from, you will be prepared to make a swatch for almost anything. Close the bottom of the tube with paper or staples so that the needles will not slip through. Cover the top with tough plastic and secure it with a rubber band. Record the sizes of all the needles and hooks you own in your notebook, and you will be less likely to collect duplicates.

Photograph: Mary Velthoven

2. Knitting Yarns

WOOL YARNS

Needless to say, all *wool* yarn is sheep's wool. Basically, it serves to keep us warm, but wool also offers a beautiful appearance when it is made into knitted or woven fabrics. It is considered to be the most versatile fiber available and has positive physical properties which have been approached but not entirely successfully reproduced by synthetic means. The warmth, stretch, and durability of wool are unsurpassed, but it is also an insulator *against* heat and sudden changes of temperature. By absorbing moisture quickly, wool helps to avoid dangerous chilling of the body.

To understand better the behavior of wool yarn in hand-knitting, it is important to know a little about the construction of the fiber itself. Many fibers are combined in the yarn we use. Seen under a microscope, each tiny fiber looks like a small straight stick covered with scales which overlap like shingles or tiles on a roof. Just under these scales lies the layer of cortical cells which look like long hairy strands under the microscope and contain small air pockets. These cortical cells provide the insulation and elasticity of the yarn. When yarn is wound too tightly into a ball or worked into some article and then rewound for use, the original elasticity of the yarn is reduced. Any strong chemical action, such as continued absorption of perspiration or use of a strong laundering agent, will also damage the elasticity of the yarn fibers and break down, to some extent, the surface scales and allow these scales to interlock. Shrinkage and matting—called felting—result, especially in socks that have been worn for a long time or subjected to heavy laundering.

Damage is also caused by the use of hot water, continued bending or twisting in the washing machine, or hard hand-rubbing. The scales on the surface of the fibers are loosened and softened so that they catch into one another, matting together to shrink the fabric. The cautions found on boxes of soap flakes and detergents stressing the use of *mild* cleansing agents and *lukewarm, tepid,* or *cold* water, the warnings, "Do Not Rub" and "Do Not Wring," should always be followed.

Manufacturers have recently found a method of treating wool and wool-and-synthetic yarns to make them machine-washable and machine-dryable. The directions on the skeins of yarn must be followed *exactly*. Be sure to read them!

HAIR YARNS

Classified with but different from sheep's wool are the types of hair yarns which must be listed as "Specialty Fibers" and which come from animals other than sheep. Most of these yarns, with the exception of mohair, are quite expensive and are used in relatively small amounts. For the most part, they are softer and more attractive and are spun in lighter weights as well as in the thickest possible yarns. In general, they have decidedly less elasticity than the true wool fibers.

MOHAIR

Mohair, the most frequently used hair yarn, comes from the coats of angora goats. Most of these goats are raised in Texas. Mohair is used to a large extent in the spinning of knitting yarns, either alone or mixed in varying percentages with wool or synthetics. The soft fibers from the mohair kids are used in combination with lamb's wool to make a lustrous yarn. It has a luxurious quality, dyes easily and brilliantly, and retains colors very well. On the labels of hand-knitting yarn, it is designated as "Super-Kid" or "Kid-Mohair."

Most of the so-called Italian and French mohair yarns originate in Texas, but the dyeing and spinning are done in Europe.

CASHMERE

Cashmere yarns are obtained from the cashmere goat, which is found only in Tibet and the northwestern provinces of China. The name of the yarn is derived not from the locality which produces it, but from the place where beautiful cashmere shawls have been made for centuries—in the province of Kashmir, in India. The difficulties of production account for the high price of this and similar yarns.

All the hair used in cashmere yarns is combed from this little goat by hand during a few short weeks in spring. Only the fleecy down from the undercoat and the hairs from the beard are used in spinning. The down, in packages of about fifty pounds, is carried great distances from small villages to larger towns. These packages are bound up in ninety-pound bales and are brought into trading posts by camel trains, then baled again and taken to the larger shipping centers. Some of this shipping flows from points in China to England. However, Russia now does a large part of this marketing, shipping the fleeces undusted, unsorted, and containing a large volume of undesirable coarse hair, to the United States. A great portion is rejected for use in knitting yarns, and the final result is that only 20 per cent or less finds its way into the finished yarn.

Cashmere has always been regarded as one of the choicest yarns for fabric weaving and hand-knitting. It is exquisitely soft, takes dyes of the subtlest shades, and is held in the highest esteem all over the world. Because it lends softness and warmth to other wools and fibers and because of the relatively small quantity available, it is often combined with less desirable materials to make yarns for hand-knitting and weaving. The cashmere content is often as low as 10 per cent, thus making it advisable for the purchaser to examine the label which must list, by law, the exact content of each type of fiber used in the final product.

ALPACA

Alpaca yarn comes from the llama, a close cousin to the camel. The differences, however, are quite apparent. Llamas are much smaller, with a characteristic long straight neck. They prefer high altitudes and are found throughout the Pacific Coast countries of South America, in the Andean regions of Ecuador, Peru, Bolivia, and Chile, roaming in great bands in the high plateaus that extend from Ecuador to Argentina. The flocks are tended almost exclusively by the local Indian tribes as they alone seem able to understand and manage them.

Alpaca yarn comes from two distinct breeds of the llama, the huacaya and the suri. It is from the suri, however, that the better grade of fleece is obtained. It is finer in texture, thicker and more lustrous. The greater quantity of alpaca yarn is consumed by the textile industry, very small amounts finding their way into the manufacture of hand-knitting yarns. Although it is very fine and soft to the touch, it is also very tough, wiry and resilient.

VICUÑA

Vicuña yarn comes from the fleece of the smallest member of the llama family. It is the very finest type of wool obtainable in the world, and centuries ago the privilege of using it was limited entirely to the Inca chiefs, the Royal Family, and others of high rank among Indians in South America before the coming of the Spanish conquistadors. Simón Bolivar, the Great Liberator, was also the great savior of this wonderful little animal which was facing complete extinction at the hands of the colonists. Not realizing the value of the vicuña fleece, the Spaniards had set about killing them in great numbers for food. In 1825, however, Simón Bolivar published two decrees: one prohibiting the killing of vicuñas, and the other permitting them to be plucked only during the three warmest months of the year. The flocks gradually began to multiply, but until recently experiments to domesticate them have failed. A few flocks are now being raised on closed ranges.

The vicuña is covered with a coat of short, very fine silky wool, and the hair on the neck is soft as down. Two fringes of long fine hair hang down from the shoulders and chest to form a sort of apron characteristic of this member of the llama family. Six to eight ounces of wool is the average yield per animal.

Exportation of vicuña fleece is closely controlled by the Peruvian government. The steady demand in the United States and elsewhere has shown that the vicuña can be a great source of national income from world markets, so there is hope that it will be more available in the future. It is by far the finest, softest, and silkiest wool fiber known and makes beautiful shawls, sweaters, and luxury items in the hand-knitting field.

ANGORA

Angora, a rabbit hair known commercially as angora yarn, has been grown and spun in France for more than a century. There are only a small number of angora breeding farms in existence, in France, the Netherlands, and Belgium. The high price per pound of imported angora rabbit wool has stimulated the breeding of this animal in the United States, where it is gradually finding a place in agricultural production, particularly in Colorado. The greatest proportion of angora wool is produced during the winter months, and each small animal yields from ten to sixteen ounces of yarn.

Extremely fluffy and very light in weight, angora wools are often blended in the carding and spinning process with other types of fibers. When blended with lamb's wool, spun rayon, cotton, silk, or synthetics, these fibers help to hold the angora hairs in place. The wool is highly prized for use in items of all descriptions. It has exceptional insulating properties, and when used in combination with wool yarn for mittens, gloves, or head coverings, it affords great protection from the cold weather. Most angora yarns, however, are spun from 100 per cent angora wool. Great is the pride of the lady who wears an angora jacket or stole, but great also is the dismay of her dark-suited escort who parts from her at the end of the evening, carrying away with him a noticeable share of the hairs it shed!

MANUFACTURE

THE HISTORY, STRUCTURE, AND PROCESSES OF MAKING WORSTED AND WOOLEN YARNS

Although Australia is the foremost wool-producing country in the world, most of our yarn comes from sheep grown in the United States. The first sheep were brought to Virginia and Massachusetts by colonists in the early seventeenth century. These sheep were of indifferent breed and were raised for food as well as for the making of yarn.

Introduction of the superior merino breed began in the eighteenth century. A great deal of attention has been given to improving the flocks and the quality of their fleece. The first full-blooded merino ram, Don Pedro by name, was brought into this country from Spain by Du Pont de Nemours and Delessert in 1801. The Du Pont family industry is known now for the production of nylon and other synthetic fibers.

Until 1809 Spain forbade the exportation of these famous sheep, on pain of death! The embargo was later lifted, due to internal strife, and many shipments were distributed to nearly every part of the United States. Their arrival laid the foundation for the production of fine wools and woolen cloth in this country.

With the advent of improved textile machinery, attempts were made to improve the quality of fleeces still further, and long-haired breeds were introduced: the Leicester from England, and the Saxony from Germany, the latter providing the familiar Saxony yarns. When better methods of spinning and weaving were employed, sheep raising became one of the foremost industries, and it is interesting to note that the 1849 census reported more than nineteen million in the United States.

The most important factors in choosing fleece are density, fineness and "crimp" (waviness), and the length of the fibers. Whatever the source of the fleece or hair, the processing of the fibers to make yarn for knitting is approximately the same.

A fleece contains anywhere from 20 to 50 per cent grease, depending on the individual animal, its breed, and the type of range it grazes. A certain amount of dirt and vegetable fiber accumulated on the range makes the fleece still heavier. The finest fleeces have the highest grease content, not only because of the protection it gives to the fleece itself while on the back of the sheep, but because of the lanolin extracted from it in processing.

Altogether, fleeces may shrink as much as 70 per cent or as little as 10 per cent, again depending on the breed of sheep, the care it is given, and the type of range it roams. All of these impurities—grease, dirt, and vegetable matter—must be removed during the *dusting* and *opening*, the *scouring* and the *burr-picking*. A relatively small amount of dirt and vegetable matter is lost when the fleeces are *sorted* or opened up, the inferior parts removed and the better sections retained for use in the manufacture of different grades of yarn. The best wools come from the shoulders and sides of the sheep. The next best, in order of value, come from the lower back, the loin, and the upper parts of the legs. The rest of the fleece is all inferior in quality and is usually put aside for use in the manufacture of cheaper grades of knitting yarns, for weaving, or the making of rugs and carpets.

Next, the fleece is *opened*—exactly what this word implies. It is run through a machine which beats the fleece over open screens, opening it up, dividing the fibers, and causing a high percentage of dirt and vegetable matter to drop through the screen. The fleece is then passed along to the most important operation: the *scouring*, the scientific washing out of dirt, grease, and other impurities. The stock is alternately washed and squeezed many times, the lumps of wool broken up more and more as it flows along from one scouring bowl to the other, until all dirt and grease have finally been removed.

The wool is rinsed, partially dried, and sent on to the burr-picking machine to extract the hard, tough little pieces of vegetable matter still sticking to the wool. Even the best mechanical device, however, cannot possibly remove every tiny burr, and one or two of these may often be encountered in knitting yarns.

The fleece is now ready for the final processing, starting with the blending of different lengths of fibers into suitable combinations for various types of knitting materials. The blend is passed onto the *carding* and *combing* machines which open up the stock still further, comb the locks and bunches, and straighten the fibers. The carding process is most important because good, even woolen yarn cannot be spun from uneven, improperly carded stock.

Worsted yarns differ considerably from other *woolen* yarns in that they are *combed* so that the short or broken fibers are disentangled and removed. The long fibers are then laid parallel and more completely disentangled.

Woolen yarns, on the other hand, are carded: various lengths are mixed and blended. Carding methodically tangles all the fibers, although minor snarls are removed to make the blend a smooth yarn in the final product.

The process varies to some extent, but, broadly speaking, worsted yarns are combed and are of longer fibers; woolen yarns are carded and of mixed lengths. In some countries where longer-haired sheep were always prevalent, the fibers were chopped into shorter lengths so that woolen yarns might be spun. This was called "brothering" and in the old days was done with an ax and a block of wood.

The combing or mixing done, the wool is then delivered to the spinning machines in the form of *roving:* a soft webby rope of from 1″ to 2″ in diameter. Roving has no twist and depends on the clinging quality of the fibers themselves to hold it together. Woolen and worsted yarns require about the same kind of finishing process, accomplished in three different operations: drafting or drawing out, twisting, and winding on.

The *drafting* or *drawing out* reduces the large roving into the thickness required for making the final product. The *twisting* gives the yarn sufficient strength for handling in the knitting operation, and the *winding on* is the final operation, delivering the yarn in the final package: the ball, hank, or skein we find on the shelves of knitting shops.

Colors are dyed into the yarns either before or after spinning. Many mills deliver specified mixtures, in the form of roving, to the yarn manufacturer, who then spins and dyes it to his own specifications. He may combine it with rayon, nylon, orlon, or other fibers, and twist it in various ways. Pompadour, one of the more familiar types of yarn, is a combination of woolen yarn with a thread of rayon or nylon wound into the mixture in the final spinning.

CHOOSING YARNS: SELECTING THE CORRECT TYPE FOR THE ARTICLE TO BE MADE

So many manufacturers, here and abroad, make so many varieties of yarn with so many trade names that it may seem difficult at first to choose the correct yarn to serve a specific purpose. Once you have determined what you are going to make, however, the article itself will suggest the weight or type of yarn to be used, and this will help you make your choice. Many varieties are interchangeable, so any one article could be made from a great number of different yarns.

WEIGHTS AND THICKNESSES

It is the *weight* and *thickness* of the yarn, its *loft* (lightness and texture), and, most particularly, the stitch gauge called for in the instructions that determine the size of the finished article.

Here, again, we must generalize, as there is no set rule to follow. We hear so much about *two-ply, three-ply,* and *four-ply* yarns, but the *ply* itself does not determine the *weight* or *thickness* of the yarn. *Ply* simply means the number of strands—two, three, or more, of any kind—which have been twisted together to form the final thickness and weight of the finished yarn. The terms *two-fold* and *three-fold* mean the same thing as two-ply and three-ply. To see for yourself the *fold* or *ply*, take a small piece of yarn in both hands, untwist it slightly, then push it together just a little, and you will be able to see immediately how many were twisted together to make the final strand.

The very lightest-weight yarns made are the hand-spun varieties from the Shetland Islands. Some run from 30,000 to 50,000 yards to the pound and are knitted by the Islanders into gossamer shawls that even in the 1930s were worth from $100 to $150 each. Records show that a Miss Ann Ives, in Lincolnshire, spun one pound of woolen yarn to the length of 168,000 yards—more than 95 miles! The same lady thought she could do still better if she had had Shetland wool to work with. This was a *single-ply* yarn, however, no thicker than a human hair, and was used in weaving. Ordinarily a single-ply yarn cannot be used in knitting as the strands would surely separate or break.

VERY LIGHT-WEIGHT YARNS

These are used for shawls (plain or lacy), infant and baby wear, sweaters, fine socks, gloves—any lacy, cobwebby, or close-knit article made on fine needles.

Very fine yarn is in small demand and therefore is often difficult to find, even in large department stores or specialty shops. Here again, if enough customers let the manufacturers know that they would like such yarn, the supply might increase. Many producers of hand-knitting yarns confine themselves, if they make light-weight yarn at all, to light colors suitable for baby wear—white, pink, and pale blue. There are, however, mail-order wholesale houses that specialize in hand-*weaving* yarns and in every imaginable color and shade. As a rule, these shops sell yarn by the pound, and one pound of very fine yarn contains many hundreds of yards, but with a little knowledge, work, and determination you can dye white yarn to any desired color and shade, or more than one shade of the same color.

Shawls and lacy stoles may be made on practically any size needle. If the yarn is hairy or fuzzy, it will afford much more warmth than a round, smooth-spun yarn. The type of the finished yarn and the manner in which it is knit determine the warmth of the garment. In fact, a very heavy ski sweater made of a smooth, round yarn may not furnish as much protection against cold and wind as two lighter-weight, more open-knit sweaters of a fuzzier hairy yarn.

Yarn for baby garments—light-weight sweaters, undergarments, stockings, socks, dresses—must be chosen with the special article in mind. The first consideration *must* be softness and non-irritation, particularly if the garment is to come into contact with the baby's tender skin. In this latter instance, the better yarn to choose is smooth, washable, treated wool or a synthetic yarn. Manufacturers have paid much attention to baby yarns, designing them to suit their special needs. They are designated by various terms, such as Baby Yarns, Two- or Three-fold Saxony, Pompadour, Dylanized, and are very soft and smooth. There are also many "nonshrink" or "shrinkproof" yarns made especially to withstand the laundering and hard wear to which baby garments are subjected.

MEDIUM-WEIGHT YARNS

This yarn is suited to practically every imaginable garment and article—dresses and suits for adults, sweaters, socks, and stockings, gloves, warm scarves for either dressy or utility wear, baby garments—everything not specifically in the very light-weight or heavy-weight category. In addition, medium-weight yarn may be doubled to make a very warm garment.

The yarn in most common use for a medium-weight article is three-ply or fingering yarn. Neither term is a true designation of the weight of the yarn itself, but through common usage they suggest medium-weight yarn which is usually woolen-spun—round and smooth—and may be used for nearly every garment or article made to a seven- or eight-stitch gauge, depending on the knitter and the size of the needle used. It goes without saying that a larger or smaller needle may be used for different types of lacy knits or fabric stitches.

For articles that must stand more rugged wear—mittens, gloves, and other outdoor garments—worsted-spun yarn is more suitable as it has greater durability and washes more easily with less tendency toward felting. Worsted-spun three-ply yarn is also excellent for lightweight afghans as it is warm and will take much abuse. As a rule, worsted-spun yarns are less expensive than woolen-spun fingering yarns, but they are also rougher in texture.

Generally speaking, all groups of three-ply yarns are available in more colors and shades than are all other types. "Heather mixtures," which are yarns dyed either in contrasting colors or in several shades of the same color mixed together before spinning to give a frosty or heather appearance, are also made in this weight. These mixture yarns are particularly suitable for socks, utility scarves, and gloves. Suits, coats, and skirts knitted of heather yarns in certain fabric stitches are difficult to distinguish from homespun, hand-woven materials.

The medium-weight range includes the greatest number of texture or specialty yarns, such as crepes and bouclés, excellent for making smart suits and dresses. A smooth, round yarn with rayon or nylon wound or spun into it is especially suitable for less casual wear, as it knits up flat, stretches less, and will work very well indeed on very small needles (#2 or smaller), and to a nine- or ten-stitch gauge, or even finer. It is attractive, too, when used for lacy or open-stitch articles.

Also in this three-ply category is slub yarn, which has knots spun into it at invervals. When knit, it has a rough texture that works well into suits, dresses, blouses, and dressy cardigans or jackets. Slub yarns can be knitted with excellent effect into articles usually designed with a smoother yarn in mind. It must be remembered, however, that a rough-textured yarn produces a rough-textured fabric.

All of these texture yarns are excellent when used in any one of the fabric stitches described in the final chapter of this book.

Classed among the medium- or a little lighter than medium-weight yarns are the various metallic yarns made of wool or nylon fibers with very fine threads of silver, gold, or copper-colored metal wound into them. These come under the heading of luxury materials and are used in the making of more formal articles and garments, such as blouses, dresses, suits, and accessories. They may be worked in so many different ways that it depends only on the personal taste of the knitter to make her choice. Used in combination with other types of yarns and ribbons, especially as a contrasting part of a design or pattern, or as part of a two-color or multicolor fabric stitch, metallic yarns lend a touch of elegance.

SPORTS-WEIGHT YARNS

These may be two-, three-, or four-ply yarns and are spun for articles and garments of a little heavier than medium-weight and a little lighter than the four-ply worsted and Germantown weights.

Sports yarns come in woolen- or worsted-spun types, in clear colors or heather mixtures, and are especially good for outdoor garments: suits and jackets, cardigans, medium-weight socks and stockings. Heather mixtures worked in one of the flat fabric stitches or multi-color fabric motifs in combination with clear-colored yarns are effective for sportswear. Worked on fine needles with a tight-gauge stitch, this yarn makes attractive bathing suits.

Shetlands and Shetland-type yarns are included in this class and are particularly beautiful. Many companies supply worsted-spun Shetland yarns for sweaters to go with matching skirt fabric. Some of these skirt materials are hand-woven from the same dye-lot as the knitting yarns. "Homespun" yarns are often matched to hand-woven skirt and suit materials.

We usually think of afghans in terms of four-ply worsteds or Germantowns, but made with this woolen-spun sports yarn, they are lighter and less "boardy," just as fine-thread laces are softer and lighter than similar lace patterns worked in heavy cotton cord.

HEAVY-WEIGHT YARNS

This type of yarn is usually four-ply, the worsteds being worsted-spun and the Germantown yarns woolen-spun. Their use is almost unlimited. The worsteds are particularly appropriate for warm garments for outdoor wear, since they afford much better insulation against cold than the woolen-spun ones and can take hard wear.

Both types of yarns offer an exceptionally wide color range. The *ombré* yarns are made in several shades of one color, or several contrasting colors, dyed in at measured intervals along the yarn. Mixture yarns may have three or four different colors—or shades of the same color—wound together in the strand, to give an attractive tweedy effect when knitted into heavy skirts, dresses, jackets, and ski sweaters.

The smooth, soft Germantown yarns are fine for warm baby things—blankets, carriage robes, snowsuits, mittens, and caps—and are unsurpassed for heavier-weight afghans.

The heavy-weight (and the lighter-weight) woolen-spun yarns may be used for making the same garments as the worsted-spun yarns. You must expect them to "rough-up," however; i.e., to acquire the unsightly and annoying little lumps known as pills or noils on the surface of the garment. Brushing them off is difficult; usually they must be plucked off by hand. This does not harm the knitted work, but for real *wear* worsted yarns are usually better.

SUPER-WEIGHT or BULKY YARNS

As has been stated, "two-ply" does not necessarily denote the weight of yarn. Many of the heaviest and thickest yarns made are two-ply—two loose heavy strands of woolen-spun yarn twisted together to form a thick heavy strand. If we took two balls of Germantown or worsted and worked with them as one, the result would be approximately the same as with bulky yarn.

Some of the Icelandic yarns have the least possible twist, and it is difficult to wind them into balls without breaking the strand. Knitting is done with this yarn coiled very softly into a box (much like the roving which is delivered to the spinner to finish). The correct amount of twist is acquired as the knitting progresses.

Other very heavy yarns are made of many strands twisted together. The strands may be twisted during spinning to make thick and thin spots along the length of the yarn. These super-weight yarns come in a wide choice of colors and mixtures. Some are spun with a certain amount of grease or lanolin left in them. This is highly prized by ski enthusiasts and fishermen. It is used exclusively by knitters of the Aran Islands in Ireland to make their famous sweaters.

MOHAIR YARN

This type of yarn is spun in almost limitless variety. The lightest weight of 100 per cent mohair is usually designated as Number One Mohair. As a rule, this is the sheerest type. It is one of the most popular yarns and can be found in so many weights, mixtures, twists, and crinkles that it is nearly impossible to name them all. Mohair yarns are also spun in combination with other types of yarns: wools, synthetics, and various mixtures of all of these.

MAN-MADE FIBERS

Rayon, nylon, orlon, dacron, and all other synthetics—and there are surely more to come—are spun into every imaginable type of yarn for hand-knitting and weaving. Orlon Sayelle is a yarn designed for hard wear and easy laundering. It is nonallergenic—a distinct asset for people who cannot tolerate wool or hair yarns. Its machine washability makes it a boon to mothers of small children, as well as to other members of the family.

Other synthetics are spun into yarns of 100 per cent inclusion or are mixed in various percentages with wool or hair to add strength and endurance.

Novelty yarns made from rayon, nylon, and other man-made fibers are used in making lacy blouses and dresses. These yarns are usually spun with a knot or slub introduced at measured intervals, and when worked in Stockinette Stitch these knots form an attractive pattern in the finished work. The size of the needle and the length of the interval between knots determine the form the pattern will assume.

Under the heading of synthetics come various ribbons used for knitting. Some are a true ribbon—the type woven just like yard goods, with a selvage at either side. Such ribbon may be found in widths from 3/16″ to 1/2″, in various combinations of silk and rayon or nylon, or in 100 per cent silk, and are woven in various types of textures—soft ribbon, taffeta, organdy (usually 100 per cent silk organdy), in all shades and colors, and some with metallic threads included at the edge or in the center. Some ribbons are woven to give a tweedy effect when knitted; others have a flecked appearance.

"Fuse-cut" ribbon is not a true ribbon at all. It is made of rayon or nylon and is cut into its particular width from a bolt of woven material which is usually a hundred yards in length. As it is cut, controlled quick heat is used to sear the edges to retard fraying.

SUMMARY

There are so many types, weights, and grades of yarn to choose from that the knitter may make almost any garment or article she has in mind. It must be understood, however, that different yarns are made to sell at various prices for a very good reason. High-quality yarns carry a high pricemark. The quality of the yarns may derive from the fibers from which they are spun or from the dyes used to color them, or both. Other determining factors are qualities of wear, such as resistance to felting, pilling, rubbing, or fading. Yarns that shrink, stretch, turn harsh and rough when washed, or lose their color by bleeding or fading can be expected to cost less than those that retain their quality under similar conditions.

Many manufacturers produce a "shrinkproof" or "shrink-resistant" wool yarn (or wool with synthetic inclusion). Such yarns have been treated chemically to reduce the felting that ordinarily occurs in non-treated fibers, and they are in great demand. They come in a variety of weights and colors, but must be knitted with a firm tension, as the finished garment, instead of shrinking, is more apt to stretch when laundered.

The dyes themselves may cause a variation in price. Better-quality dyes in permanent colors naturally cost more. Harsh, hard colors take less time and expense to produce than subtler, softer shades and are therefore less expensive.

When buying yarn, remember that if the garment is to be used for rough outdoor wear and is easy and quick to make, it is not necessary to turn to the highest-quality, higher-priced yarns. The less expensive yarns are sturdy and are practical for afghans, dolls, toys, utility shawls, golf clubhead covers, and heavy secondary socks to be worn over regular socks.

On the other hand, it is absolute folly to consider cheaper yarns for dresses, suits, sweaters, or blouses that will take many hours to knit and should give years of wear if they are made in a simple, classic style and are carefully handled and stored. A few cents' difference in price of one ounce of yarn may make a world of difference in quality and appearance, and when these pennies are multiplied by the relatively small number of ounces involved, the actual cost per garment is not great. Good-quality yarns may be used over and over again. Poor-quality yarns are even difficult to rip out!

I remember, way back in the 1930s, a knitted winter coat and skirt of a tweed mixture and a full-length coat of a bright color, both made of a high-quality four-ply worsted. They were worn for years, almost to the point of embarrassment. Both were eventually ripped out, and the yarn washed and rewound, to make a pretty afghan that is still in daily use.

As every worth-while book of instructions and every intelligent sales clerk always advises: BUY ENOUGH YARN AT ONE TIME TO MAKE THE ENTIRE ARTICLE. This warning is not given in the interests of the yarn manufacturer or the retailer, but for the customer's own good.

Great lots of yarn are dyed at one time and given a specific dye-lot number. No two dye-lots are ever exactly the same. Yarns are sold to retailers in all parts of the country in varying amounts. A "box" of yarn may contain from eight to twenty skeins or balls, and the smaller knitting shops may buy only one or two boxes. It is only reasonable to expect that, if you buy only one or two skeins or ounces, when it comes time to get more yarn of the same color, you may find, to your great disappointment, that all of the yarn in that dye-lot has been sold. It is practically impossible to match one dye-lot to another. Even *white* yarns are *dyed,* not bleached white. Yarn from another dye-lot may make a noticeable streak in the finished work. Another order from the wholesaler may take several weeks to reach the retailer and nearly always is from another dye-lot. Very few shops refuse to return the purchase price of surplus, undamaged yarn if it has not been kept too long. Buying a little extra at the beginning may help to prevent a possible knitting tragedy, later.

Some manufacturers do produce yarns that are dye-lot controlled. Only in that case can yarn be bought in small amounts, and even then it is wise to buy sufficient yarn—you'll at least avoid the delay of having to reorder. It is frustrating to have time on your hands and no yarn to work with.

SAVE YOUR LABELS or wrappers from each skein of yarn until the garment is completely finished. At the risk of seeming fussy or difficult, examine these wrappers yourself, at the counter, to be sure that all skeins or balls are marked with the same dye-lot number. If your blouse or suit turns out to be particularly beautiful, well fitting, and worthy of reproduction in some other color, the saved labels will provide you with an exact record of the number of ounces required to make it, and you can record in your permanent notebook the brand name of the yarn and the amount of yarn you have used.

When buying yarn for a suit or dress, the wise knitter will buy one or two extra ounces of yarn for possible future use. Styles and figures change, and as a result skirts may have to be lengthened or some other changes made to bring the garment up to date. If the garment is washed, wash the extra yarn at the same time. If the garment is to be cleaned, pin the yarn to the garment before it is sent out. This will keep the emergency yarn in readiness for any change that might be necessary.

Instead of buying yarn by impulse—THINK AHEAD. Doing so may pay great dividends.

3. Abbreviations and Terms

In any book of printed instructions directions *must* be condensed to fit into as small a space as possible and yet remain readable. The high cost of printing makes this especially true of knitting magazines and leaflets. Books of knitting or crocheting directions usually include a section explaining the abbreviations used. This should *always* be consulted if there is any doubt as to the interpretation of the instructions.

Some writers, however, do not take the trouble to go into detail; instead they leave much to the previous knowledge or the imagination of the reader. Many nineteenth- and early-twentieth-century books carried complicated lace instructions with little detailed explanation of terms used in the patterns. Possibly ladies of that period were much more accustomed to making needlework of all kinds and understood all the terms and abbreviations. If any question in point did arise, Grandma, Auntie, or some neighbor would surely know the answer! Many knitters guarded the secrets of their stitches as jealously as their "receipt" for preparing a certain cake, and many stitches were kept in the family as heirlooms, passed down from mother to daughter and not let out of the family until someone with particular ability could break the code.

The purpose of this chapter is to explain the abbreviations and terms that appear in instruction books, new or old. Also, in order to make the explanations in the chapters on Basic Knitting Procedures and Pattern Stitches less confusing, we have dreamed up a few of our own. In the pattern stitches, cross-references to the explanations are given as needed.

French, German, Spanish, and Swedish terms relative to knitting are also defined, as many books from abroad contain beautiful designs, instructions for which cannot be found in English. Variations between American and British terms are also compared here.

In these foreign abbreviations, "chain edge," "edge stitch," "twisted stitch," and certain other phrases unfamiliar to us are common expressions.

KNITTING ABBREVIATIONS USUALLY FOUND IN U.S. PRINT PLUS NEW ONES FOUND IN THIS BOOK

K	— Knit
P	— Purl
KP — PK, etc.	— Knit and Purl, or Purl and Knit, etc., into one stitch or yarn-over
Kb	— K into the *back* of the stitch
Pb	— P into the *back* of the stitch
st(s)	— stitch(es)
K-wise	— *Knit-wise*, or — as though to Knit
P-wise	— *Purl*-wise, or — as though to Purl
sl	— slip a st from the LH needle onto the RH needle without working it
Pat	— Pattern
tog	— together (as K 2 tog)
K 2 (3) tog	— K 2 (3) tog from the front
P 2 (3) tog	— P 2 (3) tog from the front
K 2 tog b — or K2togb	— K 2 tog from the back
P 2 tog b — or P2togb	— P 2 tog from the back
YO — yo — O	— yarn over. Wrap the yarn around the needle to form a new st (see page 71)
OO — OOO, etc.	— wrap the yarn around the needle as many times as there are O's
psso — p.s.s.o.	— pull (or pass) the slipped st over
p2so	— pull (or pass) *two* sts over
pnso — p.n.s.o.	— pull *next* (to left) st over (on the LH needle)
pn2so	— pull *next two* (to left) sts over (on the LH needle)
Sl 1, K 1, psso — *SKP* — Sl, K, and pass	— Sl 1 st, K 1 st, and pass the slipped st over the knit st — or: Slip, Knit, and pass (see page 68)
Sl 1, K2 tog, psso — SK2togP	— Sl 1 st, K 2 tog, and pass the slipped st over the st resulting from the K 2 tog
inc	— increase (a st)
dec	— decrease (a st)
inc R	— inc to the *right*
inc L	— inc to the *left*
dec R	— K 2 tog
dec L	— SKP
M 1	— make 1 st (see page 74)
Pu 1	— pick up 1 st (see page 78)
beg	— beginning (usually applied to a row or round)

rep	—repeat
rnd	—round (in circular knitting)
yf	—bring yarn to front of work
yb	—take yarn to back of work
RH	—right-hand (needle)
LH	—left-hand (needle)
in(s)	—inch(es)
SP—sp	—single-pointed (needles)
DP—dp	—double-pointed (needles), or an extra needle when cabling
Work even	—continue to work in pattern as before, without increasing or decreasing
* *	—rep whatever is written between the two * *
#—NO.—no.	—number of sts, rows, rnds, or needles
Fagot—Fag.—fag—f	—yarn over the needle as before purling and P 2 tog
"	—inch

TERMS AND ABBREVIATIONS FOUND IN BRITISH PRINT *(Not Usually Found in U.S. Print)*

BRITISH	AMERICAN
Plain Intake	—K 2 tog.
Purled Intake	—P 2 tog.
Pull over one—Take in	—SKP
Sl and b—Slip and Bind	—SKP
Take in with 3 sts	—Sl 1, K2 tog, and psso (SK2togP)
Wool forward (wl fwd)	—yarn over—or: yo—or: O
Plain intake taken from behind	—K 2 tog from the back (K2togb)
Make 1 (M 1)	—increase, either yarn over or pick up 1 st from between 2 sts (see pages 71, 74)
Stocking Stitch (S.S.)	—Stockinette Stitch
Welt	—a finish as applied—either ribbing or Quaker Stitch (Pattern Stitch #3)

TERMS AND ABBREVIATIONS FOUND IN CONTINENTAL PRINT

FRENCH	AMERICAN
À l'endroit	—front of work (or fabric)
À l'envers	—back of work (or fabric)
abréviations du tricot	—Knitting abbreviations

aiguille (aig.)	—needle
aiguille auxiliatre (aig aux)	—stitch holder
aiguille droite (aig drt)	—RH needle
aiguille gauche (aig gche)	—LH needle
ainsi de suite	—work even (etc.)
à travers	—through
attente (att)	—leave (sts) on
augmenter (aug)	—to increase
augm d'une maille levée	—inc by knitting a st between 2 sts (M 1)
augm invisible	—inc invisibly (see page 75)
auxiliaire (auxil)	—extra (needle)
bord en chainette	—selvage
bord en perle	—selvage; when edge sts are K *every row*
bouclé	—loop
boutonnière (boutonn)	—buttonhole
ce point s'exécute avec un multiple de m., plus (#) M.	—work on a multiple of (# of) sts, plus (# of sts)
changement (chang)	—change
commencer (comm)	—begin
chaque (ch)	—each, every
continuer (cont)	—continue
croiser	—to cross or twist (a st)
décolleté (decol)	—neckline
dernier (dern)	—last (row or st)
derrière (derr)	—back (of skirt or blouse)
derrière par	—back of st
devant (dev)	—front (of skirt or blouse)
diminuer (dim)	—to decrease
diminution (dim)	—decrease
diviser (div)	—divide
dos	—back
double (dbl)	—double
droite (dr)	—right side—or right needle
double jeté à l'endroit (dble jeté end)	—yarn over the needle twice
emmanchure (emman)	—armhole
endroit (end)(de l'ouvrage)	—front (of work)
ensemble (ens)	—together
épaules	—shoulders
extérieur (exte)	—outside (of work or piece)
faire un jeté	—yarn over
fermeture des mailles	—bind off. Also, the finish, the end of work
fil	—yarn
finissant (finis)	—finishing (as applied to putting together)
fois (fs)	—times (i.e., a specific number of times)
gauche (g)	—left—or Purled (side or needle)

glisser (une maille) (glis)	—slip (a st)
haut (ht)	—long (literally, high)
hauteur (haut)	—length (height)
intérieur (inter)	—inside (of work or piece)
jeté à l'endroit (jeté end)	—yarn over before a K st
jeté à l'envers (jeté env)	—yarn over before a P st
jeté le fil	—yarn over
lâcher une maille	—drop a st
laisser (lais)	—leave (on the needle)
l'aller et le retour	—K a row, P a row (i.e., over and back)
lisière (lis)	—edge
lisière chaînette	—chain edge
lisière perlé	—seam edge (K first st every row)
longueur (long)	—width, breadth
maille (m)	—stitch (st)
maille à l'endroit (m endr)	—Knit stitch
maille à l'envers (m env)	—Purl stitch
maille à l'endroit torsée	—K into back of st (Kb)
maille à l'envers torsée	—P into back of st (Pb)
maille croisée	—crossed or twisted st
maille glissée à l'endroit	—sl a st Knit-wise
maille glissée à l'envers	—sl a st Purl-wise
maille lisière (m l)	—edge st
manche	—sleeve
montage cylindrique	—cast-on round or circular knitting
montage tricoté avec aigs	—cast-on with 2 needles
montage tricoté avec une aig	—cast-on with 1 needle
monter les mailles	—cast on sts
ourlet	—hem
nombre (nbre)	—number
point (pt)	—pattern (stitch)
point de côtes 1 et 1 (2 et 2)	—ribbing—K 1, P 1, (K 2, P 2)
point de riz	—Seed Stitch
point jarretière	—Garter Stitch
point jersey	—Stockinette Stitch
première (prem)	—first (row or st)
quelque (qq)	—each, every
rabattre (fab) toutes les mailles	—bind off all sts
remaillage sur en bord	—pick up (knit up) sts from the edge
rang (rg)	—row
sous	—under
suivant (suiv)	—following (st or row)
surjet (surj)	—pass or slip (a st)
terminer (term)	—end (of)
toujours (tjrs)	—always
tous	—all—every
tout, toutes (tt, ttes)	—all—every
travail (travailler) (trav)	—work, or piece of work

tricoter (tric)	—to Knit
tricoter à l'endroit	—Knit row (or side)
ter à l'envers —	—Purl row (or side)
tricoter en ronde	—round or circular knitting
un surjet double	—sl 1, K 2 tog, psso (SK2togP)
un surjet simple	—sl 1, K 1, psso (SKP)
une diminution à droite (dim à dr)	—decrease to the right (K 2 tog)
une diminution à gauche (dim à gche)	—decrease to the left (K 2 tog b, or SKP)

GERMAN   AMERICAN

Abbildung	—illustration (Ill. or Fig.)
abheben	—to slip (a st)
abketten der Maschen	—to bind off
Abnahmen	—decrease
Abnahmegang	—decrease round or row
abnehmen	—to decrease
ab wiederholen*	—rep from*
Anschlagen	—casting on
Anschlag	—the cast-on
Arbeit	—work (or piece of work)
Arbeit wenden	—turn (the work)
auffassen	—to pick up (or knit up) sts
aufgelegt	—yarn over (the needle)
Aufnahme	—the increase
aufnehmen	—to increase
darüber	—over (such as "pull over")
die Maschen wieder aufnehmen	—to knit up or pick up sts
doppler Umschlag	—yarn over the needle twice
durch eine Masche überziehen	—sl 1, K 1, psso (SKP)
durch zwei Maschen überziehen	—sl 1, K 2 tog, psso (SK2togP)
durchziehen	—through
eine Masche überzogen	—st passed over
eine Masche abheben	—slipped st
eine Masche fallen lassen	—drop a st
Ende der Reihe	—end of the row
Faden	—yarn
Farbe	—color
Farbwechsel	—change of color
Maschen auf eine Hilfsnadel fassen	—leave (sts) on a holder
Gang	—round (rnd)
Garn	—yarn
geschlossene Arbeit	—round or circular knitting

gestrickt	—knitted
glatte (Masche)	—Knit (st)
heruntergefallen Maschen aufheben	—pick up (dropped sts)
Hilfsnadel	—stitch holder
Hohlmaschen	—hole st (made by the yarn over)
im Wechsel	—alternately
Krause (Masche)	—purl (st)
Kettenrand	—chain edge
kreuzen	—to cross (sts or cabling)
links	—left
linke	—left (or *Purl* st)
linke Nadel	—LH needle
mal(s)	—time(s)
Masche(n)	—stitch(es)
Masche links abheben	—sl a st Purl-wise
Masche rechts abheben	—sl a st Knit-wise
Maschenglied	—st (on the needle)
Maschenzahl teilbar durch	—sts (No. of) divisible by ?
Muster	—pattern (stitch)
nach hinten einstechen	—in *back* of st
Nadel	—needle
offene Arbeit	—flat knitting—2 needles
Perlenrand	—seam edge (K first st *every* row)
Rand	—side edge
Randmasche	—edge stitch
rechte (Masche)	—Knit (st)
rechte (Nadel)	—RH (needle)
rechts	—right, or *Knit* side of work
rechts abnehmen	—K 2 tog
Reihe	—row
Rückseite	—wrong side (of work)
Runde	—round (rnd)
Saum	—hem
Schlinge	—loop
Spitzen Muster	—lace pattern
Strickarbeit	—knitting (after "the")
Stricknadel	—knitting needle
überziehen	—psso
unter	—under
verdrehte	—twisted or crossed (st)
verschränkte Masche	—crossed stitch
Vorderseite	—front (or right) side of work
Zunahmen	—increase
zunehmen	—to increase
zurück stricken	—work back (to)
zusammen	—together
2 Maschen rechts zusammenstricken	—K 2 tog

SPANISH / AMERICAN

Spanish	American
aguja	—needle
aguja de punto	—knitting needle
aguja derecha	—RH needle
aguja izquierda	—LH needle
aguja de repuesta	—stitch holder
alternando	—alternately
al traves	—through
armar a timer	—cast-on
aumentar	—to increase
basta	—yarn over
borde	—edge
borde anudado	—seam edge (side edge)
borde cadeneta	—chain edge
crecido	—seam edge
dar vuelta	—turn (the work)
debajo	—under
derecha	—right (knit) needle or stitch
derecho (del trabaho)	—front, or right side (of work)
detras	—through back of st or loop
diminujendo puntos	—decrease
dobladillo	—hem
en esper—estar en suspenso	—to leave sts on a needle or holder
hacer punto	—to knit (or work in knitting)
hevilla	—loop
hilera	—round or circular knitting
hilo	—yarn
reves (del trabajo)	—wrong (side of work)
soltar un punto	—drop a stitch
tejer	—to knit
trabajo	—work (knitting)
veces	—times
volver	—work back
volver a tomar*	—rep from*
vuelta	—row

SWEDISH / AMERICAN

Swedish	American
alternativt	—alternate(ly)
arbete	—work (knitting)
återkomma	—work back
avig maska	—Purl st
avigsida (av arbetet)	—wrong side (of work)
avmaska	—bind off
avmaskad maska	—st passed over
bakifran (tagen)	—into back of st
börja on fran*	—repeat from*
falla	—hem

fánga (tappade maskor)	—pick up (dropped sts)
gáng	—times
jhälpsticka	—stitch holder
höger	—right side (of work)
höger sticka	—RH needle
igenom	—through
kant	—edge
kantmaska	—edge stitch
kastad	—yarn over
kedjesöskant	—chain edge
korsa	—cross (st)
lyfta	—slip (a st)
lyftad avig maska	—sl a st Purl-wise
lyftad rät maska	—sl a st Knit-wise
maska	—stitch
minska	—to decrease
minskningar	—decrease
montera	—cast on
montering	—casting on
mönster	—pattern stitch
ögla	—loop
öka	—to increase
ökningar	—increase
omkrets eller värv	—round or circular knitting
omslag, dubbel	—sl 1, K 2 tog, psso (SK2togP)
omslag, enkel	—sl 1, K 1, psso (SKP)—or: K 2 tog
pärlkant	—seam edge
plattstickning	—flat knitting with 2 needles
plocka upp (en maska)	—pick up or knit up sts
rät maska	—knit st
rätsica (påarbeter)	—front or right (side of work)
rundstickning	—round or circular knitting
snodd maska	—crossed or twisted st
sticka	—knit—or needle
stockning	—knitting
styng, mönster	—pattern stitch
tappa en maska	—drop a st
ta upp	—pick up or knit up (sts)
tillsammans	—together
tråd	—yarn
under	—under
uppuhåll	—leave (on a holder)
uppmaske	—to pick up loops or sts
vända	—to turn (the work)
vänster sticka	—LH needle
värv	—row

4. Basic Knitting Procedures

There is no RIGHT or WRONG way to knit. There is only a *right* or *wrong* result. Whether you use the "German" or "Continental" method or the "English" method—or any other method—it is only the result that counts, not the way you hold your needles or use your hands and fingers. One type of knitting may suit *you* but would be extremely awkward for another knitter. It is almost impossible to find any two knitters who knit *exactly* alike. It is rare that any two knitters achieve the same gauge, even if they use the same needles and the same yarn. It is the desired *result* that counts, not the manner by which the result has been achieved.

Many knitters prefer to hold the yarn in the LEFT hand while working—this method is commonly referred to as German or Continental knitting. All of the following directions, however, with the possible exception of two or three instances are given and illustrated using the English method.

It cannot be stressed too strongly that it is to any accomplished knitter's great advantage to learn both methods thoroughly, so that each operation may be done easily and with equal facility with either hand. If a garment or article is made using a small gauge and takes many hours to knit, the hands get tired of doing the same thing in the same way for long periods, no matter how easily and quickly the work may go. When the knitter is able to swap working hands every so often, from the English to the Continental method, with no visible change in tension or gauge, the hands (and also the neck and back) get tired much less quickly. It is also a decided advantage to be able to use both methods with equal facility when working with different colors in a pattern (Fair Isle or pattern knitting with two or more colors—see page 93).

CASTING ON: METHODS AND USES

In order to do any type of knitting, loops or stitches must first be put onto the needle. This is called *Casting On* or *Setting Up,* and there are several different ways to achieve as many different effects or results. Only seven having reference to the stitch patterns that follow are given here, although there are more than a dozen that can be used. In all types of casting on, the stitches to be put onto the needle must have a stretch and elasticity relating to the knitting that is to follow. Some methods will allow more stretch, have more body, or be more decorative than others, and it is quite important to know which method to employ. It is best, however, to learn *all* to begin with, and the ultimate effect that each will give; then, when any article is to be made, the best method of casting on will suggest itself. Each of the following ways of casting on stitches is accompanied by its suggested use.

METHOD I (Simple)

Make a slip knot (Fig. 1) and put it onto the needle which is held in the Left Hand. Hold the yarn lightly with the two back fingers of the Right Hand and lay the forefinger of the same hand on top of the yarn (Fig. 2). Crook this finger toward the palm and straighten it up again, applying a slight tension on the yarn, thus forming a loose type of loop on the finger. Slip this loop onto the needle from the back (Fig. 3) and pull up the yarn, not too tightly, to close the loop on the needle. Repeat this operation for the desired number of sts.

When knitting off this type of cast-on, it is advisable to insert the working needle into the *back* of the st (Fig. 4). When slipping the st from the LH needle, however, do not pull too hard on the st as you work it away from that needle. The main thing to remember about working off this type of cast-on is that it must be done with a truly light touch to keep the stitches workable.

Fig. 1

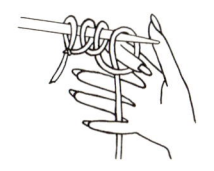

Fig. 2

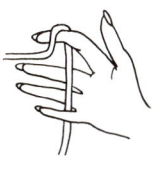

Fig. 3

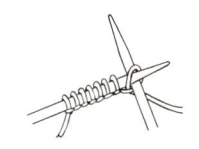

Fig. 4

Uses:

1. For the beginner who is taking a first lesson in knitting, who has never handled needles, and who has not yet developed facility.
2. For buttonholes, where only a small number of sts is required.
3. For setting up sts for lace edges or insertions, where no join of cast-on to bind-off will be required.
4. When the cast-on edge is to be used for hemming, either knitted or sewed (see page 89), working into the *fronts* of the sts on the first row.

METHOD II *(Less simple)*

Make a slip knot (Fig. 1) and put it onto the needle held in the Right Hand. Hold the yarn with the two back fingers of the Left Hand and draw the yarn in front of the thumb of the same hand, and then over and behind it (Fig. 5). Put the point of the needle into the front of this loop (Fig. 6) and slip the loop from the thumb to the needle (Fig. 7). Pull up on the yarn gently until snug—but not tight—to the needle. Repeat this operation for the desired number of sts.

When a firm edge is required in the finished piece, work this cast-on from the needle into the *fronts* of the sts (Fig. 8). If a less visible edge is desired, work it off into the *backs* of the sts (Fig. 9). For a more elastic edge, use two needles, held together, for the cast-on and, when the required number of sts has been reached, withdraw one of the needles before working off.

Uses:
1. Buttonholes (working into the *fronts* of the sts).
2. Lace edges and insertions (working into the *backs* of the sts).
3. When new sts must be added during the knitting of an article or garment, to form an addition of shaping (working into *fronts* of the sts).
4. When the cast-on edge is to be used for hemming, either knitted or sewed (working into the *backs* of the sts).

METHOD III *(Using one needle and two lengths of yarn)*

Make a slip knot some distance from the end of the yarn and slip it onto the needle which is held in the Right Hand (Fig. 10). The shorter end of the yarn is held in the Left Hand, with the yarn coming from the ball in the Right Hand.

Holding the yarn with the two back fingers of the Left Hand, draw the short end of the yarn under the thumb of the same hand and then over (Fig. 11). Insert the needle into the *front* of the loop on the thumb and, instead of slipping it onto the needle, *knit* it off with the yarn in the Right Hand (Fig. 12). This st is adjusted to the needle by pulling up snugly, but not too tightly, with the yarn in the Left Hand. Repeat this operation for the required number of sts.

The length of yarn to be held in the Left Hand must be enough to cast on for the first row, and this can be determined by working 10 sts. Pull out these sts and measure the number of inches of yarn they required, from the slip knot back to the *end* of the wrinkled yarn.

As an example: If the yarn in the Left Hand piece measures 4 inches from the knot to the end of the 10 sts used, and 40 sts must be cast on, you will need four times as much yarn for 40 sts as for 10—or 16 inches. To this add at least 6 more inches for easy accommodation in the back fingers—something to hold on to—before making the slip knot.

If the work is to be used as an edge which must have stretch and elasticity, it is advisable to use a larger needle (or two needles held together) for the cast-on than the size needle you will use for the work that is to follow. When adjusting the st to the needle, it is too easily "snugged up" and may produce an edge that is too tight if you use a small needle.

Uses:
For practically any type of wool knitting with a plain straight edge. If Stockinette Stitch is to be made, it is better to work this cast-on, on the very first row, with purling.

METHOD IV *(Using one needle and two lengths of yarn—German or Continental method)*

Make a slip knot some distance from the end of the yarn, the length to be left to be determined as in Method III.

Both lengths of yarn are held in the Left Hand, the longer end in the two back fingers and over the thumb, and the shorter end over the index finger and under the middle finger, with the middle finger controlling the tension (Fig. 13). The needle, which is held in the Right Hand, is inserted into the front of the loop on the thumb and laid on top of the yarn on the index finger (Fig. 14). *This* yarn is dipped down by the needle and pulled through the loop on the thumb (Fig. 15), forming a loop on the needle which is adjusted by placing the thumb under the yarn now coming from the needle and gently pulling back on it (Fig. 16), this same motion setting up the loop on the thumb for the next st.

Repeat this operation for the required number of sts.

For a really elastic edge, use a larger needle (or two needles held together) for the cast-on.

Uses:
Same as in Method III.

METHOD V *(This, the English method, has more stretch than all other types of casting on and makes a firmer, heavier edge.)*

Hold the yarn in the two back fingers of *both* hands (Fig. 17), the shorter end in the Left Hand. With the Right Hand, draw the yarn under the left thumb *toward you,* and then *away from you over the thumb* (Fig. 18). Then, using the index finger of the left hand as a hook (Fig. 19), lay the finger on *top* of the yarn and hook the finger toward the crotch of the thumb and forefinger, then straighten this finger up (Fig. 20). Use the resulting loop on the finger as a st, insert the RH needle into the front of it (Fig. 21) and use the yarn in the Right Hand for knitting this st onto the needle. Continue this procedure for the desired number of sts.

Casting on in this manner is a slight deviation from the usual one-needle method. The extra cross-twist (Fig. 22) in the loop on the finger gives a firmer (but not tighter) edge at the beginning of the work.

Uses:
This method makes a particularly good edge for socks, stock-

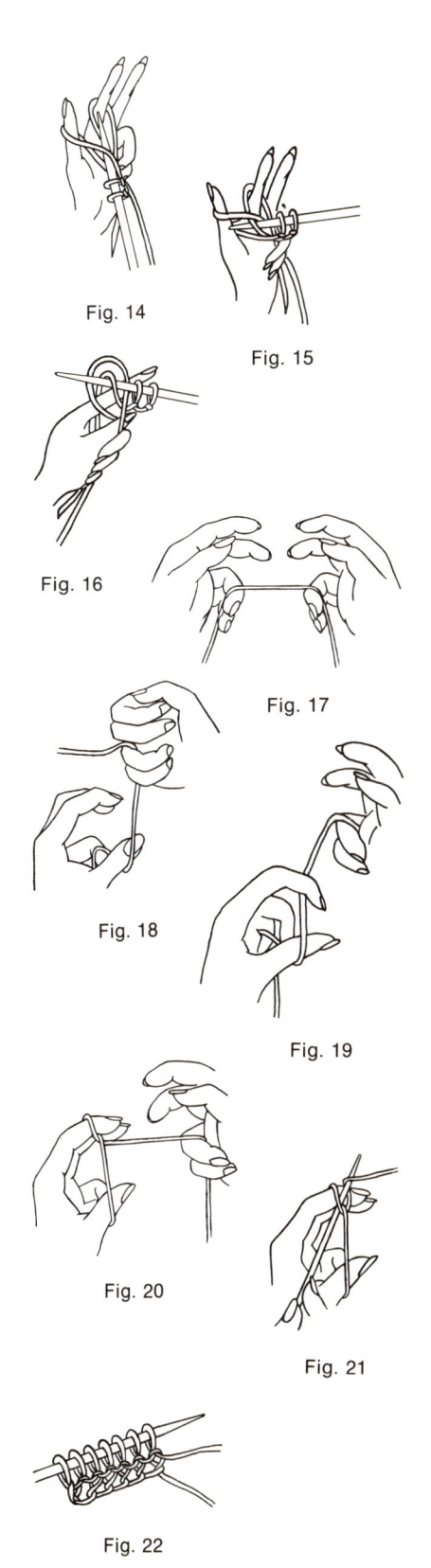

Fig. 14
Fig. 15
Fig. 16
Fig. 17
Fig. 18
Fig. 19
Fig. 20
Fig. 21
Fig. 22

ings, and any article that is to start with ribbing. It produces an edge in which the first row has been already worked during the process of casting on. If Stockinette Stitch is to be worked, it is best to purl the first row.

This is also a good method to use when two-color knitting is to follow. One color may be tied to the other, the loop being made with one color and the knitting stitch done with the other.

Because of the extra twist made in the Left Hand, more yardage must be used in the process; therefore, be sure to determine length as in Method III before putting on the sts.

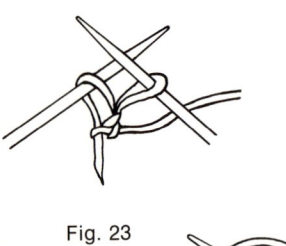

METHOD II *(Using two needles)*

Put a slip knot onto the LH needle. Holding the yarn in the Right Hand, knit into the st with the second needle and pull the loop through, but do not remove the original loop from the LH needle (Fig. 23). Put back onto the LH needle the loop that was pulled through, and twist the RH needle so that, when slipping this loop on, the two needle points are facing in the same direction. Leave the RH needle in the st, with the point under the left needle tip (Fig. 24), and adjust the yarn with the Right Hand. Continue this process for the desired number of sts.

For a firmer edge, work off into the *backs* of the sts.

Uses:

Same as Method I and Method II.

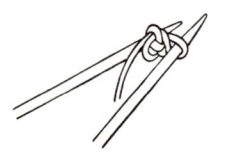

METHOD VII *(Using two needles)*

As in Method VI, put a slip knot onto the LH needle. Holding the yarn in the Right Hand, knit into the st with the second needle and pull the loop through, but do not remove the original loop from the LH needle (Fig. 25). From this point on, however, instead of knitting into this second st, insert the needle point *in between* the two sts on the needle (Fig. 26), wrap the yarn around the point, and pull this loop through *from between* the sts, not through the st itself. Twist this loop back onto the LH needle as before, inserting the needle for the following st, however, *before* adjusting the yarn to the needle.

This method of casting on gives a firmer, less loopy edge, and more like that of Method V.

Whenever you use Method VI or Method VII as an addition to sts already worked — as when adding a number of sts at a sleeve edge — take care to work the *back* of the *first st* that was cast on, so that no unsightly hole appears in that little space.

METHOD VIII *(Casting on with three needles or a circular needle)*

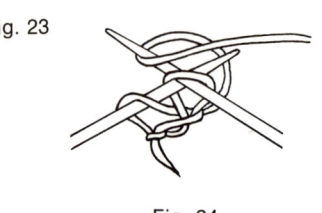

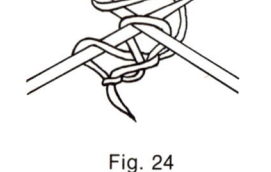

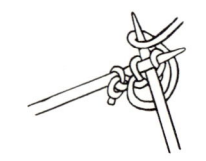

Most socks, stockings, and skirts are made in "round" or "circular" knitting. There is a very special method of casting on and working such knitting to make sure that it is not twisted in the very first operation—the cast-on and join. We know of no way to correct this unfortunate error except to rip it all out and start over again.

For socks, stockings, and some other very small articles, sts must be cast onto three needles and worked off with a fourth needle. (Only very fine steel needles come in sets of five; four are usually enough for contemporary knitting.) Circular needles are not practical for these smaller items, as explained in Chapter I.

In four-needle knitting the number of sts to each needle is defined by the number of sts required in the pattern and the kind of pattern used. If K 2, P 2 ribbing is to be made, each needle should carry a number of sts divisible by 4, so that each needle will start with K 2 and end with P 2 to ensure easier working. Thus, if a sock or stocking requires 72 sts to be cast on, each needle would be alloted 24 sts. So— cast on 24 sts on each of three needles. Lay these needles in a triangle on a flat surface (Fig. 27). Make sure that all of the sts face to the *inside* of the triangle made by the three needles. Pick them up in this very same position. The yarn remaining from the cast-on sts should be securely fastened to the first st which was cast on (Fig. 28). As you start working off the first needle, work the first few sts with the new yarn *plus* this original length (doubling the two) for about 4 to 6 sts, to insure a better join. Don't forget to work into these *double* sts on the next round!

An alternate method of casting on for more than two needles is first to cast on the required number of sts onto a single *straight* needle and then work the sts in the required pattern off from this needle onto three needles. Join, and work as specified above.

Work cast onto a circular needle is done in the same manner, except, of course, there is only one needle to contend with. If there are going to be divisions of work—such as pleats or gores—it is wise to put a marker, either a ring (Fig. 29) or a continuous thread marker (Fig. 30), at the end of each of these divisions. These markers not only indicate the divisions of work, but make counting much easier during the casting-on. The beginning thread is joined to the first of the required number, and all sts should face *inward* when placed on a flat surface as in the three-needle cast-on. Many knitters prefer to work back and forth on the cast-on sts for four or more rows, and *then* join and work in rounds. These first few rows can be joined unnoticeably with a needle when the piece is finished.

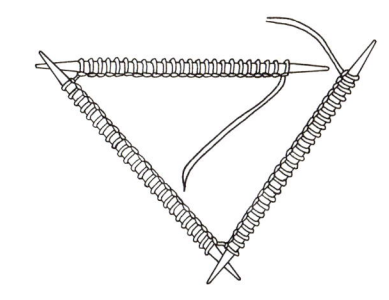

Fig. 27

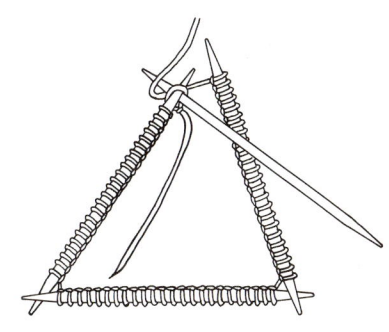

Fig. 28

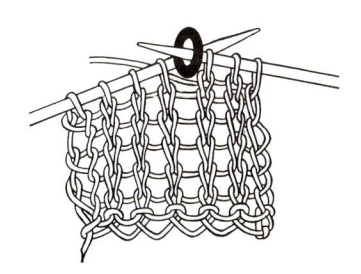

Fig. 29

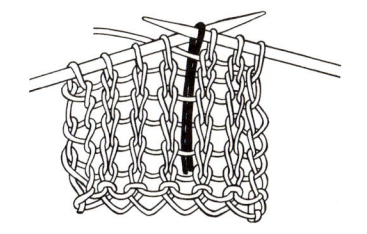

Fig. 30

KNITTING AND PURLING

"ENGLISH" METHOD

Knitting: Hold the needle with the cast-on sts in the Left Hand, with the hand *on top* of the needle. Use the thumb to hold the second st in abeyance and the forefinger in back of the first st to guide it (Fig. 31).

Wrap the knitting end of the yarn around the little finger of the

Fig. 31

Fig. 32

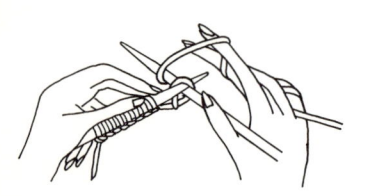

Fig. 33

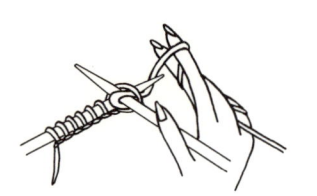

Fig. 34

Fig. 35

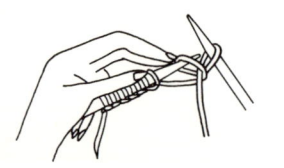

Fig. 36

Right Hand, close to the crotch (for tension) and over the first joint of the index finger (Fig. 32).

Placing the Right Hand on top of the second needle—lightly now, don't clutch it—insert the point of the needle through the *front* of the first st on the LH needle, letting it extend about an inch at back. Wrap the yarn *under* the RH needle *toward* you, and *over* it *away* from you (Fig. 33). Now, holding down on the little finger to keep the yarn from slipping, push the st on the LH needle toward the tip and off, with the left index finger, while *at the same time* drawing the loop made on the RH needle through that same st (Fig. 34). Repeat this operation across the cast-on sts. When each st has been taken off in this manner, you have completed *one row of knitting*.

FOR THE BEGINNER

Cast on about 28 sts. Continue the above knitting process until the work becomes very easy to do and starts to be fun. When a square has been completed, you have a "swatch" of Garter Stitch (K all sts every row).

Purling: The hands and needles are held in the same position for purling as for knitting, the yarn, however, being held in *front* of the work and both needles. The needle is inserted into the *front* of the st, *from back to front,* and the yarn is wrapped *over* the needle *away* from you, and *under* the needle *toward* you (Fig. 35). Then *push* the loop on the RH needle tip back through the st while sliding the st on the LH needle off with the left forefinger (Fig. 36). Repeat this operation across the cast-on sts. When each st has been taken off in this manner, you have completed *one row of purling*.

FOR THE BEGINNER

Cast on about 28 sts. Continue this purling process until it becomes very easy and fun to do. When a square has been completed, you have another swatch of Garter Stitch (P all sts every row), as this same Garter Stitch may be made by either *Knitting* all sts or *Purling* all sts.

Cast on 28 sts again. Knit one complete row, turn and put the needle with the sts on it into the Left Hand again; Purl one complete row. The alternating of these two rows will automatically result in a swatch of what is called Stockinette Stitch (See page 170).

"GERMAN" or "CONTINENTAL" METHOD

Knitting: The needle with the cast-on sts *and* the yarn are both held in the Left Hand, the yarn wrapped around the little finger for tension and over the index finger (Fig. 37). The thumb holds the second st back out of sight and the middle finger is in back of the first st, making it ready for presentation. The RH needle is held comfortably in the Right Hand with the hand on top.

60

Insert the RH needle tip into the front of the first st, *from front to back*, with the tip resting on top of the yarn held at the back (Fig. 38). Press down on the yarn with the RH needle and hook it toward the opening of the loop of that st and pull it through, pushing the st off the LH needle with the left forefinger (Fig. 39).

FOR THE BEGINNER

Cast on about 28 sts and make a Knit swatch as outlined. Then, when halfway through, change to the English method and continue in that manner, alternating German and English every two rows until each method has been accomplished with equal facility.

Purling: Hold the needle and yarn in the Left Hand in the same manner as for knitting, with the yarn held down from *in front* of the needle with the tip of the index finger (Fig. 40).

Insert the RH needle tip, *from back to front*, through the front of the first st. Release the fingertip pressure on the yarn, letting the yarn come back *over* the RH needle (Fig. 41), then press down on it again (Fig. 42). The yarn will go in *back* of the RH needle tip. This will form a loop over the needle which is held in place with the RH thumb, then pushed through the first st on the LH needle (Fig. 43), and then slipped off. Repeat this process across the row.

FOR THE BEGINNER

Cast on 28 sts and work a swatch as before. Then alternate the English and Continental methods, both in knitting and purling, practicing both methods until each is done with equal ease and the work is smooth and even in appearance.

Whenever you change from a K st to a P st, whether you are using the English or Continental method of knitting, the yarn must be brought to the front of the work between the two needle points.

To change from a P st to a K st, the yarn must be taken to the back of the work between the two needle points.

LEFT-HANDED KNITTING

If you are normally left-handed, there is really very little adjustment to be made in knitting. If you will observe your friends who knit, you will find that they use the Left Hand quite as much as they use the Right Hand, especially if they knit the German or Continental style—holding the yarn in the Left Hand and picking it through with the Right Hand. The Left Hand has entire control of the yarn. Even if they hold the yarn in the Right Hand (the English method), they use the Left Hand almost as much as the Right Hand. The fingers of the Left Hand control the sts on the needle and are also used to push the sts off the needle.

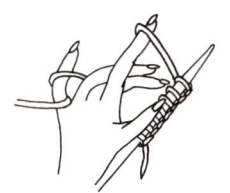

Fig. 37

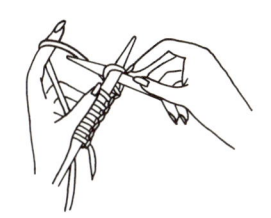

Fig. 38

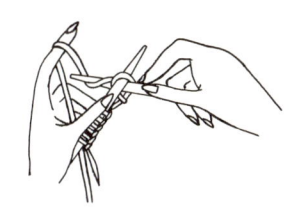

Fig. 39

Fig. 40

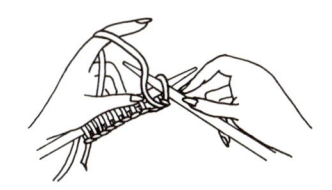

Fig. 41

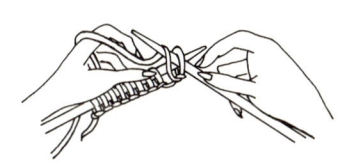

Fig. 42

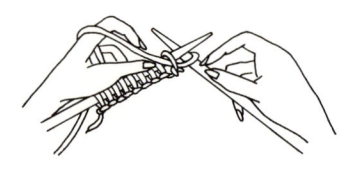

Fig. 43

In many instances in knitting, being right-handed or left-handed is a state of mind. Teachers have had much success in instructing left-handers to use the methods outlined here for the so-called right-handers.

However, if all else should fail and it seems that copying their ways of knitting cannot be managed, have one of your friends who knits work in front of a long mirror. Then sit in back of her, but just off a little to one side so that you cannot see your own reflection. Do what she does, looking at your own hands as you follow her motions. In the mirror everything she does will look left-handed to you, and it should be comparatively easy to follow the way her hands and fingers are moving.

If you have no friends who knit, follow the instructions written here for the right-handed knitter, substituting *Right* Hand for *Left* Hand and vice versa in all the instructions. All the illustrations can be held up to a mirror so that you may see just how things should look when you are working the different techniques. In all pattern stitches you should also substitute the LH for the RH and vice versa. Following the procedures in this manner should not be too difficult.

Remember two things, however, which are very important. *Your* SKP (sl 1, K 1, psso) will slant to the *right*, and *your* K 2 tog will slant to the *left*. When knitting across the needle from left to right, however, all instructions should be followed, as everything is reversed. The Knot Stitch (page 85), the Tie Stitch (page 85)—*everything* in fact—should have the needles and hands changed from right to left and left to right.

UNEVEN KNITTING

There are countless instances in which a knitter will find a marked dissimilarity in tension (the pressure applied to the yarn and needles) between Knitted and Purled rows. This lack of uniformity is not unique; practically every knitter experiences it. I would firmly advise seeking some means of overcoming this difficulty, if possible—and it *is* possible. If nothing else works, try using two sizes of needles, the smaller needle for the looser row and the larger needle for the tighter row.

VARIATIONS: HOW TO USE KNITTING AND PURLING TO FORM PATTERNS

All Knitted fabric or lace stitches are composed of these Knitted and Purled stitches as a foundation of the work. All of the following variations are simple modifications or embellishments to change the appearance of the plain Knit or plain Purled sts, turning them into fabrics or laces, depending on the sequences of the various stitches used in the progression of work.

CROSS KNIT (Italian or Twist stitch)

This is worked in the same manner as plain knitting. The needle, however, is inserted into the *back* of the st instead of into the front (Fig. 44). The Purl row is then made in plain Purl as usual.

CROSS PURL

Insert the needle into the *back* of the st instead of into the front (Fig. 45). The Knit row is worked in plain Knit.

PLAITED STOCKINETTE STITCH (See Pattern Stitch #93)

Each Knit st and Purl st is worked from the front of the st as usual. The throwing of the yarn, however, is completely reversed, the yarn being thrown *over* the needle on the Knit row (Fig. 46) and *under* the needle on the Purl row (Fig. 47). This is referred to as Reverse Stitch.

This type of stitch should always be used for knitting which includes beads or sequins.

These crossed and plaited stitches, when used as a fabric, have more elasticity than the plain Knit-and-Purl method and are recommended for such things as belts, bandages, underwear, and bathing suits, because this technique results in superior elasticity which also incorporates a definite firmness.

COMBINED CROSS AND PLAIN

In this Stockinette fabric, the needle is inserted into the *back* of the st when knitting, with the yarn thrown as in plain knitting. The Purled sts are worked from the *front* of the st, but the yarn is thrown as in Plaited Purling (Fig. 47).

This method uses less yarn than any of the others in making a Stockinette fabric and is recommended when there is any doubt about the sufficiency of yarn on hand. It is apt to result in a slightly firmer fabric and is particularly advised for knitting garments of cotton or linen yarn or chenille. Make sure, however, to establish the correct gauge first (see page 99).

For the "quick-and-easy" garments or articles made with very bulky yarns and exceptionally large needles, it is the very best stitch to use, instead of the regular Stockinette Stitch. It may not be quite so "quick" or as "easy", but a garment made by this method will retain its shape far longer than if the regular Stockinette Stitch were used.

DOUBLE THROW

This procedure can be used as a simple decorative device, or in pattern stitches to give a lacy effect, and may be made either Purled or Knitted. The needle is inserted into the st and the yarn is wound around the needle as many times as the directions call for, and then all loops are pulled through the st (Fig. 48).

Fig. 44

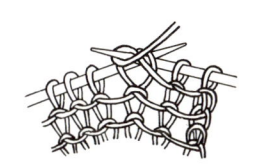

Fig. 45

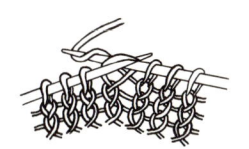

Fig. 46

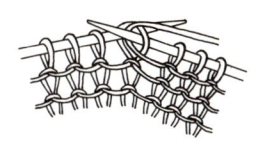

Fig. 47

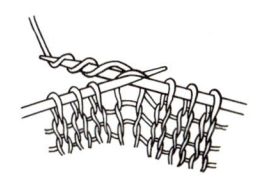

Fig. 48

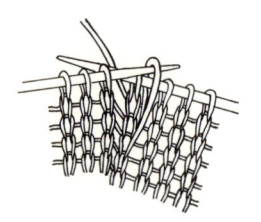

Fig. 49

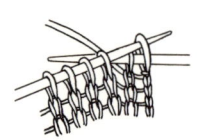

Fig. 50

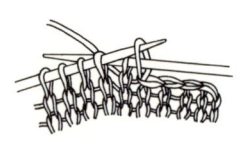

Fig. 51

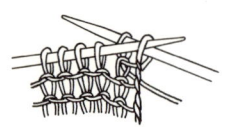

Fig. 52

The use of this st, every row throughout—or broken up by numbers of rows of Garter Stitch—with fine yarn and a medium-size needle, makes a very lacy, light-weight shawl or stole.

KNITTING A LOOP FROM BELOW

This stitch looks complicated and difficult but is very easy to make. Simply insert the RH needle point into the st indicated in the directions, knit through this st, and pull the resulting loop up to the level of the present row of knitting (Fig. 49). This loop may be passed over the next st made, or worked in whatever manner is indicated in the instructions (see Pattern Stitch #120).

BINDING OFF

Every loop, as it lies on the needle, is a loose slip stitch and, if dropped or taken off, will ravel or drop through the work. This is what happens when a run develops in a stocking. Therefore, each loop of each piece of knitting must be securely fastened at the beginning edge—the Cast-on—and the ending edge—the Bind-off.

PLAIN BIND-OFF *Knit Side*

Knit the 1st 2 sts. Then, with the LH needle point, reach over the 2nd st made and insert it into the 1st st made (Fig. 50). Pull this loop over the other st and drop it from the needle between the two needle points, making sure to retain the 2nd st made on the RH needle (Fig. 51). Knit the next st from the LH needle and repeat the pull-over. Continue in this manner until all sts are bound off, leaving one st on the RH needle. Break the yarn, leaving about 3", and pull this through the last st, thus fastening the last loop securely.

PLAIN BIND-OFF *Purl Side*

Purl 2 sts and *take the yarn to the back of the work* before pulling the 1st st over the 2nd as above. The yarn should be taken to the back each time a new st has been Purled, as this keeps the yarn out of the work area and makes the pull-over easier (Fig. 52). Fasten off as in binding off on the Knit Side.

As the bind-off process is very apt to draw and become tighter than the body of the work, great care must be taken to keep the loops loose when you pull them over. If this is found to be too difficult, try replacing the RH needle with one that is two or even three sizes larger than the needle originally used. It is much better, however, to practice the binding-off process until the correct tension has been acquired, rather than to depend on other expediencies.

RIBBING BIND-OFF

When any ribbing, even the very small amount necessary for buttonholes, is to be bound off, the sts of the ribbing *must* be worked *in their own progression* in the bind-off, the K sts worked and bound off in Knitting, and the P sts in Purling, so that the ribbing will retain its ribbed appearance throughout and not open up at the edge (Fig. 53 and Fig. 54—showing Right and Wrong).

CROCHETED BIND-OFF *(Worked with a crochet hook)*

This is a particularly good method of binding off, especially when there are many sts on the needle or needles, or when cotton, linen, or silk thread is used. The st is more evenly controlled and is less likely to bind or contract.

The yarn or thread is held in the Left Hand in back of the LH needle point. The crochet hook is inserted into the front of the 1st st, a loop is pulled through it (Fig. 55), and the st is dropped from the needle. Another loop is pulled in the same manner through both the 2nd st and the 1st loop made (Fig. 56). Continue in this manner along the entire edge, making sure not to hold the thread too firmly in the left hand or to close the loop on the hook too tightly.

As it may take a little time to achieve the required tension and ease of performance in this method, always try it out on a swatch or practice piece before using it on a garment or article.

In binding off Purled sts, bring the thread to the front of the LH needle and insert the hook into the st *Purl-wise* (Fig. 57) before pulling the loop backward through the st.

Some lace articles call for the use of a crochet hook on the finishing edge, so that crocheted loops or sts may be made between the sts that are to be bound off.

PATTERN STITCH BIND-OFF

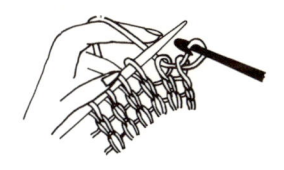

As in Ribbing Bind-off, the procedure for binding off any pattern stitch, whether it is to be bound off on either the Right or the Wrong Side of the work, remains the same as in Ribbing Bind-off. The following, however, pertains to the Right Side of the work in particular. In other words, bind off the pattern sts as they progress along the row. As an example, take Stitch Pattern #174. If this pattern were to be bound off on Row 7, reading as follows: "K 2 tog, * yo, K 3, yo, SKP, K 2, yo, SK2togP—rep to end," the bind-off would progress in the following manner:

K 2 tog and yo; pull the st made by knitting the 2 tog over the yo; (K 1, pull over)x3; yo, pull over; SKP, pull over; (K 1, pull over)x2; yo, pull over; SK2togP, pull over—and so on to the end of the row.

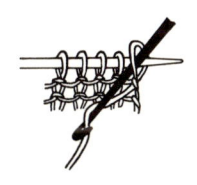

When this procedure is followed in making lace sts, and two bound-off edges are to be grafted together at a later time, the seam will be far less noticeable than if a plain bind-off was used.

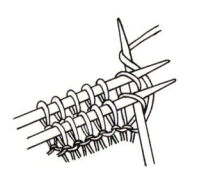

Fig. 58a

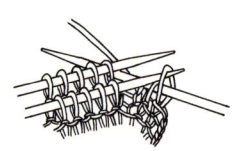

Fig. 58b

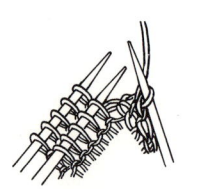

Fig. 59

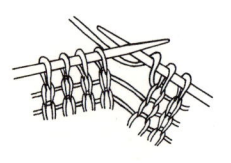

Fig. 60

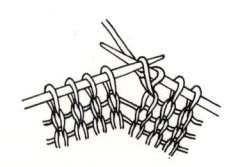

Fig. 61

When sts are Knitted and slipped in sequence, it is of particular importance that the slipped sts *be slipped* when the binding-off process is reached. Otherwise, the bound-off edge will be loose and unsightly, and it will be difficult to achieve a finished appearance.

BINDING OFF TWO PIECES TOGETHER

When two pieces of work are to be joined and each piece has an identical number of sts, they may be bound off together in an almost unnoticeable seam.

Hold the two pieces together in the Left Hand, each on its separate needle, with the right side of each piece facing the other on the inside and with the needle points facing *right*. Insert the RH needle into the front of the 1st st on both front and back needles (Fig. 58a, and Fig. 58b). Knit into these 2 sts as one st and slip them off. Knit into the next st on both needles, together, slip them off and pull over as in plain binding-off (Fig. 59).

Uses: Joining any straight edge; shoulder bind-offs on any plain sweater, using the blind TURN (page 92) if any shaping is made.

MISCELLANEOUS NOTES

Always bind off *in pattern* when any slipped sts or crossed fabric sts are used. In such cases a plain bind-off would decidedly open up the edge, as a fabric stitch is always tighter (closer gauge) than straight knitting.

When binding off a series of sts which include many yarn-overs in the instructions, the yarn-overs must also be made while binding off. If they are *not* made, the work at the edge may pucker and be too tight. Simply bring the yarn under and over the RH needle as for a yarn-over, insert the LH needle under the 1st st made on the RH needle (Fig. 60), and pull this st over the loop (Fig. 61).

When binding off a piece of work in which sts are to be dropped throughout, a chain must be made to elongate the bound-off edge to match the cast-on edge. We will suppose that the instructions, on the bind-off row, read as follows (See Pattern Stitch #151):

*Bind off 6 sts, *drop the next st*—rep from *, binding off the last 6 sts.

Before binding off the 2nd set of 6 sts, drop the next st from the LH needle and let it run. Then—bring the yarn under and over the RH needle (the regular yarn-over throw), insert the LH needle under the last st made on the RH needle, and pull this st over the loop *very loosely*.

BINDING OFF IN LACE PATTERNS

In making *Thread Laces*, the bind-off is worked in the same manner as in regular yarn knitting, but is counted in a completely different way.

When binding off articles made *with yarn,* the number of sts bound off are counted from the 1st pull-over to the number of sts designated in the instructions, and the st which is left on the RH needle is counted as the 1st st of the next group of sts.

In *Lacemaking,* however, the st which remains on the RH needle is *not* counted as part of the next group of sts worked. As an example:

K 2, K 2 tog, bind off 3 sts, K 5, SKP, K 2, K 2 tog, K 2.

This would be worked as follows: The K 2 and the K 2 tog are worked as usual. Then you bind off 3 sts. When the next 5 sts have been knitted according to the directions, the st that remains on the RH needle is *not* counted with the next K 5 sts. *Five sts are knitted,* but there were 6 sts on the RH needle before the SKP was worked.

As a contrast, in plain yarn knitting—in the making of a buttonhole or some other bound-off set of sts—the st that remains on the RH needle after the bind-off has been completed is counted as the 1st st of the following group of sts to be worked. For example:

K 5 sts, bind off 5 sts, K 6 sts, bind off 5 sts, K to end of row.

This would be worked as follows: K 5 sts, then K 2 more sts. Pull over, K another st and pull over, continuing this until 5 sts have been *pulled over.* The pattern then reads, "K 6 sts." The st that remains on the RH needle is counted as the 1st st of the K 6. You have, however, knitted only 5 sts. The second bind-off is repeated in the same way, and then the row is finished.

DECREASING

The *decrease,* as its name plainly implies, takes one st away from the total number in the row. This is done in various ways, each one of them important and each with its own definite purpose.

In lacework, symbols are used, for brevity as well as for better understanding, for the decrease also serves as a "turn" of the st to make contours in the pattern design, and it is usually compensated for, either before or after its use, by an increase.

In decreasing, when a "slipped" st is called for, *it must be slipped KNIT-WISE*—i.e., the RH needle is inserted into the st as if to knit it, and the stitch is slipped from the LH needle to the RH needle without being worked (Fig. 62).

The abbreviation "p.n.s.o." or "pnso" (pull *next* st over) is not encountered as frequently as the psso, but it has its own particular value in decreasing, as explained in the following paragraphs.

In the working of a garment, the method of decreasing and increasing is much more important than might be supposed; the one word "decrease" or "increase" is written into the instructions and it is left to the knitter to choose the best method.

Remember that a decrease can make the resulting st swing to the RIGHT (Fig. 63) or to the LEFT (Fig. 64), and *the point at which*

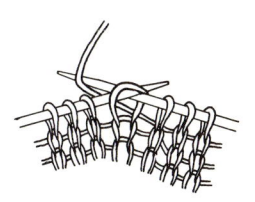

Fig. 62

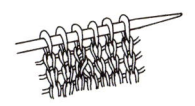

Fig. 63

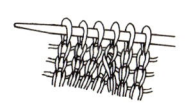

Fig. 64

Fig. 65a   Fig. 65b

Fig. 66

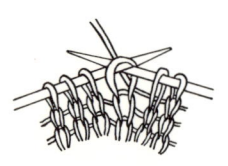

Fig. 67

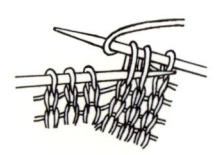

Fig. 68

Fig. 69   Fig. 70

it is used should determine which type of decrease should be made.

For example: When shaping an armhole or neck edge, the decrease *at the right* or *beginning* edge should be turned to the LEFT (Fig. 64), and the decrease *at the left* or *ending* edge should be turned to the RIGHT (Fig. 63). This is of paramount importance in the shaping of a V neck (Fig. 65a, Right; Fig. 65b, Wrong), especially when sts are to be knitted up later from that edge to make one of various finishes.

The shaping of a skirt requires the same care and attention whether it is worked from the bottom edge and decreased, or from the top (waistline) edge and increased. The paneled or plaited effects in particular require the use of two differing slants or directions of the decrease or increase to produce the best results.

KNIT DECREASES

KNIT TWO TOGETHER *(K 2 tog)*

Insert the RH needle into the front of the 2nd st on the LH needle and then through the front of the 1st st as well (Fig. 66). Wrap the yarn as for a plain K st and draw the yarn through, slipping the 2 sts off together. This makes 1 st from the 2 sts and results in a decrease to the RIGHT (Fig. 63).

SLIP, KNIT, AND PASS *(Sl 1, K 1, and psso — or SKP)*

The 1st st is slipped *Knit-wise* — i.e., insert the needle into the *front* of the st from front to back and slip it off without working it. Knit the 2nd st, then pull the slipped st over the K st (as in binding off). A decrease to the LEFT results (Fig. 64).

A less noticeable decrease, worked in almost the same manner but with a more finished appearance, is described in the following paragraph — learn this method and *use* it!

Sl the 1st st from the LH needle *Knit-wise,* and then the 2nd st in the same manner, onto the RH needle (Fig. 67). *Insert just the very tip* of the LH needle into the *fronts* of these 2 sts which are now on the RH needle, and K them together from this changed position (Fig. 68).

Both types of decreases are *absolutely essential* in making any "full-fashioned" shaping. They should also be used in making a skirt from the bottom up, using the K 2 tog for one decrease round (or row) and the SKP for the next decrease round. Alternating these two decreases will help to keep the skirt from pulling slightly on the bias, which may happen when only one kind of decrease is used.

It is also wise to develop the good habit of using these two kinds of decreases for shaping armholes and sleeves — SKP at the *beginning* of any shaping, and K 2 tog at the *end* of any shaping (Fig. 69 and

Fig. 70), including, as already noted, the shaping of the neckline of a V-neck sweater or dress.

In some of the following instructions, this SKP might be referred to as KNIT TWO TOGETHER FROM THE BACK (K 2 tog b— K2togb).

Fig. 71

KNIT THREE TOGETHER *(K 3 tog)*

Insert the RH needle into the 3rd st from the point of the LH needle, into the 2nd, and then into the 1st (Fig. 71), all at the same time. K these 3 sts off together—a double decrease made to the RIGHT (Fig. 72).

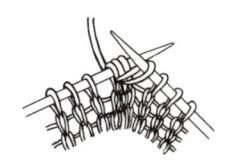

Fig. 72

KNIT THREE TOGETHER FROM THE BACK *(Knit 3 tog b—or K3togb)*

Slip the 1st 3 sts from the LH needle, separately, to the RH needle— *Knit-wise* (Fig. 73). Slip them back onto the LH needle in this new position—i.e., the sts now have the backs of the loops for presentation. Insert the RH needle into each loop, through the *back* and K them off together (Fig. 74). This is a double decrease made to the LEFT.

Any number of sts may be taken together in this manner.

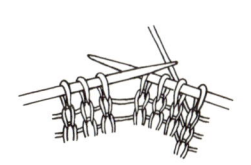

Fig. 73

RIGHT-CROSS DOUBLE DECREASE

With RH needle, sl the next st *Purl-wise;* sl next st from LH needle to a DP needle and hold in back (Fig. 75); sl next st from LH needle onto RH needle (Fig. 76); sl the st from DP needle onto LH needle (Fig. 77). Sl the 2 sts from RH needle back onto LH needle and K 2 tog twice (2 decreases made) (Fig. 78).

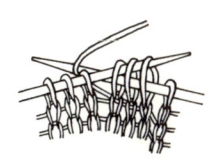

Fig. 74

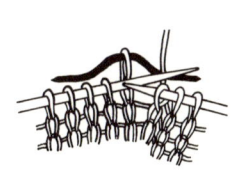

Fig. 75

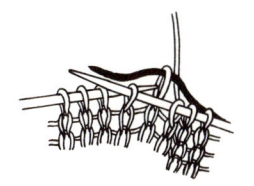

Fig. 76

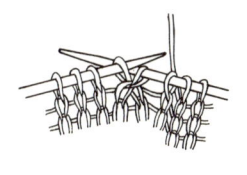

Fig. 77

Fig. 78

LEFT-CROSS DOUBLE DECREASE

With RH needle, sl next st from LH needle *Purl-wise;* sl next st to DP needle and hold in front of work (Fig. 79); sl next st from LH needle onto RH needle; sl the st from DP needle onto LH needle

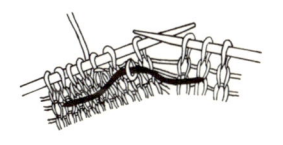

Fig. 79

Fig. 80

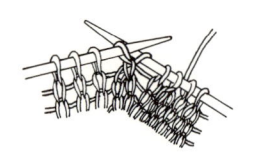

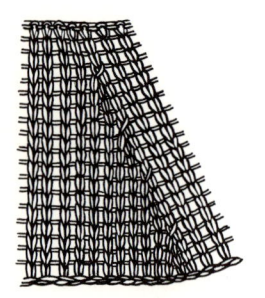

Fig. 81

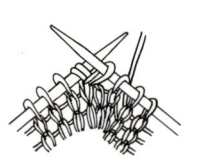

Fig. 82

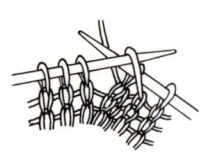

Fig. 83

(Fig. 80). Sl the 2 sts from RH needle back onto LH needle and SKP twice (2 decreases made) (Fig. 81).

These two kinds of double decreases are generally used when making raglan sleeve shapings. The *right-cross* is used at the *beginning* of any shaping, working 2 K sts before working the cross. The *left-cross* is worked 6 sts before the *end* of the row, making the double decreases and then knitting the last 2 sts.

These two types of decreases replace the K 3 tog and/or K 3 tog b, usually on a quite mannish raglan-sleeved sweater or jacket, but when they are used, the decreases should be spaced farther apart than when using the single decrease, usually every 4th row.

Also, for a special effect, the single decreases may be reversed—SKP at the beginning, usually working 2 or more sts before the decrease—and K 2 tog at the end, working the decrease at least 4 or 5 sts from the finish of the row.

SLIP, KNIT TWO TOGETHER, AND PASS
(*Sl 1, K 2 tog, and psso—or SK2togP*)

Sl the 1st st *Knit-wise*, K the next 2 sts together (Fig. 82), and pull the slipped st over the st resulting from the K 2 tog (Fig. 83). This makes 1 st from the 3 sts and pulls them together into a central point with the top of the st lying from right to left.

DOUBLE SLIP DECREASE (*Sl 1, K 1, pnso*)

Sl the 1st st *Knit-wise*, K the next st, and psso—or, better still, SKP (see Fig. 68). Put this st back onto the LH needle (Fig. 84). Then pull the 2nd st on the LH needle over this st, from Left to Right (Fig. 85), and let it drop between the points (Fig. 86). Put the resulting st back onto the RH needle. The top st will then lie from Left to Right (Fig. 87).

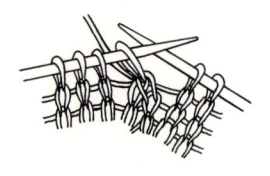

Fig. 84

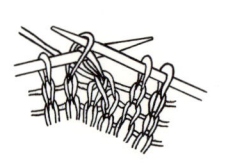

Fig. 85

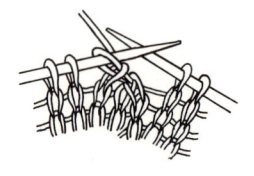

Fig. 86

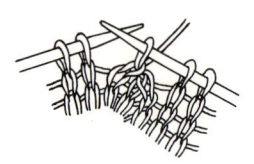

Fig. 87

PURL DECREASES

PURL TWO TOGETHER (*P 2 tog*)

Insert the RH needle point into the front of the 1st 2 sts on the LH needle and Purl them off together (Fig. 88). This decrease, made over the corresponding K 2 tog in Stockinette Stitch, slants in the same direction when the work is turned to the Knit Side of the piece.

PURL TWO TOGETHER FROM THE BACK *(P 2 tog b—or P2togb)*

This is a slightly awkward decrease to make, but when decreases are to be taken in flat knitting and must match the ones made on the Knit Side of the work, this method *must* be used.

The RH needle point is inserted into the backs of the 2nd and 1st sts, together, on the LH needle, from the back toward the front (Fig. 89), then purled together in this position. This decrease matches the SKP taken on the Right—or Knit—Side, of Stockinette Stitch.

PURL THREE TOGETHER *(P 3 tog)*

Insert the RH needle point into the 1st, 2nd, and 3rd sts on the LH needle, all at the same time, and purl them off together (Fig. 90).

This will result in the same slant of decrease on the Right—or Knit—Side of Stockinette Stitch as K 3 tog.

Any number of sts may be purled together in this manner (see Pattern Stitch #189-A).

TAKING A LARGE NUMBER OF STITCHES TOGETHER

In this case, it is easier to *Purl* sts together than to Knit them. The RH needle can be more easily inserted into a large number of sts, *Purl-wise*, than *Knit-wise*, as the needle slips into them from the point, back, on the LH needle.

DOUBLE SLIP DECREASE, PURLED *(P 2 tog pnso)*

Purl the 1st 2 sts tog. Then sl the next st *Knit-wise*, from the LH needle and place it back in its new position (Fig. 91). Put the st made from the P 2 tog back onto the LH needle and pull the next st over it (Fig. 92). Transfer *this* st onto the RH needle.

As in the Sl 1, K 2 tog, psso (SK2togP), the top of this st will lie from Right to Left on the Knit Side of Stockinette Stitch.

INCREASING

KNIT INCREASES

PLAIN YARN-OVER *(yo—or: 0)*

Bring the yarn from back to front of the work *between* the two needles and carry it over the RH needle to the back again (Fig. 93). On the following row, the st thus formed will be Knit or Purled into the *front*

Fig. 88

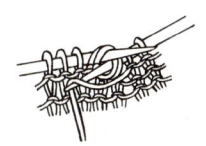

Fig. 89

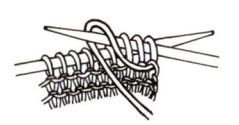

Fig. 90

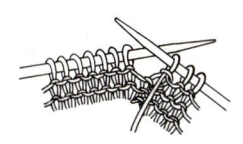

Fig. 91

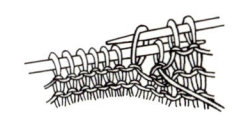

Fig. 92

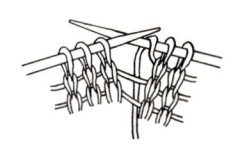

Fig. 93

Fig. 94a

Fig. 94b

of the loop and will become an extra st. This forms a hole in the work (Fig. 94a and Fig. 94b), generally used for decorative purposes.

There is no limit to the number of times the yarn may be wound around the needle to produce a lacy effect. This multiple yarn-over, however, is usually confined to lacework and will be explained in greater detail in the chapter on Pattern Stitches.

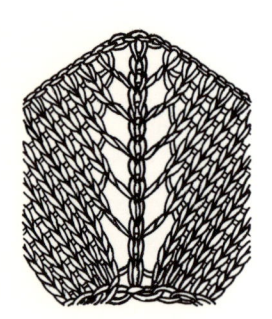

YARN-OVER WHEN CHANGING FROM KNIT TO PURL

When you are changing from a K st to a P st and a yarn-over is to be made between them, the yarn must come between the needle points toward you, over the needle away from you, and then back again toward you (Fig. 95). It is then in the correct position to work a P st.

Note: Watch closely and examine instructions carefully (especially in Thread Lace instructions), as this step is often erroneously referred to as "yarn-over twice." There are many instances, however, where two yarn-overs *are* made and where the yarn must come to Purl position before winding twice. This latter direction will most often be found in Thread Laces.

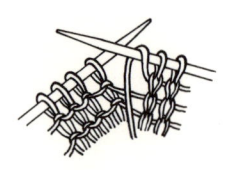

Fig. 95

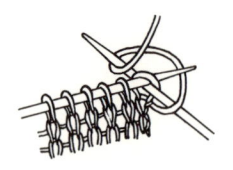

Fig. 96

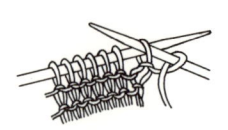

Fig. 97

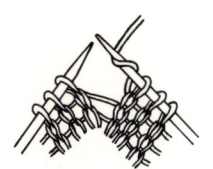

Fig. 98

YARN-OVER BEFORE WORKING THE FIRST STITCH

Knit: Put the RH needle *under* the yarn, leaving the yarn where it is, as it is now in the correct position for knitting the 1st st (Fig. 96). *Purl:* Put the needle *under* the yarn, then take the yarn over the needle to the back and bring it to the front again between the two needle points. The yarn is now in position to purl the 1st st from the LH needle (Fig. 97).

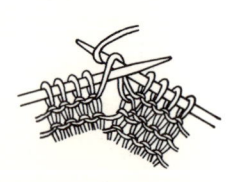

REVERSE YARN-OVER

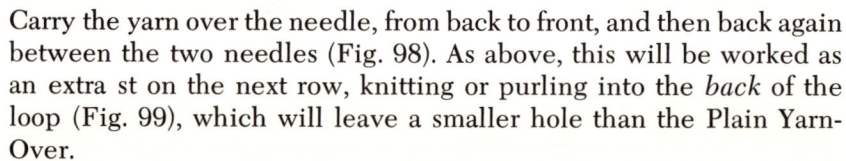

Fig. 99

Carry the yarn over the needle, from back to front, and then back again between the two needles (Fig. 98). As above, this will be worked as an extra st on the next row, knitting or purling into the *back* of the loop (Fig. 99), which will leave a smaller hole than the Plain Yarn-Over.

This method of increasing is used when an increase is to be made in Garter Stitch (Pattern Stitch #1-A) as it is less visible than any other method of increasing made in this stitch.

YARN-OVER—CROSS RIGHT

The yarn is thrown as in Reverse Yarn-Over, but on the next row it is Purled off into the *front* of the st (Fig. 100), making the resulting st cross to the RIGHT.

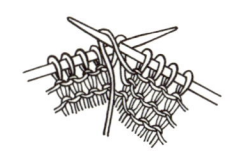

Fig. 100

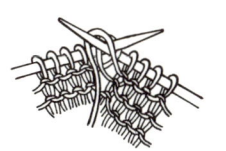

Fig. 101

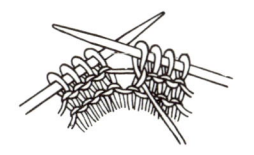

Fig. 102

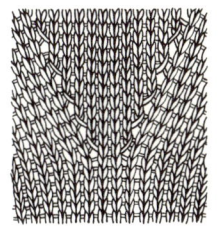

Fig. 103

YARN-OVER—CROSS LEFT

The yarn is thrown as in Plain Yarn-Over, but on the next row it is Purled off into the *back* of the st (Fig. 101), making the resulting st cross to the LEFT (Fig. 102).

Note: These two crossed yarn-overs result in a close st, with no hole made by the twisting on the following row. When these two methods of increasing are used in forming a seam st, such as in a gusset, crossing to the LEFT *before* the seam st and to the RIGHT *after* the seam st, a smooth flat seam will be attained (Fig. 103).

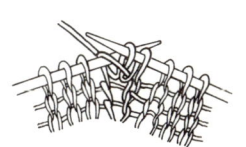

Fig. 104

PLAIN INCREASE

Insert the needle into the front of the st and *Knit, but do not slip* the worked st from the needle. Put the needle into the *back* of that same st and Knit this as another st (Fig. 104), *then* slip the 2 sts from the LH needle together. This 2nd st will have a small thread crossing over it horizontally (Fig. 105).

This increase is the one most commonly used in all knitting instructions, and it is correct to use it when the increase is to be incorporated into a seam, where it will not be noticed. The plain increase may also be used as a semidecorative stitch or as an outline in shaping. It makes an attractive seam st for a raglan shaping (Fig. 106).

When *two increases* are made, one immediately following the other, the 1st st of the 2nd increase will form an attractive chain at the center, outlined and accentuated by the horizontal threads of the two increases (Fig. 106).

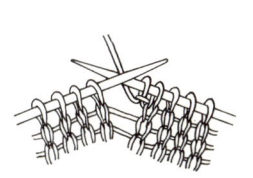

Fig. 105

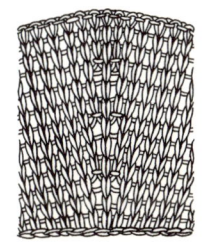

Fig. 106

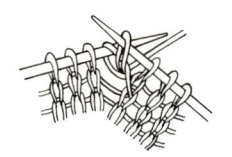

Fig. 107

This increase may also be worked to advantage if the needle is inserted into the *back* of the st and then into the *front* (Fig. 107). It should, however, be used only at the *edges* of the work—i.e., on the first st of a row, when shaping is to be made abruptly, when increasing is called for at the *beginning* and *end of every row*.

KNIT AND PURL THE SAME STITCH

This device for increasing is seldom used except perhaps at side edges where the joining of the seam will cover it. It is sometimes used when making a complicated gusset, but other means are just as good or better.

The st is Knitted without being slipped from the needle, the yarn brought to the front, and the same st is then Purled (Fig. 108). When used in the body of a Knitted fabric, this kind of increase usually leaves a rather unsightly hole and is best avoided except in very unusual circumstances.

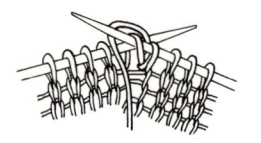

Fig. 108

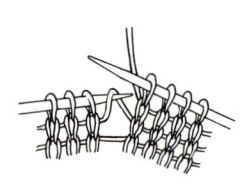

Fig. 109

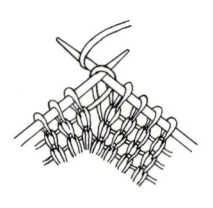

Fig. 110

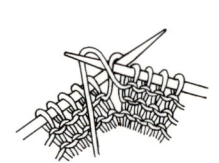

Fig. 111

LIFTED INCREASE, RIGHT *(M 1 R)*

At the point of increase insert the LH needle point, *from back to front,* under the thread between the 2 sts on opposite needles (Fig. 109). Insert the RH needle into the *front* of this new st on the LH needle and Knit it (Fig. 110) or Purl it (Fig. 111) from this position.

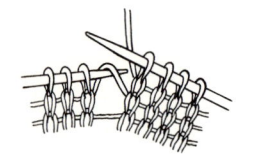

Fig. 112

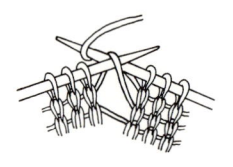

Fig. 113

Fig. 114

LIFTED INCREASE, LEFT *(M 1 L)*

Insert the LH needle point under the thread between the sts on opposite needles from *front to back* (Fig. 112). Insert the RH needle into the *back* of this new st and Knit (Fig. 113) or Purl (Fig. 114) it from this position.

INVISIBLE INCREASE, RIGHT

Turn the work on the LH needle slightly toward you so that the work on the back of that needle is visible. Insert the RH needle *tip* (just the tip, don't push the whole needle through) into the *back* of the st immediately *below* the st on the LH needle, *from the top down* (Fig. 115). Knit this as a st and then bring the needle forward and K the st on the needle from the front (Fig. 116).

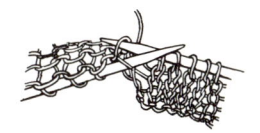

Fig. 115

INVISIBLE INCREASE, LEFT

Insert the LH needle point, *from back to front* of the work, under the st just completed on the RH needle (Fig. 117). Push back slightly on this thread, making an extra st on the LH needle. Knit this extra st into the back of the loop formed (Fig. 118).

Fig. 116

These last two methods are invaluable for working any increasing in a skirt, blouse, sweater, or jacket where the shaping must not be visible. When they are to be paired—i.e., when increases are to be made, one on either side of a central point—work an increase to the LEFT *approaching* this point, and an increase to the RIGHT *going away* from it (Fig. 119). They may also be used very effectively, one immediately following the other, first to the LEFT and then to the RIGHT. However, these increases should be used only when increasing is done gradually—i.e., *do not* use this method when increasing is being done every 2nd row or round. In that instance use LIFTED INCREASE, LEFT and LIFTED INCREASE, RIGHT.

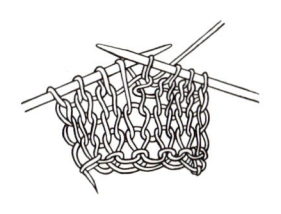

Fig. 117

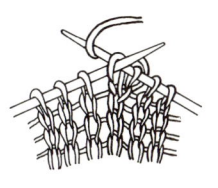

Fig. 118

Fig. 119

PURLED INCREASES

In almost any knitting, increases are generally made on the *Knit* or *front* face of the work. There are some instances, however, when shaping must be made so abruptly that increasing must be done on the Purled Side as well as the Knit Side of the work. The following methods of increasing on the Purled sts will result in the same appearance as the corresponding Knit increases.

Fig. 120

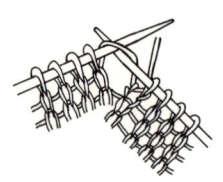

Fig. 121

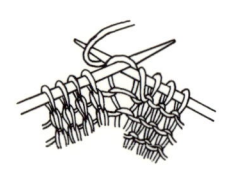

Fig. 122

PLAIN YARN-OVER

The term "Yarn-Over" is used in purling just as it is in knitting. However, in purling, the yarn is wound over the needle to the back and brought to the front between the two needle points (Fig. 120). It is worked as a separate st on the following row, into the *front* of the st (Fig. 121).

As in the Knit Yarn-Over, the yarn may be wound around the needle any required number of times.

YARN-OVER WHEN CHANGING FROM PURL TO KNIT

When changing from a Purl st to a Knit st, simply keep the yarn in front of the two needles where it is and Knit the next st (Fig. 122). This will automatically become a yarn-over.

REVERSE YARN-OVER WHEN CHANGING FROM PURL TO PURL

The yarn is brought to the back between needle points and then over the needle toward you (Fig. 123). This yarn-over is to be worked into the *front* of the st on the following row (Fig. 124).

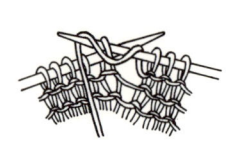

Fig. 123

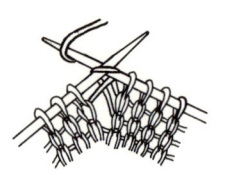

Fig. 124

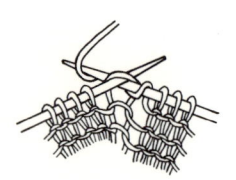

Fig. 125

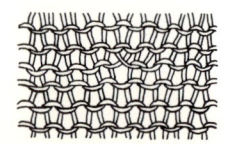

Fig. 126

REVERSE YARN-OVER WHEN CHANGING FROM PURL TO KNIT

When changing from a Purl st to a Knit st, the yarn must be taken to the back of the work between the needle points, brought over the needle toward you, then taken back again between the two needles (Fig. 125). It is then in position to work a Knit st.

YARN-OVER, CROSS RIGHT

The yarn is thrown the same as in Reverse Yarn-Over, but is worked into the *front* of the st on the next row; see Fig. 126 for the finished effect.

As in the Reverse Yarn-Over in Knitting, this cross yarn-over leaves no hole in the work; the increases are almost invisible.

YARN-OVER, CROSS LEFT

The yarn is thrown the same as in Plain Yarn-Over, but is worked into the *back* of the st on the next row; see Fig. 127 for the finished effect.

PLAIN INCREASE

Purl into the front of the st and, without removing the st from the LH needle, Purl into the *back* of the same st (Fig. 128) and then remove the 2 sts together.

As in the Knitted Plain Increase, this may be made by Purling first into the *back* of the st and then into the *front*.

INVISIBLE INCREASE, LEFT

With the LH needle tip, reach upward under the st *below* the last st made on the RH needle. Lift back slightly on this thread and Purl it from the front (Fig. 129).

INVISIBLE INCREASE, RIGHT

Insert the RH needle tip into the closed loop just below the 1st st on the LH needle and open this st just enough to be able to place the RH needle tip into it, from back to front, and purl it as a st (Fig. 130).

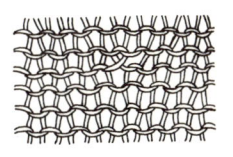

Fig. 127

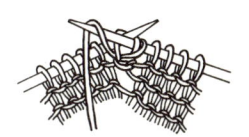

Fig. 128

Fig. 129

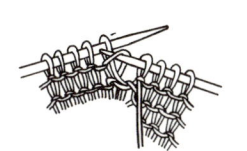

Fig. 130

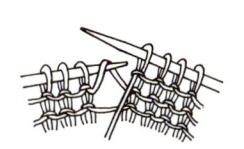

Fig. 131

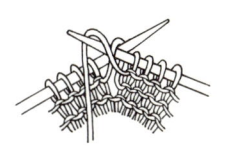

Fig. 132

LIFTED INCREASE, RIGHT *(M 1 P)*

Insert the LH needle point under the thread between the sts on the two needles, *from back to front* (Fig. 131). Purl into the *front* of this resulting loop (Fig. 132).

LIFTED INCREASE, LEFT *(M 1 P)*

Insert the LH needle point under the thread between the sts on opposite needles *from front to back* (Fig. 133). Purl into the *back* of this resulting loop (Fig. 134).

The designations Right and Left in the names of these increases indicate the direction of the slant that the st will take on the Right— or Knit—Side of the fabric.

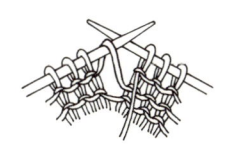

Fig. 133

Fig. 134

These types of increases, on both the Knit Side and the Purl Side, may be safely used on immediately succeeding rows when shaping must be done abruptly.

MISCELLANEOUS INCREASES

PICK UP ONE STITCH *(Pu 1) (Pattern Stitch #130)*

Insert the RH needle point under the thread lying between the two needles. Knit or Purl under this thread, using it as a st (Fig. 135). This will act as a *yarn-over*, leaving a slightly smaller hole in the work.

KP — PK — KPK — *or any variations of these*

This usually follows a row of pattern stitch where one or more yarn-overs (00 — 000 — 0000) occur. "KP" means to Knit and Purl into the yarn-overs. "PK" means to Purl and Knit into the indicated st or overs. "KPK" would make three sts.

If a KP or a PK is to be worked into a real stitch, however, it will be written in that manner.

Pattern Stitch #170, Row 2, reads as follows:

"K 1, P 3, * KP, P 3, K 1, P 3" — etc.

In this case, the KP is worked into the 00 of the previous row, the Knit st into the 1st 0, and the Purl st into the 2nd 0. It is not necessary, however, to work the KP into a yarn-over alone.

Pattern Stitch #168, Row 2, reads as follows:

"K1, * yo, K 2 tog b, K 2 tog, yo, P 2, (KPK)x2, P 2" — etc.

The row before this one has *no* yarn-overs, the K, P, and K being made into each of 2 K sts of the previous row.

In making the Knot Stitch (Pattern Stitch #32) or the Tuft Stitch (see Pattern Stitch #123) the knitting and purling into one st is done 6 or 8 times. These stitches are both fully explained under their own titles on page 85.

Note: One thing must be remembered, however: where there are more than 3 sts to be made, they *must* be made loosely enough to be worked together on the following row. In these cases, give the yo's a little extra tug on the next row.

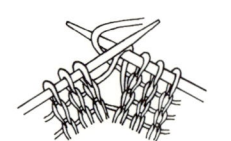

Fig. 135

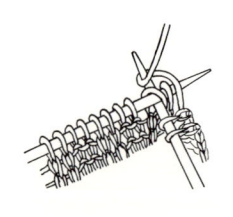

Fig. 136

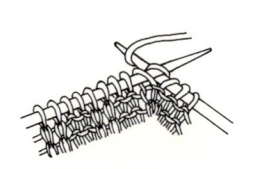

Fig. 137

78

CROSS-OVER STITCHES: CABLES

To produce a *braided*, *plaited*, or *woven* effect, a st or group of sts *beyond* or *to the left* of the st or sts at the point of the LH needle are worked *before* the sts which are skipped. There are numerous ways to work these cross-overs, and each produces a different effect.

Only the methods will be given here, the directions and uses are included with each pattern stitch.

CROSS-OVER ON TWO STITCHES, RIGHT—KNIT
(Cross R)—often called a "Mock Cable."

Insert the RH needle into the front of the 2nd st from the point of the LH needle and Knit it (Fig. 136). *Do not slip it off.* Knit into the front of the 1st (the skipped) st and *then* slip both sts off together (Fig. 137).

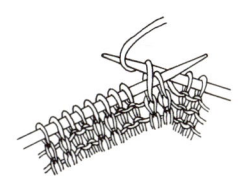

Fig. 138

CROSS-OVER ON TWO STITCHES, LEFT—KNIT *(Cross L)*

Insert the RH needle into the *back* of the 2nd st on LH needle (Fig. 138) and Knit it. Do not slip the st from the needle. Bring RH needle, with the st on it, to the front of the work and Knit the skipped st from the front, slipping both worked sts off together (Fig. 139).

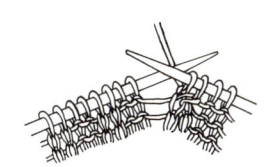

Fig. 139

CROSS-OVER ON TWO STITCHES, RIGHT—PURL *(Cross R, Purled)*

Insert the RH needle into the *front* of the 2nd st on LH needle (Fig. 140) and Purl it; do not slip the st from the needle. P the front of the 1st (the skipped) st and slip both worked sts off together (Fig. 141).

This makes a cross-over to the RIGHT on the Front—or Knit—Side of the fabric.

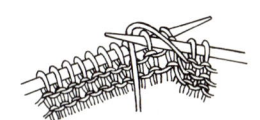

Fig. 140

CROSS-OVER ON TWO STITCHES, LEFT—PURL *(Cross L, Purled)*

With RH needle tip, pull the 2nd st on LH needle over the 1st st but do not drop it from the needle (Fig. 142). Purl it from the front of the st, slip it off, and then Purl the next st (Fig. 143). This produces a cross-over to the LEFT on the Front—or Knit—Side of the fabric.

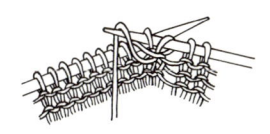

Fig. 141

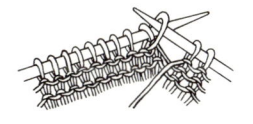

Fig. 142

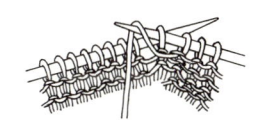

Fig. 143

Fig. 144 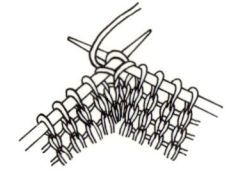   Fig. 145 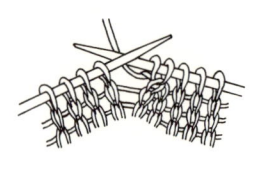   Fig. 146

CROSS THROUGH TWO STITCHES — RIGHT *(See Pattern Stitch #62)*

Insert RH needle into 2 sts on LH needle as though to Knit them together. Pull the thread through but do not take them off LH needle (Fig. 144). Instead, insert RH needle through the 1st st again and Knit it (Fig. 145). Then remove the sts from the needle (Fig. 146).

CROSS THROUGH TWO STITCHES — LEFT *(see Pattern Stitch #62)*

Insert RH needle into 2 sts on LH needle, but *through the backs* of the sts (Fig. 147). Knit them together in this position, but do not remove them from LH needle (Fig. 148). Instead, insert RH needle through the front of the 2nd st and Knit it (Fig. 149). Then remove sts from LH needle.

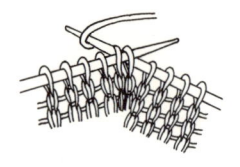

Fig. 147 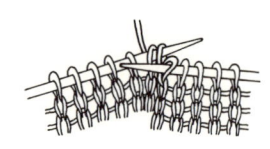   Fig. 148 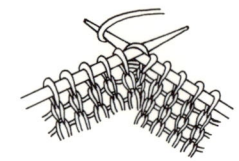   Fig. 149

MULTIPLE STITCH CROSS-OVERS

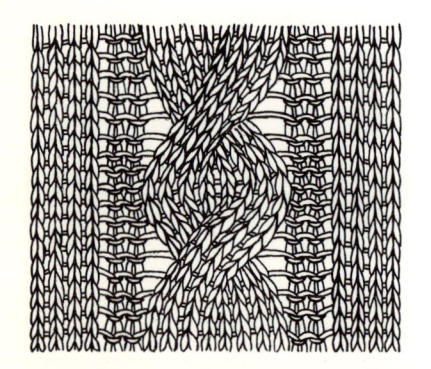

CABLE CROSS, RIGHT

In any cable which crosses the front of the fabric from LEFT to RIGHT (Fig. 150), the 1st group of sts which are held on a cable-stitch holder (or DP needle) must be held at the *back* of the work while the 2nd group is being worked. For example: A cabling row — i.e., the cross-over row — might read as follows:

P 2, cross 4 over 4 back (or R).

This would be worked as follows:

P 2 sts. Then sl the next 4 sts from LH needle onto a DP needle and hold these sts *in back of the work* (Fig. 151), away from the work

Fig. 150

area. K the next 4 sts (Fig. 152) and then either slip the 4 sts from the holder *back onto LH needle* (Fig. 153) (which is easier to do in the long run) or K them directly from the holder (which is more awkward and not advisable).

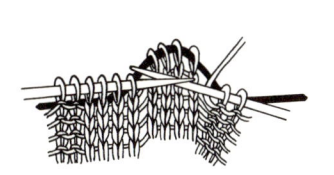

Fig. 151

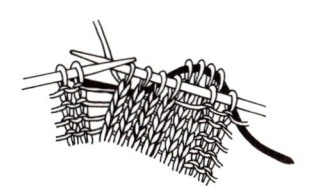

Fig. 152

Fig. 153

CABLE CROSS, LEFT

In any cable which crosses the front of the fabric from RIGHT to LEFT (Fig. 154), the 1st group of sts must be held at the *front* of the work while the 2nd group is being worked.

This is worked exactly the same as Cable Cross, Right, with this one exception; the sts are held at the *front* of the work on the DP needle instead of at the back.

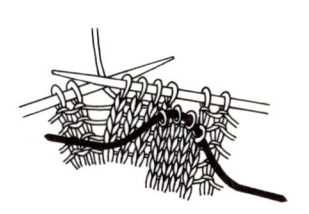

Fig. 154

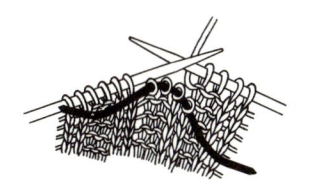

Fig. 155

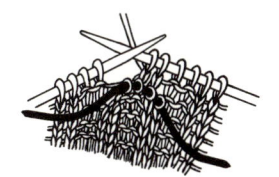

Fig. 156

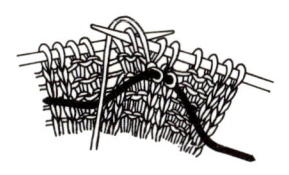

Fig. 157

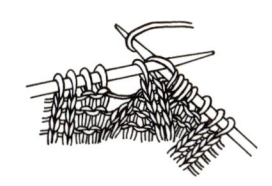

Fig. 158

MAKING A RIB CABLE *(K 2, P 2, K 2—or: K 3, P 3, K 3)*

When the pattern reads as follows:

P 2, cable 2, 2 and 2 front—

In cabling, the first 4 sts are slipped from the LH needle onto a holder (or DP needle) and held away from the work area, either back or front, as the instructions indicate (Fig. 155). The next 2 sts are Knit from LH needle (Fig. 156), then the 2 Purled sts are slipped from DP back onto LH needle and Purled (Fig. 157), then the last 2 Knit sts are Knit from DP, or placed back onto LH needle and Knit from there (Fig. 158).

The K 3, P 3, K 3 cable is worked in the same way, counting 3 instead of 2.

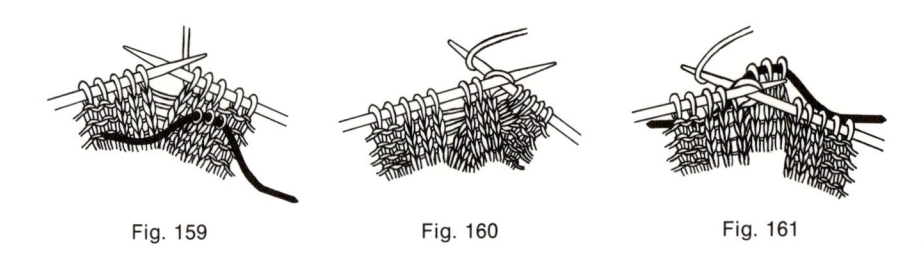

Fig. 159   Fig. 160   Fig. 161

CABLE BRAID *(see Pattern Stitch #178)*

This is worked with three groups of sts instead of two groups as in the plain cable. The 1st group is crossed over the 2nd to the LEFT. The 3rd group is crossed over the 2nd to the RIGHT. Using 9 sts as the basis of the braid, the pattern would develop as follows:

The first cross-over is made by holding the 1st 3 sts in *front* while Knitting the next 3 sts (Fig. 159). Then, when the 3 sts have been Knitted from the holder, the last 3 sts of the group are Knitted (Fig. 160).

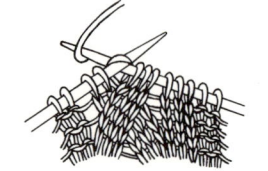

After the designated number of rows between the 1st and 2nd cabling operations have been completed, the 1st 3 sts are Knit, then the 2nd group of 3 sts are held on a holder at the *back* (Fig. 161), the 3rd group of 3 sts are Knit, and finally the 3 sts are worked from the holder or, better, put back onto LH needle and worked from that (Fig. 162a, Fig. 162b).

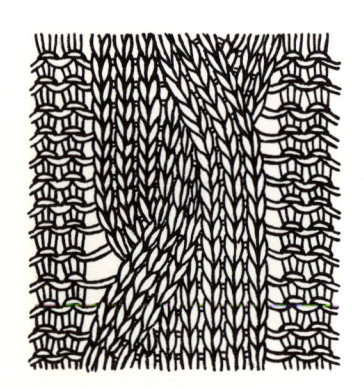

Fig. 162a

Fig. 162b

DOUBLE CABLE *(see Pattern Stitch #149)*

Often called the Smiling or Horseshoe Cable, both the Right and Left Cable Cross are used in the same cable group.

This stitch is composed of *four* groups of sts, the 1st group crossing the 2nd to the RIGHT and the 3rd group crossing the 4th to the LEFT. With 12 sts as the basis of this cable, the cabling operation would develop as follows:

Sl the 1st 3 sts onto a holder and hold them at the *back* of the work. Knit the next 3 sts (Fig. 163). The 3 sts are put back onto LH

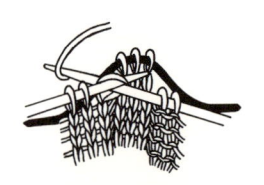

Fig. 163 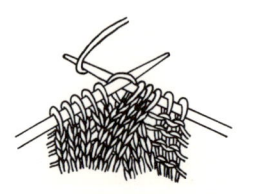   Fig. 164

82

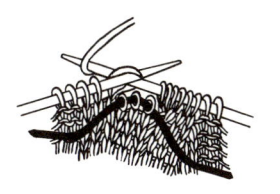

Fig. 165 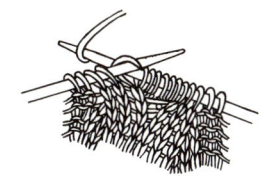   Fig. 166a

needle and Knit from that (Fig. 164). Then the 3rd group of 3 sts is held at the *front* of the work (Fig. 165), while the 4th group is worked. Then put the 3 sts from the holder back onto LH needle and Knit them (Fig. 166a, Fig. 166b).

What is called the Frowning Cable is worked in the direct opposite manner, the 1st group crossing the 2nd to the LEFT and the 3rd group crossing the 4th to the RIGHT.

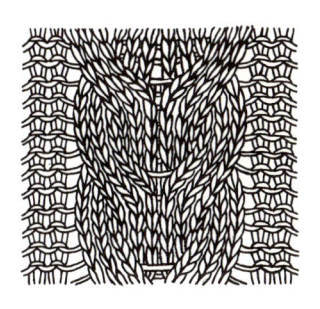

Fig. 166b

RIGHT AND LEFT *(Braid Cable) (see Pattern Stitch #148)*

This is a variation of the Cable Braid in which both the Right and Left Cross-Overs are made in the same cabling row. It produces a tighter cable and one that has less stretch. It rises and *remains* above the surface of the surrounding knitting and is used more as a decorative motif than as a cable stripe.

Fig. 167 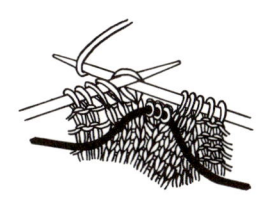   Fig. 168 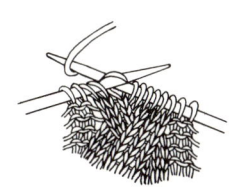   Fig. 169a

With 9 sts as the basis of this cable, the cabling operation would develop as follows:

Sl the 1st group of 3 sts onto a DP and hold them in *back* of the needles and K the next 3 sts (Fig. 167). Then bring DP, with the 3 sts on it, to the *front* of the needles (Fig. 168) and K the next 3 sts from LH needle. Then sl the 3 sts from DP to LH needle and K them (Fig. 169a, Fig. 169b).

Fig. 169b

CROSSING ON AN UNEVEN NUMBER OF STITCHES
(K 3, P 1, K 3 Cable) (see Pattern Stitch #126)

This cable is worked on 7 sts. The 1st 4 sts are put onto a DP needle and either held at the back or the front of the work as designated in the pattern. The 3 sts on LH needle are Knitted (Fig. 170). The 1 Purled st is put onto LH needle and Purled (Fig. 171). Then the last 3 sts are put onto LH needle and Knitted (Fig. 172).

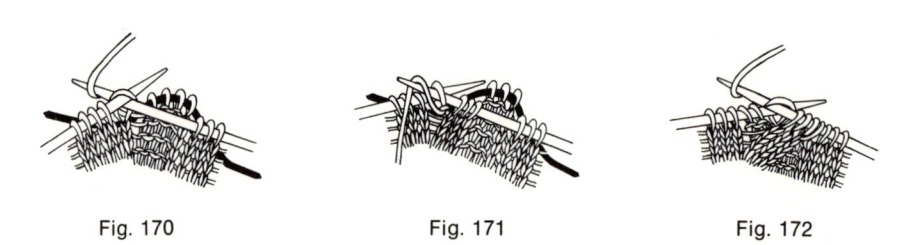

Fig. 170　　　Fig. 171　　　Fig. 172

CROSSING ON THREE STITCHES
(Cable over 2 L—Cable over 2 R) (see Pattern Stitch #60)

Cross Right. Insert RH needle into the 3rd st in a group of 3 sts on the LH needle (Fig. 173). Knit this st. Do not sl it off, but K the 1st (Fig. 174) and then the 2nd st (Fig. 175) of the 2 sts that lie before it. Sl all 3 sts off together (Fig. 176).

Cross Left. Sl the first st in a group of 3 sts on LH needle onto a DP needle and hold in front of work (or simply hold this st with LH thumb [Fig. 177]) while slipping the next 2 sts onto RH needle, in back of it. Put the 1 st across the front onto LH needle (Fig. 178) and then sl the other 2 sts back to LH needle. They are then already crossed and ready to be worked (Fig. 179).

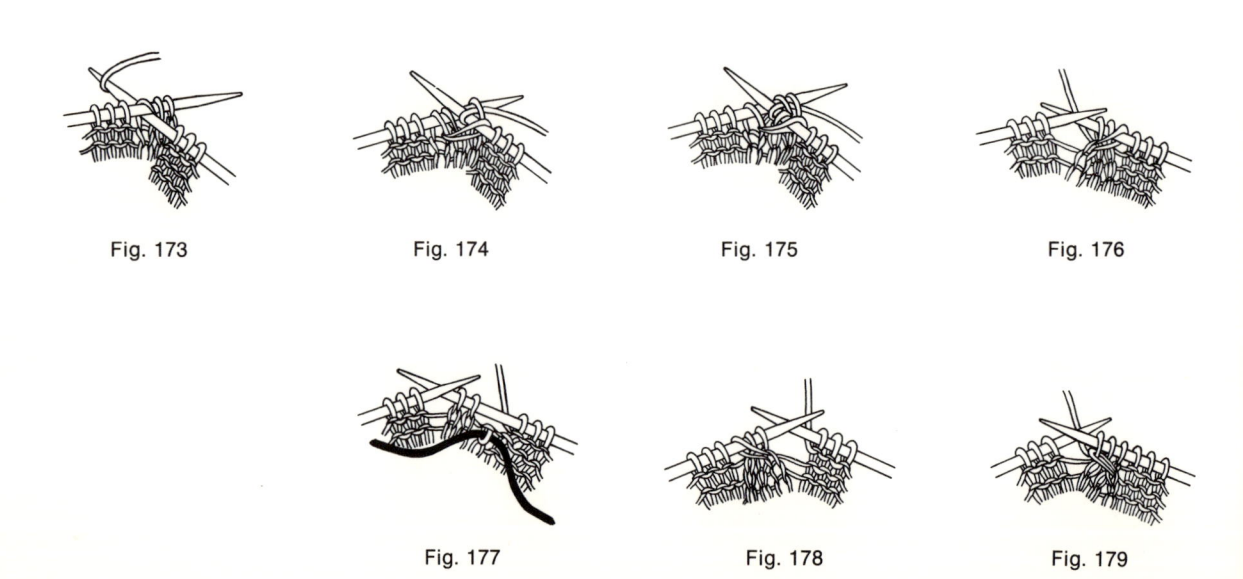

Fig. 173　　　Fig. 174　　　Fig. 175　　　Fig. 176

Fig. 177　　　Fig. 178　　　Fig. 179

MISCELLANEOUS MULTIPLE STITCHES

TIE STITCH *(see Pattern Stitch #156)*

This is sometimes called Smocking Stitch and is used to draw a number of sts together either as a false cable or to simulate smocking.

A group of sts are slipped from LH needle onto a DP needle and held away from the work area, either back or front. The yarn is then wound 2 or 3 times around these sts just under the needle which holds them (Fig. 180a). The sts are then replaced on LH needle and worked off in the manner prescribed in the instructions (Fig. 180b).

Fig. 180a

Fig. 180b

KNOT STITCH *(see Pattern Stitches #124 and #175)*

K, P, K, P, K and P — written KPKPKP in the directions — into 1 st (Fig. 181). With LH needle point, reach over the last st made and pull the next st over it, letting it drop between the two needle points (Fig. 182). Reach again with LH needle and pull next st over and let it drop as before. Repeat this pulling over of the sts until 5 in all have been pulled over, leaving the last st made — the last P st — on RH needle (Fig. 183).

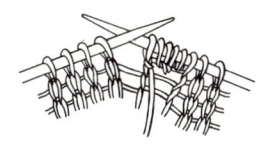

Fig. 181

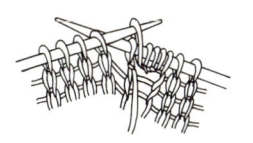

Fig. 182

Fig. 183

TUFT STITCH *(see Pattern Stitch #123)*

K, P, K, P, K, P, K and P (written KPKPKPKP, and 8 sts made) into 1 st (Fig. 184). With LH needle point, reach over to the *1st* st made in this group and pull it over the other 7 sts (Fig. 185). Then reach over again and pull the 2nd st of this group over the other 6 sts. Continue to pull 1 st over the remaining sts until only 1 st remains (Fig. 186).

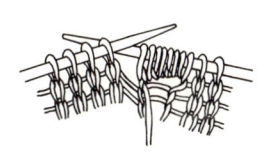

Fig. 184

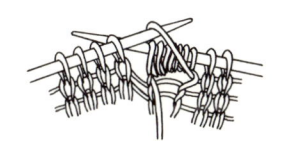

Fig. 185

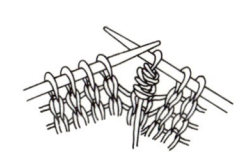

Fig. 186

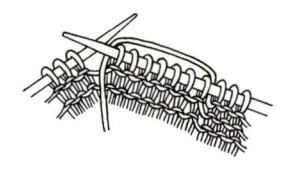

Fig. 187 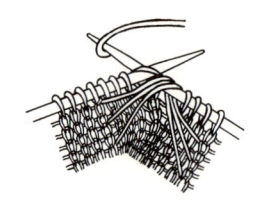   Fig. 188a 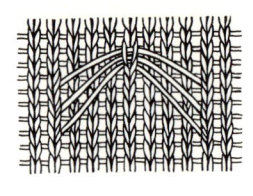   Fig. 188b

BOWKNOT or BUTTERFLY STITCH *(see Pattern Stitch #119)*

This is worked in various ways in different instructions. A strand of yarn is carried across a specified number of slipped sts (Fig. 187) on the Front — or Right — Side of the work. When the particular number of rows has been worked, these strands are then caught up into the designated row (Fig. 188a) and the strands form a bow (Fig. 188b).

Many instructions are written for the carrying of the yarn to be done on the *Knit* row and the bow to be formed on the *Purl* Side. It is just as easy, however, to carry the yarn on the Purled Side and to Knit up the strands on the Knit Side. In Pattern Stitch #119b, the strands are carried over 7 sts on the Purled side of the work for 3 Purled rows. On the following Knit row, all sts are worked to the center st of this group of 7 sts. The RH needle is then slipped under the strands and knitted off together with the next st.

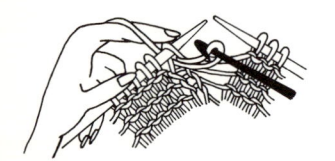

Fig. 189 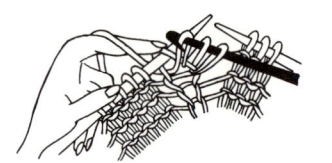   Fig. 190 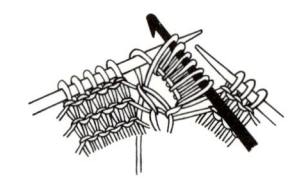   Fig. 191 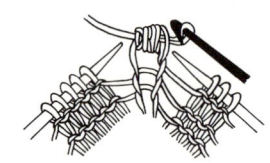   Fig. 192

ROSEBUD *(see Pattern Stitch #126)*

This is worked with a crochet hook during the knitting operation. Hold the yarn in Left Hand as for crocheting. Insert crochet hook into the designated st (Fig. 189) and pull a loop of yarn through, at least a half inch long. * Yarn over the hook and insert into the same st again and pull another loop through (Fig. 190). Rep from * twice (7 loops on hook) (Fig. 191). Yarn over hook and pull yarn through all loops, removing st from LH needle at the same time (Fig. 192). Replace this st from the hook to RH needle.

POPCORN or BUBBLE STITCH

This stitch is very often used in the famous Aran Islands sweaters.
   Work in the following manner:
   Into just one st, K 1 st and pull up loosely, yo, K another st in the same st and pull up, yo, K another st in the same st and pull up (Fig. 193). Turn the work around completely. Purl each of these 5 sts. Turn the work around again. Sl 1 st, K 4. Turn the work again and P 2 tog, P 1, P 2 tog. Turn work again and sl 1, K 2 tog, psso—(SK2togP)—POPCORN, BUBBLE made (Fig. 194 and Fig. 195).

Fig. 193

LEAF STITCH *(see Pattern Stitch #126)*

This stitch is also worked with a crochet hook. The hook is inserted *in between* 2 sts 6 rows down under the stitch marked as the "stem" stitch (Fig. 196). A loop is pulled up to the level of the knitting *loosely*, * the yarn taken around the hook, inserted again into the same spot, brought up again and once more repeated from * (Fig. 197). The yarn is pulled through the resulting 5 sts and replaced onto RH needle (Fig. 198). The second leaf is made in like manner at the designated spot 7 rows down as indicated in the instructions.

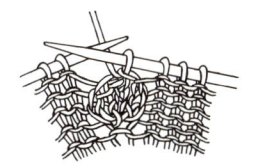

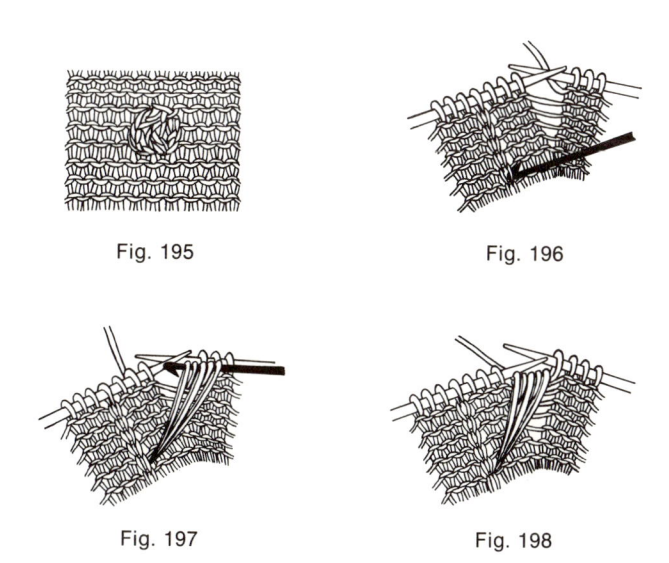

Fig. 194

Fig. 195

Fig. 196

Fig. 197

Fig. 198

SLIPPED STITCHES

As stated earlier in considering *decreased* sts, a slipped st is taken from the LH needle in a *Knit-wise* position (Fig. 62).
   In building a fabric, however, the stitch must be slipped from the needle in a *Purl-wise* position so that it will lie on the needle in the correct position for working on the next row. This must be borne in mind whenever a slipped st is called for, whether the yarn is to be carried at the front or back of the work, or on a Knitted or Purled row *(see Pattern Stitch #95).*

PICKING UP STITCHES

The term "picking up stitches" is really an erroneous one as it implies that the sts along any edge are to be picked up directly onto a single needle from the loops made by the knitted fabric itself. Common usage, however, has made this term an accepted part of the knitting language and is generally used in all modern instructions.

The operation itself is a knitting action, performed with a needle *and* yarn (or thread), and the sts are actually knitted up from the edge where additional work is to be done. As a matter of fact, sts may even be picked up from a piece of woven fabric as well as from knitted material, providing the needle can be inserted into the fabric without damaging the threads. At this point, only the manner and method of picking up sts at edges of *knit* fabrics will be taken up in detail.

No matter what particular pattern stitch has been made in the main body of the material, the number of sts which must be made at the edge in question depends on the shape or contour that this edge will ultimately assume and the stitch that will be used, and all of these *must* depend on the GAUGE upon which the new piece of work is based. As a rule, specific numbers of sts are given in instruction books. If this number is *not* specified, however, the suggestions below should be followed. We are concerned only with the *method* used in the operation.

There is one main point that must be kept in mind, particularly when picking up sts for any woolen yarn knitting. *Do not pick up too close* to the edge. With the front side of the fabric facing you, tie the yarn in at the starting point, insert the needle into the work, *at least two threads in from the edge,* wrap the yarn around the needle and pull the resulting loop through, just as though you were knitting a st from a needle (Fig. 199). Insert the needle into the next st to the left of the 1st st and repeat the process along the edge which is to be finished, usually spacing the sts as follows: Pick up 1 st in 1 space, pick up another in the space next to it, and pick up a 3rd st in the 3rd space, skipping each 4th space (Fig. 199). No matter how close together or far apart the sts are to be spaced, use one successive line of sts as a working base (Fig. 199)—i.e., follow the same side stitch in each row of the previous knitting as a guide. Of course, there must be an exception to this rule when there is a shaped edge from which these sts are to be taken up. In such a case the main point to remember is to avoid a st which presents a large open loop and choose one that will appear tighter. When 1 st is to follow close upon the heels of another in a shaped edge, choose a loop of knitting, 2 sts in from the edge for the 1st st made, and work the 2nd st into the space directly next to it.

Picking up sts with the *Wrong*—or Purled—Side of the fabric facing you is a little more difficult to do, but not at all a fearsome task. Keeping the above *Knitting* process in mind, insert the needle *Purl-wise* into the edge st and Purl it (Fig. 200). The following method may be performed more easily, however, in a *Knit-wise* fashion.

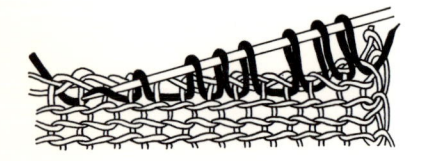

Fig. 199

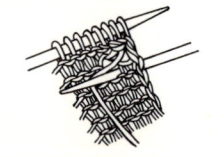

Fig. 200

With the yarn attached (or still running) at the starting point, *with the Right Side* of the fabric facing you, hold the knitting needle and fabric in the *Left Hand,* with the needle point facing *right.* Using a crochet hook in the *Right Hand,* insert it away from you, from front to back, into the correct st of the fabric (Fig. 201) and pull a loop through, slipping it onto the LH needle in the correct position for working on the next row (Fig. 202). Proceed in this manner for the desired number of sts.

When working off these sts, *always* slip the *first st Purl-wise* before working the next sts.

A new needle has been developed for the special purpose of making the process of picking up sts easier for the knitter who is unaccustomed to this procedure. This needle has a crochet hook at one end and a knitting needle point at the other. A large number of sts may be picked up on the hooked end, in one operation, and then transferred to the regular needle from the pointed end. It is a real convenience to both the amateur and the professional knitter. Be careful, though, what you use this needle on, as it is made in sizes 1, 2, and 3 only — none larger.

A crochet hook *may* be used in the same manner, but most crochet hooks are made with a bulge at the center which may be too large for the sts to pass over easily.

One more very important point: if the Right Side of the fabric consists of Purling, the picked-up sts are made in KNITTING — you would still KNIT UP the sts from the *Right Side* (the Purled Side) of the work, *not the Wrong Side.*

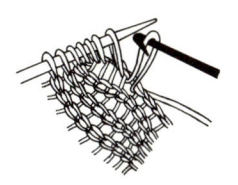

Fig. 201

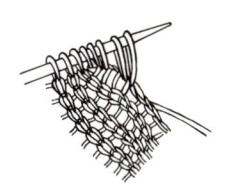

Fig. 202

KNITTED HEMS

With a needle *at least one size smaller* than the ones to be used in the fabric, and using Cast-On Method I or II, work in Stockinette Stitch for the depth of the facing of the hem. Work one Knit row on the Purled Side for a turning row, change to the regular-size needles and work the same number of rows again in Stockinette (or Pattern) Stitch, *minus one row,* ending with a Purled or Wrong Side row.

With the Knit Side of the fabric facing you, fold the work along the turning row and, with the cast-on edge immediately in back of the LH needle, insert the RH needle into the 1st st on the LH needle and into the 1st st of the cast-on edge, knitting them off together (Fig. 203). Proceed in this same manner across the row.

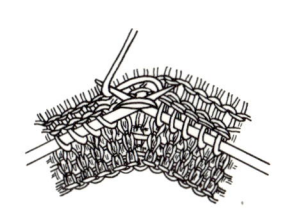

Fig. 203

ALTERNATE METHOD I

Instead of working 1 K row on the Purl Side for turning, substitute 1 row of K 1, P 1 ribbing.

89

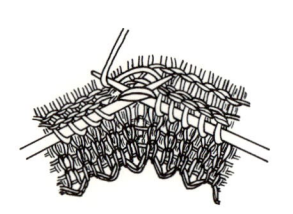

Fig. 204

ALTERNATE METHOD II

This makes a picot edge with considerable stretch. Instead of working 1 Knit row on the Purled Side for turning, work 1 row in the following manner:

P 1, * yo, P 2 tog — rep from * across the row, making sure to retain the same number of sts at the finish of the row (Fig. 204).

GRAFTING

GRAFTING FROM TWO NEEDLES (*Kitchener Stitch*)

Divide all sts onto two needles according to indicated instructions and break the yarn, making sure to leave enough to work all sts. Thread yarn into a tapestry needle. Hold the two needles together in the Left Hand, the needle points facing Right, with the finishing thread and needle held in the Right Hand. The sts on each needle must be close to the points for easy working.

Method: * Insert the tapestry needle into the *front* of the 1st st on the front needle in a knitting position (Fig. 205) and draw through this st, slipping it from the needle and drawing the yarn through at the same time. Insert the needle into the next st on the same needle in a *Purl-wise* position (Fig. 206). *Do not* slip this st from the needle, but pull the yarn through this st, leaving it on the needle (Fig. 207).

Insert the needle into the front of the first st on the back needle *from back to front* as though to Purl it (Fig. 208). Draw yarn through this st and slip it from the needle at the same time (Fig. 209). Insert needle into the next st on the same needle as though to Knit it (Fig. 210). *Do not* slip this st from the needle, but pull the yarn through this st, leaving it on (Fig. 211).

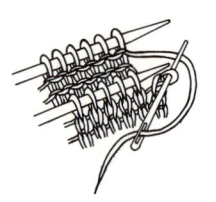

Fig. 205

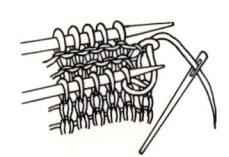

Fig. 206

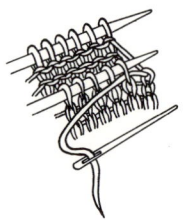

Fig. 207

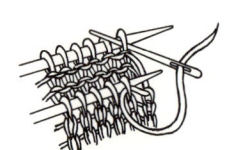

Fig. 208

Fig. 209

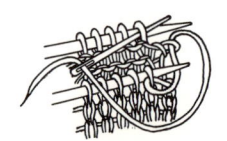

Fig. 210

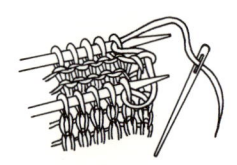

Fig. 211

Rep from * (above) across all sts on both needles until there is only one st left on each. If it is a sock or stocking, run your hand up into the work. Insert the threaded needle into the LH side of the last front loop and up into the st to the left. Sl the loop from the front needle and draw thread up gently to join loop to work. Repeat this procedure on the last loop left on the back needle. Turn work to Wrong Side and fasten thread—or, when making socks, weave the thread down and back under a few rows of knitting between the decreases.

To insure keeping the thread under the points of the two needles, keep the LH index finger over the points when the thread is being drawn through the st on the needle and the st being slipped off (Fig. 212). This also helps to keep the wrong sts from slipping off the needles.

Kitchener Stitch is the one method of grafting sts together from two needles to form an unbroken line of knitting in Stockinette Stitch. There may be instances where grafting must be made to join two pieces together where the Purled Sides of the work must match. In this case, join the work in the very same manner, the work being done on the *Wrong* Side—the Knit Side—of the work.

Fig. 212

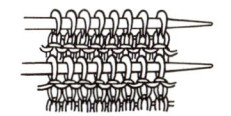

Fig. 213

GARTER STITCH GRAFTING

When two pieces of Garter Stitch must be grafted together from two needles, the two pieces of work must be properly worked for an invisible join. The top row (on the back needle) and the bottom row (on the front needle) must have the sts in the closed—or regular Purled—position (Fig. 213). The two needles are held together in the Left Hand and the yarn in the tapestry needle in the Right Hand. The grafting is then done exactly as in the above Kitchener Stitch.

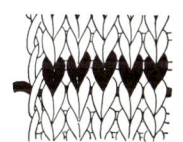

Fig. 214

HORIZONTAL GRAFTING—*on bound-off sts.*

When two bound-off edges need to be joined, grafting provides a neater-looking seam than joining with slip-stitch crochet as on side seams (see page 119). This grafting looks like another row of knitting, especially when joining two pieces of Stockinette Stitch (Fig. 214). Thread a tapestry needle with matching yarn. With the right side of both pieces facing you, hold the two pieces together with the edges touching. When you observe both pieces carefully, you can see that, on the side farthest away from you, there are *chains going away from you,* and, on the side nearest you, there are *chains coming toward you.* Each chain is a separate st. Fasten the thread at the RH edge and insert the needle under the first chain coming toward you on the near side, just below the bound-off sts (Fig. 215). The needle should be inserted *horizontally, from right to left,* and the yarn drawn through (Fig. 216). Insert the needle under the matching chain

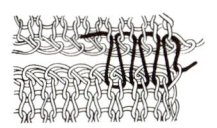

Fig. 215

Fig. 216

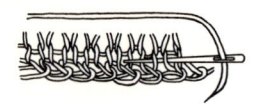

Fig. 217

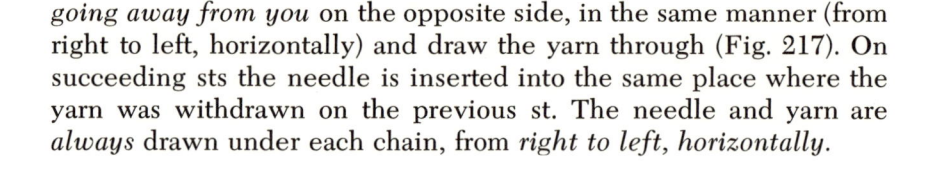

going away from you on the opposite side, in the same manner (from right to left, horizontally) and draw the yarn through (Fig. 217). On succeeding sts the needle is inserted into the same place where the yarn was withdrawn on the previous st. The needle and yarn are *always* drawn under each chain, from *right to left, horizontally.*

VERTICAL GRAFTING

This is worked in virtually the same manner as horizontal grafting, *using rows of knitting as a guide* rather than sts as in Fig. 214. When the rows of knitting match in number, the procedure is as follows: With both Right Sides of the knitting facing you, hold the two pieces together, with bottom edges at your right and edges touching. With a long piece of work, it is advisable to pin one piece to the other. Thread a tapestry needle with matching yarn and fasten it at the RH edge. Insert the needle into one st on the far side and take it under *two rows* of knitting, *at least two threads in* from the edge (Fig. 218). As in horizontal grafting, the needle should be inserted *horizontally, from right to left,* and the yarn drawn through. Then insert the needle under the two matching rows of knitting on the near side (from right to left, horizontally) and draw the yarn through (Fig. 219). Again, as in horizontal grafting, the needle is inserted into the same row of knitting where the yarn was withdraw on the previous st. This procedure is followed along the entire length of the seam.

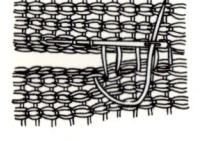

Where the number of rows on each piece are *not the same,* you may have to cheat a little; instead of going under two rows *every time,* go under just one row of the shorter piece every now and again to make the two pieces come out even.

Fig. 218

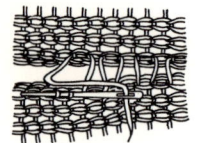

Fig. 219

Fig. 220

Fig. 221

TURNING AND SHAPING

To form a diagonal line without binding off, the work must be "turned" in the progress of Knitting and/or Purling. The most prevalent use of this turn is during the shaping of a heel on a sock or stocking (proceeding as directions indicate), although its use is not confined to just this function.

Shoulders are shaped by binding off series of sts, and then joined by sewing, slip-stitching, or grafting. They may be turned in series, however, and then joined by Kitchener Stitch, as already outlined. This turning is worked as follows:

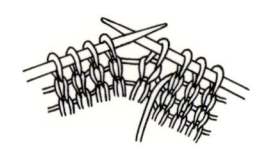

We will assume that the shoulder has 30 sts to be worked off in series of 6 sts each step. For the practice swatch: cast on 30 sts. Working in Stockinette Stitch, make about 6 rows, ending with a Purled row. Then: starting with a Knit row, K 24 sts. Bring the yarn to the front of the work and sl the next st *Purl-wise* (Fig. 220). Pass the yarn from the front to the back of the work around this slipped st (Fig. 221).

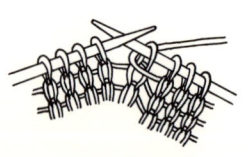

Put the slipped st back onto the LH needle without working it (Fig. 222). Turn work completely around and Purl back on all remaining sts. Again, K 18 sts; sl the next st as above. Turn the work and Purl back on the remaining sts. Continue to work 6 sts less each time before turning, until all sts have been worked and each set of 6 sts has been separated by a turned st. Bind these sts off if you wish to graft the two shoulders together, or slip the sts to a holder or spare needle, to be held until they are to be joined to each other. If these above 30 sts were to form a shoulder shaping, they would make the LEFT SHOULDER of a FRONT piece or the RIGHT SHOULDER of a BACK piece (Fig. 223).

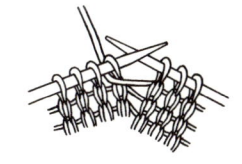

To turn the other shoulder, work as follows: Starting with a Purl row, P 24 sts. Sl the next st from the LH to the RH needle, keeping the yarn in front of the work (Fig. 224). Take the yarn to the back of the work and sl the st from the RH needle back onto the LH needle (Fig. 225). Turn the work completely around, take the yarn to the back of the work and Knit back on the remaining 24 sts. Continue to work 6 sts less each time before turning, until all sts have been worked and each set of 6 sts has been separated by a turned st (Fig. 226).

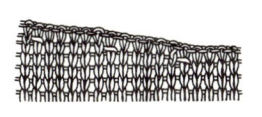

Fig. 222

Fig. 223 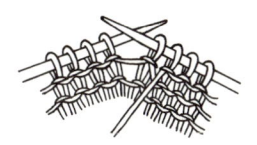   Fig. 224    Fig. 225 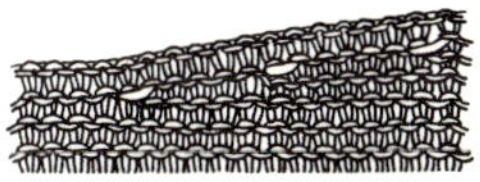   Fig. 226

KNITTING WITH MORE THAN ONE COLOR: ARGYLE, FAIR ISLE, AND SCANDINAVIAN KNITTING

In contemporary knitting the Argyle pattern is the best known and most used. Except in very unusual cases the article is made by Knitting one row and Purling the next throughout; the pattern is formed by changing colors. Each color is wound on a separate bobbin, and changes are made by following a chart. The most important thing to remember is that the colors *must* be twisted, one around the other, so that no unsightly gap divides them in the finished work and the Knit Side is smooth and even.

Before starting a sock, wind two full bobbins each of the main color or the diamond colors, and two bobbins each of the one or two cross colors. The colors are either cast on in order or tied in after a sufficient amount of cuff has been made. When changing one color for another, always wind the yarn around the next color in the sequence by putting the yarn you have just finished using *over* the yarn you are going to use next, bringing this new color up from underneath (Fig. 227). This prevents holes at the point of color change.

Fig. 227

Fig. 228

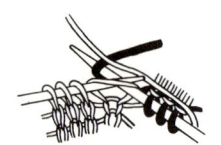

Fig. 229

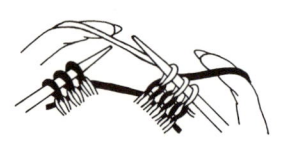

Fig. 230

Fig. 231

Fig. 232

The Fair Isle style of knitting is made in an entirely dissimilar fashion, the various colors not in use being carried along simultaneously across the back (the Purled) side of the work. This Fair Isle knitting may be successfully done in round or circular knitting, while Argyle knitting must be worked back and forth (except in a very unusual pattern). When one color is being used, the other color is carried across the back of the work and either locked in place with the working yarn (Fig. 228) or left loose if the distance is not too great (Fig. 229).

At the beginning of this chapter, it was stressed that *both* types of knitting should be learned—the English and the Continental methods—so that, if they were needed, they could be used with equal facility. This is where having learned both methods will really pay off. In working Fair Isle patterns, the Right Hand carries one color of yarn with the English method being used, and the second color is carried in the Left Hand, using the Continental method (Fig. 230).

One very important point: *always use the same hand for one color and the other hand for the other color. Don't switch hands;* it might result in an uneven appearance in the work.

As an example: we will take WHITE for the first color, and RED for the second color, with Diagram 1 to be followed. The sts on the chart are arranged 3 and 3, but traveling. WHITE is knitted for the first 3 sts, and then RED is worked for the next 3 sts (Fig. 231)—thus following the progression across the first row. The next row, the first 3 sts are purled with RED, then the sts are worked 3 and 3 to the end of the row, with WHITE having the 1st st. In this case, the two colors *are* twisted, so that there will be no gap between sts (Fig. 231). The different colors *not* being twisted in the body of the work are simply drawn across the back of the work loosely so that no puckering results (Fig. 229). This type of knitting does not require twisting of the yarn when changing colors except perhaps at the end or beginning of a row as just outlined.

When there are numbers of sts over *three* (or *five* at the most) to be carried, an entirely different manner of knitting and locking is to be followed: The English method of knitting is the easier one to use

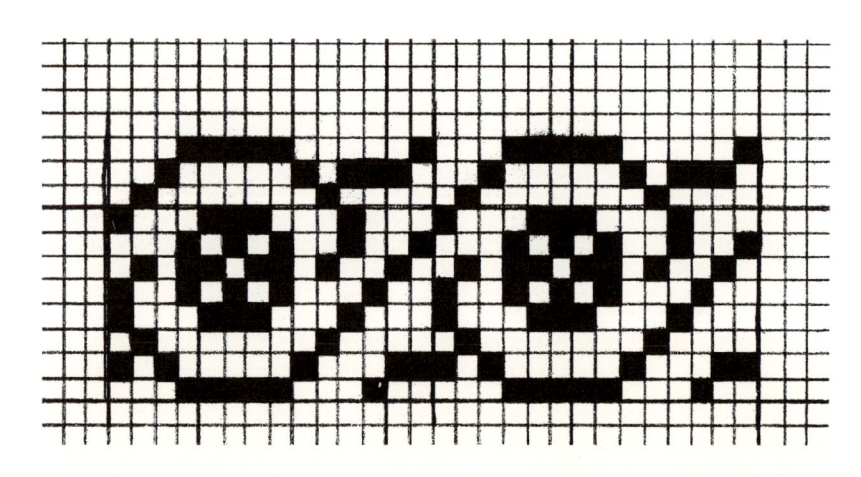

Diagram 1

in this circumstance and will be given first. We will take the number 7 for the number of sts to be worked. RED will be worked according to the English method and WHITE according to the Continental. With RED, K 3 sts as usual; then, with the Left Hand, lift WHITE slightly so that the RH needle may be inserted not only into the next st but *also* under WHITE which is in the Left Hand (Fig. 232). Knit the next st and pull RED *only* (Fig. 233) through the st. This will not only work the st but will lock WHITE at the back of the work. An entire row may be worked in this manner, with only RED appearing on the knit surface. For a practice piece, cast on 28 sts. * With RED, K 3 sts, carrying WHITE at the back loosely. Then lock WHITE with a knit st. Repeat from * across the row, locking the last st.

On the Purled Side, and still working with RED, and using the English method, Purl 3 sts as usual. Then, holding WHITE up slightly, Purl the next st with RED, inserting the RH needle into the st and *under* the WHITE strand as well (Fig. 234). Purl the RED st through, leaving the WHITE at the front and locked into position (Fig. 235). Repeat this across the row.

Work this practice swatch until you are thoroughly familiar with each movement—Knit, Purl, and lock—and you have a complete piece of RED knitting with WHITE being carried across the back of the work.

Now—using the Continental method, and carrying RED in the Left Hand, K 3 sts with RED. On the next st, and with the Right Hand, take WHITE under the needle with the regular English throw (Fig. 236); wrap RED around the needle, carry WHITE back off the needle, and complete the st with RED (Fig. 237). Work in this manner across the row, locking every 4th st.

Then, still carrying the RED yarn in the Left Hand, and using the Continental method, work with the RED yarn and carry the WHITE. P 3 sts with RED. Insert the RH needle point into the next st; carry WHITE *under* the RH needle point; wrap RED over the needle in the PURL position (Fig. 238), bring WHITE back off the needle (Fig. 239) and complete the st, thus locking WHITE into position.

Work a practice swatch, using this method, until you are thoroughly familiar with each movement—Knit, Purl, and lock. You will again have a swatch of RED, with WHITE being carried across the back.

Many knit fabrics are made, using more than one color, by just changing the colors of the yarn for one, two, or more rows. These fabrics are listed under Pattern Stitches—*not* multicolor knitting as above.

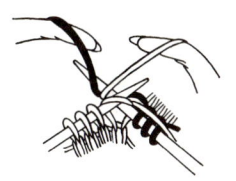

PICKING UP STITCHES FROM WOVEN MATERIAL

Knitting directly into woven material is very effective and quite easily accomplished. Finishing a neckline, the cuff of a sleeve (Fig. 240), even a knitted hemline can be done with very little effort.

As a general rule, it is wisest to use a fabric woven of wool or some fiber resembling wool. As the knitting needle is not usually used in the initial step of picking up sts, the material should be woven loosely enough so that a crochet hook may be inserted into it without damage to the fabric. The yarn used should be carefully chosen; it should be fine enough so that no threads are broken, and just heavy enough to suit the knitted finish you want to achieve.

As an example: a cuff may be knitted directly onto the bottom edge of a sleeve by working a row of single crochet directly over a very narrow hem, with the knitting sts then taken from the edge of the crochet (Fig. 241). As in all knitting, GAUGE is of prime importance and should be determined *before* the crochet work is begun, so that the sts may be close enough together or far enough apart to affect the final result. The crochet sts are made, covering the small hem, and then the knitting needle may easily pick up the sts from the double edge provided by the crochet work.

There are two alternative methods to use when picking up sts. *Method 1:* Spacing the single-crochet sts very evenly across or around the edge of the piece, knit the sts directly from these crocheted sts, and on the next row or round decrease or increase according to the number of sts necessary for the correct finish.

Method 2: Hemstitch the edge by machine. This will provide a very regular series of holes from which the knitting sts may be taken directly. On some materials this *may* result in an edge which shows traces of raveling of the fabric. Try these methods on a swatch of material before going ahead with the actual piece to be finished. You can then select the method best suited to the material.

Any of these methods may be used, whether the work is done on a flat piece (working back and forth with two needles) or worked around and around as with a cuff worked on four needles or a skirt hemline worked on a circular needle. Any one of these finishes may also be worked separately and applied later to an edge which has a crocheted line worked as outlined above. These finishes may be whipped into place on the wrong side, or joined with grafting (see page 90).

DUPLICATE STITCHING

Duplicate Stitching is a type of embroidery, worked over Stockinette Stitch, using a darning or tapestry needle and a yarn either of the same weight or heavier than that of the background knitting. It is also called Swiss Darning. The knitting stitches are embroidered over so that the pattern formed will stand out from the background. The

Diagram 2

Diagram 3

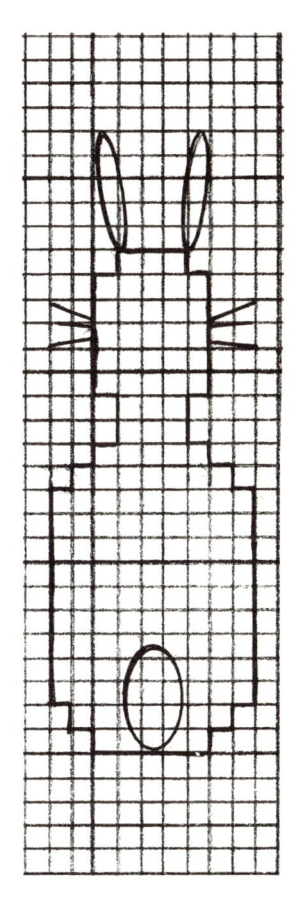

Diagram 4

97

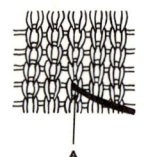

Fig. 242

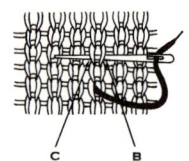

Fig. 243

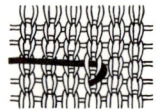

Fig. 244

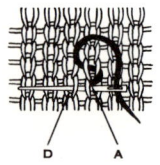

Fig. 245

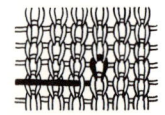

Fig. 246

design of the pattern and the style of the article to be decorated determine the kind of yarn to be used.

There are several things to consider when approaching the working of this type of stitching. The first is the fact that *knitted fabric*, especially Stockinette Stitch, does not form a true square of material, st for st and row for row. There are always more *rows* to the inch than *sts* to the inch. Therefore, if a strictly square design is to be worked, it *cannot* possibly be a square design worked out on *graph paper. It must be taller than it is wide.* A square pattern done in Duplicate Stitching will invariably turn out to be shorter and fatter than the original drawing. The design to work from should *look too high and too thin;* the resulting pattern will take form in proper proportion when the stitching has been applied. Diagram 2 will not be a true copy of the proper square shape seen in the picture. It is a good pattern to follow, but only as a traveling pattern, such as used in Fair Isle knitting, and better used in that manner. In either case, it will not be as high as it is wide.

The Sea Horse (Diagram 3), however, looks too thin on graph paper, but gains its proper proportions when worked in Duplicate Stitching, or worked in as in Fair Isle knitting.

For the practice piece, it is suggested that a swatch of Stockinette Stitch be made with 4-ply worsted or Germantown, or a similar yarn, and in white or a light color. So that the sts of the work may be more easily defined, cast on about 28 sts on size 8 or 9 needles. Work a *true square* of Stockinette Stitch. It is more than probable that you will have to work about 35 or 36 rows to make this square; thus, you will have had to make 7 or 8 *rows* more than the number of *sts across.*

Using a contrasting color, thread a tapestry needle with from 28 to 36 inches of yarn (Duplicate Stitching uses yarn quite rapidly). Following Diagram 4 of the Bunny, bring the needle, from the back to the front, up into the base of the st at A (Fig. 242). Leave about 3 inches of yarn and hold this at the back of the work so that it may be darned into the wrong side when the design has been completed.

With the point of the needle, trace the first st as it is formed in the swatch (Fig. 243). To do this, bring the needle, *from right to left,* under the two threads which form the top of this st. Draw the yarn through, from B to C (Fig. 244). Put the needle point back into A (Fig. 245) and trace the base of this st to the base of the next st to the left (under two threads) (Fig. 246). Bring needle out at D, snugging the working yarn up a little (not too closely) so as to have it stand out somewhat from the knitting itself. You will observe that the needle is *always* working from *right to left,* no matter whether it is working the *top* of the st or the *bottom* of the st. Continue to work in this manner, first working the *top* of the st and then the *bottom* of the next st to the left, until you have completed 4½ — not 5 — sts (Fig. 247).

When this last st has been reached and the top of it has been traced and worked, place the needle at the base of this last st (at E) and take the needle under the base of the next st. *Do not pull the yarn through,*

98

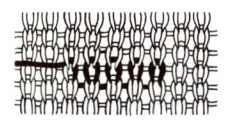

Fig. 247 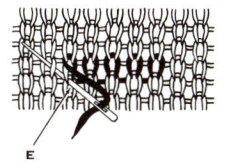   Fig. 248 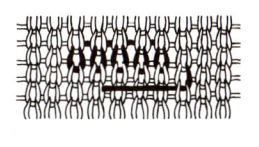   Fig. 249 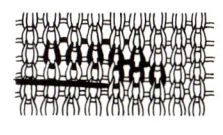   Fig. 250

Fig. 251

Fig. 252

but take the point of the needle *up* under one thread *only* on the next st above this last line worked (Fig. 248). Draw the yarn through. This will be the start of the next row. Turn work completely upside down so that the covered sts of the first row are at the top of the work (Fig. 249). You will be working in the opposite direction, but the yarn and the needle will *still* be worked *from right to left* on this next row. The sts of *this* row will be forming an upside-down V, and the needle and yarn will still be worked under two threads of both the top and the bottom of the sts (Fig. 250). Work across in this manner until you have 6½ sts. Bring the needle from the top of this st to the top of the next st (Fig. 251). *Do not* pull the yarn through, but bring the needle point *down* under just one thread (Fig. 252). Draw the yarn through. This will form the start of the first st of the next row. Turn work around again.

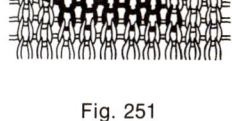

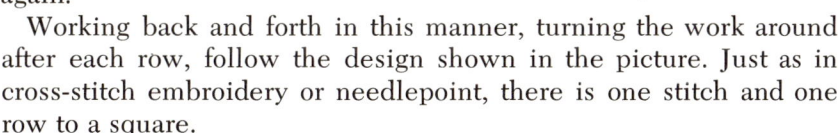

Working back and forth in this manner, turning the work around after each row, follow the design shown in the picture. Just as in cross-stitch embroidery or needlepoint, there is one stitch and one row to a square.

Many knitters prefer to make Argyle socks and sweaters by knitting just the diamonds and leaving the crossbars until after the knitting has been completed. This is a good practice to follow, as the colors used for the crossbars are apt to get a little lost when knitted in. The Duplicate Stitching for these crossbars is superimposed on the knitting, giving an attractive embossed effect. The colors may be worked exactly the same as in any other Duplicate Stitching, following the same principles outlined here.

Also, just as in good cross-stitching, the working thread should never have a knot at the end, the several short threads should be worked into the back of the stitching.

DETERMINING YOUR GAUGE

THE MOST IMPORTANT FACTOR IN THE FIT ON *ANY* KNITTED GARMENT IS *CORRECT GAUGE TIMES CORRECT MEASUREMENT.*

The *only* way to determine *your* gauge is to make a swatch (sample of knitting), using the *same stitch, same color,* and the *same kind of yarn.* Also, the swatch *must* be made on the *same size needles* you plan to use in the main part of the knitted piece. To get the best gauge, make a piece about four inches square. The number of sts *across* is your *stitch gauge* and the number of rows up and down is your *row gauge.* If the pattern stitch is not a lace one, but a type of fabric stitch, do not bind off, but remove the knitting from the needle. If it *is* a lace stitch, bind off loosely.

Smooth out the knitting or steam-press it lightly without stretching it (follow the advice given after each of the pattern stitches), and place your Knit-Check or a small transparent ruler across the *center* of the work. Count the number of sts in *two full inches* of the swatch. Half of this number will make up *your gauge* for one inch. The two inches may have an odd number of sts, leaving you with a half stitch to contend with when multiplying. DO NOT UNDERESTIMATE THE VALUE OF THIS HALF STITCH. This little half stitch becomes of the utmost importance when multiplied by the measurement. As an example: If you multiply your waistline (try 30″ for a round number), times 7½ sts (if you measured 15 sts in the 2″), you get 225 sts. Now, multiply 30″ by 8 sts (if you measured 16 sts in the 2″) and you get 240 sts. The result is a difference of 15 sts — *two whole inches!* This makes a big difference in the number of stitches to be made, the amount of yarn to be used, the knitting time, and also in the finished size, which is the most important factor.

Never use a tape measure to estimate your gauge. *Never* hold up the knitted swatch while you are measuring it or any piece of knitted work in progress — lay it flat. *Never* work a swatch for another person and *never* let another person work a swatch for you. If you are making a swatch for an instructor or teacher — or for yourself, for that matter — don't try to get out of it by saying, "I'm an *average* knitter." It is more than possible that you are *not* that average knitter.

When making a swatch of Stockinette Stitch (K 1 row, P 1 row), your *row gauge* is more easily observed if you turn the work to the Wrong Side (Purled Side). Each ridge is a row (Fig. 253). This determining of rows per inch is very useful in working a sleeve cap, decreasing for a V neckline, or in counting numbers of rows on two pieces which should match exactly when joined at the edges. In nearly every pattern stitch *there are more rows per inch than sts per inch.*

In reading instructions from a book, you will always find not only the gauge of sts per inch but the *suggested needle size* to make that gauge. You are very apt to find, however, that *that needle size* will not give *you* the required gauge. You may knit more sts to the inch than the pattern calls for. If this is the case, you are knitting more tightly than "average" and should therefore use a *larger size needle.* Conversely, if you are knitting fewer sts to the inch, you should use a *smaller size needle.* Keep changing your needles or tension until your gauge is exactly correct.

If you have made a swatch of Stockinette Stitch and then change

Fig. 253

your mind and decide on another type of pattern stitch, *you must not use* the Stockinette Stitch swatch for your gauge. You *must* test the stitch you are going to use in the main part of the body of the garment. *This is most important.* Every pattern stitch will vary to some degree in stitches-to-the-inch, and therefore the swatch must be made *in that stitch*. If more than one type of stitch is to be used in the making of the entire piece, *a swatch of each stitch* should be made and the gauge of each determined.

The popular Aran Islands sweaters are combinations of many stitches, some of them "pulling in," such as cable stitches, or "letting out," such as mesh or fishnet stitches. There *are* some types of fishnet stitches, however, that are even tighter, more pulled in than some of the cable stitches, and may even pull up lengthwise. You must be wary of *any* type of stitch if you have not already made its acquaintance.

If you wish to plan your garment or article using a loose lacy stitch, it is wise to make a swatch six or eight inches square so that the stretch, both horizontally and vertically, may be taken into account when planning. The swatch should be pressed both sideways and up and down (especially up and down) to its fullest extent before taking the gauge, so that the finished article will fit when assembled and blocked. Use this pressed swatch when determining stitch and row gauge, and make sure that you take the amount of stretch into consideration when computing the dimensions of each portion to be made.

You may be a knitter who finds that there is a marked dissimilarity in tension between the Knitted and the Purled rows. This lack of uniformity is universal, but, if it is very pronounced, you should attempt to keep your tension the same on every row, or try using two sizes of needles, the smaller needle for the looser row and the larger needle for the tighter row.

It has also been mentioned, on page 99, that the same *color* of yarn should be used for the swatch to determine the gauge. The very same yarn in another color can have a decidedly different thickness— enough to result in a marked change in the size of the completed garment.

The wise knitter keeps a constant watch for any variation in the gauge of the piece she is knitting, especially if she puts the work away for any length of time. The *tension* (pressure put upon the needles and yarn) will change with the disposition of the knitter. Worry, illness, or irritation of any kind will almost invariably tighten the gauge, while the relaxed knitter is more apt to loosen the gauge. It has also been found that the very *speedy knitter* is most likely to be a *loose knitter* and therefore more apt to have to change to a smaller-size needle than the one called for in the directions.

Watch out for any change in gauge between the making of the swatch and the knitting of the pieces of a garment. Many times a considerable number of sts on a needle will make a difference in gauge between the swatch and the larger piece of knitting. This must be watched for and promptly corrected.

When taking the gauge of bulky yarns, it is more than possible that you may measure 3 sts to the inch on a size 10 needle. It is also possible that you will still measure 3 sts to the inch on a size-larger needle. In this case, it may be wise to choose the smaller-size needle to work with. The work will be firmer, less sleazy, and will have a better texture. Usually any difference in fit can be blocked out.

When you are about to make an extremely bulky garment, using jumbo-size needles and thicker-than-usual yarn (or from two to four different strands of yarn used together), follow *to the letter* whatever instructions are given. *Never* change so much as a single stitch. *Never* put work down without finishing the row. *Never* press or block the swatch or the finished garment. *Always* work a swatch *at least* 6" square (usually 10 sts). These jumbo garments are usually worked to the gauge of 6 sts = 5" and 3 rows = 2". If your gauge measures tighter than that given in the instructions, you must not change the size of your needles, but must work a *size larger* than the one you would ordinarily have taken. If your gauge measures looser than that given, you must move down one size and work *one size smaller*. Changes in length must be carefully watched for.

KNITTING WITH RIBBONS

Ribbon knitting can be a fascinating challenge to the knitter's skill and imagination. To anyone whose knitting has been confined to working with plain yarns, it opens a whole new world of delicate and luxurious things to be made. However, knitting with ribbons does call for slightly different techniques in the way materials are handled and stitches are made.

There are many kinds and textures of ribbons and just about as many ways to work with them. Ribbons may be used alone or worked with yarns. The methods used depend on the type of garment to be made.

As stated in the chapter on yarns, ribbons are manufactured from many different kinds of materials, such as rayon, silk, nylon, or combinations of these. Some are of crisp taffeta or organdy; others are very soft and pliable and made of pure silk or silk-and-rayon mixtures; some, woven or printed, give a tweed effect, and still others have metallic threads woven into the edges or the center. There are "fuse-cut" ribbons and woven ribbons. All have their own particular uses, and these are defined in the instruction books which have designs created especially to suit the texture of the ribbon to be used. In every case the stitch is clearly described and should be carefully followed. First learn the *method* of making the stitch, get the gauge required in the instructions, and, using the rules for taking measurements (see page 115), follow all instructions exactly. As in all knitting, the size of the needle and the texture and width of the ribbon will affect the gauge. Ribbon stitches are *not all* based on the same gauge; the method used is an important factor.

Great care must be exercised to keep the ribbon flat when winding it on the needle. It is suggested that a mark be made along one side of the ribbon for a considerable length. You will then find it easier to keep the marked surface of the ribbon against the surface of the needle, thus making sure that the ribbon will not get twisted as you knit it.

Before starting, practice winding the ribbon around the needle spirally several times. You will immediately notice that it is necessary to drop the ribbon after each turn around the needle, whether you wind it over the needle toward you (Fig. 254) or under the needle toward you (Fig. 255). Just as in this practice winding, you will have to drop the ribbon after each st to readjust it for the next st, making sure that the ribbon comes out of that st *flat*. If you are in the habit of winding yarn around any of your fingers or holding it tightly, *you must not do so* in working with ribbon. You will find that you are learning entirely new ways of working.

In order to handle ribbon successfully, you will find it useful to learn an entirely different method of *Purling*. In reality, it is *Left-Hand Knitting*; the Right Side of the work faces you at all times, and the progress of the fashioning of the sts is much easier to observe. The ribbon is controlled with the Right Hand. This allows the knitter to keep the ribbon flatter with less effort, and, best of all, the ribbon is kept *ahead* of the st being worked, so that it is all less confusing and easier to handle.

When following the direction for *regular Purling*, the LH needle is inserted into the back of the st being worked on the RH needle (Fig. 256), and the ribbon is wound *over* the needle *toward* you and back *under* the needle *away* from you and pulled through the st (Fig. 257).

When the *reverse manner of Purling* is being worked, the LH needle is inserted into the back of the st on the RH needle and the ribbon is wound *under* the needle *toward* you and *over* the needle *away* from you (Fig. 258).

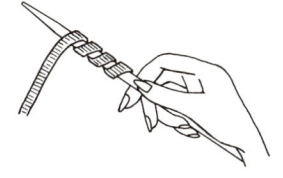

Fig. 254

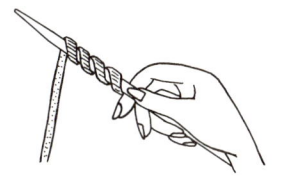

Fig. 255

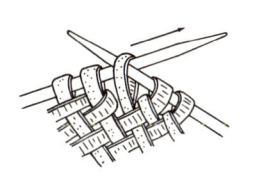

Fig. 256

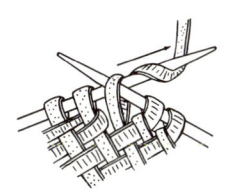

Fig. 257

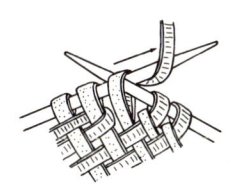

Fig. 258

FOURTEEN WAYS OF FORMING RIBBON STITCHES

RIBBON STITCH 1

Keeping the ribbon flat, wind it around the needle, inserting the needle into the *backs* of the sts on the Knit rows, and Purling in the regular manner of the Purled rows. The ribbon will continue to twist in the same direction when working this stitch.

RIBBON STITCH 2

A similar effect may be obtained by using the same method with only one exception. After inserting the needle into the st on the Knit row (into the *back* of the st), instead of bringing the ribbon toward you *under* the needle and then away, bring the ribbon toward you *over* the needle and then *away* from you under the needle (Fig. 259). Purl in the regular manner on the next row. The ribbon will twist one way going across, and untwist on the return row.

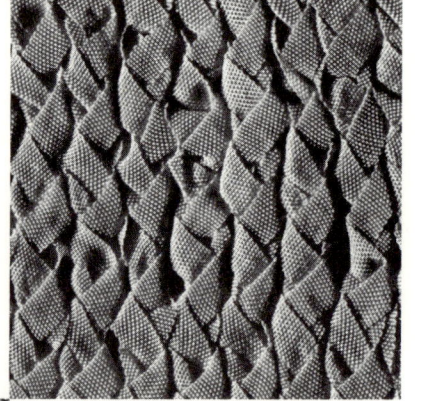

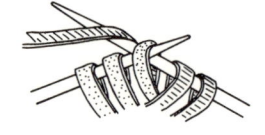

Fig. 259

RIBBON STITCH 3

This stitch produces a woven effect. When properly executed, it will produce a flat, diagonal weave with no holes appearing in the finished material. It is used to best effect with the taffeta type of ribbon.

The Knitted row is worked into the backs of the sts, and the return row is Purled in the opposite manner of regular Purling (Fig. 258). It is with this stitch in particular that the Left-Hand Purling suggested above should be used. The Right Hand has complete control of the ribbon at all times. As in all ribbon knitting, the ribbon must be kept *ahead of the needle point* at all times. This method uses a very little more ribbon than some of the others, and it also has less stretch, which is quite an advantage. The ribbon will twist one way going across and untwist on the next row. You will find it of great importance to let the ribbon spin back to its untwisted state at the *middle* of any row. In this way, the twisting will be much less annoying.

104

RIBBON STITCH 4 (*Cross-Stitch Pattern*)

This stitch is worked on two different sizes of needles, and it is important to remember which one to use on succeeding rows. You will find that using needles of different *colors* will facilitate the working of this stitch. This stitch uses an *even number* of sts.

Row 1: * On Knit Side and with *larger* needle (usually #10) insert needle through back of 1st st on LH needle and into the 2nd st as well (Fig. 260). Draw ribbon through both sts on LH needle, then K 1st st again from the *back* (Fig. 261) (a Cross-Stitch made); rep from * to end of row.

Row 2: On the Purl Side and with the *smaller* needle (usually #9) Purl in the regular manner (Fig. 257).

Row 3: On the Knit Side and with the *smaller* needle work the same as Row 1—BUT *starting and ending with K 1 st.*

Row 4: Purl all sts in the regular manner with the *larger* needle.

This stitch is more of a "see-through" stitch than most of the others. It is also a tighter stitch, so count on having more sts to the inch.

4

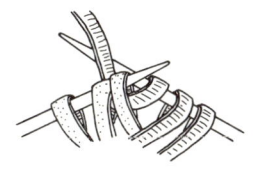

Fig. 260

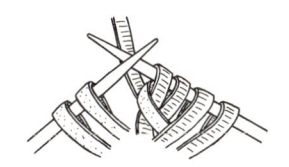

Fig. 261

Fig. 262

RIBBON STITCH 5

Always wind the ribbon, on the Knit Side, as in Ribbon Stitch 3, keeping the ribbon flat and winding in a continous spiral. Ribbon Stitch 5 also uses two different sizes of needles as in Ribbon Stitch 4; usually a #9 needle for the Knit rows and a #10 needle for the Purl rows. An *even* number of sts is used.

Row 1: * Take the *smaller* needle and insert it through the backs of 2 sts and Knit them together, BUT drop *only the* 1st of these 2 sts from LH needle (Fig. 262); rep from * until 1 st remains and K this last st through the back of the loop.

Row 2: With the *larger* needle, Purl across in the opposite of the regular manner.

This stitch resembles Ribbon Stitch 3 in appearance, but it is worked in an entirely different manner. It is a very firm stitch and will not stretch as much as most of the others. It is apt to pull a little on the bias, however, and must be very firmly blocked.

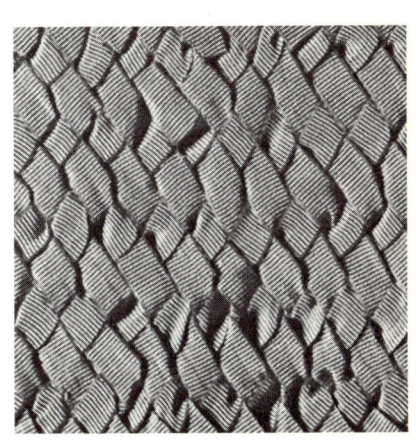

5

105

RIBBON STITCH 6

When working this stitch, it is not necessary to keep the ribbon absolutely flat. Whenever you make a Knit st, insert the needle through the back of the loop and wrap the ribbon *forward* over the needle (Fig. 259). The pattern uses an *uneven* number of sts. Purl sts are made in the regular manner.

Row 1: K 1, * bring the ribbon to the front of the work and sl 1 st as if to Purl; take the ribbon to the back of the work and K 1 — rep from * to the end of the row.

Row 2: * Take the ribbon to the back of the work, sl 1 as if to Purl, bring the ribbon to the front of the work and P 1 — rep from * to the end of the row, ending with a sl st.

Repeat these 2 rows for pattern.

This stitch has very little sidewise stretch because of the slipped sts. When binding off, always bind off *in pattern*.

6

RIBBON STITCH 7 *(Chevron Stitch)*

This pattern uses a multiple of 16 sts. It is best worked with a soft-texture ribbon, either ⅜" or ½" wide, and appropriate-size needles, either #10 or #11 — even larger if necessary.

Note: Whenever you are making a K st, insert the needle through the back of the loop and wrap ribbon forward over the top of the needle (Fig. 259).

Row 1 (Wrong Side): Purl all sts in the regular manner.

Row 2: * K 2 tog through the *fronts* of the 2 sts, K 5 sts, K in *back and front* of the next st (Fig. 263), K in *front and back* of the next st (Fig. 264), K 5, K 2 tog through the *backs* of the next 2 sts — rep from * across the row.

Repeat these 2 rows for pattern. It will form a decided *wave* at the bottom edge.

To decrease: K 2 tog (in the backs of the loops) in the plain Knit portion of the pattern. This will reduce the number of sts in this portion of the pattern.

To increase: K into the st below the next st, then K the st itself (Fig. 265). This increase must be made in a plain K st of the pattern, thus increasing the number of sts in this portion of the pattern.

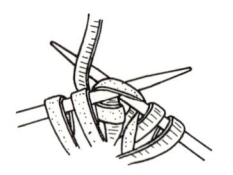

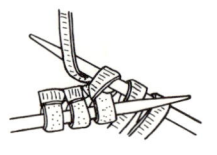

7

Fig. 263   Fig. 264   Fig. 265

106

RIBBON STITCH 8

This stitch uses an *even* number of sts.

Row 1: With the ribbon in back of the work, insert the needle through the backs of the first 2 sts together, wrap ribbon under the needle as in regular knitting (Fig. 260), draw it through, dropping only the 1st st from LH needle (Fig. 262). * Insert needle through the back of the remaining st *and* the back of the next st (Fig. 266), wrap ribbon under the needle, draw ribbon through, dropping only the 1st st from LH needle; rep from * to the last st; insert needle as before and wrap ribbon under the needle and K this last st.

Row 2: Making all Purl sts in the reverse manner of purling, * P 2 tog and drop only the first st from LH needle (Fig. 267); insert needle through the remaining st *and* the next st, P them together, and drop only the first st from LH needle (Fig. 268); rep from * to the last st, P 1.

Rep these 2 rows for Pattern Stitch.

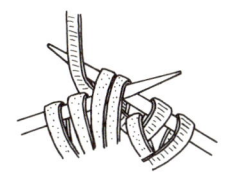

Fig. 266 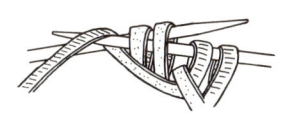   Fig. 267    Fig. 268

Ribbon Stitch 8 strongly resembles Ribbon Stitch 3 and Ribbon Stitch 5 and has practically no stretch in either direction. You may find that a larger-than-usual needle will make the work less tight (this swatch was worked on a #11 needle). It will facilitate the knitting and will be very firm. Bind off with a *smaller-size* needle.

RIBBON STITCH 9

This stitch uses an *even* number of sts.

Note: Whenever you are making a Knit st, insert the needle through the back of the st and wrap the ribbon in the regular manner.

Row 1 (Wrong Side): Purl in the reverse manner.

Row 2: * K 1; with the ribbon in front of the work, sl 1 as if to Purl, take the ribbon to the back of the work; rep from * to end of row.

Row 3: Purl in the reverse manner.

Row 4: * Bring the ribbon to the front of the work and sl 1 as if to Purl; take the ribbon to the back of the work and K 1—rep from * to end of row.

Rep these 4 rows for pattern, taking care to keep the pattern sequence when shaping.

RIBBON STITCH 10 *(Seed Stitch)*

When working this stitch, it is not necessary to keep the ribbon flat. It is worked the same as Pattern Stitch #3 on page 142, casting on an *uneven number* of sts and working *every* row as follows:

* K 1, P 1 — rep from * to end of row, ending K 1.

Seed Stitch may be pressed quite flat. Make sure to retain the pattern when shaping.

KNITTING WITH SILK ORGANDY RIBBON

The following four stitches are shown using Silk Organdy Ribbon. In knitting with this material, there is no need to keep the ribbon flat; you may use the ribbon just as if you were working with yarn. When it is finished, this type of work must be pressed quite flat (with the exception of the Popcorn Stitch), so take this under consideration in making the swatch and allow for quite a bit of stretch.

10

RIBBON STITCH 11 *(Wave Lace)*

This swatch was knitted on #3 needles and worked back and forth. It uses a multiple of 12 sts plus 1.
Row 1: K 2 tog, * yo, K 9, yo, SK2togP — rep from *, end SKP.
Row 2 and All Even-Numbered Rows: Purl all sts.
Row 3: K 2, * yo, K 3, SK2togP, K 3, yo, K 3 — rep from *, end yo, K 2.
Row 5: K 3, * yo, K 2, SK2togP, K 2, yo, K 5 — rep from *, end yo, K 3.
Row 7: K 4, * yo, K 1, SK2togP, K 1, yo, K 7 — rep from *, end yo, K 4.
Row 9: K 5, * yo, SK2togP, yo, K 9 — rep from *, end yo, K 5.
   Starting with Row 1, rep these 10 rows.
   Wave Lace made on a circular needle. Multiple of 12 sts.)
   Note: Always keep a ring marker at the beginning of each round, and make sure that it stays before the first st of every round, whether the st is a yarn-over or a Knit st.
Rnd 1 and all Odd-Numbered Rounds: K all sts.
Rnd 2: * yo, SK2togP, yo, K 9 — rep from * around.
Rnd 4: * K 3, yo, K 3, SK2togP, K 3, yo — rep from * around.
Note: Be sure to end with a yarn-over on *this* round.
Rnd 6: K 4, * yo, K 2, SK2togP, K 2, yo, K 5 — rep from *, ending yo, K 1 instead of yo, K 5.
Rnd 8: K 5, * yo, K 1, SK2togP, K 1, yo, K 7 — rep from *, ending yo, K 2 instead of yo, K 7.
Rnd 10: K 6, * yo, SK2togP, yo, K 4 — rep from *, ending yo, K 3 instead of yo, K 9.
Repeat these 10 rounds for pattern.
   This stitch, as well as any other stitch resembling it, is very effective when made into "after-five" dressy apparel.

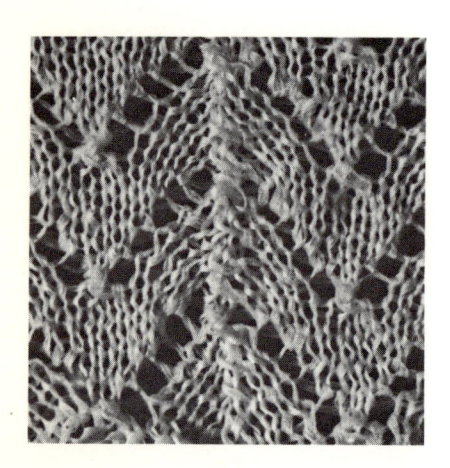

11

RIBBON STITCH 12 (*Leaf Lace*)

This stitch is the same as Pattern Stitch #176 on page 218. It was worked with #3 needles and Silk Organdy Ribbon. It uses a multiple of 10 sts plus 1 on straight needles.

Note: Purl All Even-Numbered Rows.
Row 1: K 1, * yo, K 3, SK2togP, K 3, yo, K 1 — rep from *, end same.
Row 3: K 2, * yo, K 2, SK2togP, K 2, yo, K 3 — rep from *, end yo, K 2.
Row 5: K 2 tog, * (yo, K 1)x2, SK2togP, (K 1, yo)x2, SK2togP — rep from *, end (K 1, yo)x2, SKP.
Starting with Row 1, rep these 6 rows.

This stitch may be used in the same manner as Ribbon Stitch 11. Again, this may be made "in the round."

(*Leaf Lace made on a circular needle. Multiple of 10 sts.*) The "yarn-over" at the beginning of each even-numbered round *must* have a ring marker kept before it.
Rnd 1 and All Odd-Numbered Rnds: Knit all sts.
Rnd 2: * yo, K 3, SK2togP, K 3, yo, K 2 — rep from * around.
Rnd 4: * yo, K 2, SK2togP, K 2, yo, K 3 — rep from * around.
Rnd 6: * (yo, K 1)x2, Sk2togP, (K 1, yo)x2, SK2togP — rep from * around.
Starting with Rnd 1, rep these 6 rounds.

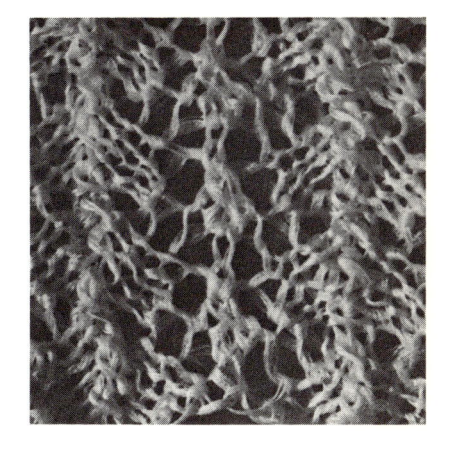

12

RIBBON STITCH 13 (*Herringbone Lace Pattern*)

Row 1 and All Odd-Numbered Rows: Purl all sts (Wrong Side)
Rows 2, 4, and 6: * K 2 tog, K 2, yo, K 2 — rep from *, end same.
Rows 8, 10, and 12: K 3, * yo, K 2, SKP, K 2 — rep from *, end yo, SKP, K 1.
Starting with Row 1, rep these 12 rows.

This stitch should not be tried on circular needles. It is best made on straight needles, working back and forth. If any shaping is required, it should be done by changing the size of the needles. For instance, if you are making a skirt, start at the bottom edge with a slightly larger-size needle, diminishing with smaller and smaller needles toward the waistline. The swatch, however, should be made on the needle on which the greatest amount of knitting is to be done, such as at the bustline of the bodice. *This* swatch was made on a #3 needle. Many of the smaller pieces can easily be *stretched* to shape with a steam iron.

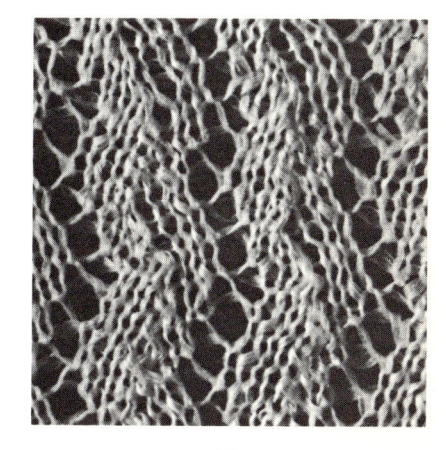

13

RIBBON STITCH 14 (*Popcorn Stitch*) Multiple of 4 sts plus 2.

Row 1: K all sts (Wrong Side).
Row 2: K 1, * PKP in next st, K 3 tog — rep from *, end K 1.
Row 3: K all sts.
Row 4: K 1, * K 3 tog, PKP in next st — rep from *, end K 1.

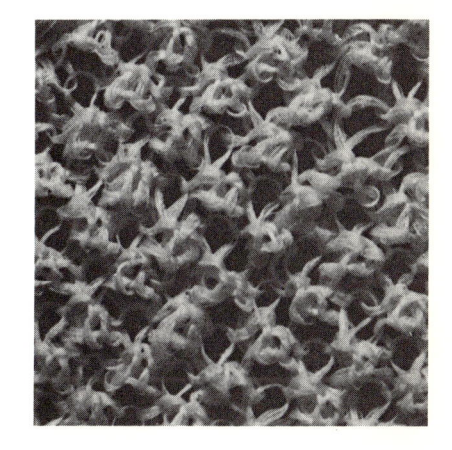

14

This stitch, when made with organdy ribbon, is very "bouncy." It was knitted on a #5 needle. It must be handled differently from other stitches made with this type of ribbon. All of the pieces should be steam-*stretched* before pinning to size and shape. This is done by holding the steam iron very close to, but not on, the Wrong Side of the work. Using as much steam as possible, *mold* the pieces to correct measurement and steam again. Let them dry thoroughly before they are taken off the board. *Do not* press the iron down or press on the Right Side of the work.

Clothing made with ribbon, in any stitch, must be just as carefully *worked to gauge* as that made with yarn. In working the *flat* ribbon stitches in particular, you must make sure that the knitting is kept flat and that the *correct gauge* is obtained. The difference of half a stitch in an inch is of great importance, as there are so few sts to an inch.

When working with ribbon of any kind, you will find it more convenient to put the ribbon on a spool in a box that is small enough to hold it comfortably, arranged so that no part of the spool touches any of the sides or bottom. Run a knitting needle through one side of the box, through the hole in the spool, and out the other side. This will allow the free passage of the ribbon so that it will unwind easily. Always pull out several yards of ribbon ahead of the knitting. As has been mentioned, many of the stitches will twist and/or untwist. When the ribbon becomes too twisted, wind as much of it as possible back onto the spool. Remove the spool from the box and put a pin through the loose ribbon and that on the spool. Let the spool hang and untwist—BUT let it twist in the other direction as much as it will while handling. This will give you a little more distance between each untwisting.

Before starting any project, make a large swatch (at least four or five inches) and bind it off. Put this swatch right side down on a well-padded pressing board and cover it with a damp cloth. Set your iron to "silk" control and press. Remove the cloth, turn to "synthetic" control, and press the swatch until thoroughly dry. Remove it from the pressing board and *then* check your gauge for sts and rows per inch. Check especially carefully the *rows per inch,* as there is usually considerable stretch *lengthwise* in ribbon knitting.

To Finish Ribbon Garments: The finishing of a knitted ribbon dress or suit requires a basic knowledge of dressmaking. Each piece must be thoroughly pressed before basting and sewing. The garment must be basted and fitted first, then the seams machine- or hand-stitched together (I prefer *hand*-stitching with doubled sewing thread), the material being treated exactly as though it were dress material. Finishing of open edges, such as the bottom of a skirt, blouse, sleeve, or neckline, may be worked in single crochet, just as in wool pieces. These points and all finishing points, such as seam allowances, darts, edges, and hems, should be pressed as the final touch.

CROCHETED FINISHES

As explained in the chapter on Equipment, a crochet hook of suitable size for finishing each knitted garment is almost a must. The size of the needle used in the knitting will nearly always determine the size of crochet hook that will be needed. To pick up sts that have been dropped, it is better to use a crochet hook of the same size as the knitting needle size—if your knitting was made on a #6 needle, a #G/6 plastic or aluminum crochet hook should be used. If quite a few rows have been lost and the stitches are picked up with a smaller hook, the fact that something wrong happened at that point will be obvious. The drawing illustrates a st that was lost six rows down. The hook should be slipped into the loop farthest down (Fig. 269). Then the *hook* part of the crochet hook should be placed *under* the straight ladder going across the top of that loop (Fig. 270), and a loop pulled through. Repeat this operation until the last ladder has been pulled through, making sure to place the hook *under* each ladder going up. This will keep the sts in the correct position as in regular knitting, and the last st placed on the LH needle in the correct position for working on the next st (Fig. 271). If the hook is placed on the last ladder incorrectly, it may show in the finished piece of knitting, and if it is placed on the LH needle in this position, the st will have to be untwisted when it is knitted onto the RH needle.

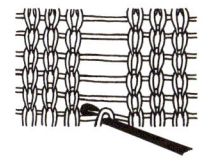

Fig. 269

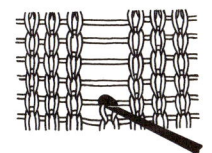

Fig. 270

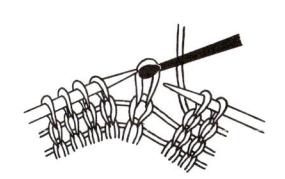

Fig. 271

CHAIN STITCH

To make a Chain Stitch in crochet, make a slip knot on the hook (Fig. 272). Hold the yarn in the Left Hand and, using a light hand and an easy touch, pull a loop through the loop on the hook—one chain stitch (ch st) made (Fig. 273). A chain made with a large hook and a heavy yarn (or several lengths of a lighter-weight yarn) is useful as a cord to run through or around a part of the garment.

SLIP STITCH

A Slip Stitch (sl st) is made by inserting the crochet hook through a st and pulling a loop through the st *and* the st on the hook (Fig. 274). This is the best stitch to use when putting two pieces together to make a seam. NEVER—but *never*—use a single crochet (see the following paragraph for directions) to join two pieces together into a seam on the *inside* of the work. *Always* use this slip stitch as outlined here (see Assembling and Finishing).

Fig. 272

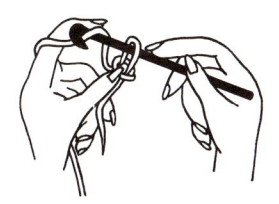

Fig. 273

Fig. 274

SINGLE CROCHET

Single Crochet (sc) is used many times to finish edges or to complement the knitting itself. As Stockinette Stitch (or any stitch that uses Stockinette as the foundation) tends to *curl up* at the top and bottom edges and *curl in* at the side edges, single crochet is very often used to take out the curl. This curl is the reason for adding a hem or some type of ribbing at the finished top or bottom edges. Frequently, however, especially on ribbon dresses, a crocheted edge is the best finishing touch, and single crochet is almost always used.

In these cases, and in slip-stitch crochet as well, a *smaller size* hook is most often used, as one the same size as the knitting needle would make the finished work look too large and clumsy and would ruffle the edge being worked.

To work Single Crochet, proceed as follows:

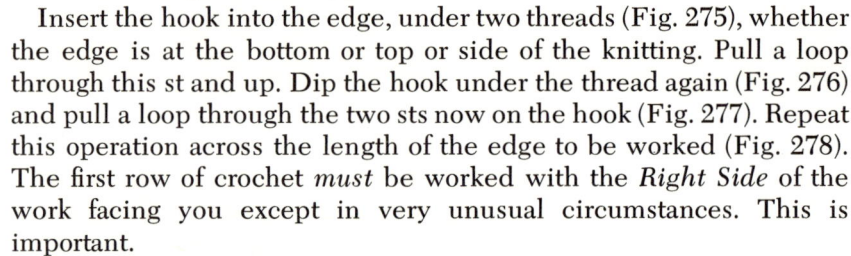

Insert the hook into the edge, under two threads (Fig. 275), whether the edge is at the bottom or top or side of the knitting. Pull a loop through this st and up. Dip the hook under the thread again (Fig. 276) and pull a loop through the two sts now on the hook (Fig. 277). Repeat this operation across the length of the edge to be worked (Fig. 278). The first row of crochet *must* be worked with the *Right Side* of the work facing you except in very unusual circumstances. This is important.

It is the usual practice to work into each st of a top or bottom edge. The procedure is different, however, on a side edge. As in Picking Up Stitches (see page 88), single crochet is usually worked into a side edge as follows: * Make a single crochet st into each of three successive edge sts in the knitting, making sure to insert the hook under two threads (Fig. 275), and skip the next st (the 4th st). Rep from * along the side edge, ch 1 st to turn (sometimes you should ch 2 sts to turn)—(see page 122). On the return row, you make the first sc into the st directly below the one on the hook (Fig. 279), and then into each st that was made on the first row.

This method of single crochet is extremely good for finishing the front edges of a cardigan where no buttonholes have been knitted directly into the work (see page 65). Work the BUTTON side as wide as necessary. The BUTTONHOLE side is usually worked as follows: Work half the width in single crochet. Mark the buttonholes

Fig. 275

Fig. 276

Fig. 277

Fig. 278

Fig. 279

112

by putting pins where the buttons will be placed. Then chain several stitches, enough to cover the width of the button—let's say 3 sts. Skip 3 sc sts, then work a number of sc sts to cover the distance between buttons. On the next row, work 3 sc sts over the ch sts of the previous row (Fig. 280), not working into the chain itself, but going under the entire chain. Then finish the rest of the width to match the button side.

To remove any doubt about how many sts to make between buttonholes, work out mathematically where each is to be placed, following these simple rules:

Let's say you want to make 7 buttonholes, and you have 69 sts on the front edge. You are going to make 3 ch sts for the buttonhole itself. At the *top* edge (the neckline), you would not wish to have more than 2 scs before the buttonhole as more than that would not make a neat finish (3 scs at the very most). First of all, subtract 5 sts from the total of 69 (this makes the 2 scs and the 3 ch sts for the first buttonhole). This leaves 64 sts to work with to make the other 6 buttonholes. You would therefore divide 64 by 6 (the number of buttonholes still to be made) This leaves 10 sts. Deduct 3 from 10—which leaves 7—the 3 sts for the chain to be made and the 7 for the scs to be worked between each buttonhole. There will be 4 sts left over for use at the *bottom* edge. Therefore, the entire row would be worked as follows:

Starting at the *top* edge, work 2 scs. Then—* ch 3, skip 3, make 7 scs—rep. from *, ending ch 3, skip 3, make 4 scs.

If the buttonholes were to be started at the bottom edge, you would reverse the order by making 4 scs to start and, following the same order, you would leave 2 scs remaining at the top edge.

Any number of sts can be worked with and any number of buttonholes can be made by following this simple procedure.

Fig. 280

Fig. 281

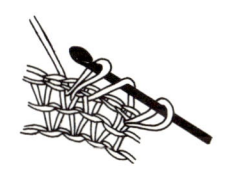

Fig. 282

DOUBLE CROCHET

Double Crochet (dc) is seldom used on a knitted garment, but if there *is* a use for it, follow this directive:

Dip the crochet hook under the yarn (Fig. 281), insert the hook into the st, and pull a loop through (Fig. 282). This leaves 3 loops on the hook. Dip the hook under the yarn and pull it through 2 loops (Fig. 283). Dip the hook under the yarn again and pull it through the remaining 2 loops on the hook—a double crochet made (Fig. 284).

Chain stitching is very often used to make a casing at the top edge of a skirt. Most directions call for one or two rows of single crochet to be made at the top edge, followed by a casing. I have found it advisable, however, to work a band about an inch or an inch and a half, either in ribbed knitting or single crochet. Also, as elastic one inch wide stays put better than a narrower piece, the casing should be made to cover the width plus a little more for allowance. It is worked as follows:

On the *inside* of the skirt, attach the yarn just one st down from the

Fig. 283

Fig. 284

top edge. Chain enough sts to slant about one inch down and fasten with a sl st at the bottom edge of the waistband. Chain the same amount of sts and fasten at a slant at the top edge again (Fig. 285). Work in this manner around the waist edge.

A skirt stays in place better, however, by working a stitched-on piece of elastic. It rarely turns out to show the elastic, and with it a skirt may be safely worn *over* a blouse or topper.

Work two rows of single crochet (or a band one and a half inches wide if preferred) around the top of the skirt at the waistline. Then cut a piece of one-inch-wide elastic to fit the waistline exactly. Overlap the edges just enough to fasten the two pieces together with narrow zigzag stitching. Pin the elastic to the inside of the waistline, just under the two rows of sc, setting the pins equadistant from each other at about eight places.

Fill the bobbin of the sewing machine with the color thread of the knitting and the spool on top to match either the white or the black of the elastic. With narrow zigzag setting, stitch one row around the top and the bottom of the elastic, and one row of wider zigzag at the center, stretching the elastic to fit the knitted or crocheted work as you sew.

Fig. 285

5. Taking Correct Measurements

When consulting a knitting or instruction book, bear in mind that the size dress, bra, or slip you wear does not *in any way* indicate the size of a hand-knitted garment. The size of a man's shirt or suit gives no indication whatever of the size of a hand-knitted sweater or jacket. Directions differ, and no two people knit exactly the same way. A man's shirt is measured around the neck, and also from the center of the back to the end of the sleeve. The sizes should be based on the *exact measurements of the person* for whom the garment is to be made. The accompanying chart gives the *knitted* measurements *usually* planned in printed directions.

Many instruction books give the approximate measurements for each size given. These are usually found just after the directions for the amounts of materials to be used in any particular garment. Read and consider them carefully, but do your own figuring as well.

The measurements given here should not be compared with the sizes found in machine-knitted sweaters or dresses, which vary a great deal. They are only a guide to help you choose the size of the *hand*-knitted garment that will fit the best. You should, first of all, take the bust or chest measurement. Compare this with the chart and then make the necessary alterations in length and width of each separate piece.

Please bear in mind that these measurements are only those that are most widely accepted and used, and that they may not apply to *your* figure (or the figure of anyone you may be knitting for) in more than one or two dimensions. We are all familiar with the *short-waisted* or *long-waisted* figure, and the *half sizes* or *tall sizes* of ready-made garments. Sleeve lengths vary to a marked degree, especially for someone who is unusually short or tall. Skirt lengths differ, as do shoulder widths and armhole depths. The chart outlined here is *only a general guide.* You must *take individual measurements carefully* for the proper fit of the garment you are going to make, and all work should be planned accordingly.

"AVERAGE" KNITTING MEASUREMENTS (in inches)

	Size	Chest or Bust	Waist	Hips	Upper Arm	Arm-hole	Sleeve Length
Infants	newborn	18			5½	3	5
	6 mo.	19			6½	3¼	6
	1 yr.	20			7	3½	7
	18 mo.	21			7¼	3¾	8
Children	2	22			7½	4	8½
	3	23			8	4¼	9½
	4	24			8½	4½	10½
	6	26			9	5	12
	8	28			10	6	13½
	10	30			11	6½	15
	12	32			12	7	16½
Women	10	32	24	34	12½	7¼	16½
	12	34	26	36	13	7½	16¾
	14	36	28	38	13½	7¾	17
	16	38	30	40	14	8	17¼
	18	40	32	42	14½	8¼	17½
	20	42	34	44	15	8½	17½
Men	36	36–38			16	9	18½
	38	38–40			16¼	9¼	18¾
	40	40–42			16½	9½	19
	42	42–44			17	10	19½
	44	44–46			17¼	10¼	20

Select the *width* across the bust or chest which will fit. Refer to the blocking measurements whenever these are given, or figure the width by *dividing the number of stitches* for each size *by the gauge given*. You can change the *length* of any section just by using the tape measure; in fact, very few instructions give a lengthwise measurement in *rows*. Increase or decrease rows may have to be spaced closer together for shorter pieces, or farther apart for longer ones. Adjustments in width are possible for Stockinette Stitch (K 1 row, P 1 row) and simple patterns with a multiple of 2 or 3 sts, but when there is a pattern stitch with a multiple that would measure more than one inch (for instance, a *multiple* of 8 sts plus 4 and a *gauge* of 4½ sts per inch), it would be better to select another style rather than to try to make your own changes unless you are an experienced knitter.

It is usually better to select a size slightly wider than one that will be even a little tight; there is no law against taking in a seam. If necessary, you can even make the back one size and the front a size larger, taking in the extra width at the shoulders with a dart or gathering. For a dress or suit, you can use one size for the skirt and a different size for the bodice or jacket.

HOW TO TAKE MEASUREMENTS

Bust Measurement (Women): Measure around the fullest part of the bust, holding the tape measure up very slightly in the back. Measure across the back from side seam to side seam as well. Often the measurement across the back is just the same as across the front, especially in older women.

Chest Measurement (Men and Children): With the chest fully expanded, measure around the fullest part of the chest.

Armhole: Measure from the *top* of the shoulder bone (Fig. 286), *straight down* to one inch below the actual armpit. Measure this *straight down; do not curve in.*

Underarm to Waist: At the side seam measure from the underarm, about one inch below the actual armpit, to the *exact* waistline. Then measure the added distance from this point, down to the length desired.

Neck to Shoulder: From the side of the neck to the *top* of the shoulder bone.

Shoulder to Waist in Front (for a full bust): Measure from the center of the Neck-to-Shoulder distance, down across the fullest part of the bust to the *exact* waistline. This will be a slightly diagonal line.

Neck to Waist in Back: Measure straight down from the prominent neck bone at the top of the spine to the *exact* waistline (Fig. 287).

Sleeve Length: Measure from about one inch below the actual armpit straight down inside of the arm to the wristbone. This measurement is for long sleeves only. Measure other lengths accordingly.

Arm: Measure the upper arm, forearm, and wrist. Take the wrist measurement exactly, the others rather loosely unless it is to be a tight-fitting sleeve.

Shoulder to Shoulder in Back: From the *top, not the side,* of the shoulder bone on one side to the same point on the other side (Fig. 287).

Length of Skirt: Hold the tape measure at the *exact* waistline. Measure from this point, down the side of the figure, to the desired length.

If the figure is large or the seat is prominent, measure from the *waistline in the front* to the bottom edge, and from the *waistline in the back* as well. These two measurements will differ considerably.

Hip: Measure the *very largest part of the seat below the waistline.* For a full figure, take the largest measurement *when seated.* Then measure from the waistline to this part of the hip.

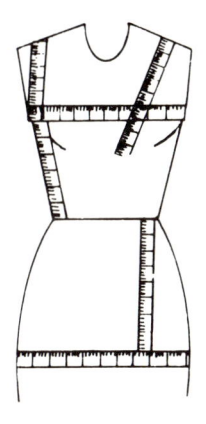

Fig. 286

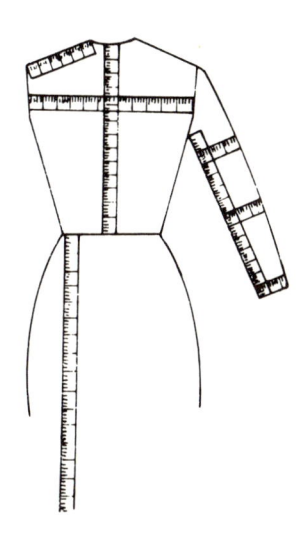

Fig. 287

HOW TO USE THESE MEASUREMENTS

Shoulder to Waist in Front: This measurement is taken because, if the bust is full, more length may be required at the side seam of the front than would usually be found in the so-called average figure. It is therefore necessary to knit this extra length and then to make a horizontal dart at the side seam, about 1½" down from the armhole, or to ease in this extra length to match the back at the side edge. However, *do not start easing in this fullness* until at least 3" above the waistline.

Neck to Waist in Back: This measurement should coincide with the side-seam measurement, plus the armhole measurement, *plus at least one more inch.* As an example; if the side seam measures 7½" and the armhole measures 8", the measurement from the back to the waist should be about 16½". *However,* if the shoulders are sharply sloped, the distance from the neck to the waist might be even more. Watch this measurement very carefully. There is nothing quite so awkward in appearance or so uncomfortable as a sweater or blouse that hikes up in the back.

Length of Skirt: If there is an exaggerated difference between the front and back measurements, there are two rules to follow:

1. If you are knitting from the bottom edge up, allow for extra length in the back by binding off, gradually, when the waistline length has been reached; on a circular skirt bind off half the number of sts for the front, then bind off series of sts toward the back on each side to make up the difference in length. On a two-panel skirt bind off a series of sts at the beginning of every row until about half the sts are bound off. Then bind off the remaining sts.

2. If you are knitting from the top edge down, cast on about one quarter of the number of sts required for the entire waistline of a circular skirt, or half the sts for a two-panel skirt back section. Then cast on at each side, gradually and in series, numbers of sts toward the sides to make up the difference in length.

Hip: To avoid that "sitting-down" look while standing up—that too tight, cupped-under-at-the-seat effect—the skirt *must* be planned so that the number of sts required at the *fullest part of the seat*, where you have taken the measurements, should be *at least* three to four inches *above that point;* i.e., if the hip measures 38" at 8" down from the waist, you should start that width and number of sts *three or four inches below the waist.*

If you observe these measurement instructions you should end up with a better-fitting garment.

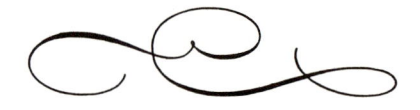

6. Assembling and Finishing

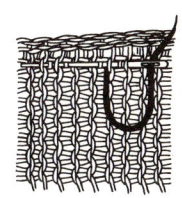

Fig. 288

Fig. 289

Fig. 290

Fig. 291

SWEATERS

There are three principal ways to join the seams of a knitted garment. Although nearly all instructions indicate that a seam should be either sewed or grafted at the side edges, I do *not* recommend either of these two methods as the best except in a few instances. Instead, I would advocate a third method: *slip-stitch crochet.* In any case, a seam should *never* be joined by *overcasting* or by *single crochet,* except in certain specified instances where the joining is meant to show on the Right Side of the work for a very special reason.

A sewed seam may be joined by using a running backstitch (Fig. 288), with yarn and a sewing needle. If you prefer to use this method, just be careful not to draw the sts too tight, as any type of joining should have as much give as the knitting itself. Of course, if the yarn is nubby, it cannot be used in this manner.

A seam may be grafted, as shown on page 91. Again, this method is very difficult if the yarn is nubby.

The following method is the one I prefer above all others, as it allows slightly more give than a sewed seam and holds a little more firmly without breaking the thread, especially when the garment is to be worn by an active person.

Hold the two edges with the right sides together at the inside. Using the same yarn as that used for the garment (except in cases where the yarn is exceptionally heavy) and a crochet hook of the appropriate size, join them with a slip stitch as follows: Insert the hook through a stitch on the front side of the seam, *one st in from the edge* (Fig. 289), and then through the corresponding st in the matching piece on the other side (Fig. 290). You must always work into the corresponding rows of knitting on both pieces. Catch the yarn with the hook, draw it through the two pieces and straight through the loop on the hook (Fig. 291). Repeat this process on the entire length of the seam, working into each row of knitting as you go. There is no great virtue in getting as close to the edge as you can possibly put the hook. If the piece is apt to be a little too large, there is no reason why the hook cannot be inserted even deeper than the second stitch. All clothes are made with seams, and a sweater is no exception.

All *side seams*, such as underarm to waist, and sleeves, should be made in this manner, but unless there is a very good and special reason for doing otherwise, work all of these seams *from the bottom edge to the top edge;* always *work up to, not down to* any given point in the work. For instance, start from the ribbing at the lower edge of the sweater and work toward the armhole. If there is a dolman sleeve, always start the joining at the edge of the sleeve and work toward the neckline. All *bound-off* seams, such as tops of shoulder shapings, should be grafted (see page 91), unless a cable, rib stitch, or some similar pattern has been used. With a simple pullover or cardigan, proceed as follows:

Graft the shoulder seams. Slip-stitch the underarm seams. If a neckband or front border is to be made, now is the time to do it, as the garment is easier to handle without the added weight of the sleeves. Then slip-stitch the sleeve seams and, without breaking the yarn, set in the sleeve as follows: Turn the sleeve right side out, body wrong side out, and put the sleeve in the armhole. Pin the center top of the sleeve to the shoulder seam, right sides together. With the *body side* of the sweater facing you, pin from the underarm toward the shoulder seam, easing in any fullness of the sleeve equally along the line as it occurs. Pin the other side to match. Then, with the *body side* still facing you, work a seam in slip stitch all around as on other seams, but after the decreases have been passed on the armhole shaping, follow the straight line of knitted rows from this point to the matching point on the other side of the armhole. This insures a very smooth straight seam, as the rows of the knitting at the armhole edges serve as a guide. Work into each row of knitting as you go, as the armhole may draw too tightly if more space between sts is allowed.

FRONT BORDERS FOR CARDIGANS

There are various ways to finish the fronts of a cardigan, and these are usually outlined in any given instructions. But if you want to plan your own cardigan, here are three different methods of finishing which are most generally approved.

KNITTED RIBBING, VERTICAL

After the waistband has been completed, the stitches from at least one inch of ribbing at the front edge should be set aside on a stitch holder. The ribbing has usually been made with a smaller-size needle than was used to make the body, and the sts are held aside so that they can be worked later with the same smaller-size needle. If the neckline is to be ribbed, the front bands should be finished *before* the neckband is made. The sts are ribbed on the smaller-size needle to form the front band, and the buttonholes are worked into the appropriate side of the front. It is wise to make the *button* side first so that the buttonholes on the opposite band can be evenly spaced. However, if you prefer, the buttonholes may be made by machine after ribbon facing has been applied. In either case the sts are transferred from the holder to the smaller-size ribbing needle and worked in the same ribbing, from waistband to neckline. BUT—and here is the difference between a passable job and a very good one—*the border is made slightly shorter* than the front sections of the cardigan, and you should *always add an extra st at the inside edge of this border* to make a better seam when grafting. In other words, pick up or make an extra st at the inside edge of these held sts before you start to work the required length, making sure to work this added st in the same type of ribbing or pattern stitch being used for the border. Next, the border is worked, not to the exact length of the front edge of the body, but at least ¾" to 1" shorter, to keep the front edge of the cardigan from drooping. A very good way to determine the length of the ribbed band is to *count the rows* along the front edge of the sweater and make the same number of rows on the ribbed band. Because of the smaller size of the needle, the border piece will automatically be a little shorter than the sweater front—just enough to make the difference. With the same number of rows on each piece, the grafting is made that much easier, and you won't have to "cheat" on the rows.

For a woman's sweater, work the Left Front band first. When it is finished, slip the sts onto a holder and break the yarn at the *inside edge*. Work the Right Front band the same length and *do not break the yarn*, but continue using this same yarn in the next operation: picking up the sts around the neckline. Knit (or Purl) 2 sts together at the inside edges of the borders to eliminate the "extra" st. When you reach the left front edge, work off in pattern the sts you had set aside on the holder and then finish the neckband, together with the two front bands, making sure to work in the top buttonhole after the first two or three rows have been completed.

Following the instructions on page 92 for Vertical Grafting, join the bands to the sweater body.

A man's sweater is finished in the same manner, but the buttonhole size has to be worked first on the Left Front.

KNITTED RIBBING, HORIZONTAL

Many a cardigan, especially a jacket of the Chanel type, calls for a border, the sts of which are picked up all around both fronts and the neckline in one operation. A circular needle is best for this, as even a 14" needle might be too short to hold all the sts.

The yarn is fastened at the lower edge of the Right Front and usually the smaller-size needle is used to pick up the required number of sts along this front to the neckline (see page 88 on Picking Up Stitches). Count the number of sts from the bottom edge to the point where the neckline begins and place a ring marker there. Pick up the sts around the neckline to the Left Front and place another ring marker on the needle at the start of the Left Front. Pick up the same number of sts down the Left Front as were counted on the Right Front. Work in ribbing (or whatever stitch is designated), making an increase on both sides of each marker, every other row, to miter these two corners, working any buttonholes into the appropriate side as you go along.

These same directions should be followed if the cardigan or jacket is to have a high, medium, or low V neckline, with one exception only. You should place the ring markers at the points on each front edge where the decreases for the V-lines begin (these should have been marked earlier).

CROCHETED BORDERS

This type of border is preferred by many because it is thicker and stronger than a knitted border and seldom needs a ribbon facing.

For working crochet on a knitted edge, the *gauge* must be *correct*. Practice on a knitted swatch, made in exactly the same stitch and with the same size needles as those used in the body of the sweater, before proceeding to work on the garment itself. The choice of crochet hook size is also very important, as the border must lie flat and smooth, neither ruffling nor puckering (see page 112).

With the *right side* of the knitting facing you, work one row of single crochet and *gauge your work* just as in picking up sts in knitting—work a st into each of three rows and then skip the fourth row. On each succeeding row, you must chain 2 to turn, and then work into each original stitch with single crochet. *Always chain 2 to turn*, and start the first st directly above the last st made on the previous row. It is also better to work single crochet *under the 2 top threads* of the previous row (see page 112), unless there is a special reason not to. Just as in a knitted border, it is wise to have the finished border very *slightly shorter* than the knitting. This can be pressed to the correct proportion on the final touching-up.

If a cardigan is to be made for a growing child, you can look to the future and make buttonholes in *both sides*. In this case, overcast the buttonholes of one side and sew the buttons over them. When the child has outgrown it, and another child of the opposite sex can use it to good advantage, simply close the buttonholes on one side and open them on the other.

INSERTING ZIPPERS

There are many instances in which a zipper is the best means of closing, such as a side opening of a dress or skirt, a back-of-the-neck opening, or the front of a cardigan. Instructions often call for an addition of sts at the side seam of a dress or skirt, to be turned in to form a facing which will accommodate the zipper with a blind placket. Usually one or two rows of single crochet around the opening or on one edge will suffice; make sure to keep this crocheting firm so that it will not stretch the knitting. Then pin the zipper in place and sew it with thread according to directions. I strongly suggest that the sewing be done *by hand*, not by machine, and that the edges of the knitting be *fulled slightly onto the zipper* to keep the zipper flat. If knitting is pulled too tight, the zipper will buckle. Instead of using regular sewing thread which might cut wool yarn, it is better to use two or three strands of six-strand embroidery floss. This is softer in texture than sewing thread and is available in a great range of colors. It may not last quite so long, but at least it won't damage the knitting, and it can always be replaced.

If the zipper still shows when the placket is finished, work another row of crocheting along the overlapping edge and tack the ends down. On the front edges of a cardigan or jacket you may insert an open-end zipper with either a fly front or a plain closing. The directions for each of these come with the package. No matter which type you use, the edges of the knitting should be finished with one or two rows of single crochet to pull them into the correct measurement before the zipper is applied. Again, *do not* fit the knitting to the zipper—fit the zipper to the knitting, making sure that the edges are not pulled.

DRY BLOCKING

There is very rarely a good reason for a full blocking operation on a bulky knit or even on many of the Shetland sweaters. (A "Quick-and-Easy" dress or sweater, made on those whopping needles and from three or four strands of yarn, should *never*, in any circumstance, feel the touch of an iron or see a blocking board.) It usually suffices to assemble the pieces and press the seams open with a steam iron (leave the ribbing alone, please). If the garment is a sweater, *just wearing it* one or two times will block it sufficiently. When a skirt, dress, or jacket does need blocking, and especially when fine yarn has been used, there are two methods which may be followed:

DRY BLOCKING A SWEATER

Lay a very damp, almost wet cotton flannel sheet on a flat surface large enough to hold the entire garment, protecting whatever is underneath it with a piece of heavy plastic. Place the garment on the damp sheet and mold it with the hands into the proper proportions, making liberal use of a tape measure and checking the dimensions to which it has been made. If the proper instructions have been followed, there should be no need for the use of pins, but if they *must* be used, be sure they are rustproof, use them sparingly, and remove them as soon as you believe the garment will retain its correct shape. (Pinholes have an annoying way of showing up after the garment is dry.) Cover the work with another wet cloth and press it down with the hands so that this dampness may penetrate the knitting. Leave the pieces in position until the knitted fabric is *completely* dry, lifting the cover cloth once in a while to reshape the garment if it is necessary. Turn the garment wrong side out and press the seams open at the sides and shoulders. This will also take away any fold lines that may have been set.

DRY BLOCKING A SKIRT

Complete any necessary finishing touches at the top and the bottom of the skirt, with the exception of applying the elastic. This should not be done until the skirt has been blocked.

The blocking should be done on a space large enough to accommodate the entire skirt — on a rug or a large table that has been thoroughly protected from heat and dampness. A folding asbestos table protector, covered with heavy paper and cloth, is ideal if you do not have a blocking screen (see pages 125–126).

Cut a piece of heavy cotton tape to half your waistline measurement, another one to half your hipline measurement, and a third to measure half the width you want the bottom of the skirt to be. For example, if your waistline is 28", your hipline 38", and the bottom of the skirt is to be 52" wide, you would cut one tape 14", one 19", and the third 26".

Cut five pieces of tape to the desired length of your skirt and follow these seven steps (Fig. 292):

1. Press the waistline tape along the top of the skirt, using tacks or pins, stretching or easing in the top edge.

2. Using one of the skirt-length tapes, press one tack into the center top of the skirt through the tape and pull the tape taut down the center line. Fasten this tape into the center of the bottom edge of the skirt.

3. At this point, establish the center of the tape to be used at the bottom width and press the bottom tack (the last one inserted) into this tape at the same point. Stretch this tape out to the sides to establish the bottom width of the skirt, and fasten the tape down temporarily at each end.

4. Using the hipline tape, measure down from the waistline to 3" *above the fullest part of the hipline* and draw this tape across the work itself at this point, just *over* the work. This tape is to be used again later on.

5. Press one of the length tapes into the top of the skirt, just inside the edge, and another into the other side. Stretch these tapes down diagonally to meet the ends of the width tape at the bottom.

6. Fasten the last two tapes to the top of the skirt, between the center and outside tapes. Pull the tapes straight and fasten them to the bottom tape.

7. Shape the skirt to these eight tapes, pressing tacks into all tapes about an inch apart, drawing the knitted material to fit the form thus made. Cover the whole thing with damp Turkish towels and leave it until thoroughly dry (Fig. 292).

Remove the skirt and turn it inside out. Press all necessary points with a steam iron without moving the iron over the surface.

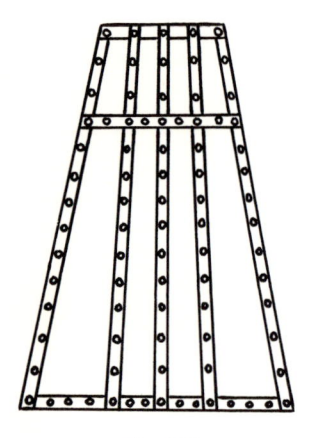

Fig. 292

124

Note: As a general rule, because of the length of time required to make it, the skirt has become somewhat soiled. Because of this and because the cleaner can do a better job of blocking, I send it to him with instructions to follow certain dimensions, such as: waist—28″, hipline—38″ at 4″ down from the waistline, plus the designated length of skirt and the width at the bottom edge. Once the skirt has been professionally blocked, it need not be done again.

WET BLOCKING: MAKING A BLOCKING SCREEN

If you are a real knitting addict and either you or the man of the house is handy with tools, you will find that a homemade blocking screen is invaluable. Blocking screens are similar to window screens, made of a heavy grade of copper or aluminum wire window screening and a wooden frame substantial enough to hold the wire taut. The size is up to you, but the screen should be large enough to block two or more pieces simultaneously. If many sweaters are being worn by the family, it is almost certain that you would never wash just one at a time! (*Note:* My screen is 36″ × 72″ and made of aluminum screening with a wooden frame and supports [Fig. 293].) Give the metal parts two or three coats of fine-grade enamel to prevent any "bleeding" of the metal, which might stain fabrics. If you are lucky enough to possess a couple of sawhorses, good! Otherwise, two chair backs should suffice as supports for the screen.

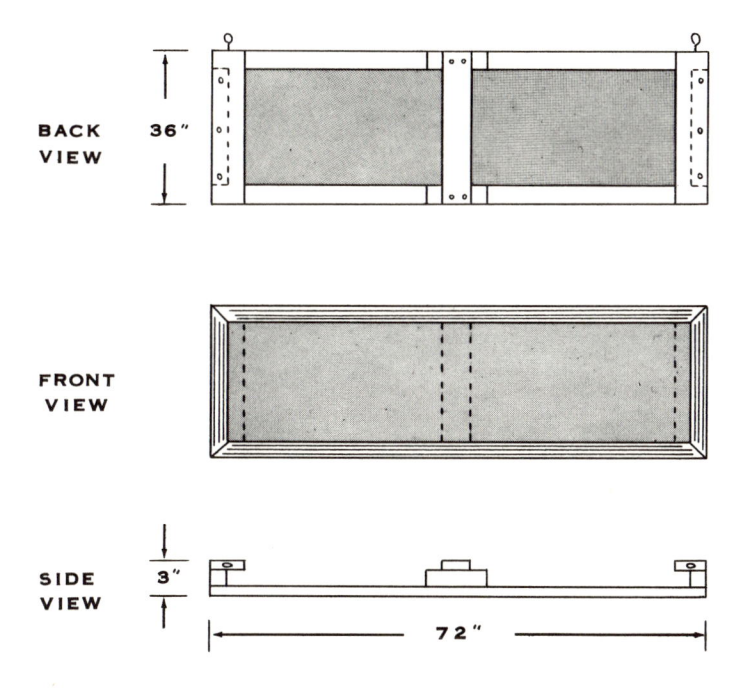

Fig. 293

Cover the screen with a light piece of cotton flannel before blocking. Wash (or wet) the garment, then remove as much moisture as possible from it and block according to the directions given under Dry Blocking. For faster drying, place an oscillating fan so that it will face directly toward the side edge of the screen and keep the air circulating under and over the cloth and the knitting. Absolutely *no* blocking or drying should be done outdoors unless it is done in *total shade*. The sun's rays can penetrate a cotton cover and bleach colors. If *white wool* has been used, it will not bleach under the sun; it will turn an ugly tan! Even as you and I, wool will sunburn if exposed to too much sunlight.

TAILORED FINISHING

The following methods are recommended for assembling, blocking, and finishing fitted garments, such as dressy blouses, dresses (either one- or two-piece), suits, and coats. These are skilled operations, and a basic knowledge of dressmaking and tailoring is extremely helpful, but not imperative. The methods given are not very difficult, but they *are* painstaking and may seem rather complicated at first glance. If you want a first-class result, however, it might be well to remember that you have put quite a bit of time into the knitting, not to mention the cost of the material. Nothing is quite comparable to the pride you will have when you wear the beautifully fitted result.

For a properly tailored finish, each piece of the garment should be blocked separately and then assembled by basting the pieces together with *wool yarn*. Always join the pieces with yarn of the same color and texture, if the original yarn cannot be used for some reason. Sewing *cannot* be done with nubby yarn as threading even a large-eye needle with this type of yarn is almost impossible. In most cases it is far better to join with slip-stitch (see page 111).

If the instructions were correctly written and have been carefully followed, the pieces should not be difficult to block. Just the use of a steam iron or a dry iron over a piece of wet cloth should be sufficient. The edges of the knitted pieces should have all of the curl removed, and if the centers of the pieces are badly wrinkled, the wrinkles should be pressed out. *Steam* all pieces flat, but do not stretch the knitting unless the instructions indicate that this must be done (on a lace dress or blouse stretching must be done to attain correct length).

When all pieces are thoroughly dry, baste the back to the front (or front sections), again with yarn, and try the garment on *wrong side out*. Any necessary adjustments, such as tucks, shirrings, or darts, should be made at this point in the fitting operation. If the garment is not to be lined, sew the pieces together (or join them with slip stitch), following the fitting lines and making sure that the stitches do not bind. Any excess material in the seams should be pressed back on the final touching-up.

Next baste the sleeve seam and baste the sleeve into the armhole, leaving about 4″ open at the top of the sleeve (2″ on each side of body shoulder seams) to allow for adjustments. Try the garment on again and pin this portion in, easing it into the remaining part of the armhole. Remove and baste, then join the sleeve seams. When all seams have been joined and all body fittings made, you are ready to put on the finishing touches.

Unless hems are indicated at the finishing (or open) edges, work one or two rows of single crochet around these edges to keep them from rolling up.

Narrow tape may be needed at the back of the neck or on the shoulder seams to retain the original fit and the shape of the garment. Use mercerized sewing cotton for this and note carefully that thread is used only at points where material other than the knitted work itself is involved.

If buttonholes have been worked into the knitting, it is advisable to face both the button and buttonhole sides with ribbon, to be put in as one of the last bits of finishing. Just as in applying ribbon at the waistline, the ribbon must be fitted to the edges before it is cut and applied, to make sure that the front edges do not droop. The two pieces of ribbon should, naturally, be of exactly equal length and pinned, basted, and whipped in. The buttonhole side should be *basted* in only until the position of the holes has been carefully marked. Then remove the ribbon and work the buttonholes in it to the proper size, either with machine or by hand. Cut holes and then apply again to position, basting carefully to match the holes in the knitting, and whip the edges. Overcast the holes made in the ribbon to the knitted buttonholes, making the stitches as unnoticeable as possible.

If hems are made on the jacket or coat, all side seams should be joined and pressed open before turning them under. Baste the hems *first* at the turning edge and then at the hemming edge. Leave *this* basting in until the final pressing. *Following one row of knitting* on the wrong side, whip the hem into position, using the knitting yarn if it is smooth or, if this is too heavy or nubby, use six-strand embroidery floss or smooth yarn of the correct color. When hemming, insert the sewing needle into *just a part of the stitch* at the back, so that the stitch will not show through to the front of the work.

LININGS AND LINING MATERIALS: HOW TO MAKE LININGS FOR JACKETS, COATS, DRESSES, SWEATERS, BLOUSES, SKIRTS

If the garment is to be lined, the patterns for each part of the lining should be made when the knitted pieces have been pressed. The back should be folded down the center, placed on a piece of wrapping paper, and moved at least an inch away from the center fold line to allow room for a pleat of about one inch. A *coat* should have a 2″

pleat allowance: a jacket a little less. Draw around the piece, leaving 1″ at all seam edges for seam allowance. This full inch may not be needed at the finish, but it is better by far to have too much than too little. If a *coat* is fitted, a dart must be allowed for at each front shoulder. Also, if there is to be a *dolman* sleeve, allow for the dart at the shoulder.

Draw around the fronts and sleeves—and if the fronts are to be faced, place the facing pieces over the front sections and draw an outline of the inner curved edges on the lining pattern. Leave at least one full inch along these edges when you cut the lining to allow it to be tucked under the facings at the finish. If facings are to be interlined, now is the time to cut the paper pattern for them. No seam allowance need be made on interlinings. In fact, a little may have to be trimmed away at the finish.

Front and sleeve pieces must have a little special attention. On the front pieces leave an allowance at the side seam edges so that darts may be taken for better fit. Make a slash at that edge, just about 2″ down from the armhole, and running about 3″ in. Open this slash enough to allow for a ¾″ dart. Open it up even more if the jacket or coat is for a full-busted person. The bottom edge will have to be cut on a slanted line to allow for this dart.

If the jacket or coat is fitted at the waist, a small allowance for a dart should be made at this point.

Sleeve top linings should measure from 1″ to 1½″ wider than those of the knitted sleeve, and should be cut about an inch longer to allow for a couple of small darts to be taken at the underarm seam at the elbow. The extra width at the top should be eased into the armhole as a final touch.

Before cutting out the actual lining pieces, cut practice pieces from an old piece of cloth or from unbleached muslin. In this way, any error in judgment can be corrected before the good lining material has been cut into.

All final finishing on a jacket or blouse should be made *before* the lining is added. Neck edges should be finished, all open edges crocheted where indicated, all details completed and pressed to the correct proportions. Any facings should be attached and interlined if necessary. Linings should be cut back to meet the facing, but leave at least ½″ of lining material to be extended under the facing. If pellon is used, insert it and tack it to the facing. All buttonholes should be cut into the lining and interlining and bound to the knitting with buttonhole stitch.

The lining pieces of a jacket should be joined and fitted into it as follows: (1) Put the jacket (or coat) on wrong side out. (2) Turn the *temporary* lining right side out and slip it on over the garment. All adjustments, such as darts and shirrings, should be made on the muslin lining and basted into the garment. (3) Turn everything right side out and try it on again. Any errors will now be detectable in this practice piece. (4) If everything fits, *then* cut the pieces of the lining on the straight of the material, put them together, and fit them into the jacket. Neck edges and fronts should be slip-stitched into place, shoulder seams sewed in, and the sleeves stitched at the armholes. The lining seams should be tacked to the seams of the knitting.

If there is a hem at the bottom of the jacket or coat, hem the lining as well and let it hang free, but the lining should be at least 1″ shorter than the garment itself. A cardigan lining should be cut in a suitable length so that a hem may be made and attached at the top of the inside of the ribbing, *always* allowing a little room for action. Sleeves may be hemmed (and the tucks made at the elbow), but the bottom of the lining hem should be tacked to the top of the sleeve hem, or to the top of the ribbing if the garment is a sweater.

If the jacket is not to be faced, and a finish of crocheting or knitting has been used around the front, neck, and bottom edges, the lining should be whipped into place along the two front edges and the neckline just inside of the finishing stitches. The lining should be allowed to hang free about an inch above the bottom edge of the jacket.

A one-piece dress is lined in virtually the same manner, but joined at the left-side seam with a zipper or other closing. The left-side pieces of the lining should be joined directly onto the knitting (don't forget the dart at the sides), and the zipper or other closing sewed into the two pieces, together. It may even be possible to buy a slip that would fit into the dress to serve as a lining. If so, open the left-side seam of the slip so that the zipper may be inserted. Tack the right seams together as well.

If a skirt has been knitted in two or more pieces, it may be lined in just the same way as a cloth skirt. Darts or tucks knitted into the skirt pieces must be duplicated in the corresponding places on the lining pieces. If the skirt has been made on a circular needle, however, it is a good idea to buy or make a half slip, dispense with the elastic at the top, and attach the slip to the skirt along with the elastic banding as outlined on page 114. In either case, circular or pieced skirt, the slip should have a slit at either side of the hem to allow for easier walking.

The lining material should be carefully chosen. Either China silk or light-weight taffeta is best. Never use crepe as it is apt to stretch or shrink when cleaned. If an excellent color match cannot be made, it is far better to use a good contrasting color.

If a hook and eye must be used anywhere, it is better to make an eye with thread. A metal eye is apt to show. Using doubled thread, attach it at the given spot, draw it under the work and up to the top again (Fig. 294), and do this about three times. Work over these threads with buttonhole stitch (Fig. 295). Be careful in fastening the garment when you are wearing it; don't let the hook go into the knitting itself.

With these basic directions in mind, follow any additional instructions for collars, facings, cuffs, just as they are given in the individual pattern. These have been carefully worked out by the designer and knitter who made up the instructions.

There are many instances where the use of shoulder pads is desirable. Often even a pullover or cardigan sweater will set better if shoulder pads are used.

Retail stores usually have a large selection of shoulder pads.

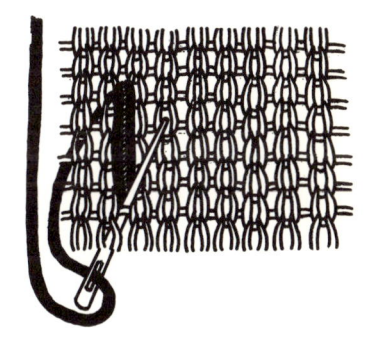

Fig. 294

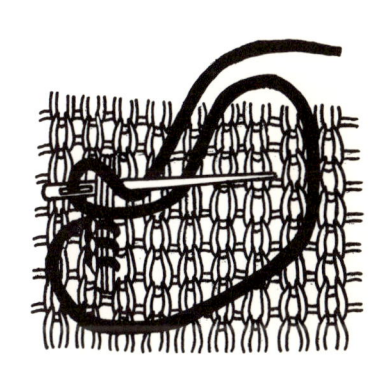

Fig. 295

However, these may be replaced with ones you can knit. Use the same yarn as that of the garment, cast on anywhere from 3" to 7" of sts, and make a small knitted square. Fold it in half corner-wise to make a triangle and tack it in place on the garment.

In the jacket of a suit and in all coats, shoulder pads make a decided difference in fit. Using shoulder pads in a cardigan may enhance the fit considerably. If you use the same yarn, the cardigan need not be cleaned or the shoulder pad removed, for the cardigan may safely be washed, knitted shoulder pads included. Commercially made shoulder pads should not be washed.

If the knitted shoulder pad is not thick enough to suit the garment, the yarn may be doubled. If a more fitted pad is desired, it may be made by following the directions of Pattern Stitch #2, using one strand of yarn for the first few rows, doubling it for several rows, and trebling it up to the center of the piece. Reverse the number of threads on the way back to the first row.

7. Knitting Stitch Patterns: How to Select and Use Them

First of all, *choose your pattern stitch very carefully!*

Whether you are going to make a sweater, suit, coat, dress, stole, shawl, or a baby garment, a pair of mittens or socks, there are several groups of stitch patterns suitable for each item. Not all stitch groups, however, are suitable for every article.

It would seldom be wise to choose a loose, lacy stitch for a tailored suit, or a close tight fabric stitch for a light-weight shawl or stole; a tight, confining ribbed pattern for a bed jacket, or an open or sleazy stitch for a bathing suit. Therefore *it is most important* to choose your pattern stitch to suit the article to be made.

The pattern stitches in this book are by no means all of the stitches that imaginative knitters have devised through the years. New ones are constantly being designed. There are no limits to what can be done, but the patterns given here represent a comprehensive selection that should suit practically every contemporary need and purpose. The stitches are grouped into different classes and are accompanied by suggestions concerning their possible uses. Appropriate yarns are also recommended, but any of the suggestions should not necessarily confine you to a particular choice. The most important point to be considered when choosing *any* pattern stitch is: "Is it right for the article I wish to make? Is it too complicated, fussy? It *is* a beautiful stitch, but will it work well into this particular garment?"

You may find illustrations or photographs of knitted suits or dresses in knitting books but not care for the particular stitch proposed by the designer; you may prefer to use one found in the next chapter. The first thing you *must* do is to observe the STITCH GAUGE in the original directions, then make a swatch of the stitch you prefer. If it compares exactly with the measurements given in the instructions or can be *made* to compare when another size of needle is used to *make* it compare, it is reasonably safe to use the stitch and follow the instructions given. If the gauge does not follow, however, and you think you can still use the pattern stitch, but at a different gauge, you must recompute the number of stitches throughout the garment.

NEVER USE *ANY* STITCH WITHOUT FIRST MAKING A SAMPLE SWATCH. *Always* work a piece *at least four inches square*, with the exact same yarn and needles you are going to use for the garment. You might have on hand a small amount of the right kind of yarn, but in another color. *Don't use it* for your swatch. Yarn of another color may vary just enough to produce a variation in gauge. As an example, I recall one knitter who made a blouse of white novelty yarn, following directions in exact detail. The blouse fitted perfectly. The knitter liked it so well that she bought the same amount of the very same novelty yarn, made in the same mill, *but dyed in another color*. She followed the same instructions and used the same size needles. The blouse turned out to be two sizes too large! She hadn't made a swatch of this new yarn to see if it compared exactly with the original. She had been warned, but she didn't believe that so much importance could possibly be attached to a change in color. It was a tragic way to learn a lesson.

The next thing to look for in your new pattern stitch is the "multiple." For instance: Pattern Stitch #7 requires a multiple of 8 sts, while Pattern Stitch #6 requires a multiple of 6 sts plus 3. You may like Pattern Stitch #7, but would prefer to make Pattern Stitch #6. The instructions may call for a total cast-on of 128 sts. This number, divided by 8 (the multiple of Pattern Stitch #7) is 16—meaning that there are 16 patterns of that stitch. The number 128 divided by 6 is 21 with 2 left over. Therefore, switching from Pattern Stitch #7 to Pattern Stitch #6 would require the addition of one more stitch in the total number. The original number—128—should be changed to 129 to allow for the extra st required in Pattern Stitch #6. The difference of the one st between the two patterns is easily absorbed in the last row of the piece to be worked, or in some other place, such as an armhole shaping or, in this case, in the neckline, where an additional st would make no difference at all in size or fit.

Many instruction books, however, do not give the multiple of the sts used in the directions. They should, but they may not. In this case, it is not very difficult to find the multiple for yourself. Look first for the two asterisks—the two * *—one of them at or near the beginning of the numbers in the row, and one near the end. As an example, Pattern Stitch #103 reads as follows:

Row 1: K 1, * sl 1, K 3—rep from *, end sl 1, K 1.

To find the multiple, count *from* the first * *to* the dash (—), or the second *. This row consists of one slipped st and 3 Knit sts, adding up to 4 altogether. The one Knit st *before* the first * and the slipped st and one Knit st *after* the last * adds to 3 sts. Thus—a multiple of 4 sts plus 3 (the 1 st found at the beginning, plus the 2 sts at the end of the pattern). This is not *always* dependable, however, and each pattern, if you cannot rely on the information available, should be worked out by itself. First: Cast on the number of sts *before* the first *, then, counting the number of sts between the * * (the number of sts forming the pattern itself), cast on *at least* twice this number of sts. (If the pattern is made up of a small number of sts, cast on 4 or 5 repeats of the number.)

We will use Pattern Stitch #72 as an example of a stitch in which the *multiple* of sts is easy to determine, but the extra number of sts for the edges is vague. It reads as follows:
Row 1: P 2, * K 2, P 2, K 1, P 1, K 1, P 2, K 2, P 3 — rep from *, end P 2. The number of sts between the two * * adds up to 14 sts in all. If you did not *know* (because we told you so) that the multiple was 14 *plus 1*, you would cast on 28 sts (for the number, times 2, of the pattern itself) and then 2 more sts for the P 2 *before* the first * and 2 more sts for the P 2 *after* the last *. Then, working from the beginning of the row — P 2, * K 2, P 2, K 1, P 1, K 1, P 2, K 2, P 3 — go back to the * and work K 2, P 2, K 1, P 1, K 1, P 2, K 2 and P 3 again. However, this will give you 3 sts too many, so — P 2 tog 3 times on the last 6 sts, or simply drop the 3 extra sts. Counting the sts on your needle, you will find they add up to 29 altogether (14 × 2, plus 1). This means that 3 of the sts in the pattern itself were to be used as part of the edge. This does not *always* work out in this manner but, following this general procedure, the multiple — plus the extra sts — can be determined satisfactorily.

When counting the multiple, however, do *not* count any of the *Made Sts* — M 1, yo, or Pu 1. These sts are added while the row is being worked. Do, however, count 2 sts for each plain dec. and 3 sts for "SK2togP," etc.

In some pattern stitches the multiple does not remain constant throughout all rows; sts are added or subtracted during the working of the rows. When the first row in the sequence is reached again, however, the numbers will have regained their regular count.

Every pattern stitch in the following chapter has been worked to an exact multiple, plus the extra sts which must be used. All have been proved workable by actual experience. The patterns have been grouped informally into eight different categories:

1. Reversible Stitches I: stitches which are alike (or similar) on both sides — #1 through #23
2. Reversible Stitches II: those that are as good on one side as on the other — #24 through #42
3. Ribbing Stitches: #43 through #66
4. Fabric Stitches: texture patterns — #67 through #124
5. Non-reversible: good on one side only — #125 through #141
6. "Small" Stitches: for use where a print or contrast fabric would ordinarily be used in woven materials — #142 through #157
7. Cable Stitches: #158 through #179
8. Lace Stitches: #180 through #200

These stitches are *very* loosely grouped, for it is quite difficult in some cases to state precisely that each stitch belongs to only one group. Some patterns are interchangeable with other groups. Others are not. For example, some reversible stitches may be used for fabric stitches and vice versa. Some of the smaller pattern lace stitches may be used in place of some "small" stitches. The larger lace patterns, however, could by no means replace the fabric stitches nor could the cable stitches be substituted for lace stitches. Heed the warnings beside some of the stitches. Don't just look at the photograph and select a stitch without first making a swatch. It may *act* different from what you might expect when worked into a piece. The stitch may have no give when you need it, or it might stretch when you want it to be firm. The photograph cannot show this reaction, and the yarn you use might give the stitch a decidedly different effect from the one pictured.

You may notice that all plain ribbing stitches have been omitted. This has been done intentionally, as all ribbing is a matter of simple multiplication: K 2, P 2 ribbing is a multiple of 4 sts — K 3, P 3 ribbing a multiple of 6 sts — etc. Any uneven ribbing such as K 3, P 1 or K 4, P 2, is just as simply figured out. There are so many beautiful patterns that could be included in the limited total of 200 that space has been alloted only to those of greater interest.

Some of the patterns carry a warning: "Set-Up Row — *Do Not Repeat.*" This "Set-Up" row will prepare the sts for the first row of the pattern stitch itself.

Space does not permit detailed explanation of each separate operation involved in each pattern stitch. If the chapter on Basic Knitting Procedures has been carefully studied, you have already been made aware of most of the procedures to be followed. If you have not yet examined it thoroughly, you will find many helpful cross-references in the Pattern Stitch directions, so that you will not be left in doubt as to which procedure to follow in any particular instance.

Try to ignore what may seem to be the complexity of the stitch *as written*, or the details of the stitch shown in the photograph. Many of these patterns (and others found elsewhere) may appear at a casual glance to contain so many rows — or so many sts in the multiple — as to seem too complicated to tackle. Once you have made a swatch, however, and completed two or three repeats, the imagined difficulties dissolve as you see the pattern come to life in your hands. Give the patterns a chance! You may find that it is fun to work them out and that you really prefer the challenge of a pattern stitch to the repetition of plainer stitches.

Develop the *rhythm* of knitting a pattern stitch. It facilitates your work and becomes faster and easier to do as you go along. This is particularly true of the fabric stitches where only a small number of sts are used in each unit. "K 1, yf, sl 1, yb" — works out to a 4 beat — 1 for "K 1," 2 for "yf," 3 for "sl 1," and 4 for "yb" — etc.

Inevitably pattern stitches have to be increased or decreased for shaping a garment, especially in pieces which make up a blouse or jacket. This is where the use of graph paper is most applicable. In working these decreases or increases, part of the pattern is taken away or added to. Work out on graph paper the position of the sts *as they appear from the Right Side* of the material to be worked. Pattern Stitch #20 is shown here on diagrammed graph paper. Eight increases and decreases are to be made on each side during the shaping; therefore, start the working of the diagram *at least* 8 sts in from each edge. On the paper, mark out 30 squares—14 sts for each pattern—plus the 2 extra sts for the edges. On the first row of the pattern, place an X where the sts are purled. On the next row of the pattern, place an X in the spaces where the sts are to be *Knitted* and leave the spaces blank for the *Purled* sts, as this is the way they appear on the *Right Side* of the work. The accompanying diagram shows that 4 increases have been made, and then that 4 decreases have followed. With a stitch gauge of five and one-half to each inch, and eight rows to each inch, it will be seen that increases have been made after each one-half inch, and then the decreases worked in the same manner.

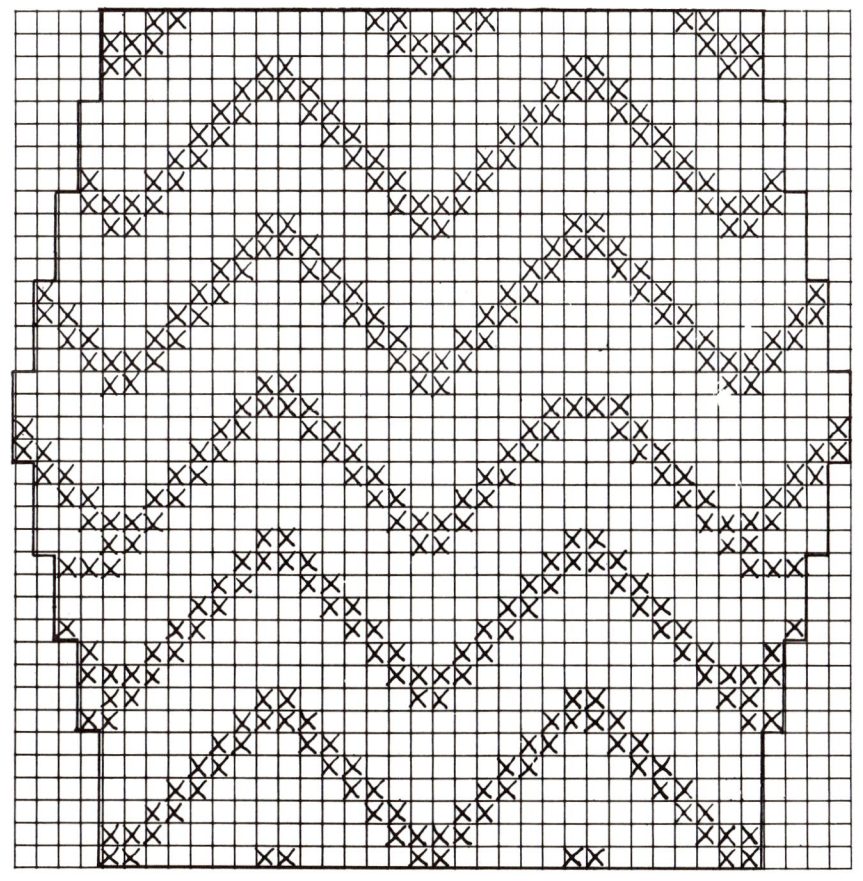

Another precautionary measure must be mentioned here. When two or more pattern stitches are to be used in the same article or garment, *the stitch gauge of each of them* must be determined before changing from one to the other. It is all too likely that the gauges are entirely different and sts may have to be added or taken away in the first row (or set-up row) of the new pattern stitch. As an example: If you are working Stockinette Stitch at the bottom of a blouse, with an 8-st gauge, and you wish to change to a looser or tighter stitch (making the guage smaller or larger), you must first find out whether your new stitch gauge will be the same as the Stockinette. If it is not, you must either change the size of your needle or take out or add the difference —*in each inch*—of the number of sts that the new pattern stitch requires.

Finally, these things must be expected of certain pattern stitches:

1. Fabric stitches which include *slipped* sts which cross other *worked* sts have less tendency to stretch when they are blocked or while they are worn than those patterns in which *all* sts are *worked*. Pattern Stitches #81-A and #81-B, #95 and #96 are good examples. This same rule applies to patterns that include much "crossing" or "pulling over" of sts—see Pattern Stitches #85 and #105.

2. Many "yarn-overs" in one row, that are *worked* in the following row, may make the work loose and stretchy.

3. Any cabling will pull the sts (and the final fabric) in to a great extent, as will any tight ribbing.

TO REACH THE *EXACT* GAUGE OF ANY STITCH, BLOCK THE SWATCH before the gauge is taken. This is particularly important when light- or medium-weight yarn is to be worked on needles that are larger than those ordinarily used for that particular weight of yarn. I recall a one-piece dress made with a very full skirt, in a medium-weight yarn—a mixture of rayon and wool—on #5 needles. (This yarn would usually be worked on #1 or #2 needles.) The pattern stitch included a six-row insertion of a small lace stitch every two or three inches (Pattern Stitch #158) This lace stitch was outlined with two rows of Garter Stitch. The skirt length blocked out to 23″. It had been made, however, to measure 18″ before blocking. It had stretched 5 inches in the blocking! The amount of stretch an entire garment will have when blocked can be measured by taking the gauge of the stitches and rows in the swatch *before* and *after* blocking, and comparing the difference in the two gauges.

When Purled sts are alternated with Knit sts in *vertical* lines, the Knit sts rise and remain more prominent in the fabric, and the Purled sts sink into the background. This is called *Ribbing*.

When a small number of rows of Stockinette Stitch are alternated, the Purled side of the work rises to the surface and the Knit side sinks into the background. This is often called "Welting" (Pattern Stitch #2), although there are many other arrangements of stitches that also produce a welted effect.

An ALL KNIT or ALL PURL fabric (Garter Stitch) will remain flat, and pattern stitches with any amount of Garter Stitch included in the design will tend to remain flat as well. Any pattern stitches which include any variation of SEED STITCH (Pattern Stitch #3) will also tend to remain flat.

On the other hand, Stockinette Stitch (K 1 row, P 1 row) will inevitably curl inward at the side edges, and outward at the bottom and top edges. Therefore, unless these edges are to be caught into a seam, they should have some type of stitch that will remain flat to start them, surround them, or outline them—either any type of Seed or Garter Stitch, or a combination of the two. If Stockinette Stitch is to be used as the basis of a blouse or sweater, and ribbing is to be used at the start, the edges do not require a finishing. Otherwise the bottom edges must have some type of finish that will take out the curl—usually one or two rows of single crochet—to keep it flat.

Many of the following pattern stitches may be made "in the round" —worked on 4 double-pointed needles or on a circular needle— particularly some of the lace patterns, such as Pattern Stitches #165, #176, and #180. These patterns are worked with the design made on the KNIT SIDE only, and then the next row is Purled. In circular knitting this second row (or round) would be Knitted, not Purled. Problems in working these patterns may arise when making the beginning and end of the round, where possible yarn-overs might appear and must be watched for.

When these lace patterns are adapted for garments such as one-piece dresses or skirts, there is another very important factor to be taken into consideration—fitting and shaping. First, a CORRECT GAUGE of the swatch is taken on the CORRECT SIZE OF NEEDLE for the parts of the garment that *must fit*—i.e., bodice or waist, waistline, and hip. The gauge in these cases would be taken on the correct size of needle for the yarn being used; then, if working from the hemline *up*, it would be proper to cast on the sts and work them, for the first few inches, on a needle about 2 or 3 sizes larger than the one used for the original swatch (see page 99 on taking gauge and making a swatch). The sts should be worked for the first few inches on the largest size needle, then the next smaller, on down to the smallest needle, the one used for the main swatch. When using *any* of these sts on two or three sizes of needles, it is of paramount importance to watch out for the amount of stretch that each size of needle will give to the fabric being knitted, especially the vertical stretch, so that the *correct length* of the garment or article may be ascertained. Therefore, make a swatch of the pattern stitch on *each* size of needle, press the swatches so that the ultimate amount of stretch may be determined, and plan your knitting accordingly.

The type of yarn used will affect the "line" and "drape" of the finished piece of work. *All* knitting has a tendency to slant a little on the bias, particularly when most of the sts are knitted on one row and purled on the next, and especially when made in a circular fashion. Linen and cotton yarns are particularly subject to this tendency, because most of them have extremely little "loft"; their tight twist requires special treatment. The chapter on Basic Knitting Procedures stresses this point. The "Combined Cross and Plain" knitting should be used whenever linen and cotton yarns are used, except in certain lace stitches that include many yarn-overs, K 2 togs, SKPs and SK2togPs. The frequent use of these last three types of stitches will keep the material from going bias; the K2tog pulls the work to the right, the SKP pulls it to the left, and the SK2togP pulls it upright. Pattern Stitches #176 and #180 are prime examples of such stitches and may be worked as the instructions are written, without worrying about the Reverse Stitch usually specified for cotton and linen.

8. Pattern Stitches

LIST OF PATTERN STITCHES

REVERSIBLE STITCHES I

#1-A Garter Stitch
#1-B Garter Stitch Worked on the Bias
#2 Horizontal Ribbing or Welting (Often called Quaker Stitch)
#3 Seed, Moss, or Rice Stitch
#4-A Diagonal Ribbing or Chevron (Right Slant)
#4-B Diagonal Ribbing or Chevron (Left Slant)
#4-C Chevron (A and B combined)
#5 Small Check
#6 Ribbing and Welt
#7 Broken Check
#8 Alternating Broken Check
#9 Ribbing and Garter
#10 Broken Ribbing I
#11 Broken Ribbing II
#12 Broken Ribbing III
#13 Brioche Stitch
#14 Open Seed-Stitch Blocks
#15 Open-Laced Cross-Stitch
#16 Basket Weave
#17 Uneven Basket Weave
#18 Broken Ribbing IV
#19 Modified Ribbing
#20 Wide Chevron
#21 Tall Diamond, Outlined I
#22 Tall Diamond II
#23 Lozenge

REVERSIBLE STITCHES II

#24 Tall Diamond in Relief III
#25 Flat Diamond, Outlined
#26 Vertical Chevron
#27 Large and Small Diamonds
#28 Horizontal Leaf
#29 Small Cross-Stitch Pattern

#30 Gathered Fabric Stitch
#31 Waved Ribbing
#32 Knot Stitch Fabric
#33 Drop Stitch Pattern
#34 Baby Variegated Ribbing
#35 Shirred Ribbing
#36 Eyelet Fabric
#37 Striped Fagoting
#38 Open Wave Lace
#39 Ear of Corn
#40 Fagot and Cable Stripe
#41 Acorn Pattern
#42 Lace Triangles

RIBBING STITCHES

#43 Eyelet Diamond
#44 Diamond Ribbing Pattern
#45 Open Blocks
#46-A Diagonal Lace Stripe I
#46-B Diagonal Lace Stripe II
#47 Zigzag Ribbing
#48 Cockleshells
#49 Spider Web Lace
#50 Crossed Ribbing I
#51 Stocking Heel Stitch (Slipped Ribbing)
#52 Decorative Ribbing
#53 Baby Cross-Stitch Stripe
#54 Baby Cross-Braid Stripe
#55 Cross-Stitch Ribbing
#56 Ribbing with Tight Braid
#57 Crossed Ribbing II
#58 Piqué Stitch
#59 Leaf Ribbing
#60 Baby Zigzag Cable
#61 Split Cable and Stripe
#62 Herringbone Ribbing
#63 Teardrop Ribbing
#64 Cross-Braid Ribbing

#65 Fancy Ribbing Stitch
#66 Baby Cross-Cable Ribbing

FABRIC STITCHES

#67 Stockinette Stitch
#68 Shirred Stockinette Stitch
#69 Broken Ribbing V
#70-A Diagonal Seed Stitch I
#70-B Diagonal Seed Stitch II
#70-C Chevron Seed Stitch
#71 Open Chevron
#72 Broken Chevron
#73 Waved Welt
#74 Seed Stitch Blocks
#75 Flat Diamond I
#76 Triangles
#77 Basket Weave (Combined Rib and Welt)
#78 Seed and Stockinette Diamond
#79 Modified Seed Stitch
#80 Double Seed, Moss, or Rice Stitch
#81-A Slip Diagonal Fabric I
#81-B Slip Diagonal Fabric II
#82 Vertical Herringbone
#83 Fabric Stitch
#84 Herringbone Stripe
#85 Zigzag Stockinette Fabric
#86 Striped Fabric Stitch
#87 Mock Cable Fabric
#88-A Diagonal Cross Fabric—Right
#88-B Diagonal Cross Fabric—Left
#88-C Herringbone Cross Fabric
#89 Modified Schiaparelli
#90-A Schiaparelli, Cross Right
#90-B Schiaparelli, Cross Left
#91 Waffle Fabric Stitch
#92 Double English Knitting
#93 Braided Stitch
#94 Slip Fabric Stitch
#95 Woven Fabric Stitch I
#96 Woven Fabric Stitch II
#97 Staggered Check
#98 Fabric Block
#99 Heavy Woven Bias Fabric
#100 Flat Diamond II
#101 Cross-Weave Fabric
#102 Staggered Slip Check
#103 Slip Check
#104 Stockinette Stitch Wave
#105 Ribbing with Diagonal Slip Stitches
#106 Cross-Stitch Block
#107 Gathered Ribbing
#108 Waffle Stitch
#109-A Palm Leaf *Knit* Fabric
#109-B Palm Leaf *Purl* Fabric

#110 Cross-Stitch Diamond Fabric
#111 Diamond Cross
#112 Traveling Diamond and Ribbing
#113 Smocked Honeycomb
#114 Knotted Trellis Stitch
#115 Overlay Stitch
#116-A Cross-Stitch Fabric I
#116-B Cross-Stitch Fabric II
#116-C Cross-Stitch Fabric III
#117 Cable Bowknot
#118 Slip Cross Fabric
#119-A Bowknot Stitch (Butterfly Stitch) I
#119-B Bowknot Stitch II
#120 Lazy Daisy
#121 Leaf Fabric
#122 Embossed Leaf Pattern
#123 Tufted Rosette
#124 Oblique Knot Stitch

NON-REVERSIBLE STITCHES

#125 Clover and Diamond
#126 Rambler Rose
#127 Winding Vine and Stripe
#128 Tiny Tower
#129 Small Diamond Dot
#130 Bridal Veil Stitch
#131 Triplet Ribbing
#132 Tiny Eyelet Ribbing
#133 Open Stripe
#134 Tear Drop
#135 Simple Lace Pattern
#136 Purl Fabric Stitch
#137 Piqué Stitch
#138 Tiny Leaf Fabric
#139 Diamond in a Diamond
#140 Simple Lace Stitch
#141 Butterfly Lace Stitch

"SMALL" STITCHES

#142 Alternate Ribbing and Cable
#143 Traveling Cross Cable
#144 Fancy Cable
#145 Tiny Twisted Ribbing
#146 Flat Cable Fabric
#147 Spreading Cable
#148 Plaited Cable
#149 Horseshoe Cable Stripe
#150 Staggered Horseshoe Cable
#151 Open Drop-Stitch Cable
#152 Basket-Weave Cable
#153 Stockinette Cable Fabric
#154 Heavy Cable and Garter Stitch
#155 Fagot and Cable
#156 Smocked Ribbing
#157 Pullover (Mock) Cable

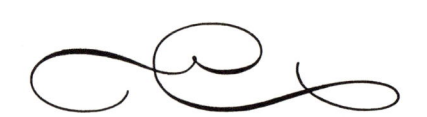

CABLE STITCHES

#158 Lattice Stitch I
#159 Lattice Stitch II
#160 Fancy Horizontal Stripe
#161 Open Cross Lattice Stitch
#162 Pointed Lace Pattern
#163 Zigzag and Fagot
#164 Crossed Cable and Fagot
#165 Herringbone Lace Pattern
#166 Woven Cable
#167 Lace Rosebud and Leaf
#168 Twinberry Stripe
#169 Baby Fern Stitch
#170 Arrowhead Stitch
#171 Grapevine Stitch
#172 Cross-Over Leaf Lace
#173 Baby Fan
#174 Open Diamond Stitch Lace
#175 Diamond and Knot Stitch
#176 Lace Leaf
#177 Fan with Ribbing
#178 Cable and Fan
#179 Simple Lace Diamond

LACE STITCHES

#180 Baby Leaf Lace
#181 Diamond Leaf Lace
#182 Large Leaf Pattern
#183 Pointed Leaf
#184 Leaf and Twig
#185 Lace Wings
#186 Popcorn
#187 Bell Pattern
#188 Bell Stitch Pattern
#189-A Bluebells I
#189-B Bluebells II
#190 Eyelet Crown (Crown of Glory or Cat's Paw)
#191 Lace Drop Stitch Pattern
#192 Sunburst
#193 Leaf Lace
#194 Fern Pattern
#195 Lady Slipper
#196 Pineapple Lace Stitch
#197 Open Leaf or Pineapple
#198 Eccentric Zigzag
#199 Double Leaf and Fagot
#200 Leaf Scallop

REVERSIBLE STITCHES I

#1-A GARTER STITCH—*Any number of sts.*

Knit all sts or Purl all sts, every row.

When working any *square* piece, work the same number of ridges (2 rows make one ridge) as the number of sts on the needle. Bind off on the *Wrong* Side on the last row.

Garter Stitch may be used in many ways and combinations. Used alone, it is just plain uninteresting, but in combination or in conjunction with other pattern stitches it is most valuable. Many of the following patterns are made up of Garter Stitch *plus* variations of other sts. The combinations are worked out in the pattern stitches themselves.

Articles that must "grow up" with an infant are often made in Garter Stitch because it has considerable lengthwise stretch. It is also a very warm stitch, no matter what weight of yarn is used. Its very nature produces a sort of double thickness and provides more warmth and insulation than other flat stitches.

When working a strip, such as a scarf or a large or small rectangle or square—for a shawl or for pieces for an afghan—many people prefer to start each row with a slipped st, this st to be slipped *Knit-wise*. When edges are to be picked up and worked in another direction, it is wise to *slip the first st* on every row and to *Purl the last st* of every row. This produces a chain at each edge which facilitates the knitting process. Also, when picking up sts, it is easy to pick up to gauge, as you can rely on Garter Stitch edges to be one st to one ridge, which will make the added piece exactly match the original piece in size and gauge. When an increase is to be made, use the Yarn-Over—Cross Right explained in #1-B, which follows. It is practically invisible.

#1-A

#1-B GARTER STITCH WORKED ON THE BIAS

Note: All increases are made as follows:

Throw yarn over needle from back to front and then take to back again between the two needles. The st is knitted from the *front* on the return row (Yarn-Over—Cross Right—see page 73).

Cast on 3 sts.
Row 1: K 1, yo, K 1, yo, K 1.
Row 2: K 5.
Row 3: K 1, yo, K 3, yo, K 1.
Row 4: K 7.

Continue to increase in this manner, every Odd-Numbered Row, just after the first st and before the last st, until the side edges measure the required number of inches or rows.

To Decrease:
All Odd-Numbered Rows: K 1, SKP, K to last 3 sts, K 2 tog, K 1.
All Even-Numbered Rows: Knit all sts.

#1-B

Continue in this manner until there are 5 sts remaining. Then:
K 1, SK2togP, K 1.
K 3 sts.
Bind off.

This swatch was increased and decreased at the edges. This stitch is the traditional method used for making the famous Shetland Islands shawls. To make a rectangular piece, proceed exactly the same as in making a diagonal square until the desired *width* of the rectangle is attained. Working the increase at one edge and the decrease at the other, continue until the desired length is reached and then continue to decrease at *both* edges and finish in the same manner as the square.

#2 **HORIZONTAL RIBBING or WELTING** (*Often called Quaker Stitch*)—*Any number of sts.*

Row 1: Knit.
Row 2: Purl.
Row 3: Knit.
Row 4: Knit.
Row 5: Purl.
Row 6: Knit.

Starting with Row 1, rep these 6 rows.

As may be seen by the directions, this pattern is made up of a number of rows of Stockinette Stitch showing the *face* of the stitch alternating with the *reverse* or *Purled* Side of the same stitch, in regular groups. It is very attractive when used as a yoke, as crosswise or horizontal shirring, as a trim at widthwise edges, or as a finishing frill. It can be used at the bottom edge of a sleeve to provide a push-up effect, and when the amount of yarn on hand is not quite enough for a full-length sleeve, this is a good solution.

#2

#3 **SEED, MOSS, or RICE STITCH**—*Any uneven number of sts.*

* K 1, P 1—rep from *, ending K 1.

Repeat this row throughout.

This stitch is one of the most versatile of all plain stitches. It serves in place of Garter Stitch and is much more interesting. It combines easily with any other stitch and makes a beautiful contrast when used with Stockinette Stitch. Like Garter Stitch, it provides warmth and insulation, as it is another of the double-weight stitches. It is exactly the same on both sides, so it can be used for any reversible article. When used for coats or jackets, it does not need to be faced or lined. It is unexcelled as a trim, border, or edge. As a fabric stitch (for suits, dresses, or jackets) it appears slightly rough in texture.

#3

142

#4-A DIAGONAL RIBBING or CHEVRON (*Right Slant*)—*Multiple of 8 sts.*

Row 1: K 2, * P 4, K 4—rep from *, end K 2.
Row 2: P 3, * K 4, P 4—rep from *, end K 4, P 1.
Row 3: * P 4, K 4—rep from *, end same.
Row 4: K 1, * P 4, K 4—rep from *, end K 3.
Row 5: P 2, * K 4, P 4—rep from *, end K 4, P 2.
Row 6: K 3, * P 4, K 4—rep from *, end K 1.
Row 7: * K 4, P 4—rep from *, end same.
Row 8: P 1, * K 4, P 4—rep from *, end K 4, P 3.
  Starting with Row 1, rep these 8 rows.

#4-A

#4-B DIAGONAL RIBBING or CHEVRON (*Left Slant*)—*Multiple of 8 sts.*

Row 1: K 2, * P 4, K 4—rep from *, end K 2.
Row 2: P 1, * K 4, P 4—rep from *, end K 4, P 3.
Row 3: * K 4, P 4—rep from *, end same.
Row 4: K 3, * P 4, K 4—rep from *, end P 4, K 1.
Row 5: P 2, * K 4, P 4—rep from *, end K 4, P 2.
Row 6: K 1, * P 4, K 4—rep from *, end P 4, K 3.
Row 7: * P 4, K 4—rep from *, end same.
Row 8: P 3, * K 4, P 4—rep from *, end K 4, P 1.
  Starting with Row 1, rep these 8 rows.

#4-B

#4-C CHEVRON (*A and B combined*)—*Multiple of 16 sts.*

To combine #4-A and #4-B to make this Chevron welting, cast on a multiple of 16 sts, placing a running or ring marker between the two center sts.
Work Row 1 of A across entire pattern (4 Knit sts at center).
Work Row 2 of B to marker, and Row 2 of A beyond marker to end (6 P sts at center).
Work Row 3 of A to marker, and Row 3 of B beyond marker to end (8 K sts at center).
Work Row 4 of B to marker, and Row 4 of A beyond marker to end (2 K sts at center).
Work Row 5 of A to marker, and Row 5 of B beyond marker to end (4 P sts at center).
Work Row 6 of B to marker, and Row 6 of A beyond marker to end (6 K sts at center).
Work Row 7 of A to marker, and Row 7 of B beyond marker to end (8 P sts at center).
Work Row 8 of B to marker, and Row 8 of A beyond marker to end (2 P sts at center).
  Starting with Row 1, rep these 8 rows.

#4-C

This directional stitch has many uses. Using A as the Left Front and sleeve of a sweater (either pullover or cardigan type) and B as the Right Front and sleeve, and combining A and B to make Pattern C for the back, creates a most interesting design. Pattern Stitch #4-C has many uses in itself—as the center of a crib blanket, shawl, or stole, or to form the panels of a skirt. It is neither as flat a stitch as plain Stockinette nor as rough as Seed or Garter Stitch. Except in unusual circumstances, it is better to use a yarn of a 3-ply or heavier weight. The pattern loses some of its effect in lighter-weight yarns.

Suggested Trim: Stockinette, either side.

Suggested Ribbing: K 2, P 2 or K 1, P 1.

#5

#5 SMALL CHECK—*Multiple of 6 sts plus 3.*

Rows 1 and 3: * K 3, P 3—rep from *, end K 3.
Rows 2 and 4: * P 3, K 3—rep from *, end P 3.
Rows 5 and 7: Same as Row 2.
Rows 6 and 8: Same as Row 1.
  Starting with Row 1, rep these 8 rows.

This pattern is good for scarves, sweaters, jackets, and any article that must be the same on both sides. It is very useful for blankets and afghans or as the border of either. Any weight of yarn may be used to good effect. The pattern shows up better, however, in medium-weight or heavier yarns.

Suggested Ribbing: K 1, P 1.

#6

#6 RIBBING AND WELT—*Multiple of 6 sts plus 3.*

Rows 1 and 3: * K 3, P 3—rep from *, end K 3.
Row 2: * P 3, K 3—rep from *, end P 3.
Rows 4 and 6: Knit all sts.
Row 5: Purl all sts.
Rows 7 and 9: Same as Row 1.
Row 8: Same as Row 2.
Rows 10 and 12: Purl all sts.
Row 11: Knit all sts.
  Starting with Row 1, rep these 12 rows.
  Bind off on either Row 3 or Row 9.
  Same uses as #5.

#7

#7 BROKEN CHECK—*Multiple of 8 sts.*

Row 1: * P 7, K 1—rep from *, end same.
Row 2: * P 2, K 6—rep from *, end same.
Row 3: * P 5, K 3—rep from *, end same.
Row 4: * P 4, K 4—rep from *, end same.
Row 5: * P 3, K 5—rep from *, end same.
Row 6: * P 6, K 2—rep from *, end same.

144

Row 7: * P 1, K 7—rep from *, end same.
Row 8: Purl all sts.
   Starting with Row 1, rep these 8 rows.
   Bind off on Row 8.
   Same uses as #5.

#8 ALTERNATING BROKEN CHECK—*Multiple of 8 sts.*

Row 1: * P 7, K 1—rep from *, end same.
Row 2: * P 2, K 6—rep from *, end same.
Row 3: * P 5, K 3—rep from *, end same.
Row 4: * P 4, K 4—rep from *, end same.
Row 5: * P 3, K 5—rep from *, end same.
Row 6: * P 6, K 2—rep from *, end same.
Row 7: * P 1, K 7—rep from *, end same.
Row 8: Purl all sts.
Row 9: * K 1, P 7—rep from *, end same.
Row 10: * K 6, P 2—rep from *, end same.
Row 11: * K 3, P 5—rep from *, end same.
Row 12: * K 4, P 4—rep from *, end same.
Row 13: * K 5, P 3—rep from *, end same.
Row 14: * K 2, P 6—rep from *, end same.
Row 15: * K 7, P 1—rep from *, end same.
Row 16: Purl all sts.
   Starting with Row 1, rep these 16 rows.

#8

#9 RIBBING AND GARTER—*Multiple of 10 sts plus 5.*

Row 1: (K 1, P 1)x2, * K 7, P 1, K 1, P 1—rep from *, end (P 1, K 1)x2.
Row 2: * (P 1, K 1)x2, P 1, K 5—rep from *, end (P 1, K 1)x2, P 1.
Rows 3 and 5: Same as Row 1.
Rows 4 and 6: Same as Row 2.
Row 7: * K 5, (P 1, K 1)x2, P 1—rep from *, end K 5.
Row 8: K 6, * P 1, K 1, P 1, K 7—rep from *, end P 1, K 1, P 1, K 6.
Rows 9 and 11: Same as Row 7.
Rows 10 and 12: Same as Row 8.
   Starting with Row 1, rep these 12 rows.
   Same uses as #5.

#9

#10 BROKEN RIBBING I—*Multiple of 12 sts.*

Rows 1 and 3: K 2, * P 2, K 4—rep from *, end P 2, K 2.
Rows 2 and 4: P 2, * K 2, P 4—rep from *, end K 2, P 2.
Rows 5 and 7: K 1, * P 4, K 2—rep from *, end P 4, K 1.
Rows 6 and 8: P 1, * K 4, P 2—rep from *, end K 4, P 1.
   Starting with Row 1, rep these 8 rows.
   This is an interesting stitch to make and is effective for sweaters and

#10

145

jackets for all sizes and age groups. It should have some other stitch, either a ribbing or border stitch, for a proper finish—it is unwise to use it alone.

Suggested Trim: Stockinette, either side, or Seed Stitch.
Suggested Ribbing: K 1, P 1 or K 3, P 3.

#11 **BROKEN RIBBING II**—*Multiple of 4 sts plus 1.*

* K 2, P 2—rep from *, end K 1.
Repeat this one row throughout.

Any article made with two exposed sides, such as a scarf or jacket, can use this pattern to advantage. It is very good for garments which need an elastic quality—high socks or stockings, close-fitting underwear, gloves—and it is quite appropriate for bathing suits and bathing trunks. In this latter case, use a heavier than medium-weight yarn on a needle smaller than would ordinarily be used for that weight of yarn. This ribbing will stretch in the width but will snap back into its original size when dry, better than many other ribbing stitches.

Suggested Trim: Seed Stitch.
Suggested Ribbing: K 2, P 2—or: K 1, P 1.

#12 **BROKEN RIBBING III**—*Multiple of 6 sts plus 1.*

Row 1: * K 1, P 1—rep from *, end K 1.
Row 2: P 2, * K 3, P 3—rep from *, end P 2.
Repeat these 2 rows throughout.
Same uses as #11.

#13 **BRIOCHE STITCH**—*Any even number of sts.*

Note: Method of yo before the first st is found on page 72.
Set-Up Row—*Do Not Repeat:* * yo, sl 1 Purl-wise, K 1—rep from * across.
Working Row: * yo, sl 1 Purl-wise, K 2 tog (the st and the yo)—rep from * across.

Repeat this working row throughout, casting on and binding off very loosely.

Brioche Stitch may be used for any loose stretchy fabric which must be alike on both sides—for instance, stoles, scarves, baby covers. It is also very good where a double thickness is desired. Watch out, though! It has a tendency to stretch lengthwise.

Bind off as follows: * K 1, K 2 tog and psso—rep from * across the row as you bind off.

146

#14 OPEN SEED-STITCH BLOCKS—*Multiple of 12 sts plus 8.*

Rows 1, 3, 5, 7, and 9: (K 1, P 1)x3, K 1, * (yo, K 2 tog)x3, (P 1, K 1)x3—rep from *, end (P 1, K 1)x3, P 1.
Rows 2, 4, 6, 8, and 10: * P 1, K 1—rep from *, end same.
Rows 11, 13, 15, 17, and 19: K 1, * (yo, K 2 tog)x3, (P 1, K 1)x3—rep from *, end (yo, K 2 tog)x3, P 1.
Rows 12, 14, 16, 18, and 20: Same as Row 2.
    Starting with Row 1, rep these 20 rows.
  This stitch may be used with practically any weight of yarn, depending upon the article to be made. The very nature of the stitch will produce a lighter, cooler fabric than a solid stitch. Use Seed Stitch for trim.

#14

#15 OPEN-LACED CROSS-STITCH—*Multiple of 8 sts.*

  To Start: Knit 4 rows.
Row 1: K 1, then K every st with 3 throws.
Row 2: * Sl 1st 8 sts from L to R needle, letting the extra loops drop. With LH needle reach over the 1st 4 sts nearest to RH needle tip and pull over the 4 sts beyond these onto LH needle. Slip the 4 skipped sts back onto LH needle and K these 8 sts; rep from * across, taking care not to twist the sts when crossing or knitting them.
Rows 3, 4, 5, and 6: Knit all sts.
Row 7: Same as Row 1.
Row 8: Work the same as Row 2, crossing the 1st *4 sts* to begin, and then crossing 8 sts for remainder of row, ending with cross 4.
Rows 9, 10, 11, and 12: Knit all sts.
    Starting with Row 1, rep these 12 rows.
  This is another stitch which is exactly the same on both sides and may be used in practically any weight of yarn. It is best suited to the plain-spun yarns; its effectiveness is somewhat lost when novelty yarns are used. It is virtually a double-weight stitch, heavier than the photograph may reveal, and excellent for baby blankets or similar articles, as it is warm and will remain flat without blocking. Using just one repeat of this pattern, with the ridge of Garter Stitch before and after crossing, makes it a very good insertion pattern.
  Suggested Trim: Garter Stitch only.

#15

#16 BASKET WEAVE—*Multiple of 6 sts plus 2.*

Rows 1 and 3: * K 2, P 4—rep from *, end K 2.
Rows 2 and 4: * P 2, K 4—rep from *, end P 2.

#16

Row 5: Knit all sts.
Row 6: Purl all sts.
Rows 7 and 9: P 3, * K 2, P 4 — rep from *, end K 2, P 3.
Rows 8 and 10: K 3, * P 2, K 4 — rep from *, end P 2, K 3.
Row 11: Knit all sts.
Row 12: Purl all sts.
    Starting with Row 1, rep these 12 rows.
    Same uses as #5.
  When used as a sweater, any accompanying ribbing at bottom edges should be K 2, P 1; this ribbing will run right up into the pattern stitch without breaking.

#17 UNEVEN BASKET WEAVE — *Multiple of 12 sts plus 6.*

Row 1: * K 6, P 6 — rep from *, end K 6.
Row 2: * P 6, K 6 — rep from *, end P 6.
Row 3: Knit all sts.
Row 4: Purl all sts.
Row 5: Same as Row 1.
Row 6: Same as Row 2.
Rows 7, 9, 11, and 13: * P 2, K 2, P 2, K 6 — rep from *, end P 2, K 2, P 2.
Rows 8, 10, 12, and 14: * K 2, P 2, K 2, P 6 — rep from *, end K 2, P 2, K 2.
Row 15: Same as Row 1.
Row 16: Same as Row 2.
Row 17: Knit all sts.
Row 18: Purl all sts.
    Starting with Row 1, rep these 18 rows.
  Same uses as #5. This pattern is also the same on both sides. It is classed with Garter and Seed Stitches as a flat stitch. Garter, Seed, and Double Seed Stitches (#1, #3, and #80) are good trimming stitches.
    Suggested Ribbing: K 1, P 1 — K 2, P 2 — or Broken Ribbing I, #10, may be used at bottom edges.

#18 BROKEN RIBBING IV — *Multiple of 4 sts.*

Row 1: P 1, K 1, * P 1, K 3 — rep from *, end P 1, K 1.
Row 2: * P 1, K 3 — rep from *, end same.
Row 3: * K 1, P 3 — rep from *, end same.
Row 4: K 1, P 1, * K 3, P 1 — rep from *, end K 1, P 1.
    Starting with Row 1, rep these 4 rows.
  This stitch could easily be classed in each of three groups: among those equally good on both sides, in the ribbing group, and in the fabric or texture group. It is quickly and easily worked, is good for jackets and cardigans, and is especially smart for suits and dresses. Its use should be confined to smooth-textured yarns, as crepes or nubby yarns would spoil its effectiveness. The vertical stitch emphasizes *height*.
  Suggested Trim: Seed Stitch.
  Suggested Ribbing: K 1, P 1.

148

#19 MODIFIED RIBBING—*Multiple of 5 sts plus 2.*

Row 1: P 3, * K 1, P 4—rep from *, end K 1, P 3.
Row 2: K 2, * P 1, K 1, P 1, K 2—rep from *, end same.
Row 3: P 2, * K 1, P 1, K 1, P 2—rep from *, end same.
Row 4: K 3, * P 1, K 4—rep from *, end P 1, K 3.
    Starting with Row 1, rep these 4 rows.
    Same uses as #18.
    Suggested Trim: Seed Stitch.
    Suggested Ribbing: K 1, P 1.

#19

#20 WIDE CHEVRON—*Multiple of 14 sts plus 2.*

Row 1: * P 2, K 5—rep from *, end P 2.
Row 2: K 3, * P 10, K 4—rep from *, end K 3.
Row 3: * K 2, P 2, K 8, P 2—rep from *, end K 2.
Row 4: P 3, * K 2, P 6, K 2, P 4—rep from *, end P 3.
Row 5: K 4, * P 2, K 4, P 2, K 6—rep from *, end K 4.
Row 6: P 5, * K 2, P 2, K 2, P 8—rep from *, end P 5.
Row 7: P 1, K 5, * P 4, K 10—rep from *, end P 4, K 5, P 1.
Row 8: * K 2, P 5—rep from *, end K 2.
Row 9: P 3, * K 10, P 4—rep from *, end P 3.
Row 10: * P 2, K 2, P 8, K 2—rep from *, end P 2.
Row 11: K 3, * P 2, K 6, P 2, K 4—rep from *, end K 3.
Row 12: P 4, * K 2, P 4, K 2, P 6—rep from *, end P 4.
Row 13: K 5, * P 2, K 2, P 2, K 8—rep from *, end K 5.
Row 14: K 1, P 5, * K 4, P 10—rep from *, end K 4, P 5, K 1.
    Starting with Row 1, rep these 14 rows.
    Same uses as #4-C.

#20

#21 TALL DIAMOND, OUTLINED I—*Multiple of 10 sts plus 1.*

Row 1: K 4, * P 3, K 7—rep from *, end P 3, K 4.
Row 2: P 4, * K 3, P 7—rep from *, end K 3, P 4.
Row 3: K 3, * P 2, K 1, P 2, K 5—rep from *, end P 2, K 1, P 2, K 3.
Row 4: P 3, * K 2, P 1, K 2, P 5—rep from *, end K 2, P 1, K 2, P 3.
Row 5: K 2, * P 2, K 3—rep from *, end P 2, K 2.
Row 6: P 2, * K 2, P 3—rep from *, end K 2, P 2.
Row 7: * K 1, P 2, K 5, P 2—rep from *, end K 1.
Row 8: * P 1, K 2, P 5, K 2—rep from *, end P 1.
Row 9: P 2, * K 7, P 3—rep from *, end K 7, P 2.
Row 10: K 2, * P 7, K 3—rep from *, end P 7, K 2.
Row 11: Same as Row 7.
Row 12: Same as Row 8.
Row 13: Same as Row 5.
Row 14: Same as Row 6.
Row 15: Same as Row 3.
Row 16: Same as Row 4.
    Starting with Row 1, rep these 16 rows.

#21

Same uses as #4 and #5. In an eight- or nine-st gauge, it is appropriate for a scarf and glove set, with the pattern stitch used only on the *back* of the glove. In any weight of yarn, it is good for sweaters of all kinds and sizes.

Suggested Trim: Stockinette, either side, or Seed Stitch.
Suggested Ribbing: K 1, P 1.

#22 **TALL DIAMOND II**—*Multiple of 8 sts plus 7.*

All Even-Numbered Rows: Purl all sts.
Row 1: K 3, * P 1, K 7—rep from *, end P 1, K 3.
Row 3: K 2, * P 1, K 1, P 1, K 5—rep from *, end P 1, K 1, P 1, K 2.
Row 5: K 1, * P 1, K 3—rep from *, end P 1, K 1.
Row 7: P 1, * K 5, P 1, K 1, P 1—rep from *, end K 5, P 1.
Row 9: * K 7, P 1—rep from *, end K 7.
Row 11: Same as Row 7.
Row 13: Same as Row 5.
Row 15: Same as Row 3.
  Starting with Row 1, rep these 16 rows.
  Same uses as #21.

#23 **LOZENGE**—*Multiple of 8 sts plus 1.*

Row 1: K 3, * P 1, K 1, P 1, K 5—rep from *, end K 3.
Row 2: P 3, * K 1, P 1, K 1, P 5—rep from *, end P 3.
Row 3: Same as Row 1.
Row 4: Same as Row 2.
Row 5: K 2, * P 1, K 3—rep from *, end K 2.
Row 6: P 2, * K 1, P 3—rep from *, end P 2.
Row 7: K 1, P 1, * K 5, P 1, K 1, P 1—rep from *, end P 1, K 1.
Row 8: P 1, K 1, * P 5, K 1, P 1, K 1—rep from *, end K 1, P 1.
Row 9: Same as Row 7.
Row 10: Same as Row 8.
Row 11: Same as Row 5.
Row 12: Same as Row 6.
  Starting with Row 1, rep these 12 rows.
  Same uses as #18, #5 and #21.

REVERSIBLE STITCHES II

#24 **TALL DIAMOND IN RELIEF III**—*Multiple of 14 sts plus 9.*

Row 1: (K 1, P 1)x4, * K 7, (P 1, K 1)x3, P 1—rep from *, end (P 1, K 1)x4.
Row 2: (P 1, K 1)x4, * P 7, (K 1, P 1)x3, K 1—rep from *, end (K 1, P 1)x4.
Row 3: K 2, * (P 1, K 1)x2, (P 1, K 4)x2—rep from *, end (P 1, K 1)x2, P 1, K 2.
Row 4: P 2, * (K 1, P 1)x2, (K 1, P 4)x2—rep from *, end (K 1, P 1)x2, K 1, P 2.

150

Row 5: K 3, * P 1, K 1, P 1, K 4—rep from *, end P 1, K 1, P 1, K 3.
Row 6: P 3, * K 1, P 1, K 1, P 4—rep from *, end K 1, P 1, K 1, P 3.
Row 7: * K 4, P 1, K 4, (P 1, K 1)x2, P 1—rep from *, end K 4, P 1, K 4.
Row 8: * P 4, K 1, P 4, (K 1, P 1)x2, K 1—rep from *, end P 4, K 1, P 4.
Row 9: P 1, * K 7, (P 1, K 1)x3, P 1—rep from *, end K 7, P 1.
Row 10: K 1, * P 7, (K 1, P 1)x3, K 1—rep from *, end P 7, K 1.
Row 11: Same as Row 7.
Row 12: Same as Row 8.
Row 13: Same as Row 5.
Row 14: Same as Row 6.
Row 15: Same as Row 3.
Row 16: Same as Row 4.
    Starting with Row 1, rep these 16 rows.
    Same uses as #5 and #21.
    Suggested Trim: Seed Stitch.
    Suggested Ribbing: K 1, P 1.

#25

#25 FLAT DIAMOND, OUTLINED—*Multiple of 10 sts plus 1.*

Row 1: K 4, * P 3, K 7—rep from *, end P 3, K 4.
Row 2: P 3, * K 2, P 1, K 2, P 5—rep from *, end K 2, P 1, K 2, P 3.
Row 3: K 2, * P 2, K 3—rep from *, end P 2, K 2.
Row 4: P 1, * K 2, P 5, K 2, P 1—rep from *, end K 2, P 1.
Row 5: P 2, * K 7, P 3—rep from *, end K 7, P 2.
Row 6: Same as Row 4.
Row 7: Same as Row 3.
Row 8: Same as Row 2.
    Starting with Row 1, rep these 8 rows.
    Same uses as #5 and #21.

#26

#26 VERTICAL CHEVRON—*Multiple of 6 sts plus 2.*

All Even-Numbered Rows: Purl all sts.
Row 1: K 4, * P 3, K 3—rep from *, end P 4.
Row 3: K 1, P 1, * K 3, P 3—rep from *, end K 3, P 2, K 1.
Row 5: K 1, P 2, * K 3, P 3—rep from *, end K 3, P 1, K 1.
Row 7: K 1, * P 3, K 3—rep from *, end K 4.
Row 9: Same as Row 5.
Row 11: Same as Row 3.
    Starting with Row 1, rep these 12 rows.
    Same uses as #5, #19, and #21.
    Suggested Trim: Garter or Seed Stitch.
    Suggested Ribbing: K 1, P 1.

#27 LARGE AND SMALL DIAMONDS—*Multiple of 15 sts plus 2.*

Row 1: * K 2, P 13—rep from *, end K 2.
Row 2: P 3, * K 11, P 4—rep from *, end P 3.

#27

Row 3: K 4, * P 9, K 6—rep from *, end P 9, K 4.
Row 4: P 5, * K 7, P 8—rep from *, end K 7, P 5.
Row 5: K 6, * P 5, K 10—rep from *, end P 5, K 6.
Row 6: * K 2, P 5, K 3, P 5—rep from *, end K 2.
Row 7: P 3, * K 5, P 1, K 5, P 4—rep from *, end K 5, P 3.
Row 8: Same as Row 3.
Row 9: Same as Row 7.
Row 10: Same as Row 6.
Row 11: Same as Row 5.
Row 12: Same as Row 4.
Row 13: Same as Row 3.
Row 14: Same as Row 2.
  Starting with Row 1, rep these 14 rows.

 This stitch is not alike on both sides, but it is good on either side. It may be used for a man's scarf or sweater; one unit of the pattern could be used for the jacket of a suit. Smooth yarn helps to emphasize the pattern.

 Suggested Trim: Purled Side of Stockinette.
 Suggested Ribbing: K 1, P 1.

#28 HORIZONTAL LEAF—*Multiple of 10 sts.*

Rows 1 and 3: Purl all sts.
Rows 2 and 4: Knit all sts.
Row 5: Knit all sts.
Row 6: * K 5, P 5—rep from *, end same.
Row 7: K 4, * P 5, K 5—rep from *, end K 1.
Row 8: P 2, * K 5, P 5—rep from *, end P 3.
Row 9: K 2, * P 5, K 5—rep from *, end K 3.
Row 10: Knit all sts.
Row 11: P 1, * K 5, P 5—rep from *, end P 4.
Row 12: K 3, * P 5, K 5—rep from *, end K 2.
Row 13: P 3, * K 5, P 5—rep from *, end P 2.
Row 14: K 1, * P 5, K 5—rep from *, end K 4.
Row 15: Knit all sts.
Row 16: Purl all sts.
  Starting with Row 1, rep these 16 rows.

 Same uses as #27, except that it should be used for women's—not men's—apparel, as it is definitely a more feminine stitch. One or two repeats of this pattern, made to run vertically, creates a good set-in pattern for a dressy blouse.

 Suggested Trim: Purled side of Stockinette, Horizontal Ribbing or Welting (#2).
 Suggested Ribbing: None (preferably).

#28

#29 SMALL CROSS-STITCH PATTERN—*Multiple of 6 sts.*

Note: Method of cross R, cross L is found on page 79.
Row 1: P 2, * K 2, P 4—rep from *, end K 2, P 2.
Row 2: K 2, * P 2, K 4—rep from *, end P 2, K 2.
Row 3: P 1, * cross R, cross L, P 2—rep from *, end P 1.
Row 4: K 1, P 1, * K 2, P 1—rep from *, end K 1.
Row 5: * cross R, P 2, cross L—rep from *, end same.
Row 6: P 1, * K 4, P 2—rep from *, end P 1.
Row 7: K 1, * P 4, K 1—rep from *, end K 1.
Row 8: Same as Row 6.
Row 9: * cross L, P 2, cross R—rep from *, end same.
Row 10: Same as Row 4.
Row 11: P 1, * cross L, cross R, P 2—rep from *, end P 1.
Row 12: Same as Row 2.
  Starting with Row 1, rep these 12 rows.

This stitch is very elastic, but firm. Novelty yarn, either crepe or nubby, is appropriate for it. This versatile stitch is excellent when used as a contrast, but it is just as good for sweaters (either pullover or cardigan). Made with heavier-weight yarns, it is a very warm fabric. Worked with heavy yarn and on small needles, it is good for bathing suits and bathing trunks. It requires very little blocking and should *not* be pressed.

  Suggested Trim: Stockinette Stitch, either side.
  Suggested *as* a Trim: Upper part of blouses or jackets, pockets, sleeves (or parts of sleeves), as a gathering at yokes.
  Suggested Ribbing: K 1, P 1.

#29

#30 GATHERED FABRIC STITCH—*Multiple of 4 sts plus 2.*

Row 1: P 2, * K 2, P 2—rep from *, end same.
Row 2: K 2, * P 2, K 2—rep from *, end same.
Row 3: P 2, * K 2 tog and K the first st again before removing, P 2—rep from *, end same.
Row 4: Same as Row 2.
Row 5: Same as Row 2.
Row 6: Same as Row 1.
Row 7: * K 2 tog and K the first st again, P 2—rep from *, end K 2 tog and K the first st again.
Row 8: Same as Row 1.
  Starting with Row 1, rep these 8 rows.
BE CAREFUL WITH THIS STITCH. It needs close watching for the first few patterns.
  Same uses as #29.

  Suggested Trim: Stockinette, either side, or Seed Stitch.
  Suggested Ribbing: K 2, P 2—or: K 1, P 1.

#30

#31 **WAVED RIBBING**—*Multiple of 18 sts plus 1.*

Note: All following *Made* sts (M 1) are Purled.
Row 1: * P 1, K 3, P 11, K 3—rep from *, end P 1.
Row 2: * K 1, P 3, K 11, P 3—rep from *, end K 1.
Row 3: * P 1, M 1, K 3, P 2 tog, P 7, P 2 tog b, K 3, M 1—rep from *, end M 1, P 1.
Row 4: K 2, * P 3, K 9, P 3, K 3—rep from *, end K 2.
Row 5: P 2, * M 1, K 3, P 2 tog, P 5, P 2 tog b, K 3, M 1, P 3—rep from *, end M 1, P 2.
Row 6: K 3, * P 3, K 7, P 3, K 5—rep from *, end K 3.
Row 7: P 3, * M 1, K 3, P 2 tog, P 3, P 2 tog b, K 3, M 1, P 5—rep from *, end M 1, P 3.
Row 8: K 4, * P 3, K 5, P 3, K 7—rep from *, end K 4.
Row 9: P 4, * M 1, K 3, P 2 tog, P 1, P 2 tog b, K 3, M 1, P 7—rep from *, end M 1, P 4.
Row 10: K 5, * P 3, K 3, P 3, K 9—rep from *, end K 5.
Row 11: P 5, * M 1, K 3, P 3 tog, K 3, M 1, P 9—rep from *, end M 1, P 5.
Row 12: K 6, * P 3, K 1, P 3, K 11—rep from *, end K 6.
Row 13: P 6, * K 3, P 1, K 3, P 11—rep from *, end P 6.
Row 14: Same as Row 12.
Row 15: P 4, * P 2 tog b, K 3, M 1, P 1, M 1, K 3, P 2 tog, P 7—rep from *, end P 4.
Row 16: K 5, * P 3, K 3, P 3, K 9—rep from *, end K 5.
Row 17: P 3, * P 2 tog b, K 3, M 1, P 3, M 1, K 3, P 2 tog, P 5—rep from *, end P 3.
Row 18: K 4, * P 3, K 5, P 3, K 7—rep from *, end K 4.
Row 19: P 2, * P 2 tog b, K 3, M 1, P 5, M 1, K 3, P 2 tog, P 3—rep from *, end P 2.
Row 20: K 3, * P 3, K 7, P 3, K 5—rep from *, end K 3.
Row 21: * P 1, P 2 tog b, K 3, M 1, P 7, M 1, K 3, P 2 tog—rep from *, end P 1.
Row 22: K 2, * P 3, K 9, P 3, K 3—rep from *, end K 2.
Row 23: P 2 tog b, * K 3, M 1, P 9, M 1, K 3, P 3 tog—rep from *, end P 2 tog.
Row 24: K 1, * P 3, K 11, P 3, K 1—rep from *, end same.
   Starting with Row 1, rep these 24 rows.

#31

Waved Ribbing is fine for sports pullovers or cardigans, using either side as the Right Side. The two sides are totally dissimilar, but both are attractive. A single repeat of this stitch makes an unusual trim for a sweater or jacket of either the Knit or Purled side of Stockinette.
   Suggested Trim: Either side of Stockinette.
   Suggested Ribbing: P 1, K 3 ribbing; cast on a multiple of 16 sts plus 1 for each multiple of 18 sts plus 1 in the pattern stitch. Work the required amount of ribbing in the following manner:
Row 1: * P 1, K 3—rep from *, end P 1.
Row 2: * K 1, P 3—rep from *, end K 1.
   On the last row of ribbing (Row 2), increase across one row as fol-

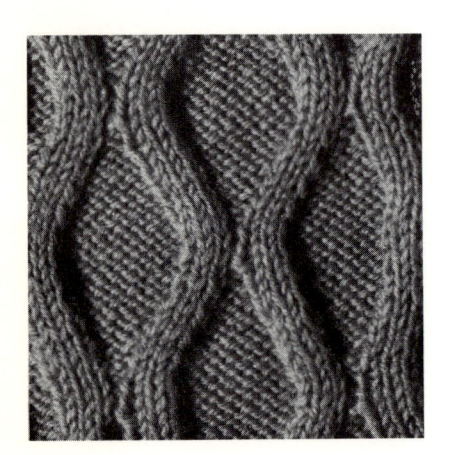

lows: K 1, P 3, * (K 1, P 3, inc)x2, (K 1, P 3)x2—rep from *, end K 1, P 3, K 1.

This will place the sts in proper position for the first row of the pattern stitch.

#32 **KNOT STITCH FABRIC**—*Multiple of 8 sts plus 6.*

Rows 1 and 3: Knit all sts.
Rows 2 and 4: Purl all sts.
Row 5: Purl all sts.
Row 6: Knit all sts.
Row 7: * P 6, KPKP twice—rep from *, end P 6.
Row 8: * K 6, P 4 tog twice—rep from *, end K 6.
Row 9: Same as Row 7.
Row 10: Same as Row 8.
Row 11: Purl all sts.
Row 12: Knit all sts.
Row 13 through Row 18: rep from Row 1 through Row 6.
Row 19: * P 2, KPKP twice; rep between * * in Row 7, end KPKP twice, P 2.
Row 20: K 2, * P 4 tog twice, K 6—rep from *, end P 4 tog twice, K 2.
Row 21: Same as Row 19.
Row 22: Same as Row 20.
Row 23: Purl all sts.
Row 24: Knit all sts.
　　Starting with Row 1, rep these 24 rows.

Knot Stitch Fabric works very well with any weight of yarn, from the finest two-ply to the thickest yarns, and may be knitted vertically (from side to side) as well as horizontally.

It is an excellent pattern for jackets and, in fine yarns, for blouses and sweaters. As it is a variation of Horizontal Ribbing or Welting (#2), it may be used in its place; the additional knots make it a little more interesting.

　Suggested Trim: Either side of Stockinette.
　Suggested Ribbing: K 2, P 2.

#33 **DROP STITCH PATTERN**—*Multiple of 10 sts plus 4.*

　Set-Up Row—*Do Not Repeat:* K 2, * yo, K 10—rep from *, end yo, K 2.
Rows 1, 3, and 5: Purl all sts.
Rows 2 and 4: Knit all sts.
Row 6: K 2, * drop 1, K 5, yo, K 5—rep from *, end drop 1, K 2.
Rows 7, 9, and 11: Purl all sts.
Rows 8 and 10: Knit all sts.
Row 12: K 2, * yo, K 5, drop 1, K 5—rep from *, end yo, K 2.
　　Starting with Row 1, rep these 12 rows.

This stitch may be substituted for plain Stockinette anywhere except as trim. It is particularly effective as a contrast fabric in combination with Stockinette, using either the Knit or Purled Side as the Right Side.

#32

#33

155

#34

#34 BABY VARIEGATED RIBBING—*Multiple of 4 sts plus 3.*

Row 1: P 1, * K 3, P 1—rep from *, end K 2.
Row 2: P 2, * K 1, P 3—rep from *, end K 1.
Row 3: Same as Row 1.
Row 4: P 2 tog, * yo, K 1, yo, P 3 tog—rep from *, end yo, K 1.
Row 5: K 2, * P 1, K 3—rep from *, end P 1.
Row 6: K 1, * P 3, K 1—rep from *, end P 2.
Row 7: Same as Row 5.
Row 8: K 1, yo, * P 3 tog, yo, K 1, yo—rep from *, end P 2 tog.
 Starting with Row 1, rep these 8 rows.

 The two sides of this stitch are entirely different, but both are handsome. The lacy side is excellent for blouses and baby sweaters, or for contrast touches, particularly when worked in fine wool or cotton yarns. The ribbed side is good for mild-weather cardigans, using medium- to heavier-weight yarns, as the stitch itself is an open one. It works very well as a contrast fabric in small touches (see #29).
 Suggested Trim: Purled Side of Stockinette.
 Suggested Ribbing: K 1, P 3—or: K 1, P 1.
 Use a very light hand when blocking.

#35

#35 SHIRRED RIBBING—*Multiple of 8 sts plus 3.*

Row 1: P 3, * K 5, P 3—rep from *, end same.
Row 2: K 3, * P 5, K 3—rep from *, end same.
Row 3: P 3, * pu 1 P-wise, K 1, P 3 tog, K 1, pu 1 P-wise, P 3—rep from *, end same.
Row 4: Same as Row 2.
 Starting with Row 1, rep these 4 rows.

 This adaptable stitch is excellent for sweaters of all types and weights and is particularly good when used with heavier than medium-weight yarns, with small-size needles, for bathing suits or bathing trunks. It is also good as trimming touches (as in #29). It is most effective in smooth yarns, but when used as a trimming stitch, nubby or novelty yarns, particularly linen or cotton, are suitable.
 One unit of the pattern (one multiple) makes an attractive outline for paneling in a dress or skirt. Do not overblock.
 Suggested Trim: Purled side of Stockinette.
 Suggested Ribbing: K 1, P 1.

#36

#36 EYELET FABRIC—*Multiple of 4 sts plus 3.*

Row 1: Purl all sts.
Row 2: K 2, * yo, K 2 tog, K 2—rep from *, end yo, K 2 tog, K 3.
Row 3: Purl all sts.
Row 4: K 4, * yo, K 2 tog, K 2—rep from *, end yo, K 2 tog, K 1.
 Starting with Row 1, rep these 4 rows.

 This open stitch is ideal for light-weight garments—sweaters of light- to medium-weight yarn, blouses and trimmings made with linen or cotton thread, and soft undergarments.

Suggested Trim: Stockinette, either side; Seed Stitch—in fact, any trimming stitch.

#37 STRIPED FAGOTING—*Multiple of 8 sts plus 4.*

Row 1: * P 4, K 2 tog, yo, K 2—rep from *, end P 4.
Row 2: * K 4, P 2 tog, yo, P 2—rep from *, end K 4.
  Repeat these 2 rows throughout.
  This stitch is good in a smooth yarn, but nubby and crepe yarns can also be used. It is particularly effective in a one-piece dress, with all increases and decreases made in the Stockinette portions between the fagoting. In very fine to light-weight yarn it provides that little extra warmth in cool weather. One unit (one multiple of the pattern) makes a pleasing trim. Placed where lace insertions might appear in a fabric blouse, it is very pretty and easily planned.
  Suggested Ribbing: K 2, P 2—or (very good): #52 or #55.
  Do not overblock.

#37

#38 OPEN WAVE LACE—*Multiple of 10 sts.*

Note: For making a yo before working a st at beg of row, see page 72.
Row 1: K 5, * yo, K 1, 00, K 1, 000, K 1, 00, K 1, yo, K 6—rep from *, ending yo, K 1.
Row 2: Knit across, dropping all overs without working them.
Row 3: Knit all sts.
Row 4: Knit all sts.
Row 5: * yo, K 1, 00, K 1, 000, K 1, 00, K 1, yo, K 6—rep from *, end same.
Row 6: Same as Row 2 (Watch out! Don't knit the yo on the last st).
Row 7: Knit all sts.
Row 8: Knit all sts.
  Starting with Row 1, rep these 8 rows.
  This lacy stitch is adaptable to light-, medium-, or heavy-weight yarns, depending upon the weight of the article. Smooth yarn should be used to emphasize the wavy contours. Both sides are exactly the same. Too fussy for any practical garment, the stitch is used chiefly for bed jackets, shawls, and baby sacques.
  Suggested Trim: Garter Stitch only.

#38

#39 EAR OF CORN—*Multiple of 8 sts plus 4.*

Rows 1, 3, 5, and 7: P 4, * K 2, yo, SKP, P 4—rep from *, end same.
Rows 2, 4, 6, and 8: K 4, * P 2, yo, P 2 tog, K 4—rep from *, end same.
Rows 9, 11, 13, and 15: K 2, yo, SKP, * P 4, K 2, yo, SKP—rep from *, end same.
Rows 10, 12, 14, and 16: P 2, yo, P 2 tog, * K 4, P 2, yo, P 2 tog—rep from *, end same.
  Starting with Row 1, rep these 16 rows.

#39

This small pattern stitch, good either as trim or as an all-over stitch for light-weight sweaters and bed jackets, is completely different on each side, the Purl Side suggesting an ear of corn and the Knit Side showing more of an outlined diamond.

Suggested Trim: Stockinette, either side, or Seed Stitch.
Suggested Ribbing: K 2, P 2.

#40 FAGOT AND CABLE STRIPE —*Multiple of 6 sts plus 2.*

Row 1: K 2, * P 2 tog, yo, P 2, K 2 — rep from *, end same.
Row 2: P 2, * SKP, yo, K 2, P 2 — rep from *, end same.
Rows 3, 5, 7, 9, and 11: Same as Row 1.
Rows 4, 6, 8, and 10: Same as Row 2.
Row 12: P 2, * sl 2 on DP front, SKP, and yo from LH needle, K 2 from DP, P 2 — rep from *, end same.
    Starting with Row 1, rep these 12 rows.

This stitch, a true cable, is very springy, good for gathering, for trimming touches, or as an all-over pattern. Light- to medium-weight yarns are best for it; the stitch serves no real purpose in heavy-weight yarns. Crepe yarns may be used, but nubby yarns obscure the pattern.

Suggested Ribbing: K 2, P 2.
Use only the lightest of blocking.

#41 ACORN PATTERN —*Multiple of 12 sts plus 3.*

Row 1: K 2, * yo, K 2, P 7, K 2, yo, K 1 — rep from *, end yo, K 2.
Row 2: P 5, * K 2, SK2togP, K 2, P 7 — rep from *, end P 5.
Row 3: K 3, * yo, K 2, P 5, K 2, yo, K 3 — rep from *, end same.
Row 4: P 6, * K 1, SK2togP, K 1, P 9 — rep from *, end P 6.
Row 5: K 4, * yo, K 2, P 3, K 2, yo, K 5 — rep from *, end yo, K 4.
Row 6: P 7, * SK2togP, P 11 — rep from *, end P 7.
Row 7: P 5, * K 2, yo, K 1, yo, K 2, P 7 — rep from *, end P 5.
Row 8: K 1, K 2 tog, K 2, * P 7, K 2, SK2togP, K 2 — rep from *, end K 2, SKP, K 1.
Row 9: P 4, * K 2, yo, K 3, yo, K 2, P 5 — rep from *, end P 4.
Row 10: K 1, K 2 tog, K 1, * P 9, K 1, SK2togP, K 1 — rep from *, end K 1, SKP, K 1.
Row 11: P 3, * K 2, yo, K 5, yo, K 2, P 3 — rep from *, end same.
Row 12: K 1, K 2 tog, * P 11, SK2togP — rep from *, end SKP, K 1.
    Starting with Row 1, rep these 12 rows.

This chunky little pattern has a rough-textured appearance in any weight of yarn and should be used carefully. Excellent for trimming touches, it should be used sparingly as an all-over pattern and then only for warm garments or articles, particularly crib or carriage covers. It is a good gathering pattern. As a background stitch, it works very well in bedspread cotton. Blocked lightly, it remains quite springy, but it may be blocked out entirely to show the acorn more clearly. Work and block a swatch before using this pattern.

Suggested Trim: Stockinette, Purl Side.
Suggested Ribbing: K 2, P 2 — or, even better, none.

#42 **LACE TRIANGLES**—*Multiple of 11 sts plus 5.*

All Odd-Numbered Rows: Purl all sts.
Row 2: * K 3, (yo, SKP)x4—rep from *, end K 5.
Row 4: K 4, * (yo, SKP)x3, K 5—rep from *, end K 6.
Row 6: K 5, * (yo, SKP)x2, K 7—rep from *, end same.
Row 8: K 6, * yo, SKP, K 9—rep from *, end K 8.
Row 10: K 1, (K 2 tog, yo)x2, * K 3, (K 2 tog, yo)x4—rep from *, end (K 2 tog, yo)x3, K 2.
Row 12: K 2, K 2 tog, yo, * K 5, (K 2 tog, yo)x3—rep from *, end (K 2 tog, yo)x3, K 1.
Row 14: K 1, K 2 tog, yo, * K 7, (K 2 tog, yo)x2—rep from *, end (K 2 tog, yo)x2, K 2.
Row 16: * K 2 tog, yo, K 9—rep from *, end K 2 tog, yo, K 3.
   Starting with Row 1, rep these 16 rows.

This semi-lace stitch is good for many articles: lighter-weight sweaters, underwear; in fact, any of the uses given for #33. It combines well with either side of Stockinette Stitch as the basic fabric.
   Suggested Trim: Stockinette, either side.
   Suggested Ribbing: K 2, P 2—K 1, P 1—or any of the small variety ribbing stitches.

#42

RIBBING STITCHES

#43 **EYELET DIAMOND**—*Multiple of 28 sts plus 4.*

Note: In the following pattern, on every *alternate* Purl row, Purl and Knit the double overs (00) of the preceding row.
All Other Even-Numbered Rows: Purl all sts.
Rows 1, 5, 9, 13, 17, 21, 25, 29, and 33: Knit all sts.
Row 3: K 2, (K 2 tog, 00, SKP)x2, * K 4, K 2 tog, 00, SKP, K 4, (K 2 tog, 00, SKP)x4—rep from *, end (K 2 tog, 00, SKP)x2, K 2.
Row 7: (K 2 tog, 00, SKP)x2, * K 4, (K 2 tog, 00, SKP)x2, K 4, (K 2 tog, 00, SKP)x3—rep from *, end (K 2 tog, 00, SKP)x2.
Row 11: K 2, K 2 tog, 00, SKP, * K 4, (K 2 tog, 00, SKP)x3, K 4, (K 2 tog, 00, SKP)x2—rep from *, end K 4, K 2 tog, 00, SKP, K 2.
Row 15: K 2 tog, 00, SKP, * K 4, (K 2 tog, 00, SKP)x4, K 4, K 2 tog, 00, SKP—rep from *, end K 4, K 2 tog, 00, SKP.
Row 19: K 6, * (K 2 tog, 00, SKP)x5, K 8—rep from *, end K 6.
Row 23: Same as Row 15.
Row 27: Same as Row 11.
Row 31: Same as Row 7.
Row 35: (K 2 tog, 00, SKP)x3, * K 8, (K 2 tog, 00, SKP)x5—rep from *, end K 8, (K 2 tog, 00, SKP)x3.
Row 36: Purl all sts, making a Purl and Knit in each double over.
   Starting with Row 1, rep these 36 rows.

#43

159

HOWEVER, for working a swatch, cast on 32 sts. Follow the same directives as at the beg of the pattern stitch:

Row 3: K 2, (K 2 tog, 00, SKP)x2, K 4, K 2 tog, 00, SKP, K 4, (K 2 tog, 00, SKP)x2, K 2.

Row 7: * (K 2 tog, 00, SKP)x2, K 4 — rep from *, end (K 2 tog, 00, SKP)x2.

Row 11: K 2, K 2 tog, 00, SKP, K 4, (K 2 tog, 00, SKP)x3, K 4, K 2 tog, 00, SKP, K 2.

Row 15: K 2 tog, 00, SKP, K 4, (K 2 tog, 00, SKP)x4, K 4, K 2 tog, 00, SKP.

Row 19: K 6, (K 2 tog, 00, SKP)x5, K 6.

Row 23: Same as Row 15.

Row 27: Same as Row 11.

Row 31: Same as Row 7.

Row 35: (K 2 tog, 00, SKP)x3, K 8, (K 2 tog, 00, SKP)x3.

Starting with Row 1, rep these 36 rows.

This large pattern is a good contrast fabric with either side of Stockinette as the foundation fabric. The eyelets make it a little cooler than any solid fabric stitch, and it is easily made. Any light- to medium-weight yarn may be used to good effect. Cotton and linen are particularly suitable, but should have the Purled rows worked in Reverse Stitch as outlined on page 63.

Suggested Trim: Stockinette, either side.
Suggested Ribbing: None.
This stitch may be blocked flat.

#44 DIAMOND RIBBING PATTERN — *Multiple of 8 sts plus 2.*

Row 1: P 4, * K 2, P 6 — rep from *, end K 2, P 4.
Row 2: K 4, * P 2, K 6 — rep from *, end P 2, K 4.
Row 3: P 3, * K 2 tog, yo, SKP, P 4 — rep from *, end P 3.
Row 4: K 3, * P 1, K into *back and front* of next st, P 1, K 4 — rep from *, end K 3.
Row 5: P 2, * K 2 tog, yo, K 2, yo, SKP, P 2 — rep from *, end same.
Row 6: K 2, * P 6, K 2 — rep from *, end same.
Row 7: K 1, * K 2 tog, yo, K 2 tog, (yo, SKP)x2 — rep from *, end K 1.
Row 8: P 4, * K into *front and back* of next st, P 6 — rep from *, end P 4.
Row 9: K 1, * (yo, SKP)x2, K 2 tog, yo, K 2 tog — rep from *, end yo, K 1.
Row 10: K 1, Kb 1, * P 6, K into *back and front* of next st — rep from *, end Kb 1, K 1.
Row 11: P 2, * yo, K 3 tog b, yo, K 3 tog, yo, P 2 — rep from *, end same.
Row 12: K 2, * Kb 1, P 1, K into *back and front* of next st, P 1, Kb 1, K 2 — rep from *, end same.
Row 13: P 3, * yo, SKP, K 2 tog, yo, P 4 — rep from *, end yo, P 3.
Row 14: K 3, * Kb 1, P 2, Kb 1, K 4 — rep from *, end K 3.

Starting with Row 1, rep these 14 rows.

As an all-over pattern, this stitch is excellent for dressy cardigans, but better used as a small pattern contrast stitch, like #29, which has

#44

160

the same characteristic springy quality, but is a little more elaborate. Diamond Ribbing Pattern is very effective in light- to medium-weight yarns. As a background stitch for any article made of cotton or linen yarn, it is most effective but should be *knitted as wool is knitted—not* with the Reverse Stitch (see page 63) usually recommended for these materials.

Suggested Trim: Purl Side of Stockinette.
Suggested Ribbing: K 1, P 1.
Block very lightly.

#45 **OPEN BLOCKS**—*Multiple of 10 sts plus 8.*

Rows 1, 3, 5, 7, and 9: K 7, * yo, SKP, K 2 tog, yo, K 6—rep from *, end K 7.
Rows 2, 4, 6, 8, and 10: Purl all sts.
Rows 11, 13, 15, 17, and 19: K 2, * yo, SKP, K 2 tog, yo, K 6—rep from *, end yo, SKP, K 2 tog, yo, K 2.
Rows 12, 14, 16, 18, and 20: Purl all sts.
  Starting with Row 1, rep these 20 rows.
 This stitch is the same as #14 except that the stitch foundation is Stockinette instead of Seed Stitch. It has the same uses.
 Suggested Trim: Stockinette, either side.
 Suggested Ribbings: K 2, P 2—or: K 1, P 1.

#46-A **DIAGONAL LACE STRIPE I**—*Multiple of 10 sts plus 3.*

Row 1: * P 3, yo, SKP, K 5—rep from *, end P 3.
Row 2: * K 3, P 4, P 2 tog b, yo, P 1—rep from *, end K 3.
Row 3: * P 3, K 2, yo, SKP, K 3—rep from *, end P 3.
Row 4: * K 3, P 2, P 2 tog b, yo, P 3—rep from *, end K 3.
Row 5: * P 3, K 4, yo, SKP, K 1—rep from *, end P 3.
Row 6: * K 3, P 2 tog b, yo, P 5—rep from *, end K 3.
Row 7: * P 3, K 7—rep from *, end P 3.
Row 8: * K 3, P 7—rep from *, end K 3.
  Starting with Row 1, rep these 8 rows.
 This stitch is good for cool-weather pullovers and cardigans and as a trimming stitch. It combines well with Stockinette and, using one repeat of the pattern, is an interesting trimming or outlining pattern stitch.
 Suggested Trim: Stockinette, either side.
 Suggested Ribbing: K 1, P 1.
 Do not overblock.

#46-B **DIAGONAL LACE STRIPE II**—*Multiple of 10 sts plus 3.*

Row 1: * P 3, K 5, K 2 tog, yo—rep from *, end P 3.
Row 2: * K 3, P 1, yo, P 2 tog, P 4—rep from *, end K 3.
Row 3: * P 3, K 3, K 2 tog, yo, K 2—rep from *, end P 3.

#45

#46-A

Row 4: * K 3, P 3, yo, P 2 tog, P 2 — rep from *, end K 3.
Row 5: * P 3, K 1, K 2 tog, yo, K 4 — rep from *, end P 3.
Row 6: * K 3, P 5, yo, P 2 tog — rep from *, end K 3.
Row 7: * P 3, K 7 — rep from *, end P 3.
Row 8: * K 3, P 7 — rep from *, end K 3.
  Starting with Row 1, rep these 8 rows.

 This stitch (not illustrated) is, of course, #46-A in reverse direction and is used in the same way.

 Try #46-A and #46-B together, using the first 8 rows of A as far as the center of the work (marked with a ring or running marker), and then switch to the first 8 rows of B — to make C — another interesting variation of this pattern.

#47 ZIGZAG RIBBING — *Multiple of 13 sts.*

All Odd-Numbered Rows: K 3, * P 7, K 6 — rep from *, end P 7, K 3.
Row 2: P 3, * K 4, K 2 tog, yo, K 1, P 6 — rep from *, end P 3.
Row 4: P 3, * K 3, K 2 tog, yo, K 2, P 6 — rep from *, end P 3.
Row 6: P 3, * K 2, K 2 tog, yo, K 3, P 6 — rep from *, end P 3.
Row 8: P 3, * K 1, K 2 tog, yo, K 4, P 6 — rep from *, end P 3.
Row 10: P 3, * K 2 tog, yo, K 5, P 6 — rep from *, end P 3.
Row 12: P 3, * K 1, yo, SKP, K 4, P 6 — rep from *, end P 3.
Row 14: P 3, * K 2, yo, SKP, K 3, P 6 — rep from *, end P 3.
Row 16: P 3, * K 3, yo, SKP, K 2, P 6 — rep from *, end P 3.
Row 18: P 3, * K 4, yo, SKP, K 1, P 6 — rep from *, end P 3.
Row 20: P 3, * K 5, yo, SKP, P 6 — rep from *, end P 3.
  Starting with Row 1, rep these 20 rows.
  Same uses as #46.

#47

#48 COCKLESHELLS — *Multiple of 19 sts.*

Note: The number of sts increases during the first 10 rows. They regain the original count, however, on Row 11.
Row 1: Knit all sts.
Row 2: K 1, * 00, K 2 tog, K 13, K 2 tog, 00, K 2 — rep from *, end 00, K 1.
Row 3: K 1, * KP, K 15, KP, K 2 — rep from *, end KP, K 1.
Row 4: Knit all sts.
Row 5: Knit all sts.
Row 6: K 1, * (00, K 2 tog)x2, K 11, (K 2 tog, 00)x2, K 2 — rep from *, end 00, K 1.
Row 7: * (K 1, KP)x2, K 13, (KP, K 1)x2 — rep from *, end same.
Row 8: Knit all sts.
Row 9: K 6, * (00, K 1)x14, K 11 — rep from *, end K 5.
Row 10: K 1, * (00, K 2 tog)x2, 00 as before Purling, sl the next 15 sts from L to R needle, letting all overs drop. Sl the LH needle back into these 15 sts, in back of loops, wrap yarn around RH needle point, and pull loop through all 15 sts, Purling them together. Draw

#48

162

this st up close and pull work down to even up the shell; then: (00, K 2 tog)x2, 00, K 2 — rep from *, end 00, K 1.
Row 11: * (K 1, KP)x3, K 1, (KP, K 1)x3 — rep from *, end same.
Row 12: Knit all sts.
   Starting with Row 1, rep these 12 rows.
   This lacy stitch, almost identical on both sides, should be limited to such items as bed jackets, crib covers, and shawls, depending on the weight of yarn used. The stitch works best when a smooth yarn is used.
   Suggested Trim: Garter Stitch.

#49 SPIDER WEB LACE — *Multiple of 12 sts plus 5.*

Set-Up Row — *Do Not Repeat:* K 2, * P 1, K 5, 000, SKP, K 4 — rep from *, end P 1, K 2.
Row 1: P 2, K 1, * P 3, P 2 tog b, 000, drop the overs of the last row, P 2 tog, P 3, K 1 — rep from *, end K 1, P 2.
Row 2: K 2, * P 1, K 2, K 2 tog, 000, drop overs as before, SKP, K 2 — rep from *, end P 1, K 2.
Row 3: P 2, K 1, * P 1, P 2 tog b, 000, drop overs, P 2 tog, P 1, K 1 — rep from *, end K 1, P 2.
Row 4: K 2, * P 1, K 2 tog, 000, drop overs, SKP — rep from *, end P 1, K 2.
Row 5: P 2, K 1, * P 1, drop overs, cast on 4 sts (with cast-on Method II), P under the 5 dropped loops (making a P st), cast on 4 sts, P 1, K 1 — rep from *, end K 1, P 2.
Row 6: K 2, * P 1, K 4, K 2 tog, 000, pick up a st *from the back of the last st made and Knit this st, with the next st, together;* K 4 — rep from *, end P 1, K 2.
   Starting with Row 1, rep these 6 rows.
   This stitch is equally attractive on either side. Despite its open appearance, the stitch keeps its shape well, is quite springy, and makes a very good up-and-down pattern when used as an all-over stitch. One or two repeats of the pattern form a good trim. Practically any weight of yarn may be used, but the effect is lost in any but the smooth or fine crepe yarns.
   Suggested Trim: Stockinette, either side.
   Suggested Ribbing: K 1, P 1, making the K rib match the K rib in the pattern stitch, on the last row.

#50 CROSSED RIBBING — *Multiple of 2 sts plus 1.*

Row 1: * P 1, Kb 1 — rep from *, end P 1.
Row 2: * K 1, P 1 — rep from *, end K 1.
   Repeat these 2 rows throughout.
   This is a simple variation of K 1, P 1 ribbing, but it pulls in a little tighter and holds its elasticity much better than the untwisted stitch. Crossed Ribbing is always used on the finest handmade articles

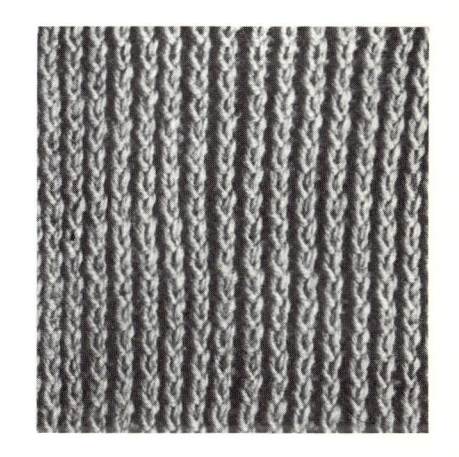

from Italy and Switzerland, not only because it is attractive, but because it retains its original shape better even though it stretches well.

It is used as any similar ribbing is used, and also as a simple gathering stitch.

#51 STOCKING HEEL STITCH (Slipped Ribbing)
—Any uneven number of sts.

Row 1: * K 1, sl 1—rep from *, end K 1.
Row 2: Purl all sts.

Repeat these 2 rows throughout.

This slip-stitch ribbing is usually found at the heels of socks, where heavy wear is encountered, but it is very useful at other points as well and may be used in many ways. It is a good gathering stitch for waistlines and shoulders, as it pulls in about one-third, much more than plain Stockinette Stitch.

#52 DECORATIVE RIBBING—Multiple of 4 sts plus 3.

Row 1: K 1, Pb 1, * K 3, Pb 1—rep from *, end K 1.
Row 2: P 1, * Kb 1, P 1, K 1, P 1—rep from *, end Kb 1, P 1.

Repeat these 2 rows throughout.

This stitch is very similar to #50 in performance, but it does not pull in quite so tightly, nor is it quite so elastic. It is a little more elaborate and can be used as an all-over pattern stitch as well as for ribbing. When heavy-weight yarn and small-size needles are used, it is excellent for bathing suits or bathing trunks.

The stitch may be blocked fairly flat without losing its outlines, and it need not be blocked at all if it is used as ribbing.

#53 BABY CROSS-STITCH STRIPE—Multiple of 7 sts plus 5.

Row 1: P 1, * K 3, P 1, cross R, P 1—rep from *, end K 3, P 1.
Row 2: K 1, * P 3, K 1, P 2, K 1—rep from *, end P 3, K 1.

Repeat these 2 rows throughout.

This easily made all-over pattern stitch gives any smooth yarn an interesting up-and-down stripe. It has a good elastic quality and may be blocked flat without detracting from its appearance. In heavy-weight yarn, with small-size needles, it is good for bathing wear. Any weight of yarn may be used in making sweaters of any size in this stitch. Using just one repeat of the pattern stitch, increasing or decreasing in the Stockinette portion of the pattern, is an excellent way of making a one-piece dress.

Suggested Trim: Stockinette, either side.
Suggested Ribbing: Any of the Cross-Stitch ribs.

#54 BABY CROSS-BRAID STRIPE—*Multiple of 8 sts plus 3.*

Row 1: * K 3, P 1, cross R, K 1, P 1—rep from *, end K 3.
Row 2: * P 3, K 1—rep from *, end P 3.
Row 3: * K 3, P 1, K 1, cross R, P 1—rep from *, end K 3.
Row 4: Same as Row 2.
   Starting with Row 1, rep these 4 rows.
   Same uses as #53.
   Suggested Ribbing: #55.

#55 CROSS-STITCH RIBBING—*Multiple of 3 sts plus 1.*

Row 1: P 1, * cross R, P 1—rep from *, end same.
Row 2: K 1, * P 2, K 1—rep from *, end same.
   Repeat these 2 rows throughout.
   This very springy stitch retains its elasticity through much wear and washing. It is a particularly good ribbing stitch for cotton or linen knitting as it retains its ribbed appearance and elasticity without going flat as plain ribbing might do.

#56 RIBBING WITH TIGHT BRAID—*Multiple of 5 sts plus 2.*

   Set-Up Row—*Do Not Repeat:* * P 2, K 2, sl 1 P-wise with yarn in back—rep from *, end P 2.
Row 1: * K 2, yf, sl 1, P 2—rep from *, end K 2.
Row 2: * P 2, yb, sl 2 sts to DP back, K next st, then K 1, sl 1 from DP—rep from *, end P 2.
   Repeat these 2 rows throughout.
   This stitch is quite similar to #55 and has all of its uses.

#57 CROSSED RIBBING II—*Multiple of 12 sts plus 2.*

See illustration overleaf.

Rows 1, 3, 7, and 9: * K 2, P 2—rep from *, end K 2.
Rows 2, 4, 8, and 10: * P 2, K 2—rep from *, end P 2.
Row 5: * K 2, P 4—rep from *, end K 2.
Row 6: * P 2, K 4—rep from *, end P 2.
Row 11: P 3, * K 2, P 4—rep from *, end K 2, P 3.
Row 12: K 3, * P 2, K 4—rep from *, end P 2, K 3.
   Starting with Row 1, rep these 12 rows.
   This is a fine all-over pattern stitch with a ribbed effect. It is quite elastic, excellent for garments that must have some stretchability. Use smooth-type or crepe yarns, however, as nubby yarns compete with the pattern.
   Suggested Trim: Stockinette, either side, or Seed Stitch.
   Suggested Ribbing: K 2, P 2.
   Block very lightly.

#54

#55

#56

#57

#58

#59

#58 PIQUÉ STITCH—*Multiple of 10 sts.*

Rows 1 and 3: * P 3, K 1, P 3, K 3—rep from *, end same.
Row 2: * P 3, K 3, P 1, K 3—rep from *, end same.
Row 4: Knit all sts.
   Starting with Row 1, rep these 4 rows.
Same uses as #57.
   Suggested Trim: Stockinette, either side, or Seed Stitch.
   Suggested Ribbing: K 1, P 1.

#59 LEAF RIBBING—*Multiple of 12 sts plus 1.*

Row 1: * K 1, P 1, (K 1, P 3)x2, K 1, P 1—rep from *, end K 1.
Row 2: * P 1, K 1, (P 1, K 3)x2, P 1, K 1—rep from *, end P 1.
Row 3: * K 1, P 1, K 2, P 2, K 1, P 2, K 2, P 1—rep from *, end K 1.
Row 4: * P 1, K 1, P 2, K 2, P 1, K 2, P 2, K 1—rep from *, end P 1.
Row 5: * K 1, P 1, K 3, P 1, K 1, P 1, K 3, P 1—rep from *, end K 1.
Row 6: * P 1, K 1, P 3, K 1, P 1, K 1, P 3, K 1—rep from *, end P 1.
Row 7: * K 1, P 2, K 2, P 1, K 1, P 1, K 2, P 2—rep from *, end K 1.
Row 8: * P 1, K 2, P 2, K 1, P 1, K 1, P 2, K 2—rep from *, end P 1.
Row 9: * K 1, P 3, (K 1, P 1)x2, K 1, P 3—rep from *, end K 1.
Row 10: * P 1, K 3, (P 1, K 1)x2, P 1, K 3—rep from *, end P 1.
   Starting with Row 1, rep these 10 rows.
   This is another subtle all-over small pattern stitch that has a certain amount of elasticity. It loses its delicate outline in any but the smooth yarns. It is attractive on either side, so that it is a very useful stitch for any reversible article.
   Suggested Trim: Stockinette, either side, or Garter or Seed Stitch.
   Suggested Ribbing: K 1, P 1.

#60 BABY ZIGZAG CABLE—*Multiple of 8 sts plus 1.*

Note: Method of cabling on odd numbers of sts on page 84.
Row 1: K 1, * P 2, K 3, P 2, K 1—rep from *, end same.
Row 2—and all Even-Numbered Rows: P 1, * K 2, P 3, K 2, P 1—rep from *, end same.
Row 3: K 1, * P 2, cable 1 over 2R, P 2, K 1—rep from *, end same.
Row 5: Same as Row 1.
Row 7: K 1, * P 2, cable 1 over 2 L, P 2, K 1—rep from *, end same.
   Starting with Row 1, rep these 8 rows.
   This all-over stitch is fine used alone and is unsurpassed for bathing wear when made with heavier-weight yarns and a small-size needle. It also serves as a good gathering stitch when used as a trim, and one repeat of the pattern makes a smart outline or vertical trimming stitch.
   Suggested Trim: Stockinette, either side.
   Suggested Ribbing: Any ribbing used with this stitch should be carefully treated because the stitch itself pulls in well. Ribbing to be used with this pattern can be made in the following manner:
   Cast on a multiple of 7 sts plus 1 for each multiple of 8 sts plus 1 in the pattern stitch and work as follows:

166

Row 1: * K 1, P 2, K 2, P 2 — rep from *, end K 1.
Row 2: * P 1, K 2, P 2, K 2 — rep from *, end P 1.
 Repeat these 2 rows for the desired amount of ribbing and increase, on the last row (Row 2), as follows:
* P 1, K 2, P 2, inc., K 1 — rep from *, end P 1.
 This prepares the number of sts for the first row of the pattern stitch itself.

#61 SPLIT CABLE AND STRIPE — *Multiple of 23 sts plus 9.*

Row 1: * (K 1, P 1)x4, K 1, P 6, K 2, P 6 — rep from *, end (K 1, P 1)x4, K 1.
Row 2: * (P 1, K 1)x4, P 1, K 6, P 2, K 6 — rep from *, end (P 1, K 1)x4, P 1.
Row 3: Same as Row 1.
Row 4: Same as Row 2.
Row 5: * (K 1, P 1)x4, K 1, P 6, cross R, P 6 — rep from *, end (K 1, P 1)x4, K 1.
Row 6: Same as Row 2.
Row 7: * (K 1, P 1)x4, K 1, P 5, cross R, cross L, P 5 — rep from *, end (K 1, P 1)x4, K 1.
Row 8: * (P 1, K 1)x4, P 1, K 5, P 1, K 2, P 1, K 5 — rep from *, end (P 1, K 1)x4, P 1.
Row 9: * (K 1, P 1)x4, K 1, P 4, cross R, P 2, cross L, P 4 — rep from *, end (K 1, P 1)x4, K 1.
Row 10: * (P 1, K 1)x4, (P 1, K 4)x3 — rep from *, end (P 1, K 1)x4, P 1.
Row 11: * (K 1, P 1)x4, K 1, P 3, cross R, P 4, cross L, P 3 — rep from *, end (K 1, P 1)x4, K 1.
Row 12: * (P 1, K 1)x4, P 1, K 3, P 1, K 6, P 1, K 3 — rep from *, end (P 1, K 1)x4, P 1.
Row 13: * (K 1, P 1)x4, K 1, P 2, cross R, P 6, cross L, P 2 — rep from *, end (K 1, P 1)x4, K 1.
Row 14: * (P 1, K 1)x4, P 1, K 2, P 1, K 8, P 1, K 2 — rep from *, end (P 1, K 1)x4, P 1.
Row 15: * (K 1, P 1)x5, cross R, P 8, cross L, P 1 — rep from *, end (K 1, P 1)x4, K 1.
Row 16: * (P 1, K 1)x5, P 1, K 10, P 1, K 1 — rep from *, end (P 1, K 1)x4, P 1.
Row 17: * (K 1, P 1)x5, K 1, P 10, K 1, P 1 — rep from *, end (K 1, P 1)x4, K 1.
Rows 18, 20, 22, and 24: Same as Row 16.
Rows 19, 21, and 23: Same as Row 17.
Row 25: * (K 1, P 1)x5, cross L, P 8, cross R, P 1 — rep from *, end (K 1, P 1)x4, K 1.
Row 26: * (P 1, K 1)x4, P 1, K 2, P 1, K 8, P 1, K 2 — rep from *, end (P 1, K 1)x4, P 1.
Row 27: * (K 1, P 1)x4, K 1, P 2, cross L, P 6, cross R, P 2 — rep from *, end (K 1, P 1)x4, K 1.

#60

#61

Row 28: * (P 1, K 1)x4, P 1, K 3, P 1, K 6, P 1, K 3 — rep from *, end (P 1, K 1)x4, P 1.
Row 29: * (K 1, P 1)x4, K 1, P 3, cross L, P 4, cross R, P 3 — rep from *, end (K 1, P 1)x4, K 1.
Row 30: * (P 1, K 1)x4, (P 1, K 4)x3 — rep from *, end (P 1, K 1)x4, P 1.
Row 31: * (K 1, P 1)x4, K 1, P 4, cross L, P 2, cross R, P 4 — rep from *, end (K 1, P 1)x4, K 1.
Row 32: * (P 1, K 1)x4, P 1, K 5, P 1, K 2, P 1, K 5 — rep from *, end (P 1, K 1)x4, P 1.
Row 33: * (K 1, P 1)x4, K 1, P 5, cross L, cross R, P 5 — rep from *, end (K 1, P 1)x4, K 1.
Row 34: Same as Row 2.
Row 35: Same as Row 5.
Row 36: Same as Row 2.
  Starting with Row 1, rep these 36 rows.
  This is an excellent stitch for sports sweaters, particularly pullovers for adults.

  Suggested Ribbing: K 1, P 1 ribbing, casting on a multiple of 22 sts, plus 9 for each multiple of 23 sts, plus 9 in the pattern stitch, increasing, on the first row of the pattern stitch itself, in the following manner: *(K 1, P 1)x4, K 1, P 5, inc., K 1, K 2 tog, P 5, inc — rep from *, end (K 1, P 1)x4, K 1.
  Continue with the pattern stitch, starting with Row 2.

#62 HERRINGBONE RIBBING — *Multiple of 9 sts plus 3.*

Note: Method of crossing *through* sts is found on page 80.
Row 1: * P 3, cross through 2 sts R, 3 times — rep from *, end P 3.
Row 2: * K 3, P 6 — rep from *, end K 3.
Row 3: * P 3, K 1, cross through 2 sts R twice, K 1 — rep from *, end P 3.
Row 4: Same as Row 2.
  Starting with Row 1, rep these 4 rows.

  Yarn that has little natural elasticity, such as camel's hair or cashmere — in fact, any smooth yarn — is well-suited to this stitch as it is very elastic and pulls in tightly where needed. Don't block it, however, if you want the pattern stitch itself to show up. One multiple of the stitch (outlined on each side of the stripe by the 3 Purled sts) makes a very suitable trim for cardigans, suit jackets, and skirts. It is especially good when used with other sts in Aran Islands patterns.

  Suggested Trim: Stockinette, either side.
  Suggested Ribbing: K 1, P 1, increasing 1 st for each crossed rib in the final row as follows:
  Cast on a multiple of 8 sts plus 3 for each multiple of 9 sts plus 3 in the pattern stitch. Work K 1, P 1 ribbing and increase, on the last row, as follows:
* (K 1, P 1)x4, K 1, inc. — rep from *, ending K 1, P 1, K 1.

#62

168

#63 **TEARDROP RIBBING** — *Multiple of 7 sts plus 1.*

Rows 1, 3, 5, and 7: * K 1, P 2, K 2, P 2 — rep from *, end K 1.
Rows 2, 4, 6, and 8: * P 1, K 2, P 2, K 2 — rep from *, end P 1.
Row 9: * K 1, P 2, insert needle into the next 2 sts as though to K 2 tog; however, using these 2 sts as one st, KPKP and K (making 5 sts), P 2 — rep from *, end K 1.
Row 10: * P 1, K 2, P 5, K 2 — rep from *, end P 1.
Row 11: * K 1, P 2, SKP, K 3 tog, P 2 — rep from *, end K 1.
Row 12: Same as Row 2.
  Starting with Row 1, rep these 12 rows.

This stitch reacts in about the same way as #62 and its uses are similar, although it is a little smaller stitch. It is good as an all-over stitch as well, or where an elastic stitch is needed.

Suggested Trim: Stockinette, either side.
Suggested Ribbing: K 2, P 1, K 1, P 1 — or: Cast on a multiple of 7 sts plus 1 in the pattern stitch and work in K 1, P 2 ribbing. Increase on the final row as follows:
 * P 1, K 2, P 1, inc, K 2 — rep from *, ending P 1.

#64 **CROSS-BRAID RIBBING** — *Multiple of 5 sts plus 2.*

Row 1: P 2, * cross R, K 1, P 2 — rep from *, end same.
Row 2: K 2, * P 3, K 2 — rep from *, end same.
Row 3: P 2, * K 1, cross R, P 2 — rep from *, end same.
Row 4: Same as Row 2.
  Starting with Row 1, rep these 4 rows.
Same uses as #62.

Suggested Ribbing: K 2, P 2 ribbing, casting on a multiple of 4 sts plus 2 for each multiple of 5 sts plus 2 in the pattern stitch, and increasing 1 st in each P 2 on the final row of ribbing.

#65 **FANCY RIBBING STITCH** — *Multiple of 8 sts plus 3.*

Note: Use Method II (see page 56) for the cast-on stitch on Row 4.
Row 1: K 4, * P 3, K 5 — rep from *, end P 3, K 4 (Wrong Side).
Row 2: P 4, * K 3, P 5 — rep from *, end K 3, P 4.
Row 3: K 3, * P 5, K 3 — rep from *, end same.
Row 4: P 3, * cast on 1 st, K 1, SK2togP, K 1, cast on 1 st, P 3 — rep from *, end same.
  Starting with Row 1, rep these 4 rows.
Same uses as #62. Also good for bathing wear.

Suggested Trim: Stockinette, either side, or Seed Stitch.
Suggested Ribbing: K 1, P 1.

169

#66

#66 BABY CROSS-CABLE RIBBING—*Multiple of 8 sts plus 3.*

Rows 1, 3, and 5: * K 3, P 5—rep from *, end K 3 (Wrong Side).
Rows 2 and 4: * P 3, K 5—rep from *, end P 3.
Row 6: * P 3, sl 4 sts to DP and hold in back, K next st, sl 3 sts back to LH needle and bring remaining st on DP to front, K the 3 sts from LH needle, then K the 1 st from DP—rep from *, end P 3.
  Starting with Row 1, rep these 6 rows.

Like #62, this is a very versatile stitch. It is handsome used alone or as a trimming stitch, makes a good gathering stitch, and works well with any type of yarn. One repeat of the pattern provides an attractive trimming stitch. It is very good for use in bathing suits, even in medium-weight yarns on fine needles.

Suggested Trim: Stockinette, either side.
Suggested Ribbing: K 1, P 1.

FABRIC STITCHES

#67

#67 STOCKINETTE STITCH—*Any number of sts.*

Row 1: Knit all sts.
Row 2: Purl all sts.
  Repeat these 2 rows throughout.

Stockinette is the foundation of every kind of knitting; only the addition of any yarn-overs, decreases, or increases, whatever form they may take, makes the various knitting pattern stitches different from one another. There is only *one* stitch that does not require both knitting and purling, and that is Garter Stitch, which is either all knitted or all purled.

#68

#68 SHIRRED STOCKINETTE STITCH—*Any number of sts.*

Work 6 rows of Stockinette Stitch.
Row 7 (Knit row): Increase in every st across the row, using the invisible increases #1 and #2 on alternate sts.
Counting this increase row as the first row, work 6 rows of Stockinette.
Row 13 (Knit row): * K 2 tog, SKP—rep from * across the row.
  Counting this decrease row as the first row again, rep from beginning.

This pattern may, of course, be worked with any number of rows, both between the shirring and for the shirring itself.

It is useful either as an all-over stitch or as trimming. This description is intended only to show a method, as a means to an end; it is not meant to be a set pattern in itself. Try your own variations.

170

#69 **BROKEN RIBBING V**—*Multiple of 2 sts plus 1.*

Row 1: Knit all sts.
Row 2: Purl all sts.
Row 3: * K 1, P 1—rep from *, end K 1.
Row 4: * P 1, K 1—rep from *, end P 1.
   Starting with Row 1, rep these 4 rows.

This petite pattern stitch is a pleasing texture or fabric stitch and should not be blocked as it practically blocks itself. It is better suited to smooth yarns and works very well in heavy-weight wool or cotton yarns for jackets and other outer garments.

Suggested Trim: Stockinette, either side, Garter Stitch, or Seed Stitch.

Suggested Ribbing: K 1, P 1.

#69

#70-A **DIAGONAL SEED STITCH I**—*Multiple of 10 sts plus 1.*

Row 1: K 2, * (P 1, K 1)x3, P 1, K 3—rep from *, end K 2.
Row 2: * P 3, (K 1, P 1)x3, K 1—rep from *, end K 1, P 1.
Row 3: * (P 1, K 1)x3, P 1, K 3—rep from *, end P 1.
Row 4: P 1, K 1, * P 3, (K 1, P 1)x3, K 1—rep from *, end (K 1, P 1)x3.
Row 5: (P 1, K 1)x2, P 1, * K 3, (P 1, K 1)x3, P 1—rep from *, end K 3, P 1, K 1, P 1.
Row 6: (P 1, K 1)x2, * P 3, (K 1, P 1)x3, K 1—rep from *, end P 3, (K 1, P 1)x2.
Row 7: P 1, K 1, P 1, * K 3, (P 1, K 1)x3, P 1—rep from *, end K 3, (P 1, K 1)x2, P 1.
Row 8: (P 1, K 1)x3, * P 3, (K 1, P 1)x3, K 1—rep from *, end P 3, K 1, P 1.
Row 9: P 1, * K 3, (P 1, K 1)x3, P 1—rep from *, end same.
Row 10: P 1, * (K 1, P 1)x3, K 1, P 3—rep from *, end same.
   Starting with Row 1, rep these 10 rows.

#70-A

#70-B **DIAGONAL SEED STITCH II**—*Multiple of 10 sts plus 1.*

Row 1: K 2, * (P 1, K 1)x3, P 1, K 3—rep from *, end K 2.
Row 2: P 1, * (K 1, P 1)x3, K 1, P 3—rep from *, end same.
Row 3: P 1, * K 3, (P 1, K 1)x3, P 1—rep from *, end same.
Row 4: (P 1, K 1)x3, * P 3, (K 1, P 1)x3, K 1—rep from *, end K 1, P 1.
Row 5: P 1, K 1, P 1, * K 3, (P 1, K 1)x3, P 1—rep from *, end K 3, (P 1, K 1)x2, P 1.
Row 6: (P 1, K 1)x2, * P 3, (K 1, P 1)x3, K 1—rep from *, end P 3, (K 1, P 1)x2.
Row 7: (P 1, K 1)x2, P 1, * K 3, (P 1, K 1)x3, P 1—rep from *, end K 3, P 1, K 1, P 1.
Row 8: P 1, K 1, * P 3, (K 1, P 1)x3, K 1—rep from *, end (K 1, P 1)x3.
Row 9: * (P 1, K 1)x3, P 1, K 3—rep from *, end P 1.
Row 10: * P 3, (K 1, P 1)x3, K 1—rep from *, end P 1.
   Starting with Row 1, rep these 10 rows.

#70-B

#70-C CHEVRON SEED STITCH—*Multiple of 30 sts plus 2.*

Place a running or ring marker between the 2 center sts.
Row 1: Same as Row 1 of either #70-A or #70-B to the marker. Then start the row again from the *beginning*, not the *, and work to the end (4 K sts at center).
Row 2: Same as Row 2 of #70-B to the marker, and same as Row 2 of #70-A to the end (6 purled sts at center).
Row 3: Same as Row 3 of #70-A to the marker, and same as Row 3 of #70-B to the end (2 purled sts at center for all remaining rows).
Row 4: Same as Row 4 of #70-B to the marker, and same as Row 4 of #70-A to the end.
Row 5: Same as Row 5 of #70-A to the marker, and same as Row 5 of #70-B to the end.
Row 6: Same as Row 6 of #70-B to the marker, and same as Row 6 of #70-A to the end.
Row 7: Same as Row 7 of #70-A to the marker, and same as Row 7 of #70-B to the end.
Row 8: Same as Row 8 of #70-B to the marker, and same as Row 8 of #70-A to the end.
Row 9: Same as Row 9 of #70-A to the marker, and same as Row 9 of #70-B to the end.
Row 10: Same as Row 10 of #70-B to the marker, and same as Row 10 of #70-A to the end.
   Starting with Row 1, rep these 10 rows.
   These three patterns may be used in exactly the same manner as #4-A, #4-B, and #4-C, and are good in any weight of yarn. They may be treated in the same manner and used for the same types of articles.
   Suggested Trim: Seed Stitch.

#71 **OPEN CHEVRON**—*Multiple of 8 sts plus 1.*

Row 1: * P 1, K 3—rep from *, end P 1.
Row 2: * P 1, K 1, P 5, K 1—rep from *, end P 1.
Row 3: K 2, * P 1, K 3—rep from *, end K 2.
Row 4: P 3, * K 1, P 1, K 1, P 5—rep from *, end P 3.
   Starting with Row 1, rep these 4 rows.
   This rough-textured stitch works beautifully in any smooth yarn for sweaters, suits, gloves—any garment requiring a fabric stitch or plain knitting. The basic stitch is Stockinette, and this slight elaboration of it reacts in much the same way, except that it remains flatter while it is being worked.
   Suggested Trim: Seed Stitch.
   Suggested Ribbing: K 1, P 1—K 2, P 2—or any of the small type of ribbings.
   Block very lightly.

172

#72 **BROKEN CHEVRON**—*Multiple of 14 sts plus 1.*

Row 1: P 2, * K 2, P 2, K 1, P 1, K 1, P 2, K 2, P 3—rep from *, end P 2.
Row 2: K 3, * P 2, K 5—rep from *, end P 2, K 3.
Row 3: * P 1, K 1, P 2, K 2, P 3, K 2, P 2, K 1—rep from *, end P 1.
Row 4: * K 1, P 2, K 2, P 2—rep from *, end K 1.
   Starting with Row 1, rep these 4 rows.
   This useful stitch is very good for garments or articles that show both sides of the fabric, as it needs no lining or facing stitch for finishing. (See #71 for specific uses.) Heavy-weight wool or cotton yarns bring out the pattern.
   Suggested Trim: Seed Stitch.
   Suggested Ribbing: K 1, P 1.

#72

#73 **WAVED WELT**—*Multiple of 8 sts plus 1.*

Row 1: * P 1, K 7—rep from *, end P 1.
Row 2: K 2, * P 5, K 3—rep from *, end P 5, K 2.
Row 3: P 3, * K 3, P 5—rep from *, end K 3, P 3.
Row 4: K 4, * P 1, K 7—rep from *, end P 1, K 4.
Row 5: * K 1, P 7—rep from *, end K 1.
Row 6: P 2, * K 5, P 3—rep from *, end K 5, P 2.
Row 7: K 3, * P 3, K 5—rep from *, end P 3, K 3.
Row 8: P 4, * K 1, P 7—rep from *, end K 1, P 4.
   Starting with Row 1, rep these 8 rows.
   This stitch is the same on both sides—an advantage to be considered in selecting a stitch for some articles. A broad stitch, it conveys an appearance of width, so consider this also when planning. Any type of yarn may be used, and the contours may be blocked out entirely or left unblocked, as in Horizontal Ribbing or Welting (#2). Waved Welt may be used as a trim as in #2.
   Suggested Trim: Stockinette, either side, or Seed Stitch.
   Suggested Ribbing: Practically any kind, depending on the garment.

#73

#74 **SEED STITCH BLOCKS**—*Multiple of 10 sts plus 5.*

Rows 1, 3, 5, and 7: * (P 1, K 1)x2, P 1, K 5—rep from *, end (P 1, K 1)x2, P 1.
Rows 2, 4, and 6: (P 1, K 1)x2, * P 7, K 1, P 1, K 1—rep from *, end (K 1, P 1)x2.
Rows 8, 10, 12, and 14: * P 5, (K 1, P 1)x2, K 1—rep from *, end P 5.
Rows 9, 11, and 13: K 5, * P 1, K 1, P 1, K 7—rep from *, end K 7.
   Starting with Row 1, rep these 14 rows.
   Seed Stitch Blocks may be used in any manner plain Seed Stitch is used, except as trimming.

#74

173

#75

#75 FLAT DIAMOND I—*Multiple of 10 sts plus 3.*

Row 1: * P 1, K 1, P 1, K 7—rep from *, end P 1, K 1, P 1.
Row 2: (P 1, K 1)x2, * P 5, (K 1, P 1)x2, K 1—rep from *, end (K 1, P 1)x2.
Row 3: (P 1, K 1)x2, P 1, * K 3, (P 1, K 1)x3, P 1—rep from *, end (P 1, K 1)x2, P 1.
Row 4: * P 3, (K 1, P 1)x3, K 1—rep from *, end P 3.
Row 5: K 4, * (P 1, K 1)x2, P 1, K 5—rep from *, end (P 1, K 1)x2, P 1, K 4.
Row 6: P 5, * K 1, P 1, K 1, P 7—rep from *, end K 1, P 1, K 1, P 5.
Row 7: Same as Row 5.
Row 8: Same as Row 4.
Row 9: Same as Row 3.
Row 10: Same as Row 2.
  Starting with Row 1, rep these 10 rows.
  Same uses as #74.

#76

#76 TRIANGLES—*Multiple of 12 sts plus 1.*

Row 1: Knit all sts.
Row 2: Purl all sts.
Row 3: * P 1, K 11—rep from *, end P 1.
Row 4: K 2, * P 9, K 3—rep from *, end K 2.
Row 5: P 3, * K 7, P 5—rep from *, end P 3.
Row 6: K 4, * P 5, K 7—rep from *, end K 4.
Row 7: P 5, * K 3, P 9—rep from *, end P 5.
Row 8: Purl all sts.
Row 9: Knit all sts.
Row 10: P 6, * K 1, P 11—rep from *, end P 6.
Row 11: K 5, * P 3, K 9—rep from *, end K 5.
Row 12: P 4, * K 5, P 7—rep from *, end P 4.
Row 13: K 3, * P 7, K 5—rep from *, end K 3.
Row 14: P 2, * K 9, P 3—rep from *, end P 2.
  Starting with Row 1, rep these 14 rows.
This version of Stockinette may be used in combination with either side of that stitch forming the foundation. It is an excellent all-over small pattern as well as a good trimming or contrast stitch, and the pattern shows up very well on either side.
  Suggested Trim: Stockinette, either side, or Seed Stitch.
  Suggested Ribbing: Practically any small ribbing stitch.

#77

#77 BASKET WEAVE (*Combined Rib and Welt*)—*Multiple of 8 sts.*

Row 1: K 3, * P 2, K 6—rep from *, end P 2, K 3 (Wrong Side).
Row 2: P 3, * K 2, P 6—rep from *, end K 2, P 3.
Row 3: Same as Row 1.
Row 4: Knit all sts.
Row 5: K 7, * P 2, K 6—rep from *, end K 7.
Row 6: P 7, * K 2, P 6—rep from *, end P 7.

174

Row 7: Same as Row 5.
Row 8: Knit all sts.
    Starting with Row 1, rep these 8 rows.
  This stitch works well both as a trimming stitch and as an all-over stitch. It is very good for cardigans or jackets in any size and in any weight of smooth yarn; crepe or nubby yarns hide the pattern. The stitch makes a good border for a baby's afghan or as a strip in a large afghan.
    Suggested Trim: Stockinette, either side.
    Suggested Ribbing: K 2, P 2 only.
    Requires no blocking.

#78 SEED AND STOCKINETTE DIAMOND
—Multiple of 28 sts plus 1.

Row 1: * P 1, K 13 — rep from *, end P 1.
Row 2: P 1, * K 1, P 11, K 1, P 1 — rep from *, end same.
Row 3: K 2, P 1, * K 9, (P 1, K 1)x2, P 1, K 9, P 1, K 3, P 1 — rep from *, end K 9, P 1, K 2.
Row 4: P 3, K 1, * P 7, (K 1, P 1)x3, K 1, P 7, K 1, P 5, K 1 — rep from *, end P 7, K 1, P 3.
Row 5: K 4, P 1, * K 5, (P 1, K 1)x4, P 1, K 5, P 1, K 7, P 1 — rep from *, end K 5, P 1, K 4.
Row 6: P 5, K 1, * P 3, (K 1, P 1)x5, K 1, P 3, K 1, P 9, K 1 — rep from *, end P 3, K 1, P 5.
Row 7: K 6, * (P 1, K 1)x8, P 1, K 11 — rep from *, end K 6.
Row 8: P 7, * (K 1, P 1)x7, K 1, P 13 — rep from *, end P 7.
Row 9: Same as Row 7.
Row 10: Same as Row 6.
Row 11: Same as Row 5.
Row 12: Same as Row 4.
Row 13: Same as Row 3.
Row 14: Same as Row 2.
Row 15: Same as Row 1.
Row 16: * P 1, K 1, P 11, K 1 — rep from *, end K 1, P 1.
Row 17: P 1, K 1, P 1, * K 9, P 1, K 3, P 1, K 9, (P 1, K 1)x2, P 1 — rep from *, end P 1, K 1, P 1.
Row 18: (P 1, K 1)x2, * P 7, K 1, P 5, K 1, P 7, (K 1, P 1)x3, K 1 — rep from *, end (K 1, P 1)x2.
Row 19: (P 1, K 1)x2, P 1, * K 5, P 1, K 7, P 1, K 5, (P 1, K 1)x4, P 1 — rep from *, end (P 1, K 1)x2, P 1.
Row 20: (P 1, K 1)x3, * P 3, K 1, P 9, K 1, P 3, (K 1, P 1)x5, K 1 — rep from *, end (K 1, P 1)x3.
Row 21: (P 1, K 1)x4, P 1, * K 11, (P 1, K 1)x8, P 1 — rep from *, end (P 1, K 1)x4, P 1.
Row 22: (P 1, K 1)x4, * P 13, (K 1, P 1)x7, K 1 — rep from *, end (K 1, P 1)x4.
Row 23: Same as Row 21.
Row 24: Same as Row 20.

#78

#79

Row 25: Same as Row 19.
Row 26: Same as Row 18.
Row 27: Same as Row 17.
Row 28: Same as Row 16.
    Starting with Row 1, rep these 28 rows.
    This geometric stitch is effective worked in any weight of smooth yarn, and can be used for cardigans, pullovers, for the center of a baby's afghan, or for afghan strips.
    Suggested Trim: Seed Stitch.
    Suggested Ribbing: K 1, P 1.

#79 MODIFIED SEED STITCH—*Any even number of sts.*

Rows 1 and 3: Knit all sts.
Row 2: * K 1, P 1—rep from *, end same.
Row 4: * P 1, K 1—rep from *, end same.
    Starting with Row 1, rep these 4 rows.
    This may be used in place of Seed Stitch with only one exception—it is *not* the same on both sides and therefore may need to be faced or lined.
    Suggested Trim: Same stitch or Seed Stitch.
    Suggested Ribbing: K 1, P 1 only.

#80

#80 DOUBLE SEED, MOSS, or RICE STITCH —*Multiple of 4 sts plus 2.*

Row 1: * K 2, P 2—rep from *, end K 2.
Row 2: * P 2, K 2—rep from *, end P 2.
Row 3: Same as Row 2.
Row 4: Same as Row 1.
    Starting with Row 1, rep these 4 rows.
    This stitch may be substituted for Seed Stitch with no exceptions; the only difference between the two is that Double Seed, Moss, or Rice Stitch has a slightly rougher texture. It is especially good in medium- to heavy-weight wool or cotton yarns for jackets and requires no facing or lining as it is exactly the same on both sides.
    Suggested Ribbing: K 2, P 2 only.
    Requires very little blocking.

#81-A

#81-A SLIP DIAGONAL FABRIC I—*Multiple of 3 sts.*

Row 1: * P 2, yb, sl 1, yf—rep from *, end yf, sl 1.
Row 2: * yf, sl 1, P 2—rep from *, end same.
Row 3: * yb, sl 1, yf, P 2—rep from *, end same.
Row 4: * P 2, yf, sl 1—rep from *, end same.
Row 5: P 1, * yb, sl 1, yf, P 2—rep from *, end P 1.
Row 6: P 1, * yf, sl 1, P 2—rep from *, end P 1.
    Starting with Row 1, rep these 6 rows.

#81-B SLIP DIAGONAL FABRIC II—*Multiple of 3 sts.*

Note: This KNIT fabric matches the PURL fabric in #81-A, the pattern running in the opposite diagonal.
Row 1: * K 2, yf, sl 1, yb—rep from *, end *yb*, sl 1.
Row 2: * yb, sl 1, K 2—rep from *, end same.
Row 3: * yf, sl 1, yb, K 2—rep from *, end same.
Row 4: * K 2, yb, sl 1—rep from *, end same.
Row 5: K 1, * yf, sl 1, yb, K 2—rep from *, end K 1.
Row 6: K 1, * yb, sl 1, K 2—rep from *, end K 1.
    Starting with Row 1, rep these 6 rows.

When making a garment with this stitch, one side of the front or back should be made with the Purled fabric, and the other with the Knit fabric.

This serviceable flat fabric stitch includes slipped sts, so the resulting fabric has little stretch when blocked or worn. As it holds its shape well, it is excellent for suits and jackets. Made with heavy-weight yarn, on small-size needles, it is very good for bathing wear.

Suggested Trim: Stockinette or Seed Stitch.
Suggested Ribbing: None.
This pattern stitch may be fully blocked.

#82 VERTICAL HERRINGBONE—*Multiple of 9 sts plus 1.*

Note: In the following instructions, all *Made sts* (M 1) are knitted.
Row 1: Purl all sts.
Row 2: * K 2 tog, K 3, M 1, K 4—rep from *, end K 5.
Row 3: Purl all sts.
Row 4: K 4, * M 1, K 4, K 2 tog, K 3—rep from *, end K 4, K 2 tog.
    Starting with Row 1, rep these 4 rows.

This up-and-down fabric stitch will stretch in either direction, but it is elastic enough to snap back into position. It is very good for tailored suits and dresses. In knitting a skirt made in separate panels, it is best to make all increases at the edges. When this stitch is made on a circular needle, the stripes may be increased individually.

When using cotton or linen yarns, the Reverse Stitch (page 63) must be used, as advised for this material. Therefore, for each K 2 tog in the pattern stitch, substitute SKP.

#83 FABRIC STITCH—*Multiple of 4 sts plus 3.*

Row 1: * K 3, sl 1—rep from *, end K 3.
Row 2: * K 3, yf, sl 1, yb—rep from *, end K 3.
Row 3: K 1, sl 1, * K 3, sl 1—rep from *, end K 1.
Row 4: K 1, yf, sl 1, yb, * K 3, yf, sl 1, yb—rep from *, end K 1.
    Starting with Row 1, rep these 4 rows.

This stitch looks like #79 and has the same uses. It is a firmer stitch, however, and has less stretch because of the slipped sts in the pattern. Its elasticity makes it good for bathing suits if it is made with heavy-weight yarn on small-size needles, and it is excellent for jackets of wool or heavier-weight cotton yarns.

#84

#85

#86

#84 HERRINGBONE STRIPE—*Multiple of 18 sts plus 5.*

Row 1: Purl all sts.
Row 2: * K 5, M 1, K 2, SKP, K 5, K 2 tog, K 2, M 1—rep from *, end K 5.
  Repeat these 2 rows throughout.

This is very similar to and has the same uses as #82. It works up quite tightly and is excellent for tailored suits and skirts. All increases and decreases should be done in the plain Stockinette portion.

#85 ZIGZAG STOCKINETTE FABRIC—*Multiple of 9 sts plus 6.*

All Odd-Numbered Rows: Purl all sts.
Row 2: K 4, * (cross L)x3, K 3—rep from *, end cross L.
Row 4: cross L, K 3, * (cross L)x3, K 3—rep from *, end K 4.
Row 6: K 1, cross L, K 3, * (cross L)x3, K 3—rep from *, end same.
Row 8: (cross L)x2, K 3, * (crossL)x3, K 3—rep from *, end K 2.
Row 10: (cross R)x2, K 3, * (cross R)x3, K 3—rep from *, end K 2.
Row 12: K 1, cross R, K 3, * (cross R)x3, K 3—rep from *, end same.
Row 14: cross R, K 3, * (cross R)x3, K 3—rep from *, end K 4.
Row 16: K 4, * (cross R)x3, K 3—rep from *, end cross R.
  Starting with Row 1, rep these 16 rows.

This stitch is very effective for dressy cardigans or pullovers, as an all-over pattern for a trimming stitch on a foundation of Stockinette, or as a pattern stripe for afghans. Crepe or nubby yarns are suitable, but the pattern shows up better when a smooth yarn is used.

Suggested Trim: Stockinette, Knit Side.
Suggested Ribbing: K 1, P 1, making the K 1 match the K 1 in the zigzag stripes.

#86 STRIPED FABRIC STITCH—*Multiple of 22 sts plus 8.*

Set-Up Row—*Do Not Repeat:* * (K 1, P 1)x4, K 2, sl 1 with yarn in back, (K 1, P 1)x4, sl 1 with yarn in back, K 2—rep from *, end (K 1, P 1)x4.
Row 1: P 10, * sl 1 with yarn in front, P 8, sl 1 with yarn in front, P 12—rep from *, end P 10.
Row 2: * (P 1, K 1)x4, cross 3rd st on LH needle in front of 1st 2 sts, working K 1, sl 1 on these 2 sts, (P 1, K 1)x4, cross 1st st on LH needle in front of next 2 sts, working sl 1, K 1 on these 2 sts—rep from *, end (P 1, K 1)x4.
Row 3: Same as Row 1.
Row 4: * (K 1, P 1)x4, cross 3rd st over 2 as above, (K 1, P 1)x4, cross 1st st over 2 as above—rep from *, end (K 1, P 1)x4.
  Starting with Row 1, rep these 4 rows.

The foundation of this stitch is the same as #79 (Modified Seed Stitch); the two may be used in combination and are fine complements for a two-piece outfit. Increases are easily made in the center portions, which may be wider than those in the accompanying directions, with the striped cross sts used to outline the panels. This stitch is particularly appropriate for a one-piece dress designed on princess or fitted lines.

Suggested Trim: #79.

Suggested Ribbing: Either repeats of the cross-stitch line with one Purled st between, or none at all.

#87 MOCK CABLE FABRIC — *Multiple of 4 sts plus 2.*

Row 1: Purl all sts.
Row 2: K 1, * cross L, K 2 — rep from *, end K 3.
Row 3: Purl all sts.
Row 4: K 3, * cross R, K 2 — rep from *, end K 1.
  Starting with Row 1, rep these 4 rows.

This very elastic stitch belies its appearance. An interesting variation of Stockinette, it may be used in its place, but increases should *not* be made at any place except the side edges. The stitch should be made up only in the smooth yarns, either wool, cotton, or linen.

#87

#88-A DIAGONAL CROSS FABRIC — RIGHT
— *Multiple of 4 sts plus 1.*

All Odd-Numbered Rows: Purl all sts.
Row 2: * K 2, cross R — rep from *, end K 1.
Row 4: K 1, * cross R, K 2 — rep from *, end same.
Row 6: * cross R, K 2 — rep from *, end K 3.
Row 8: K 3, * cross R, K 2 — rep from *, end cross R.
  Starting with Row 1, rep these 8 rows.

#88-B DIAGONAL CROSS FABRIC — LEFT
— *Multiple of 4 sts plus 1.*

All Odd-Numbered Rows: Purl all sts.
Row 2: K 1, * cross L, K 2 — rep from *, end same.
Row 4: * K 2, cross L — rep from *, end K 1.
Row 6: K 3, * cross L, K 2 — rep from *, end cross L.
Row 8: * cross L, K 2 — rep from *, end K 3.
  Starting with Row 1, rep these 8 rows.

#88-A

#88-C HERRINGBONE CROSS FABRIC — *Cast on a multiple of 8 sts plus 2, placing a marker between the 2 center sts.*

All Odd-Numbered Rows: Purl all sts.
Row 2: Work Row 2 of #88-A to marker and Row 2 of #88-B to end.
Row 4: Work Row 4 of #88-A to marker and Row 4 of #88-B to end.
Row 6: Work Row 6 of #88-A to marker and Row 6 of #88-B to end.
Row 8: Work Row 8 of #88-A to marker and Row 8 of #88-B to end.
  Starting with Row 1, rep these 8 rows.

This stitch, not illustrated, along with #88-A and #88-B, may be used in the same manner as any of the variations of #70 or #81. They pull in tighter than #70 or #80, however, and are more elastic.

#88-B

#89

#89 MODIFIED SCHIAPARELLI—*Multiple of 4 sts plus 2.*

Note: For method of yo before knitting the first st, see page 72.
Row 1: * K 2, yo, K 2 and pull the yo over the K 2 — rep from *, end K 2.
Row 2: Purl all sts.
Row 3: * yo, K 2 and pull the yo over the K 2, K 2 — rep from *, end yo, K 2 and pull over.
Row 4: Purl all sts.
  Starting with Row 1, rep these 4 rows.

  This fabric stitch is pretty as an all-over pattern or as a trim for Stockinette. It is a good stitch for jackets and coats in medium- to heavy-weight yarns. In heavy-weight yarns, used with small-size needles, it is well adapted to bathing wear. Watch it, though! This stitch must be firmly blocked to counteract the bias tendency.

#90-A SCHIAPARELLI, CROSS RIGHT—*Any even number of sts.*

Row 1: * cross R — rep from *, across the row.
Row 2: Purl all sts.
Row 3: K 1, * cross R — rep from *, across the row, end K 1.
Row 4: Purl all sts.
  Starting with Row 1, rep these 4 rows.

#90-A

#90-B SCHIAPARELLI, CROSS LEFT—*Any even number of sts.*

  This is worked in the same manner as #90-A, crossing LEFT instead of crossing RIGHT.
  These stitches have considerable vertical but little side stretch. They are elastic, however, and will snap back into place. They are therefore excellent for tailored jackets or short coats, preferably made with smooth yarns.

#90-B

#91 WAFFLE FABRIC STITCH—*Multiple of 2 sts plus 1.*

Row 1: Knit all sts.
Row 2: * K 1, K the st *under* the next st, removing both sts from LH needle as one—rep from *, end K 1.
Row 3: Knit all sts.
Row 4: K 2, * K the st under the next st as above, K 1—rep from *, end K 2.
    Starting with Row 1, rep these 4 rows.
    This elastic variation of a waffle stitch, because of its nearly double thickness, is good for use in short coats and jackets. Its warmth makes it very useful for baby garments and blankets, and it is an attractive variety stitch for afghan strips. It shows up and reacts best in smooth yarns.
    Suggested Trim: Seed Stitch.
    Suggested Ribbing: K 1, P 1.

#91

#92 DOUBLE ENGLISH KNITTING—*Any even number of sts.*

Set-Up Row—*Do Not Repeat:* * yo, sl 1, K 1—rep from *, end same.
Row 1: * yf, sl 1, yo, P 2 tog, (the st and the yo)—rep from *, end same.
Row 2: P 1, * sl 1, (the yo), P 2—rep from *, end sl 1, P 1.
Row 3: * P 2 tog, (the st and the yo), sl 1, yo—rep from *, end P 2 tog, P 1.
Row 4: yo, sl 1, P 1, * sl 1, (the yo), P 2—rep from *, end same.
    Starting with Row 1, rep these 4 rows.
    When binding off, do it on Row 2 or Row 4, knitting the yo together with the st before it, and counting this K 2 tog as one st.
    This stitch resembles #91 but is made in an entirely different manner. It has considerably more stretch and so should be used with caution. It produces a double-thick fabric ideal for cold-weather garments.
    Suggested Trim: Stockinette.
    Suggested Ribbing: K 1, P 1.

#92

#93 BRAIDED STITCH—*Any even number of sts.*

Note: This stitch is worked with two sizes of needles, the Purl row with a needle 2 sizes larger than the one used on the Knit row.
    Cast on with the smaller needle.
Row 1: Purl all sts with the larger-size needle.
Row 2—with the smaller-size needle: * cross R, lifting the st over before knitting it—rep from * across row.
    Repeat these 2 rows throughout.
    This small pattern stitch is excellent for suits, jackets, and short coats, and makes a good gathering stitch or a conservative trimming for Stockinette. As a foundation stitch, it works very well in sweaters of all types and sizes in every weight of yarn.
    Suggested Trim: Stockinette, either side, or Seed Stitch.
    Suggested Ribbing: K 1, P 1—or: K 2, P 2.

#93

#94 **SLIP FABRIC STITCH**—*Any even number of sts.*

Row 1: * K 1, yf, sl 1, yb—rep from *, end same.

Row 2: Purl all sts.

Row 3: * yf, sl 1, yb, K 1—rep from *, end same.

Row 4: Purl all sts.
   Starting with Row 1, rep these 4 rows.

This smooth, firm stitch is particularly appropriate for tailored suits, skirts, and jackets. It has very little stretch because of the slipped sts, and it blocks out flat. It is good when made with smooth yarns and is quite effective as a flat fabric when crepe or nubby yarns are used. It is not recommended for growing children's garments.
   Suggested Trim: Stockinette.

#94

#95 **WOVEN FABRIC STITCH I**—*Any even number of sts.*

Note: This stitch may be made with a needle 2 sizes larger than the size ordinarily used for the weight of yarn being worked. Do not allow for much stretch in the material. A smaller needle *must* be used for the cast-on.

Row 1: * K 1, yf, sl 1, yb—rep from *, end same.

Row 2: * P 1, yb, sl 1, yf—rep from *, end same.
   Repeat these 2 rows throughout.

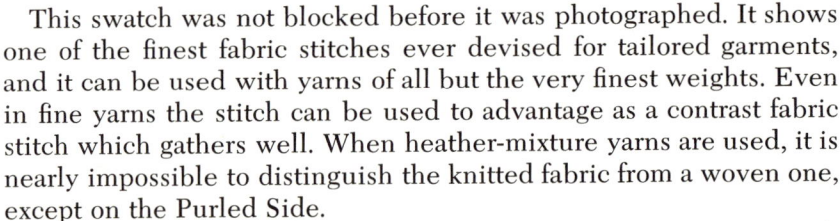

This swatch was not blocked before it was photographed. It shows one of the finest fabric stitches ever devised for tailored garments, and it can be used with yarns of all but the very finest weights. Even in fine yarns the stitch can be used to advantage as a contrast fabric stitch which gathers well. When heather-mixture yarns are used, it is nearly impossible to distinguish the knitted fabric from a woven one, except on the Purled Side.
   This stitch is best used in making flat pieces—i.e., working each piece of the pattern separately and then tailoring all of them together as any woven fabric is tailored. A skirt may be worked on a circular needle but must have special treatment. An *odd number* of sts must be cast on, and directions for *Row 1 only* are to be worked. The circular-knit skirt is worked from the waistline down and increased for shaping. All increases must be made in the following manner, with an *odd number of rows* between increases:
   Use a running marker at the point of shaping and, in the st *just before* this marker and *immediately after it*, Knit the front of the st and bring the yarn to the front of the work without removing the st; then slip the needle into the *back* of the same st and remove the st from the needle.
   This stitch blocks flat and may be pressed thoroughly.
   Suggested Trim: Same stitch, either side.

#95

182

#96 **WOVEN FABRIC STITCH II**—*Multiple of 4 sts plus 2.*

Note: When carrying the yarn in front of sts, carry it fairly loosely.
Rows 1, 5, and 9: * K 2, yf, sl 2, yb—rep from *, end K 2.
Rows 2, 6, and 10: P 1, * yb, sl 2, yf, P 2—rep from *, end P 3.
Rows 3, 7, and 11: * yf, sl 2, yb, K 2—rep from *, end yf, sl 2.
Rows 4, 8, and 12: P 3, * yb, sl 2, yf, P 2—rep from *, end P 1.
Rows 13, 17, and 21: * yf, sl 2, yb, K 2—rep from *, end yf, sl 2.
Rows 14, 18, and 22: P 1, * yb, sl 2, yf, p 2—rep from *, end P 3.
Rows 15, 19, and 23: K 2, * yf, sl 2, yb, K 2—rep from *, end same.
Rows 16, 20, and 24: P 3, * yb, sl 2, yf, P 2—rep from *, end P 1.
    Starting with Row 1, rep these 24 rows.
  This woven fabric stitch creates a striped twill effect and should be worked from side to side, rather than from end to end, of any pattern piece if a lengthwise stripe is preferred. As shown, it is excellent for jackets and coats. Used vertically, with the stripe running up and down, it may be used for any tailored garment for which heavier-weight woven fabric would be suitable.

#96

#97 **STAGGERED CHECK**—*Multiple of 6 sts plus 5.*

Row 1: * (K 1, yf, sl 1, yb)x2, K 1, P 1—rep from *, end (K 1, yf, sl 1, yb)x2, K 1.
Row 2: yb, * (sl 1, yf, P 1, yb)x2, sl 1, K 1, yb—rep from *, end (sl 1, yf, P 1, yb)x2, yb, sl 1.
Rows 3, 5, 7, 9, and 11: Same as Row 1.
Rows 4, 6, 8, and 10: Same as Row 2.
Row 12: Purl all sts.
Row 13: yf, sl 1, yb, K 1, P 1—rep from * to * in Row 1, end K 1, yf, sl 1.
Row 14: P 1, yb, sl 1, K 1—rep from * to * in Row 2, end sl 1, yf, P 1.
Rows 15, 17, 19, 21, and 23: Same as Row 13.
Rows 16, 18, 20, and 22: Same as Row 14.
Row 24: Purl all sts.
    Starting with Row 1, rep these 24 rows.
  The foundation of this stitch is the same as #95. The two together—this check pattern for the jacket and #95 for the skirt—are a happy combination. The check is *not* advised for skirts, however, as it is difficult to shape. It is better to use it for straight coats and jackets.
  Suggested Trim: #95.

#97

#98 **FABRIC BLOCK**—*Multiple of 6 sts plus 8.*

Note: In the following pattern, "y around needle" means to bring the yarn to the front of the work, over the needle again, and around to the front again. This yo, together with the slipped st, makes a cross st.

#98

183

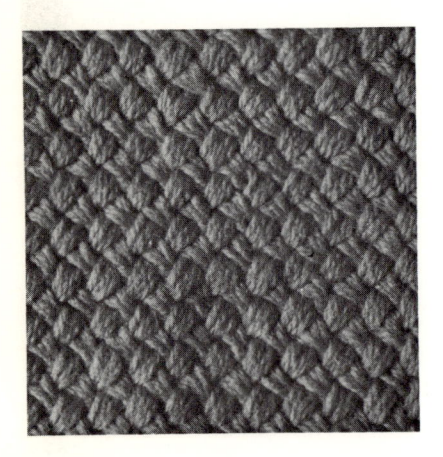

These 2 sts are knitted together on the next row.
Row 1: Knit all sts.
Row 2: K 1, yf, sl 1, y around needle, sl 1 keeping yarn in front (making a yo), * K 2, yf, (sl 1, y around needle)x3, sl 1, yo—rep from *, end K 2, yf, sl 1, y around needle, sl 1, yo, K 1.
Row 3: K 1, K 2 tog b (the yo and the sl st) twice, * K 2, (K 2 tog b)x4—rep from *, end K 2, (K 2 tog b)x2, K 1.
Rows 4, 6, 8, and 10: Same as Row 2.
Rows 5, 7, 9, and 11: Same as Row 3.
Row 12: Purl all sts.
Row 13: Knit all sts.
Row 14: Rep between * * on Row 2—end K 2.
Row 15: Rep between * * on Row 3—end K 2.
Rows 16, 18, 20, and 22: Same as Row 14.
Rows 17, 19, 21, and 23: Same as Row 15.
Row 24: Purl all sts.
   Starting with Row 1, rep these 24 rows.
   This is a beautiful stitch for coats and jackets. Its use should be confined to heavy-weight yarns and a slightly smaller-size needle than would ordinarily be used for a heavy weight of yarn. If too large-size a needle is used, the fabric may stretch and lose its shape. With the smaller-size needle, it will safely retain its outline.
   If these suggestions have been followed, the fabric may be fully blocked.

#99

#99 HEAVY WOVEN BIAS FABRIC—*Any even number of sts.*

Note: The photograph shows this stitch worked with doubled yarn.
Row 1: * K the 2nd st from the back, then the 1st st from the front—rep from *, end same.
Row 2: P 1, * P the 2nd st and then the 1st st—rep from *, end P 1.
   Repeat these 2 rows throughout.
   This is an ideal stitch for heavy coats and jackets. It is extremely firm and holds its shape very well indeed. In addition to being an unusually good gathering stitch for very fine yarn on baby garments, it is a good trimming stitch for Stockinette. By itself it needs no trim.

#100 FLAT DIAMOND II—*Multiple of 8 sts plus 7.*

Row 1: K 3, * P 1, K 7—rep from *, end P 1, K 3.
Row 2: P 2, * K 1, P 1, K 1, P 5—rep from *, end K 1, P 1, K 1, P 2.
Row 3: K 1, * P 1, K 3—rep from *, end P 1, K 1.
Row 4: K 1, * P 5, K 1, P 1, K 1—rep from *, end P 5, K 1.
Row 5: * K 7, P 1—rep from *, end K 7.
Row 6: Same as Row 4.
Row 7: Same as Row 3.
Row 8: Same as Row 2.
   Starting with Row 1, rep these 8 rows.
   This easily made all-over pattern stitch may be used by itself or as

#100

184

a trimming stitch. As Stockinette is the foundation, it is good when the two are used in combination. Excellent for use in sweaters of all types.

    Suggested Trim: Stockinette, either side, or Seed Stitch.
    Suggested Ribbing: K 1, P 1.

#101 CROSS-WEAVE FABRIC—*Multiple of 4 sts plus 3.*

Row 1: * P 3, K 1 with 2 wraps—rep from *, end P 3.
Row 2: * K 3, P 1 and drop second wrap—rep from *, end K 3.
Row 3: Knit all sts.
Row 4: Purl all sts.
Row 5: P 1, * K 1 with 2 wraps, P 3—rep from *, end K 1 with 2 wraps, P 1.
Row 6: K 1, * P 1 and drop 2nd wrap, K 3—rep from *, end P 1 and drop 2nd wrap, K 1.
Row 7: Knit all sts.
Row 8: Purl all sts.
    Starting with Row 1, rep these 8 rows.

This rough-textured fabric should be handled carefully as it is apt to be quite stretchy. This may be overcome by working with smaller-size needles than the weight of yarn used would ordinarily call for. Despite its stretchiness, this pattern stitch is also elastic and will spring back into shape. It may be used in place of any small basket-weave stitch. The basis of this pattern is Garter Stitch, so it remains flat and makes a good framing stitch. It is excellent for sweaters where a little bulk is desired.

    Suggested Trim: Stockinette, either side, or (very sparingly) Garter Stitch.
    Suggested Ribbing: K 1, P 1 only.
    Block very lightly.

#102 STAGGERED SLIP CHECK—*Multiple of 4 sts plus 3.*

Row 1: K 1, * sl 1, K 3—rep from *, end sl 1, K 1.
Row 2: P 1, * sl 1, P 3—rep from *, end sl 1, P 1.
Row 3: Same as Row 1.
Row 4: Knit all sts.
Row 5: * K 3, sl 1—rep from *, end K 3.
Row 6: * P 3, sl 1—rep from *, end P 3.
Row 7: Same as Row 5.
Row 8: Knit all sts.
    Starting with Row 1, rep these 8 rows.

Rough-textured and quite firm, this fabric retains its original shape and elasticity. Equally good as an all-over pattern or as a trimming stitch, it works up well for jackets and coats. When heavy-weight yarn and small-size needles are used, this stitch is appropriate for bathing wear.

    Suggested Trim: Same stitch or Stockinette.
    Suggested Ribbing: K 1, P 1 only.

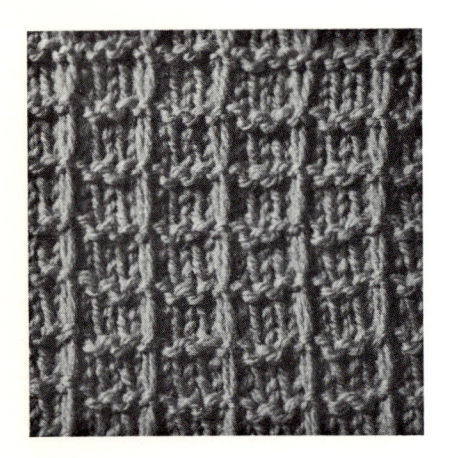

#103 (image)

#104 (image)

#105 (image)

#103 SLIP CHECK—*Multiple of 4 sts plus 3.*

Row 1: K 1, * sl 1, K 3—rep from *, end sl 1, K 1.
Row 2: P 1, * sl 1, P 3—rep from *, end sl 1, P 1.
Row 3: Same as Row 1.
Row 4: Knit all sts.
  Starting with Row 1, rep these 4 rows.
  Same uses, in all respects, as #102. Slip Check has even less vertical stretch than #102.

#104 STOCKINETTE STITCH WAVE—*Multiple of 8 sts plus 3.*

To Start: Purl 1 Row.
Rows 1 and 3: Purl all sts.
Rows 2 and 4: Knit all sts.
Row 5: Knit all sts.
Row 6: K 1, * K into the st 6 rows below the next st (under the ridge) and pull up a loop (not too high). Slip it to LH needle and Knit it. K next st and pull 2nd st on RH needle over the 1st st on the same needle; K 7—rep from *, end pull up and over as before, K 1.
Rows 7 and 9: Purl all sts.
Rows 8 and 10: Knit all sts.
Row 11: Knit all sts.
Row 12: K 5; rep between * * on Row 6, end K 5.
  Starting with Row 1, rep these 12 rows.
  This is a very easy stitch to knit and is useful in making crib blankets, afghans, and similar articles, but it should be planned carefully. It works particularly well in very fine yarn for baby sweaters.
  Suggested Trim: Seed Stitch or Garter Stitch.
  Suggested Ribbing: K 1, P 1 only.
  This stitch may be fully blocked.

#105 RIBBING WITH DIAGONAL SLIP STITCHES
  —*Multiple of 9 sts plus 3.*

Row 1: P 3, * yo, K 3, pull the yo over the K 3, K 3, P 3—rep from *, end same.
Row 2 and All Even-Numbered Rows: K 3, * P 6, K 3—rep from * across.
Row 3: P 3, * K 1, yo, K 3, pull yo over as before, K 2, P 3—rep from *, end same.
Row 5: P 3, * K 2, yo, K 3, pull yo over as before, K 1, P 3—rep from *, end same.
Row 7: P 3, * K 3, yo, K 3, pull yo over as before, P 3—rep from *, end same.
  Starting with Row 1, rep these 8 rows.
  This is an interesting stitch for suit jackets, short coats, and dressy sweaters for adults. When you use this pattern for a suit jacket, it is wise to choose a plain tailored pattern for the skirt. It is an excellent trimming stitch with good gathering qualities.

186

#106 **CROSS-STITCH BLOCK**—*Multiple of 8 sts plus 2.*

Rows 1, 3, 5, and 7: Knit all sts.
Rows 2, 4, 6, and 8: * K 2, P 6—rep from *, end K 2.
Row 9: K 7, * sl 1, K 2, sl 1, K 4—rep from *, end K 7.
Row 10: K 7, * yf, sl 1, yb, K 2, yf, sl 1, yb, K 4—rep from *, end K 7.
Row 11: Same as Row 9.
Row 12: Same as Row 10.
Row 13: K 7, * sl 3 on DP and hold in back, K next st, sl 2 from DP to LH needle and bring DP with the 1 st to front, K 2 from LH needle and K 1 from DP, K 4—rep from *, end K 7.
Row 14: Same as Row 2.
    Starting with Row 1, rep these 14 rows.
  This is an unusually good stitch for crib blankets or afghans using medium- to heavy-weight yarns, also for slightly bulky coat-sweaters or jackets.
  Suggested Trim: Garter Stitch.
  No ribbing.
  This stitch needs little or no blocking.

#106

#107 **GATHERED RIBBING**—*Multiple of 6 sts plus 3.*

Rows 1 and 3: * P 3, K 3—rep from *, end P 3.
Rows 2 and 4: * K 3, P 3—rep from *, end K 3.
Row 5: * P 3, K 3rd st on LH needle, then 2nd, and then 1st—rep from *, end P 3.
Rows 6 and 8: Purl all sts.
Row 7: Knit all sts.
Rows 9 and 11: * K 3, P 3—rep from *, end K 3.
Rows 10 and 12: * P 3, K 3—rep from *, end P 3.
Row 13: * K 3rd st on LH needle, then 2nd, and then 1st, P 3—rep from *, end as at beginning.
Rows 14 and 16: Purl all sts.
Row 15: Knit all sts.
    Starting with Row 1, rep these 16 rows.
  This is a good all-over stitch as well as a good trimming stitch for coat-sweaters or jackets. Smooth yarns emphasize the pattern, but crepe and nubby yarns may be used to make a contrast fabric for Stockinette.
  Suggested Trim: Stockinette, either side.
  Suggested Ribbing: K 3, P 3—or: K 1, P 1.
  May be blocked out flat or left unblocked, depending on the article.

#107

#108 **WAFFLE STITCH**—*Multiple of 3 sts plus 2.*

Row 1: * K 2, K 1 with 2 wraps—rep from *, end K 2.
Row 2: * P 2, sl 1, dropping the extra loop—rep from *, end P 2.
Row 3: * K 2, sl 1—rep from *, end K 2.
Row 4: * K 2, yf, sl 1, yb—rep from *, end K 2.
    Starting with Row 1, rep these 4 rows.

#108

187

This versatile pattern is appropriate for jackets or coat-sweaters. Unusually springy, it is one of the best stitches for accessories, such as purses, hats, and slippers. Its double thickness makes it especially warm. Because of its superior elasticity, it is well adapted for bathing wear if heavy-weight yarn and small-size needles are used. It is an excellent trimming and gathering stitch. In brief, it is an unusually good all-around stitch.

#109-A PALM LEAF *KNIT* FABRIC—*Multiple of 14 sts plus 8.*

All Odd-Numbered Rows: Purl all sts (Wrong Side).
Row 2: K 2, * cross R, cross L, K 10—rep from *, end cross R, cross L, K 2.
Row 4: K 1, * cross R, K 2, cross L, K 8—rep from *, end cross R, K 2, cross L, K 1.
Row 6: Same as Row 2.
Row 8: K 3, * cross through 2 sts R, K 12—rep from *, end cross through 2 sts R, K 3.
Row 10: Knit all sts.
Row 12: K 9, * cross R, cross L, K 10—rep from *, end K 9.
Row 14: K 8, * cross R, K 2, cross L, K 8—rep from *, end K 8.
Row 16: Same as Row 12.
Row 18: K 10, * cross through 2 sts R, K 12—rep from *, end K 10.
Row 20: Knit all sts.

Starting with Row 1, rep these 20 rows.

#109-A

#109-B PALM LEAF *PURL* FABRIC—*Multiple of 14 sts plus 8.*

Row 1: K 3, * P 2, K 12—rep from *, end P 2, K 3 (Wrong Side).
Row 2: P 2, * cross R, cross L, P 10—rep from *, end cross R, cross L, P 2.
Row 3: K 2, * P 4, K 10—rep from *, end P 4, K 2.
Row 4: P 1, * cross R, K 2, cross L, P 8—rep from *, end cross R, K 2, cross L, P 1.
Row 5: K 1, * P 6, K 8—rep from *, end P 6, K 1.
Row 6: P 1, * K 1, cross R, cross L, K 1, P 8—rep from *, end K 1, cross R, cross L, K 1, P 1.
Row 7: Same as Row 3.
Row 8: P 2, * K 1, cross through 2 sts R, K 1, P 10—rep from *, end K 1, cross through 2 sts R, K 1, P 2.
Row 9: Same as Row 1.
Row 10: P 3, * K 2, P 12—rep from *, end K 2, P 3.
Row 11: K 10, * P 2, K 12—rep from *, end K 10.
Row 12: P 9, * cross R, cross L, P 10—rep from *, end P 9.
Row 13: K 9, * P 4, K 10—rep from *, end K 9.
Row 14: P 8, * cross R, K 2, cross L, P 8—rep from *, end same.
Row 15: K 8, * P 6, K 8—rep from *, end same.
Row 16: P 8, * K 1, cross R, cross L, K 1, P 8—rep from *, end same.
Row 17: Same as Row 13.

#109-B

188

Row 18: P 9, * K 1, cross through 2 sts R, K 1, P 10 — rep from *, end P 9.
Row 19: Same as Row 11.
Row 20: P 10, * K 2, P 12 — rep from *, end P 10.
  Starting with Row 1, rep these 20 rows.

These stitches, and similar ones throughout this collection, have many uses. They might easily be compared to print fabrics in woven materials and are used in approximately the same manner. Some form very small patterns and may be used much like a small print or as contrast fabrics.

Either of these two stitches is good used alone in dressy coat-sweaters. Combined with Stockinette (either side), #109-A or #109-B adds interest to a one-piece dress or, in suits, as a contrast jacket with a plain Knit skirt. Either stitch shows up best using smooth yarn, but crepe and nubby yarns may also be used to advantage. This makes an excellent contrast stitch in cotton or linen yarn, but be sure to use the Reverse Stitch (see page 63) as the background knitting.

#110 CROSS-STITCH DIAMOND FABRIC — *Multiple of 6 sts plus 2.*

Note: All Even-Numbered Rows: Purl all sts.
Row 1: K 3, * cross R, K 4 — rep from *, end K 3.
Row 3: * K 2, cross R, cross L — rep from *, end K 2.
Row 5: K 1, * cross R, K 2, cross L — rep from *, end K 1.
Row 7: * cross R, K 4 — rep from *, end cross R.
Row 9: K 1, * cross L, K 2, cross R — rep from *, end K 1.
Row 11: * K 2, cross L, cross R — rep from *, end K 2.
  Starting with Row 1, rep these 12 rows.

This stitch has the same uses as #109. The crossed stitches make it a little more elastic. The diamonds show up very well in crepe and nubby yarns. The fabric may be blocked flat or left entirely unblocked, according to the use it is being put to.

#110

#111 DIAMOND CROSS — *Multiple of 10 sts.*

Row 1: P 4, * yb, sl 2, yf, P 8 — rep from *, end yb, sl 2, yf, P 4.
Row 2: K 4, * yf, sl 2, yb, K 8 — rep from *, end yf, sl 2, yb, K 4.
Row 3: P 2, * yb, sl 3 sts from L to R needle, sl next st to DP and hold in front, sl the 3 sts back to the LH needle and K the st from DP; P 2, sl next st to DP and hold in front, P 2, yb and K the st from DP, yf, P 4 — rep from *, end P 2.
Row 4: K 2, P 1, * K 4, P 1 — rep from *, end K 2.
Row 5: P 2, * yb, sl 1, yf, P 4 — rep from *, end yb, sl 1, yf, P 2.
Row 6: K 2, * yf, sl 1, yb, K 4 — rep from *, end yf, sl 1, yb, K 2.
Row 7: * sl 2 sts from L to R needle, sl next st to DP and hold in front, sl the 2 sts back to LH needle, K the st from DP, yf, P 6, sl next st to DP and hold in front, P 2, yb, K the st from DP — rep from *, end same.
Row 8: P 1, * K 8, P 2 — rep from *, end K 8, P 1.
Row 9: K 1, * P 8, yb, sl 2, yf — rep from *, end P 8, K 1.

#111

Row 10: P 1, * K 8, yf, sl 2, yb — rep from *, end K 8, P 1.
Row 11: * sl 1 st to DP and hold in front, yf, P 2, yb and K the st from DP, P 4, sl 3 sts from L to R needle, sl next st to DP and hold in front, sl the 3 sts back to LH needle, yb and K the st from DP, P 2, yb — rep from *, end sl 2 from LH needle, sl next st to DP and hold in front, sl the 2 sts back to LH needle, K the st from DP and P 2.
Row 12: K 2, P 1, * K 4, P 1 — rep from *, end K 2.
Row 13: Same as Row 5.
Row 14: Same as Row 6.
Row 15: P 2, * sl next st to DP and hold in front, P 2, yb, K the st from DP, sl next 2 sts from L to R needle, sl next st to DP and hold in front, sl the 2 sts back to LH needle, yb and K the st from DP, P 6 — rep from *, end P 4.
Row 16: K 4, * P 2, K 8 — rep from *, end P 2, K 4.
   Starting with Row 1, rep these 16 rows.
Very similar to #110, this stitch has the same uses. It is even more elastic than #110 because the sts are slipped as well as crossed. It combines the Knit crossed sts on a Purled background and so may be combined with either side of Stockinette as the Right Side of the foundation fabric.

#112 **TRAVELING DIAMOND AND RIBBING**
   —*Multiple of 9 sts plus 1.*

Row 1: K 1, * P 3, cross R, P 3, K 1 — rep from *, end same.
Row 2: P 1, * K 3, P 2, K 3, P 1 — rep from *, end same.
Row 3: K 1, * P 2, cross R, cross L, P 2, K 1 — rep from *, end same.
Row 4: P 1, * K 2, P 1 — rep from *, end same.
Row 5: K 1, * P 1, cross R, P 2, cross L, P 1, K 1 — rep from *, end same.
Row 6: P 1, * K 1, P 1, K 4, P 1, K 1, P 1 — rep from *, end same.
Row 7: K 1, * cross R, P 4, cross L, K 1 — rep from *, end same.
Row 8: P 2, * K 6, P 3 — rep from *, end P 2.
Row 9: K 1, * cross L, P 4, cross R, K 1 — rep from *, end same.
Row 10: Same as Row 6.
Row 11: K 1, * P 1, cross L, P 2, cross R, P 1, K 1 — rep from *, end same.
Row 12: Same as Row 4.
Row 13: K 1, * P 2, cross L, cross R, P 2, K 1 — rep from *, end same.
Row 14: Same as Row 2.
   Starting with Row 1, rep these 14 rows.
This stitch has the same uses and may be treated in exactly the same manner as #111. The only difference is the vertical stripe, which emphasizes height in a finished garment.

#113 **SMOCKED HONEYCOMB** — *Multiple of 8 sts plus 3.*

   Note: Method of making Tie Stitch on page 85.
   Rows 1, 3, 5, and 7: K 3, * P 1, K 3 — rep from *, end same.

#112

#113

190

Rows 2, 4, and 6: P 3, * K 1, P 3 — rep from *, end same.
Row 8: P 3, * Tie Stitch on 5 sts, work off K 1, P 3, K 1, then P 3 — rep from *, end same.
Rows 9, 11, 13, and 15: Same as Row 1.
Rows 10, 12, and 14: Same as Row 2.
Row 16: P 3, K 1, P 3, * Tie Stitch as above, P 3 — rep from *, end K 1, P 3.
    Starting with Row 1, rep these 16 rows.
  Similar in appearance to #111, this pattern is made with a Tie Stitch which draws the fabric in a little closer and makes it quite elastic. For a little closer smocking, Rows 6, 7, 14, and 15 may be omitted, making a 12-row pattern. It is a beautiful trimming stitch for gatherings at the yoke, waist, and sleeves of baby garments. A contrasting color may be worked over the knitted smocking points.

#114 **KNOTTED TRELLIS STITCH** — *Multiple of 8 sts.*

Set-Up Row — *Do Not Repeat:* P 3, * K 2, P 6 — rep from *, end K 2, P 3 (Right Side).
Row 1: K 3, * yf, sl 2, yb, K 6 — rep from *, end yf, sl 2, yb, K 3.
Row 2: P 3, * cross R, P 6 — rep from *, end cross R, P 3.
Row 3: K 3, * (KPK)x2, K 6 — rep from *, (KPK)x2, K 3.
Row 4: P 3, * K 3 tog, K 3 tog b, P 6 — rep from *, end K 3 tog, K 3 tog b, P 3.
Row 5: Same as Row 1.
Row 6: Same as Row 2.
Row 7: Same as Row 1.
Row 8: P 2, * cross R, cross L, P 4 — rep from *, end P 2.
Row 9: K 2, * yf, sl 1, yb, K 2, yf, sl 1, yb, K 4 — rep from *, end K 2.
Row 10: P 1, * cross R, P 2, cross L, P 2 — rep from *, end P 1.
Row 11: K 1, * yf, sl 1, yb, K 4, yf, sl 1, yb, K 2 — rep from *, end K 1.
Row 12: * cross R, P 4, cross L — rep from *, end same.
Row 13: P 1, * K 6, yf, sl 2, yb — rep from *, end P 1.
Row 14: K 1, * P 6, cross R — rep from *, end K 1.
Row 15: KPK, * K 6, (KPK)x2 — rep from *, end KPK.
Row 16: K 3 tog b, * P 6, K 3 tog, K 3 tog b — rep from *, end K 3 tog.
Row 17: Same as Row 13.
Row 18: Same as Row 14.
Row 19: Same as Row 13.
Row 20: * cross L, P 4, cross R — rep from *, end same.
Row 21: Same as Row 11.
Row 22: P 1, * cross L, P 2, cross R, P 2 — rep from *, end P 1.
Row 23: Same as Row 9.
Row 24: P 2, * cross L, cross R, P 4 — rep from *, end P 2.
    Starting with Row 1, rep these 24 rows.
  This is a more elaborate variation of #111 and may be used in the same manner. Carry the yarn *loosely* when slipping sts.

#114

191

#115

#115 OVERLAY STITCH—*Multiple of 4 sts plus 1.*

Row 1: P 1, * yb, sl 3, yf, P 1—rep from *, end same.
Row 2: Knit all sts.
Row 3: Purl all sts.
Row 4: K 2, * K under loop below and next st on LH needle, together, K 3—rep from *, end K 2.
Row 5: P 3, * yb, sl 3, yf, P 1—rep from *, end P 3.
Row 6: Knit all sts.
Row 7: Purl all sts.
Row 8: K 4, * K under loop and st as before, K 3—rep from *, end K 4.
  Starting with Row 1, rep these 8 rows.

This petite simulation of #110, made in an entirely different manner, may be used in the same way for more diminutive purposes, such as an all-over pattern for baby garments or as a trimming stitch.

#116-A CROSS-STITCH FABRIC I—*Multiple of 3 sts plus 1.*

Row 1: * K 1, sl 1 K-wise, K in front and back of next st and psso—rep from *, end K 1.
Row 2: Purl all sts.
  Repeat these 2 rows throughout.

#116-B CROSS-STITCH FABRIC II—*Multiple of 3 sts plus 1.*

Row 1: * K 1, sl 1 K-wise, K in front and back of next st and psso—rep from *, end K 1.
Row 2: Purl all sts.
Row 3: * sl 1 K-wise, K in front and back of next st and psso, K 1—rep from *, end K 2.
Row 4: Purl all sts.
  Starting with Row 1, rep these 4 rows.

#116-A

#116-C CROSS-STITCH FABRIC III—*Multiple of 3 sts plus 1.*

Note: All Odd-Numbered Rows: Purl all sts.
Row 2: * K 1, sl 1 K-wise, K in front and back of next st, psso—rep from *, end K 1.
Row 4: * sl 1 K-wise, K in front and back of next st, psso, K 1—rep from *, end K 1.
Row 6: K 2, * sl 1 K-wise, K in front and back of next st, psso, K 1—rep from *, end sl 1, K in front and back of next st, psso.
  Starting with Row 1, rep these 6 rows.

All three versions of #116 are very elastic indeed, perfect for fabrics that must be not too close, yet must not stretch. It is one of the finest fabric stitches for use with cotton or linen yarns. Pattern Stitch #116-A gives a narrow striped effect, #116-B a little wider stripe, and #116-C an all-over pattern. All are good for any weight of yarn, fine for trimming or contrast but not suitable as a gathering stitch because the gauge is nearly the same gauge as Stockinette when made on the same size needles.

#116-B

#117 **CABLE BOWKNOT**—*Multiple of 16 sts plus 1.*

Row 1: Purl all sts.
Row 2: Knit all sts.
Row 3: P 6, * K 1, P 3, K 1, P 11—rep from *, end P 6.
Row 4: K 6, * P 1, K 3, P 1, K 11—rep from *, end K 6.
Row 5: Same as Row 3.
Row 6: Same as Row 4.
Row 7: P 6, * sl 4 sts on DP front, K next st, sl 3 sts from DP to LH needle and P these 3 sts, then K the st from DP, P 11—rep from *, end P 6.
Row 8: Same as Row 4.
Row 9: Same as Row 3.
Row 10: Same as Row 4.
Row 11: Same as Row 7.
Row 12: Same as Row 4.
Row 13: Same as Row 3.
Row 14: Same as Row 4.
Row 15: Purl all sts.
Row 16: Knit all sts.
Row 17: P 14, * K 1, P 3, K 1, P 11—rep from *, end P 14.
Row 18: K 14, * P 1, K 3, P 1, K 11—rep from *, end K 14.
Row 19: Same as Row 17.
Row 20: Same as Row 18.
Row 21: * P 14, cross as in Row 7, P 11—rep from *, end P 14.
Row 22: Same as Row 18.
Row 23: Same as Row 17.
Row 24: Same as Row 18.
Row 25: Same as Row 21.
Row 26: Same as Row 18.
Row 27: Same as Row 17.
Row 28: Same as Row 18.
  Starting with Row 1, rep these 28 rows.

This pretty stitch is good for trimming or contrast in any type or weight of yarn, and may be combined with either side of Stockinette as the foundation fabric. It is most attractive used as the yoke or top of a one-piece dress, or as a suit jacket or a separate short coat or cardigan.

  Suggested Trim: Stockinette, either side.
  Suggested Ribbing: K 1, P 1.

#118 **SLIP CROSS FABRIC**—*Multiple of 4 sts plus 1.*

  Note: Method of crossing 1 over 2, R and L, on page 79.
Row 1: P 1, * P 1 with 2 wraps, P 3—rep from *, end same.
Row 2: * K 3, sl 1 with yarn in back, letting the extra loop drop—rep from *, end K 1.
Row 3: P 1, * sl 1 with yarn in front, P 3—rep from *, end same.

#116-C

#117

#118

193

Row 4: * K 1, cross 1 over 2 R—rep from *, end K 1.
Row 5: P 4, * P 1 with 2 wraps, P 3—rep from *, end P 4.
Row 6: K 4, * sl 1 with yarn in back, letting the extra loop drop, K 3—rep from *, end K 4.
Row 7: P 4, * sl 1 with yarn in front, P 3—rep from *, end P 4.
Row 8: K 4, * cross 1 over 2 L, K 1—rep from *, end K 2.
    Starting with Row 1, rep these 8 rows.
  Same uses as in #116. In addition, Slip Cross Fabric acts as a good gathering stitch.

#119-A BOWKNOT STITCH I (often called Butterfly Stitch)—*Multiple of 14 sts plus 9.*

Note: Method of working is fully explained on page 86.
Rows 1, 3, and 5: Purl all sts.
Rows 2, 4, and 6: Knit all sts.
Rows 7, 9, and 11: P 8, * yb and sl 7 sts, yf, P 7—rep from *, end P 8.
Rows 8 and 10: Knit all sts.
Row 12: K 11, * make bowknot, K 13—rep from *, end K 11.
Rows 13, 15, and 17: Purl all sts.
Rows 14, 16, and 18: Knit all sts.
Rows 19, 21, and 23: P 1—rep between * * on Row 7—end P 1.
Rows 20 and 22: Knit all sts.
Row 24: K 4—rep between * * on Row 12—end K 4.
    Starting with Row 1, rep these 24 rows.

#119-A

#119-B BOWKNOT STITCH II—*Multiple of 14 sts plus 9.*

Rows 1, 3, and 5: Knit all sts.
Rows 2, 4, and 6: Purl all sts.
Rows 7, 9, and 11: K 8, * sl 7 with yarn in back, K 7—rep from *, end K 8.
Rows 8 and 10: Purl all sts.
Row 12: P 11, * make bowknot (with a Knit st), P 13—rep from *, end P 11.
Rows 13, 15, and 17: Knit all sts.
Rows 14, 16, and 18: Purl all sts.
Rows 19, 21, and 23: K 1—rep between * * on Row 7—end K 1.
Row 24: P 4; rep between * * on Row 12—end P 4.
    Starting with Row 1, rep these 24 rows.
  These charming stitches must be considered carefully when you plan your design. They should be used as an all-over pattern, only for garments and articles where the bowknot sts are not apt to be caught and ripped. In heavy-weight yarn (4-ply worsted, Germantown, and heavier) they are fine for carriage or crib blankets outlined by three or more inches of a suitable framing stitch.

#119-B

#120 **LAZY DAISY**—*Multiple of 10 sts plus 5.*

Note: Purl one row to begin.
Rows 1, 3, 9, and 11: Knit all sts.
Rows 2, 4, 8, 10, and 12: Purl all sts.
Row 5: K 5, * insert needle into a st 5 rows beneath the 3rd st from point of LH needle and pull up a loop, K 5, pull up another loop from the same st below, K 5—rep from *, end same.
Row 6: P 4, * P 2 tog b, P 5, P 2 tog, P 3—rep from *, end P 4.
Row 7: K 7, * pull up a loop from the same st below where loops were made in Row 5, place it on LH needle and K through back of loop and front of next st, together, K 9—rep from *, end K 7.
Row 13: K 10—rep between * * of Row 5—end K 10.
Row 14: P 9—rep between * * of Row 6—end P 9.
Row 15: K 12—rep between * * of Row 7—end K 12.
Row 16: Purl all sts.
   Starting with Row 1, rep these 16 rows.
This is another stitch that looks difficult but is really easy to make and is pretty either as an all-over pattern or a contrast or trimming stitch. It works equally well in smooth and novelty yarns and is attractive made with fine yarns for baby garments.

#120

#121 **LEAF FABRIC**—*Multiple of 16 sts plus 1.*

Row 1: P 8, * K 1, yo, P 7—rep from *, end P 8.
Row 2: K 8, * P 2, K 7—rep from *, end K 8.
Row 3: P 8, * K 2, yo, P 7—rep from *, end P 8.
Row 4: K 8, * P 3, K 7—rep from *, end K 8.
Row 5: P 8, * K 3, yo, P 7—rep from *, end P 8.
Row 6: K 8, * P 4, K 7—rep from *, end K 8.
Row 7: P 8, * K 4, yo, P 7—rep from *, end P 8.
Row 8: K 8, * P 5, K 7—rep from *, end K 8.
Row 9: P 8, * K 5, yo, P 7—rep from *, end P 8.
Row 10: K 8, * P 6, K 7—rep from *, end K 8.
Row 11: P 8, * K 6, yo, P 7—rep from *, end P 8.
Row 12: K 8, * P 7, K 7—rep from *, end K 8.
Row 13: P 8, * K 5, K 2 tog, P 7—rep from *, end P 8.
Row 14: K 8, * P 2 tog, P 4, K 7—rep from *, end K 8.
Row 15: P 8, * K 3, K 2 tog, P 7—rep from *, end P 8.
Row 16: K 8, * P 2 tog, P 2, K 7—rep from *, end K 8.
Row 17: P 8, * K 1, K 2 tog, P 7—rep from *, end P 8.
Row 18: K 8, * P 2 tog, P 7—rep from *, end K 8.
Row 19: P 4, * K 1, yo, P 7—rep from *, end K 1, yo, P 4.
Row 20: K 4, * P 2, K 7—rep from *, end K 4.
Row 21: P 4, * K 2, yo, P 7—rep from *, end K 2, yo, P 4.
Row 22: K 4, * P 3, K 7—rep from *, end K 4.
Row 23: P 4, * K 3, yo, P 7—rep from *, end K 3, yo, P 4.
Row 24: K 4, * P 4, K 7—rep from *, end K 4.

#121

195

Row 25: P 4, * K 4, yo, P 7 — rep from *, end K 4, yo, P 4.
Row 26: K 4, * P 5, K 7 — rep from *, end K 4.
Row 27: P 4, * K 5, yo, P 7 — rep from *, end K 5, yo, P 4.
Row 28: K 4, * P 6, K 7 — rep from *, end K 4.
Row 29: P 4, * K 6, yo, P 7 — rep from *, end K 6, yo, P 4.
Row 30: K 4, * P 7, K 7 — rep from *, end K 4.
Row 31: P 4, * K 5, K 2 tog, P 7 — rep from *, end P 4.
Row 32: K 4, * P 2 tog, P 4, K 7 — rep from *, end K 4.
Row 33: P 4, * K 3, K 2 tog, P 7 — rep from *, end P 4.
Row 34: K 4, * P 2 tog, P 2, K 7 — rep from *, end K 4.
Row 35: P 4, * K 1, K 2 tog, P 7 — rep from *, end P 4.
Row 36: K 4, * P 2 tog, K 7 — rep from *, end K 4.

Starting with Row 1, rep these 36 rows.

Used correctly, this embossed fabric is very effective. As an all-over fabric it is apt to be rather heavy and clumsy, but used sparingly, it makes a very good contrast or trimming stitch. All types of yarns may be used for it.

#122 EMBOSSED LEAF PATTERN — *Multiple of 16 sts plus 15.*

Note: The 1st Made st (M 1) is a Make 1 Right, and the 2nd Made st is a Make 1 Left — see page 74.

Row 1: * P 15, M 1, K 1, M 1 — rep from *, end P 15.
Row 2: * K 15, P 3 — rep from *, end K 15.
Row 3: * P 15, M 1, K 3, M 1 — rep from *, end P 15.
Row 4: * K 15, P 5 — rep from *, end K 15.
Row 5: * P 15, M 1, K 1, SKP, K 2, M 1 — rep from *, end P 15.
Row 6: * K 15, P 6 — rep from *, end K 15.
Row 7: * P 15, M 1, K 2, SKP, K 2, M 1 — rep from *, end P 15.
Row 8: * K 15, P 7 — rep from *, end K 15.
Row 9: * P 15, M 1, K 3, SKP, K 2, M 1 — rep from *, end P 15.
Row 10: * K 15, P 8 — rep from *, end K 15.
Row 11: * P 15, K 4, SKP, K 2 — rep from *, end P 15.
Row 12: * K 15, P 7 — rep from *, end K 15.
Row 13: * P 15, SKP, K 1, SKP, K 2 tog — rep from *, end P 15.
Row 14: * K 15, P 4 — rep from *, end K 15.
Row 15: * P 15, SKP, K 2 tog — rep from *, end P 15.
Row 16: * K 15, P 2 tog — rep from *, end K 15.
Rows 17 and 19: Purl all sts.
Rows 18 and 20: Knit all sts.
Row 21: P 7, * M 1, K 1, M 1, P 15 — rep from *, end M 1, K 1, M 1, P 7.
Row 22: K 7, * P 3, K 15 — rep from *, end P 3, K 7.
Row 23: P 7, * M 1, K 3, M 1, P 15 — rep from *, end M 1, K 3, M 1, P 7.
Row 24: K 7, * P 5, K 15 — rep from *, end P 5, K 7.
Row 25: P 7, * M 1, K 1, SKP, K 2, M 1, P 15 — rep from *, end M 1, K 1, SKP, K 2, M 1, P 7.
Row 26: K 7, * P 6, K 15 — rep from *, end P 6, K 7.
Row 27: P 7, * M 1, K 2, SKP, K 2, M 1, P 15 — rep from *, end M 1, K 2, SKP, K 2, M 1, P 7.
Row 28: K 7, * P 7, K 15 — rep from *, end P 7, K 7.

#122

Row 29: P 7, * M 1, K 3, SKP, K 2, M 1, P 15 — rep from *, end M 1, K 3, SKP, K 2, M 1, P 7.
Row 30: K 7, * P 8, K 15 — rep from *, end P 8, K 7.
Row 31: P 7, * K 4, SKP, K 2, P 15 — rep from *, end K 4, SKP, K 2, P 7.
Row 32: K 7, * P 7, K 15 — rep from *, end P 7, K 7.
Row 33: P 7, * SKP, K 1, SKP, K 2 tog, P 15 — rep from*, end SKP, K 1, SKP, K 2 tog, P 7.
Row 34: K 7, * P 4, K 15 — rep from *, end P 4, K 7.
Row 35: P 7, * SKP, K 2 tog, P 15 — rep from *, end SKP, K 2 tog, P 7.
Row 36: K 7, * P 2 tog, K 15 — rep from *, end P 2 tog, K 7.
Rows 37 and 39: Purl all sts.
Rows 38 and 40: Knit all sts.
    Starting with Row 1, rep these 40 rows.
Same uses, in every respect, as #121.

#123 TUFTED ROSETTE—*Multiple of 12 sts plus 9.*

Note: For method of making a Tuft, see page 85.
All Even-Numbered Rows: Purl all sts.
Rows 1 and 3: Knit all sts.
Row 5: K 10, * Make an 8 st tuft (KPKPKPKP) in next st, K 11 — rep from *, end K 10.
Row 7: * K 9, tuft, K 1, tuft — rep from *, end K 9.
Row 9: Same as Row 7.
Row 11: Same as Row 5.
Rows 13 and 15: Knit all sts.
Row 17: K 4, * tuft, K 11 — rep from *, end K 4.
Row 19: K 3, * tuft, K 1, tuft, K 9 — rep from *, end K 3.
Row 21: Same as Row 19.
Row 23: Same as Row 17.
Row 24: Purl all sts.
    Starting with Row 1, rep these 24 rows.
This beautiful trimming or contrast stitch can be made in any yarn, but it is best in a smooth one. In very fine yarns it makes a dainty yoke for a baby's or little girl's dress. For an evening blouse, sew a pearl bead in the center of each rosette.

#123

#124 OBLIQUE KNOT STITCH—*Multiple of 6 sts.*

Note: Each knot is worked KPKPKP into one st — see page 85.
Row 1: * K 2, knot, P 3 — rep from *, end same.
Row 2: * K 3, P 3 — rep from *, end same.
Row 3: P 1, * K 2, knot, P 3 — rep from *, end P 2.
Row 4: K 2, * P 3, K 3 — rep from *, end K 1.
Row 5: P 2, * K 2, knot, P 3 — rep from *, end P 1.
Row 6: K 1, * P 3, K 3 — rep from *, end K 2.
Row 7: * P 3, K 2, knot — rep from *, end P 3, K 3.
Row 8: * P 3, K 3 — rep from *, end same.
Row 9: K 1, * P 3, K 2, knot — rep from *, end K 2.
Row 10: P 2, * K 3, P 3 — rep from *, end P 1.
Row 11: K 2, * P 3, K 2, knot — rep from *, end K 1.
Row 12: P 1, * K 3, P 3 — rep from *, end P 2.

#124

197

Starting with Row 1, rep these 12 rows.

This stitch is better used as a trimming or contrast than as an all-over pattern. Smooth yarns should be used, although crepe yarns are also adaptable to it.

NON-REVERSIBLE STITCHES

#125 CLOVER AND DIAMOND—*Multiple of 15 sts.*

Note: Numbers of sts change between rows.
Set-Up Row—*Do Not Repeat:* P 3, * K 9, P 6—rep from *, end P 3.
Row 1: K 2, * SKP, P 3, yo, P 2 tog, P 2, K 2 tog, K 2, yo, K 2—rep from *, end K 2 tog, K 2.
Row 2: * P 3, K 7, P 3, K 1—rep from *, end P 3.
Row 3: K 2, * SKP, P 6, K 3, yo, P 1, yo, K 2—rep from *, end K 3.
Row 4: * P 3, K 6, P 3, K 3—rep from *, end P 3.
Row 5: K 2, * SKP, P 4, K 2 tog, K 2, yo, P 3, yo, K 2—rep from *, end K 2 tog, K 2.
Row 6: * P 3, K 4, P 3, K 5—rep from *, end P 3, K 4, P 3.
Row 7: K 2, * SKP, P 2, K 2 tog, K 2, yo, P 5, yo, K 2—rep from *, end K 2 tog, K 2.
Row 8: * P 3, K 2, P 3, K 7—rep from *, end P 3.
Row 9: K 2, * SKP, K 2 tog, K 2, yo, P 1, P 2 tog, yo, P 1, yo, P 2 tog, P 1, yo, K 2—rep from *, end SKP, K 2 tog, K 2.
Row 10: * cable 3 and 3 Purled front, K 9—rep from *, end cable 3 and 3 Purled front.
Row 11: K 3, * yo, K 2, SKP, P 3, yo, P 2 tog, P 2, K 2 tog, K 2—rep from *, end yo, K 3.
Row 12: P 3, * K 1, P 3, K 7, P 3—rep from *, end K 1, P 3.
Row 13: K 3, * yo, P 1, yo, K 2, SKP, P 5, K 2 tog, K 2—rep from *, end yo, P 1, yo, K 3.
Row 14: P 3, * K 3, P 3, K 5, P 3—rep from *, end K 3, P 3.
Row 15: K 3, * yo, P 3, yo, K 2, SKP, P 3, K 2 tog, K 2—rep from *, end yo, P 3, yo, K 3.
Row 16: P 3, * K 5, P 3, K 3, P 3—rep from *, end K 5, P 3.
Row 17: K 3, * yo, P 5, yo, K 2, SKP, P 1, K 2 tog, K 2—rep from *, end yo, P 5, yo, K 3.
Row 18: P 3, * K 7, P 3, K 1, P 3—rep from *, end K 7, P 3.
Row 19: K 3, * yo, P 1, P 2 tog, yo, P 1, yo, P 2 tog, P 1, yo, K 2, SKP, K 3—rep from *, end yo, K 3.
Row 20: P 3, * K 9, cable 3 and 3 Purled front—rep from *, end K 9, P 3.

Starting with Row 1, rep these 20 rows.

This true cable stitch is very elastic. Good as a trimming stitch or as an all-over pattern on baby blankets or afghan strips, it shows up best in smooth yarns.

#125

198

#126 **RAMBLER ROSE**—*Multiple of 22 sts plus 1.*

Note: All increases (M 1) in the following pattern are made P-wise.

Method of working Rosebud (RB) and Leaf is found on pages 86–87. Method of cabling K 3, P 1, K 3 is found on page 84.

Row 1: * P 1, M 1, K 3, P 2 tog, P 5, K 1, P 5, P 2 tog b, K 3, M 1—rep from *, end M 1, P 1.
Row 2: K 2, * P 3, K 6, P 1, K 6, P 3, K 3—rep from *, end K 2.
Row 3: P 2, M 1, * K 3, P 2 tog, P 4, RB, P 4, P 2 tog b, K 3, M 1, P 3, M 1—rep from *, end M 1, P 2.
Row 4: K 3, * P 3, K 11, P 3, K 5—rep from *, end K 3.
Row 5: P 3, M 1, * K 3, P 2 tog, P 7, P 2 tog b, K 3, M 1, P 2, K 1, P 2, M 1—rep from *, end M 1, P 3.
Row 6: K 4, * P 3, K 9, P 3, K 3, P 1, K 3—rep from *, end K 4.
Row 7: P 4, M 1, * K 3, P 2 tog, P 5, P 2 tog b, K 3, M 1, P 3, K 1, P 3, M 1—rep from *, end M 1, P 4.
Row 8: K 5, * P 3, K 7, P 3, K 4, P 1, K 4—rep from *, end K 5.
Row 9: P 5, M 1, * K 3, P 2 tog, P 3, P 2 tog b, K 3, M 1, P 4, K 1, P 4, M 1—rep from *, end M 1, P 5.
Row 10: K 6, * P 3, K 5, P 3, K 5, P 1, K 5—rep from *, end K 6.
Row 11: P 6, M 1, * K 3, P 2 tog, P 1, P 2 tog b, K 3, M 1, P 5, K 1, P 5, M 1—rep from *, end M 1, P 6.
Row 12: K 7, * P 3, K 3, P 3, K 6, P 1, K 6—rep from *, end K 7.
Row 13: P 7, M 1, * K 3, P 3 tog, K 3, M 1, P 6, K 1, P 6, M 1—rep from *, end M 1, P 7.
Row 14: K 8, * P 3, K 1, P 3, K 7, P 1, K 7—rep from *, end K 8.
Row 15: P 8, * cable K 3, P 1 and K 3, back, P 4, Leaf 6 rows down, P 3, K 1, P 3, Leaf 7 rows down, P 4, cable K 3, P 1 and K 3, front—rep from *, end P 8.
Row 16: K 8, * P 3, K 1, P 3, K 3, K 2 tog, K 3, P 1, K 3, K 2 tog b, K 3—rep from *, end K 8.
Row 17: P 6, P 2 tog b, * K 3, M 1, P 1, M 1, K 3, P 2 tog, P 5, K 1, P 5, P 2 tog b—rep from *, end P 2 tog, P 6.
Row 18: K 7, * P 3, K 3, P 3, K 6, P 1, K 6—rep from *, end K 7.
Row 19: P 5, P 2 tog b, * K 3, M 1, P 3, M 1, K 3, P 2 tog, P 4, RB, P 4, P 2 tog b—rep from *, end P 2 tog, P 5.
Row 20: K 6, * P 3, K 5, P 3, K 11—rep from *, end K 6.
Row 21: P 4, P 2 tog b, * K 3, M 1, P 2, K 1, P 2, M 1, K 3, P 2 tog, P 7, P 2 tog b—rep from *, end P 2 tog, P 4.
Row 22: K 5, * P 3, K 3, P 1, K 3, P 3, K 9—rep from *, end K 5.
Row 23: P 3, P 2 tog b, * K 3, M 1, P 3, K 1, P 3, M 1, K 3, P 2 tog, P 5, P 2 tog b—rep from *, end P 2 tog, P 3.
Row 24: K 4, * P 3, K 4, P 1, K 4, P 3, K 7—rep from *, end K 4.
Row 25: P 2, P 2 tog b, * K 3, M 1, P 4, K 1, P 4, M 1, K 3, P 2 tog, P 3, P 2 tog b—rep from *, end P 2 tog, P 2.
Row 26: K 3, * P 3, K 5, P 1, K 5, P 3, K 5—rep from *, end K 3.
Row 27: P 1, P 2 tog b, * K 3, M 1, P 5, K 1, P 5, M 1, K 3, P 2 tog, P 1, P 2 tog b—rep from *, end P 2 tog, P 1.

#126

Row 28: K 2, * P 3, K 6, P 1, K 6, P 3, K 3 — rep from *, end K 2.
Row 29: P 2 tog b, * K 3, M 1, P 6, K 1, P 6, M 1, K 3, P 3 tog — rep from *, end P 2 tog.
Row 30: K 1, * P 3, K 7, P 1, K 7, P 3, K 1 — rep from *, end same.
Row 31: P 1, K 3, * P 4, Leaf, P 3, K 1, P 3, Leaf, P 4, cable K 3, P 1 and K 3 back, P 4, Leaf, P 3, K 1, P 3, Leaf, P 4, cable K 3, P 1 and K 3 front — rep from *, end K 3, P 1.
Row 32: K 1, P 3, * K 3, K 2 tog, K 3, P 1, K 3, K 2 tog b, K 3, P 3, K 1, P 3 — rep from *, end P 3, K 1.
   Starting with Row 1, rep these 32 rows.
   Same uses as #125. Very good-looking when used as the two fronts of Aran Islands-style cardigans. This is a very feminine stitch.

#127 WINDING VINE AND STRIPE — *Multiple of 6 sts.*

Row 1: Knit all sts (Right Side).
Row 2: P 2, * K 2, P 4 — rep from *, end P 2.
Row 3: K 1, * cross L, K 4 — rep from *, end K 3.
Row 4: P 2, * K 1, P 1, K 1, P 3 — rep from *, end P 1.
Row 5: K 2, * cross L, K 4 — rep from *, end K 2.
Row 6: P 3, K 2, * P 4, K 2 — rep from *, end P 1.
Row 7: Knit all sts.
Row 8: Same as Row 6.
Row 9: K 2, * cross R, K 4 — rep from *, end K 2.
Row 10: Same as Row 4.
Row 11: K 1, * cross R, K 4 — rep from *, end K 3.
Row 12: Same as Row 2.
   Starting with Row 1, rep these 12 rows.
   This stitch is equally attractive as an all-over pattern or as a contrast or trimming stitch. It may be used for pullovers, or cardigans in all sizes for children or adults, as sections of these, or for a suit jacket to go with a skirt in which Stockinette predominates. One pattern multiple may be used as an outline of panels in the skirt, spaced either closely or far apart.
   Suggested Trim: Stockinette, either side, Garter Stitch, or Seed Stitch.
   Suggested Ribbing: K 1, P 1.
   Block lightly.

#128 TINY TOWER — *Multiple of 8 sts plus 1.*

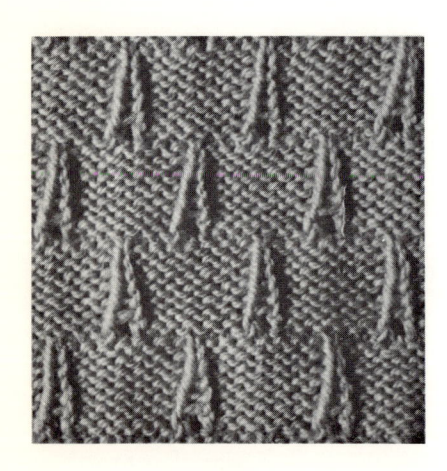

Row 1: P 4, * yo, P 2 tog, P 6 — rep from *, end yo, P 2 tog, P 3.
Rows 2, 4, and 6: K 4, * P 1, K 7 — rep from *, end K 4.
Rows 3, 5, and 7: P 4, * K 1, P 7 — rep from *, end P 4.
Row 8: Purl all sts.
Row 9: P 8, * yo, P 2 tog, P 6 — rep from *, end P 2 tog, P 7.
Rows 10, 12, and 14: K 8, * P 1, K 7 — rep from *, end K 8.
Rows 11, 13, and 15: P 8, * K 1, P 7 — rep from *, end K 1, P 8.
Row 16: Purl all sts.
   Starting with Row 1, rep these 16 rows.

This all-over pattern stitch is adaptable to almost any type of garment or article: sweaters, afghans, baby garments; nearly everything where Stockinette can be used. It is particularly effective as a suit jacket or top (or part of the top) of a one-piece dress. Smooth or crepe yarns are advised, as the pattern does not show up as well with nubby yarns.

#129 SMALL DIAMOND DOT—*Multiple of 8 sts plus 7.*

Row 1: Knit all sts.
Row 2: P 3, * K 1, P 7 – rep from *, end K 1, P 3.
Row 3: K 2, * P 3, K 5 – rep from *, end P 3, K 2.
Row 4: P 1, * K 5, P 3 – rep from *, end K 5, P 1.
Row 5: * P 2, P 2 tog, yo, P 3, K 1 – rep from *, end P 2, P 2 tog, yo, P 3.
Row 6: Same as Row 4.
Row 7: Same as Row 3.
Row 8: Same as Row 2.
   Starting with Row 1, rep these 8 rows.
   Same uses as #128, but this pattern is slightly more open. It should be fully blocked.

#130 BRIDAL VEIL STITCH—*Multiple of 4 sts plus 2.*

All Odd-Numbered Rows: Purl all sts.
Row 2: K 1, * pu 1 (K-wise), K 1, pu 1, SK2togP – rep from *, end K 1.
Row 4: K 1, * SK2togP, pu 1, K 1, pu 1 – rep from *, end (pu 1, K 1)x2.
   Starting with Row 1, rep these 4 rows.
   This versatile stitch may be used as an all-over pattern or as a trimming stitch, and is shown here worked with medium-weight yarn on #3 needles. It may be used as the basic stitch for cool-weather sweaters, either pullovers or cardigans, for blouses or trimming for blouses (either as a contrast fabric or with one or two repeats of the pattern). When knitted in a smooth novelty yarn which includes some rayon, it may be used for evening wear, either blouses or dresses. This stitch is easy to work and knits up very quickly on large needles.
   WARNING! If you use larger-than-normal-size needles, be sure to take the gauge both *before* and *after* blocking.
   Suggested Trim: Stockinette or any good trimming stitch.
   Suggested Ribbing: K 1, P 1.

#131 TRIPLET RIBBING—*Multiple of 12 sts plus 7.*

All Odd-Numbered Rows: K 2, * P 3, K 3 – rep from *, end P 3, K 2.
Row 2: P 2, * Kb 3 times, P 3 – rep from *, end Kb 3 times, P 2.
Row 4: P 2, * yo, SK2togP, yo, P 3, Kb 3 times – rep from *, end yo, SK2togP, yo, P 2.
Row 6: Same as Row 2.
Row 8: P 2, * Kb 3 times, P 3, yo, SK2togP, yo, P 3 – rep from *, end Kb 3 times, P 2.
   Starting with Row 1, rep these 8 rows.

#129

#130

#131

201

This is another versatile stitch and may be used in the same ways as #127 and #128. It is more elastic, as is any ribbing stitch. Since it is a vertical stitch, it might be more flattering to some figures than the more horizontal #128.

One pattern multiple makes an outline or trimming pattern for panels of a skirt. The pattern is excellent for linen or cotton yarns, and is also good for heavy-weight yarns.

#132 TINY EYELET RIBBING—*Multiple of 5 sts plus 2.*

Row 1: * P 2, K 3—rep from *, end P 2.
Row 2: * K 2, P 3—rep from *, end K 2.
Row 3: * P 2, sl 1, K 2 and pass the sl st over the K 2—rep from *, end P 2.
Row 4: * K 2, P 1, yo, P 1—rep from *, end K 2.
    Starting with Row 1, rep these 4 rows.
Same uses as #131.

#133 OPEN STRIPE—*Multiple of 5 sts plus 6.*

Row 1: K 2, * yo, K 2 tog, K 3—rep from *, end yo, K 2 tog, K 2.
Row 2: P 2, * yo, P 2 tog, P 3—rep from *, end yo, P 2 tog, P 2.
    Repeat these 2 rows throughout.
Same uses as #131. However, this is a somewhat more conservative pattern.

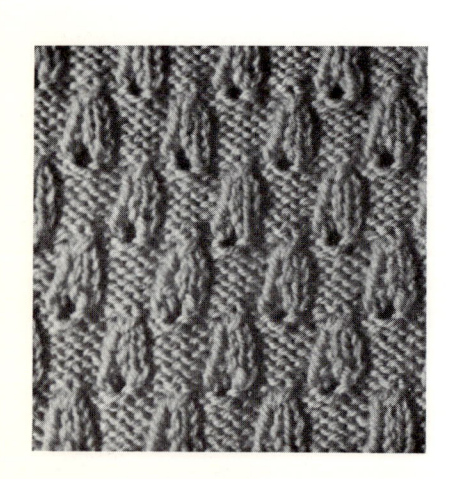

#134 TEAR DROP—*Multiple of 6 sts plus 5.*

Row 1: P 5, * K 1, yo, P 5—rep from *, end same (Right Side).
Row 2: K 5, * P 2, K 5—rep from *, end same.
Row 3: P 5, * K 2, P 5—rep from *, end same.
Row 4: Same as Row 2.
Row 5: Same as Row 3.
Row 6: K 5, * P 2 tog, K 5—rep from *, end same.
Row 7: P 2, * K 1, yo, P 5—rep from *, end K 1, yo, P 2.
Row 8: K 2, * P 2, K 5—rep from *, end P 2, K 2.
Row 9: P 2, * K 2, P 5—rep from *, end K 2, P 2.
Row 10: Same as Row 8.
Row 11: Same as Row 9.
Row 12: K 2, * P 2 tog, K 5—rep from *, end P 2 tog, K 2.
    Starting with Row 1, rep these 12 rows.
This stitch may be used in the same ways as #127.

#135 SIMPLE LACE PATTERN—*Any Odd Number of Sts.*

Rows 1 and 3: Knit all sts.
Rows 2 and 4: Purl all sts.
Row 5: K 2 tog all across the row, end K 1.
Row 6: * K 1, pu 1 K-wise—rep from *, end pu 1, K 1.
Row 7: Knit all sts.
Row 8: Purl all sts.

Row 9: K 1—then K 2 tog across the row to the end.
Row 10: Same as Row 6.
    Starting with Row 1, rep these 10 rows.

This stitch is made with very little effort. The decorative pattern may be more widely spaced, or Rows 1 and 2 may be omitted to bring it closer together. It is excellent when worked from side to side for a blouse. If you choose linen or cotton yarns, make sure to use the Reverse Stitch (page 63).

#135

#136 PURL FABRIC STITCH—*Multiple of 6 sts plus 5.*

Rows 1, 3, and 5: Purl all sts (Right Side).
Rows 2 and 4: Knit all sts.
Row 6: K 5, * K a loop from 5 rows below next st, draw up and K next st; pass loop over this st, K 5—rep from *, end same.
Rows 7, 9, and 11: Purl all sts.
Rows 8 and 10: Knit all sts.
Row 12: K 2; rep between * * in Row 6, end K a loop as before, pull over and K 2.
    Starting with Row 1, rep these 12 rows.

This stitch may be used in the same ways as #127.

#137 PIQUÉ STITCH—*Multiple of 6 sts plus 5.*

Rows 1, 3, and 5: P 2, * Kb 1, P 5—rep from *, end Kb 1, P 2.
Rows 2, 4, and 6: K 2, * Pb 1, K 5—rep from *, end Pb 1, K 2.
Rows 7, 9, and 11: * P 5, Kb 1—rep from *, end P 5.
Rows 8, 10, and 12: * K 5, Pb 1—rep from *, end K 5.
    Starting with Row 1, rep these 12 rows.

Same uses as #127. However, Piqué Stitch is firmer and more elastic.

#136

#138 TINY LEAF FABRIC—*Multiple of 8 sts plus 7.*

See illustration overleaf.
Row 1: * P 7, KPK—rep from *, end P 7.
Row 2: * K 7, P 3—rep from *, end K 7.
Row 3: * P 7, K 3—rep from *, end P 7.
Row 4: Same as Row 2.
Row 5: Same as Row 3.
Row 6: * K 7, P 3 tog—rep from *, end K 7.
Row 7: P 3, * KPK, P 7—rep from *, end P 3.
Row 8: K 3, * P 3, K 7—rep from *, end K 3.
Row 9: P 3, * K 3, P 7—rep from *, end P 3.
Row 10: Same as Row 8.
Row 11: Same as Row 9.
Row 12: K 3, * P 3 tog, K 7—rep from *, end K 3.
    Starting with Row 1, rep these 12 rows.

This stitch offers the same uses as #127.

#137

#138

#139 DIAMOND IN A DIAMOND—*Multiple of 8 sts plus 1.*

All Odd-Numbered Rows: Purl all sts.
Row 2: K 2, * yo, SKP, K 6—rep from *, end yo, SKP, K 5.
Row 4: K 3, * yo, SKP, K 3, K 2 tog, yo, K 1—rep from *, end yo, SKP, K 4.
Row 6: K 4, * yo, SKP, K 1, K 2 tog, yo, K 3—rep from *, end yo, SKP, K 3.
Row 8: K 2, K 2 tog, * yo, K 5, yo, SK2togP—rep from *, end yo, K 5.
Row 10: K 6, * yo, SKP, K 6—rep from *, end yo, SKP, K 1.
Row 12: K 4, K 2 tog, yo, * K 1, yo, SKP, K 3, K 2 tog, yo—rep from *, end yo, K 3.
Row 14: K 3, * K 2 tog, yo, K 3, yo, SKP, K 1—rep from *, end K 2 tog, yo, K 4.
Row 16: K 5, * yo, SK2togP, yo, K 5—rep from *, end yo, SKP, K 2.
   Starting with Row 1, rep these 16 rows.

This pattern approaches the lace stitches but is a small motif and should be used mostly as a trim for blouses and dresses. It also makes exquisite bed jackets and baby garments when used as an all-over pattern. It can be worked as the center portion of light-weight crib or carriage robes, or as a strip for afghans. Judiciously used, it may add an interesting note to cardigans. Any type and weight of yarn may be used.

#139

#140 SIMPLE LACE STITCH—*Multiple of 6 sts plus 1.*

Row 1: Knit all sts (Wrong Side)
Row 2: Purl all sts.
Row 3: Knit all sts.
Row 4: K 1, * yo, K 1, SK2togP, K 1, yo, K 1—rep from *, end same.
Row 5: Purl all sts.
Row 6: Same as Row 4.
Row 7: Purl all sts.
Row 8: Same as Row 4.
   Starting with Row 1, rep these 8 rows.

For a rather elaborate-looking stitch, this is very easily worked. It is most appropriate for shawls, stoles, bed jackets, and baby garments, such as sacques. It is particularly effective when worked with very fine yarns on a #4 or larger-size needle. Just one repeat of the pattern makes a lovely scalloped edging for panties, baby dresses, or collars and cuffs.

#141 BUTTERFLY LACE STITCH—*Multiple of 12 sts plus 5.*

Row 1: P 1, * (K 1, yo)x2, K 1, P 9—rep from *, end (K 1, yo)x2, K 1, P 1.
Row 2: K 1, * P 5, K 9—rep from *, end P 5, K 1.
Rows 3 and 5: P 1, * K 5, P 9—rep from *, end K 5, P 1.

#140

204

Rows 4 and 6: Same as Row 2.
Row 7: P 1, * K 1, insert RH needle into st 6 rows beneath 2nd st on LH needle. Drop 3 sts from LH needle and pull them all loose down to where RH needle is placed. K this st and pull resulting loop up to level of present row (a butterfly made); K 1, P 9 — rep from *, end K 1, butterfly, K 1, P 1.
Row 8: K 1, * P 1, K 1, P 1, K 9 — rep from *, end (P 1, K 1)x2.
Row 9: P 7, * (K 1, yo)x2, K 1, P 9 — rep from *, end P 7.
Row 10: K 7, * P 5, K 9 — rep from *, end K 7.
Rows 11 and 13: P 7, * K 5, P 9 — rep from *, end P 7.
Rows 12 and 14: Same as Row 10.
Row 15: P 7, * K 1, butterfly, K 1, P 9 — rep from *, end P 7.
Row 16: K 7, * P 1, K 1, P 1, K 9 — rep from *, end K 7.
    Starting with Row 1, rep these 16 rows.

This stitch may be used in the same ways as #127 but is more lacy and elaborate. It is a little more difficult to work, however, and should be practiced before using.

#141

"SMALL" STITCHES

#142 ALTERNATE RIBBING AND CABLE
—*Multiple of 16 sts plus 2.*

Note: Method cabling 2, 2, and 2 may be found on page 81.
All Odd-Numbered Rows: * K 2, P 2 — rep from *, end K 2.
Rows 2, 4, 6, and 8: * P 2, K 2 — rep from *, end P 2.
Row 10: P 2, * cable 2, 2, and 2 *front*, (P 2, K 2)x2, P2 — rep from *, end same.
Rows 12, 14, 16, and 18: Same as Row 2.
Row 20: * (P 2, K 2)x2, P 2, cable 2, 2, and 2 *back* — rep from *, end P 2.
    Starting with Row 1, rep these 20 rows.

A bold pattern for all types of sports sweaters, in all but the very smallest sizes. Any weight of yarn may be used. In any of the dressy yarns — crepe, nubby, or even those with a metallic thread, this stitch makes beautiful cardigans.

#142

#143 TRAVELING CROSS CABLE —*Multiple of 8 sts plus 6.*

All Odd-Numbered Rows: * K 2, P 2 — rep from *, end K 2.
Rows 2, 4, and 6: * P 2, K 2 — rep from *, end P 2.
Row 8: * P 2, cable 3 over 3 *front* — rep from *, end P 2, K 2, P 2.
Rows 10, 12, and 14: Same as Row 2.
Row 16: P 2, K 2, P 2, * cable 3 over 3 *back*, P 2 — rep from *, end same.
    Starting with Row 1, rep these 16 rows.
Same uses as #142.

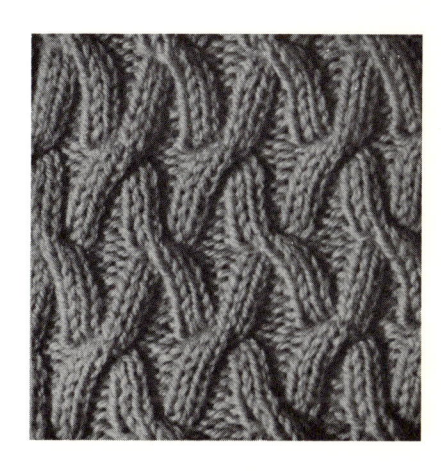

#143

#144   **FANCY CABLE**—*Multiple of 16 sts plus 2.*

Rows 1, 3, 5, 7, 9, and 11: K 2, * P 2, K 2—rep from *, end same.
Rows 2, 4, 6, 8, 10, and 12: P 2, * K2, P 2—rep from *, end same.
Row 13: * K 2, P 2, cable 5 over 5 *back*, P 2—rep from *, end P 2, K 2.
Rows 14, 16, and 18: * P 2, K 2, P 10, K 2—rep from *, end K 2, P 2.
Rows 15 and 17: * K 2, P 2, K 10, P 2—rep from *, end P 2, K 2.
Row 19: Same as Row 13.
Row 20: Same as Row 2.
Rows 21, 23, 25, 27, 29, and 31: Same as Row 1.
Rows 22, 24, 26, 28, 30, and 32: Same as Row 2.
Row 33: * cable 5 over 5 *back*, P 2, K 2, P 2—rep from *, end K 2.
Rows 34, 36, 38: P 2, * K 2, P 2, K 2, P 10—rep from *, end same.
Rows 35 and 37: * K 10, P 2, K 2, P 2—rep from *, end K 2.
Row 39: Same as Row 33.
Row 40: Same as Row 2.
    Starting with Row 1, rep these 40 rows.

  This stitch and its uses are similar to #143. Fancy Cable is slightly more elaborate, however, and pulls in a little tighter because of the double twist in the cabling.

#145   **TINY TWISTED RIBBING**—*Multiple of 8 sts plus 6.*

Row 1: K 2, * P 2, K 1, P 4, K 1—rep from *, end P 2, K 2.
Row 2: P 2, * K 2, P 1, K 4, P 1—rep from *, end K 2, P 2.
Row 3: Same as Row 1.
Row 4: P 2, * K 2, P 1, cable 2 over 2 front, P 1—rep from *, end K 2, P 2.
Row 5: Same as Row 1.
Row 6: Same as Row 4.
Row 7: K 1, * P 4, K 1, P 2, K 1—rep from *, end P 4, K 1.
Row 8: P 1, * K 4, P 1, K 2, P 1—rep from *, end K 4, P 1.
Row 9: Same as Row 7.
Row 10: P 1, * cable 2 over 2 front, P 1, K 2, P 1—rep from *, end cable 2 over 2 front, P 1.
Row 11: Same as Row 7.
Row 12: Same as Row 10.
    Starting with Row 1, rep these 12 rows.

  This is a little too elaborate an all-over ribbing for any yarns heavier than medium weight, but it is excellent for very fine light-weight yarns worked on a #3 or #4 needle.
  Suggested Ribbing: K 2, P 2 only.

#146   **FLAT CABLE FABRIC**—*Multiple of 11 sts plus 1.*

Rows 1 and 3: K 3, * P 6, K 5—rep from *, end P 6, K 3.
Row 2: P 3, * K 6, P 5—rep from *, end K 6, P 3.

#144

#145

#146

206

Row 4: P 3, * sl 5 sts to DP front, K 1, sl 1st 4 sts from DP to LH needle and take DP, with the 1 st, to back. K 4 from LH needle and then the 1st st from DP, P 5 — rep from *, end P 3.
Rows 5 and 7: Same as Row 1.
Rows 6 and 8: Same as Row 2.
  Starting with Row 1, rep these 8 rows.

Although this does not resemble a cable stitch in appearance, it is a true cable. Unusually elastic, it may be used both as an all-over fabric and as a contrast where gathering is needed (same as #144). Just one repeat of the pattern makes a very good single-cable trim.

#147 **SPREADING CABLE** — *Multiple of 18 sts plus 6.*

Rows 1, 3, 5, and 7: * K 6, P 3 — rep from *, end K 6.
Rows 2, 4, and 6: * P 6, K 3 — rep from *, end P 6.
Row 8: * P 6, sl 3 on DP front, P 3 from LH needle, then K 3 from DP, sl next 3 sts on DP back, K 3 from LH needle, then P 3 from DP — rep from *, end P 6.
Rows 9, 11, 13, and 15: K 9, * P 6, K 12 — rep from *, end K 9.
Rows 10, 12, and 14: P 9, * K 6, P 12 — rep from *, end P 9.
Row 16: * P 6, sl 3 on DP back, K 3, then P 3 from DP, sl 3 to DP front, P 3, then K 3 from DP — rep from *, end P 6.
  Starting with Row 1, rep these 16 rows.

Same uses as #146.

#148 **PLAITED CABLE** — *Multiple of 20 sts plus 8.*

All Odd-Numbered Rows: K 2, * P 4, K 2, P 12, K 2 — rep from *, end P 4, K 2.
Rows 2, 4, 6, and 8: P 2, * K 4, P 2, K 12, P 2 — rep from *, end K 4, P 2.
Row 10: P 2, * K 4, P 2, sl 8 sts to DP front, K 4 sts from LH needle, sl 4 sts from DP to LH needle and take DP to back, K 4 sts from LH needle, then K 4 sts from DP, P 2 — rep from *, end K 4, P 2.
  Starting with Row 1, rep these 10 rows.

This stitch is best used for sports sweaters. However, one cable, used alone, makes an attractive trim on dressy blouses. Any weight and type of yarn may be used.

#149 **HORSESHOE CABLE STRIPE** — *Multiple of 16 sts plus 8.*

Rows 1 and 3: P 2, * K 4, P 2, K 8, P 2 — rep from *, end K 4, P 2.
Rows 2 and 4: K 2, * P 4, K 2, P 8, K 2 — rep from *, end P 4, K 2.
Row 5: P 2, K 4, * P 2, cable 2 over 2 back, cable 2 over 2 front, P 2, K 4, P 2 — rep from *, end K 4, P 2.
Row 6: Same as Row 2.
  Starting with Row 1, rep these 6 rows.

Same uses as #146 and #148.

#147

#148

#149

#150

#150 STAGGERED HORSESHOE CABLE—*Multiple of 20 sts plus 2.*

All Even-Numbered Rows: * K 2, P 8 — rep from *, end K 2.
Row 1: Knit all sts.
Row 3: * K 2, cable 2 and 2 back, cable 2 and 2 front, K 12 — rep from *, end same.
Rows 5, 9, 14, 17, and 21: Knit all sts.
Rows 7, 11, 15, and 19: Same as Row 3.
Row 23: * K 12, cable 2 and 2 back, cable 2 and 2 front — rep from *, end K 2.
Rows 25, 29, 33, and 37: Knit all sts.
Rows 27, 31, 35, and 39: Same as Row 23.
    Starting with Row 1, rep these 40 rows.

  This is a most attractive cable stitch for somewhat dressier sportswear. It offers the same uses as #146 and #148 and is a very good stitch pattern for socks.

#151

#151 OPEN DROP-STITCH CABLE—*Multiple of 7 sts plus 6.*

Rows 1, 3, 5, and 7: Purl all sts.
Rows 2, 4, and 6: Knit all sts.
Row 8: * cross 3 over 3 front, K 1 — rep from *, end cross 3 over 3 front.
    Starting with Row 1, rep these 8 rows.

  When binding off, drop every 7th stitch. Let these sts drop through the entire row (see page 66 for binding off).

  This stitch must be carefully considered before use. Because of the drop stitch, the threads are apt to be caught and broken, so do not use it for rough wear. A good all-over stitch for light-weight, cool-weather wear, it is also a pleasing trimming or contrast stitch when used carefully.

  The stitch must be specially set up when it is to be used as a trimming or contrast; otherwise the drop stitch may run through the entire piece of work. *Two* extra sts must take the place of the *one* st in the pattern — the one which is dropped, so the row *before* the first row of the pattern stitch must have a multiple of 8 sts plus 6 for every multiple of 7 sts plus 6 in the pattern stitch.

  This Set-Up Row must follow this procedure: K 5, * K 2 tog, yo, SKP, K 4 — rep from *, end yo, SKP, K 5.

  Then follow the pattern stitch from Row 1.

  Be sure to let the sts drop in the swatch *before* taking the gauge. This is most important.

#152

#152 BASKET-WEAVE CABLE—*Multiple of 6 sts.*

All Odd-Numbered Rows: Purl all sts.
Rows 2 and 4: Knit all sts.
Row 6: * cable 3 over 3 front — rep from *, end same.
Rows 8 and 10: Knit all sts.
Row 12: K 3, * cable 3 over 3 back — rep from *, end K 3.
    Starting with Row 1, rep these 12 rows.

208

This adaptable cable stitch may be used as an all-over pattern or as a trimming or contrast stitch. All weights and types of yarns may be used to advantage. In the very fine two-ply yarns, it makes an attractive warm sweater for babies, children, and women. It is an excellent gathering stitch, especially when Stockinette is the basic fabric.

#153 STOCKINETTE CABLE FABRIC—*Multiple of 6 sts.*

All Odd-Numbered Rows: Purl all sts.
Row 2: Knit all sts.
Row 4: * K 2, cable 2 and 2 back—rep from *, end same.
Row 6: Knit all sts.
Row 8: * cable 2 and 2 front, K 2—rep from *, end same.
 Starting with Row 1, rep these 8 rows.
 Same uses, in every respect, as #152. Stockinette Cable Fabric does not pull in quite so tightly.

#154

#154 HEAVY CABLE AND GARTER STITCH—
Multiple of 23 sts plus 4.

For Swatch: cast on 50 sts. The Make 1 (M 1) is knitted.
 Note: The number of sts varies in some of the rows.
Row 1: K 2, * M 1, K 4, SKP, K 11, K 2 tog, K 4—rep from *, end M 1, K 2.
Row 2: K 3, * P 5, K 11, P 5, K 1—rep from *, end K 3.

Row 3: K 3, * M 1, K 4, SKP, K 9, K 2 tog, K 4, M 1, K 1—rep from *, end M 1, K 3.
Row 4: K 4, * P 5, K 9, P 5, K 3—rep from *, end K 4.
Row 5: K 4, * M 1, K 4, SKP, K 7, K 2 tog, K 4, M 1, K 3—rep from *, end M 1, K 4.
Row 6: * K 5, P 5, K 7, P 5—rep from *, end K 5.
Row 7: K 5, * M 1, K 4, SKP, K 5, K 2 tog, K 4, M 1, K 5—rep from *, end same.
Row 8: K 6, * P 5, K 5, P 5, K 7—rep from *, end K 6.
Row 9: K 6, * M 1, K 4, SKP, K 3, K 2 tog, K 4, M 1, K 7—rep from *, end M 1, K 6.
Row 10: K 7, * P 5, K 3, P 5, K 9—rep from *, end K 7.
Row 11: K 7, * M 1, K 4, SKP, K 1, K 2 tog, K 4, M 1, K 9—rep from *, end M 1, K 7.
Row 12: K 8, * P 5, K 1, P 5, K 11—rep from *, end K 8.
Row 13: K 8, * sl 3 on DP front, K 2 tog and K 4 from LH needle, then K 3 from DP, K 13—rep from *, end K 10 (1 st lost in each cable).
Row 14: K 8, * P 10, K 11—rep from *, end K 8.
Rows 15, 17, and 19: Knit all sts.
Rows 16, 18, and 20: Same as Row 14.
Row 21: K 8, * cable 5 over 5 front, K 11—rep from *, end K 8.
Row 22: Same as Row 14.
Row 23: K 13, * M 1, K 21—rep from *, end M 1, K 13.

209

Row 24: Same as Row 12.
Row 25: K 7, * K 2 tog, K 4, M 1, K 1, M 1, K 4, SKP, K 9 — rep from *, end K 7.
Row 26: Same as Row 10.
Row 27: K 6, * K 2 tog, K 4, M 1, K 3, M 1, K 4, SKP, K 7 — rep from *, end K 6.
Row 28: Same as Row 8.
Row 29: K 5, * K 2 tog, K 4, M 1, K 5, M 1, K 4, SKP, K 5 — rep from *, end same.
Row 30: Same as Row 6.
Row 31: K 4, * K 2 tog, K 4, M 1, K 7, M 1, K 4, SKP, K 3 — rep from *, end K 4.
Row 32: Same as Row 4.
Row 33: K 3, * K 2 tog, K 4, M 1, K 9, M 1, K 4, SKP, K 1 — rep from *, end K 3.
Row 34: Same as Row 2.
Row 35: K 19; rep between * * in Row 13 — end K 21.
Row 36: K 3, P 5, * K 11, P 10 — rep from *, end P 5, K 3.
Rows 37, 39, and 41: Knit all sts.
Rows 38, 40, and 42: Same as Row 36.
Row 43: K 19, * cable 5 over 5 front, K 11 — rep from *, end K 19.
Row 44: Same as Row 36.
Row 45: K 24, * M 1, K 21 — rep from *, end K 24.
Row 46: K 3, * P 5, K 11, P 5, K 1 — rep from *, end K 3.

Starting with *Row* 3, rep through Row 46 (44 rows in pattern).
This is one of the heaviest cable stitches and one of the most elaborate to make. It is definitely a sportswear stitch, for pullovers or cardigans, and it stands out best in medium- to heavy-weight smooth yarns. It may also be used effectively as the center of a blanket or as a strip for an afghan.

Suggested Trim: Garter Stitch only.
Suggested Ribbing: K 1, P 1.

#155

#155 FAGOT AND CABLE — *Multiple of 33 sts plus 9.*

Rows 1, 3, 5, and 7: * (P 3, K 3)x2, P 3, (yo, P 2 tog, P 3)x3, K 3 — rep from *, end P 3, K 3, P 3.
Rows 2, 4, and 6: * (K 3, P 3)x2, K 3, (yo, P 2 tog, K 3)x3, P 3 — rep from *, end K 3, P 3, K 3.
Row 8: * (K 3, P 3)x2, sl 3 on DP front, K 3, yo, P 2 tog from LH needle, then K 3 from DP, yo, P 2 tog, cable as before, P 3 — rep from *, end K 3, P 3, K 3.
Rows 9, 11, 13, and 15: Same as Row 1.
Rows 10, 12, and 14: Same as Row 2.
Row 16: * (K 3, P 3)x2, K 3, yo, P 2 tog, sl 5 on DP back, K 3, yo, P 2 tog from LH needle, then K 3 from DP, yo, and P 2 from DP, K 3, P 3 — rep from *, end K 3, P 3, K 3.

Starting with Row 1, rep these 16 rows.
This elaborate stitch is definitely feminine but should be used with

restraint, as too much of it in one garment is apt to look fussy and clumsy. A single repeat of the pattern, eliminating the 9 sts before and after the cable pattern, functions as a trimming stitch on a sweater or as a strip for an afghan.

#156 SMOCKED RIBBING—*Multiple of 16 sts plus 2.*

Note: Method of working Tie Stitch is given on page 85.
All Odd-Numbered Rows: * K 2, P 2—rep from *, end K 2 (Wrong Side).
Rows 2, 4, 6, 10, 12, and 14: * P 2, K 2—rep from *, end P 2.
Row 8: * P 2, Tie St on 6 sts, working off K 2, P 2, K 2, (P 2, K 2)x2—rep from *, end P 2.
Row 16: * (P 2, K 2)x2, P 2, Tie St on 6 sts as before—rep from *, end P 2.
　　Starting with Row 1, rep these 16 rows.
This is not a true cable, but may be treated in the same manner as any cable stitch. It is elastic, easy to make, and most attractive. It may be used in the same ways as #142 and #143.

#156

#157 PULLOVER (MOCK) CABLE—*Multiple of 8 sts plus 2.*

All Odd-Numbered Rows: * K 2, P 2—rep from *, end K 2 (Wrong Side).
Row 2: * P 2, K 2—rep from *, end P 2.
Row 4: * P 2, insert RH needle, from front to back, between 6th and 7th sts on LH needle and K a loop through. Slip this loop onto LH needle and K through this loop and the next st, together; K 1, P 2, K 2—rep from *, end P 2.
Row 6: Same as Row 2.
Row 8: P 2, K 2; rep between * * on Row 4, end K 2, P 2.
　　Starting with Row 1, rep these 8 rows.
This is another pattern which may be used as a cable stitch but is not a true cable. It is very easy to make and has the same uses as #142, #143, and #152, but with the added advantage of being an excellent trimming, contrast, or gathering stitch. Unlike most of the cable stitches, it retains its beauty even when fully blocked. Any weight or type of yarn may be used to good advantage.

#157

CABLE STITCHES

#158 LATTICE STITCH I—*Multiple of 3 sts.*

Note: Method of working a yo before the first st may be found on page 72.
All Even-Numbered Rows: Purl all sts.
Row 1: K 2, * yo, K 3, pull first st of the K 3 over the other 2 sts—rep from *, end K 1.
Row 3: K 1, * yo, K 3, pull over as before—rep from *, end K 2.

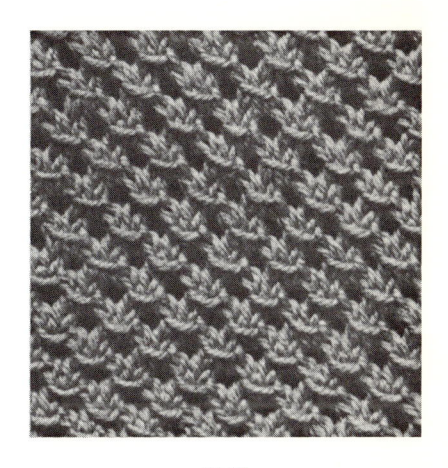

#158

211

Row 5: * yo, K 3, pull over as before—rep from *, end same.
        Starting with Row 1, rep these 6 rows.

Take care! Do *not* yarn-over at the end of Rows 1 and 3, before the final sts.

This easily made stitch is pleasing as an all-over pattern or as a trimming. Using just one full pattern, outlined by one ridge of Garter Stitch, it makes an excellent insertion stitch. It may be used for light-weight garments—dressy sweaters for adults, sweaters for children or babies, but it is best used as a trimming stitch in these cases.

#159 LATTICE STITCH II—*Multiple of 3 sts.*

Row 1: Purl all sts.
Row 2: K 2, * yo, K 3, pull first st of the K 3 over the other 2 sts—rep from *, end K 1.
Row 3: Purl all sts.
Row 4: K 1, * yo, K 3, pull over as before—rep from *, end K 2.
        Starting with Row 1, rep these 4 rows.
        Same uses as #158.

#159

#160 FANCY HORIZONTAL STRIPE—*Multiple of 8 sts.*

Row 1: Purl all sts (Right Side).
Row 2: K 1, * yo, K 2 tog—rep from *, end K 1.
Row 3: Same as Row 2.
Row 4: Knit all sts.
Row 5: Knit all sts.
Row 6: Purl all sts.
Row 7: K 3, P 2, * K 6, P 2—rep from *, end K 3.
Row 8: P 2, K 4, * P 4, K 4—rep from *, end P 2.
Row 9: K 1, P 2, * K 2, P 2—rep from *, end K 1.
Row 10: K 2, P 4, * K 4, P 4—rep from *, end K 2.
Row 11: Same as Row 8.
Row 12: P 1, K 2, * P 2, K 2—rep from *, end P 1.
Row 13: Same as Row 10.
Row 14: P 3, K 2, * P 6, K 2—rep from *, end P 3.
Row 15: Knit all sts.
Row 16: Purl all sts.
        Starting with Row 1, rep these 16 rows.

This stitch may be used as an attractive all-over pattern, either as a horizontal design or worked from side seam to side seam to make a vertical design. Just one repeat of the pattern, plus Rows 1, 2, 3, and 4, makes a beautiful trimming or insertion stitch. It is best confined to smooth yarns as nubby yarns tend to obscure the design.

In a flat piece, such as a blanket, this pattern should not be bound off until Row 5 has been worked again. Bind off, on the next row, in knitting.

#160

212

#161   OPEN CROSS-LATTICE STITCH—*Multiple of 4 sts.*

Note: Method of making a yo before working the first st may be found on page 72.
Row 1: K 3, * K 2 tog, yo, K 2—rep from *, end yo, K 3.
Row 2: * yo, P 2 tog, P 2—rep from *, end same.
Row 3: K 1, * K 2 tog, yo, K 2—rep from *, end K 2 tog, yo, K 1.
Row 4: * P 2, yo, P 2 tog—rep from *, end same.
Row 5: * yo, SKP, K 2—rep from *, end same.
Row 6: P 1, * P 2 tog b, yo, P 2—rep from *, end P 2 tog b, yo, P 1.
Row 7: * K 2, yo, SKP—rep from *, end same.
Row 8: P 3, * P 2 tog b, yo, P 2—rep from *, end P 2 tog b, yo, P 3.
   Starting with Row 1, rep these 8 rows.
This all-over small lace pattern may be used for light-weight garments or articles—baby sacques, light-weight dressy sweaters, blouses, bed jackets, shawls—and may also be used as a trimming or contrast stitch. It should be fully blocked. It washes very well.

#161

#162   POINTED LACE PATTERN—*Multiple of 9 sts plus 1.*

Row 1: Purl all sts.
Row 2: K 1, * yo, K 2, K 2 tog, SKP, K 2, yo, K 1—rep from *, end same.
   Repeat these 2 rows throughout.
This is one of a very few lace stitches which might be classed as tailored. It is conservative, extremely easy to make, and the directions are easy, with only two rows to follow. Even the bottom edge requires no finishing if a ridge or two of Garter Stitch is worked before the pattern is started. It is a good all-over pattern, useful as a trimming or contrast stitch where a slightly open effect is desired. It is fine for baby sacques and sweaters, and for bed jackets, light-weight robes, and afghans. It works very well for light-weight cool-weather cardigans used in part or for all of the top of a one-piece dress, or as a jacket for a dressy two-piece dress or suit. Any type of yarn may be used. Light- to medium-weight yarns are best for this stitch.

#162

#163   ZIGZAG AND FAGOT—*Multiple of 9 sts plus 4.*

All Odd-Numbered Rows are worked as follows: K 2 tog, yo, K 2,
   * P 5, K 2 tog, yo, K 2—rep from *, end same.
Row 2: K 2 tog, yo, K 2, * yo, SKP, K 3, K 2 tog, yo, K 2—rep from *, end same.
Row 4: K 2 tog, yo, K 3, * yo, SKP, K 2, K 2 tog, yo, K 3—rep from *, end yo, K 2.
Row 6: K 2 tog, yo, K 4, * yo, SKP, K 1, K 2 tog, yo, K 4—rep from *, end yo, K 2.
Row 8: K 2 tog, yo, K 5, * yo, SKP, K 2 tog, yo, K 5—rep from *, end yo, K 2.

#163

Row 10: K 2 tog, yo, K 4, * K 2 tog, yo, K 1, K 2 tog, yo, K 4 — rep from *, end yo, K 2.
Row 12: K 2 tog, yo, K 3, * K 2 tog, yo, K 2, K 2 tog, yo, K 3 — rep from *, end yo, K 2.
Row 14: K 2 tog, yo, K 2, * K 2 tog, yo, K 3, K 2 tog, yo, K 2 — rep from *, end same.
Row 16: K 2 tog, yo, K 1, * K 2 tog, yo, K 4, K 2 tog, yo, K 1 — rep from *, end yo, K 2.
    Starting with Row 1, rep these 16 rows.

Another tailored lace stitch, a little more elaborate than #162, this is very easy to make despite the number of rows in the pattern. It offers all of the uses of #162 as well as being very good as a contrast stitch for suits and dresses.

#164 CROSSED CABLE AND FAGOT — *Multiple of 9 sts plus 7.*

Row 1: K 2, * yo, SK2togP, yo, K 1, 00, K 4, 00, K 1 — rep from *, end yo, SK2togP, yo, K 2.
Row 2: P 5, * sl 1 with yarn in front, drop the 00, P 4, turn; K 4, turn; P 4, drop the 00, sl 1 with yarn in front, P 3 — rep from *, end P 5.
Row 3: K 2, * yo, SK2togP, yo, sl 5 sts on DP back, K next st, sl 4 from DP to LH needle and bring the 1 st on DP to front. K 4 sts from LH needle and then the 1st st from DP — rep from *, end yo, SK2togP, yo, K 2.
Row 4: Purl all sts.
Row 5: K 2, * yo, SK2togP, yo, K 6 — rep from *, end yo, SK2togP, yo, K 2.
Row 6: Purl all sts.
    Starting with Row 1, rep these 6 rows.

Although this is not a true cable stitch, it combines the elasticity of cable with an openwork stripe and may be used as an all-over pattern for dressy sweaters, or as a trimming or contrast stitch in very light-weight through medium-weight yarns. Crepes and smooth novelty yarns may be used, but nubby yarns compete with the pattern.
    Bind off on Row 4.

#164

#165 HERRINGBONE LACE PATTERN — *Multiple of 6 sts.*

All Odd-Numbered Rows: Purl all sts (Wrong Side).
Rows 2, 4, and 6: * K 2 tog, K 2, yo, K 2 — rep from *, end same.
Rows 8, 10, and 12: K 3, * yo, K 2, SKP, K 2 — rep from *, end yo, SKP, K 1.
    Starting with Row 1, rep these 12 rows.

This, like #162, is a tailored lace stitch. Besides all the uses of #162, it goes very well with Stockinette as a contrast stitch trimming or used for a dressy jacket for a suit.

#165

#166 WOVEN CABLE—*Multiple of 7 sts plus 2.*

Rows 1, 3, 5, 7, and 9: K 2, * P 5, K 2 — rep from *, end same.
Rows 2, 4, 6, and 8: P 2, * SKP, yo, K 1, yo, K 2 tog, P 2 — rep from *, end same.
Row 10: P 2, * sl 3 on DP back, K 2, sl 1 from DP to LH needle and bring DP to front, K 1 from LH needle, then K 2 from DP, P 2 — rep from *, end same.
Rows 11, 13, 15, 17, and 19: Same as Row 1.
Rows 12, 14, 16, and 18: Same as Row 2.
Row 20: P 2, * sl 3 on DP front, K 2, sl 1 from DP to LH needle and take DP to back, K 1 from LH needle, then K 2 from DP, P 2 — rep from *, end same.
    Starting with Row 1, rep these 20 rows.

This stitch should be used sparingly as a trimming or contrast stitch. Very elastic, it is a good gathering stitch but should not be used as an all-over pattern except in unusual cases. It may be quite firmly blocked.

#167 LACE ROSEBUD AND LEAF—*Multiple of 8 sts plus 3.*

Row 1: * P 3, K 2, yo, Kb 1, yo, K 2 — rep from *, end P 3.
Row 2: * K 3, P 3, Kb 1, P 3 — rep from *, end K 3.
Row 3: * P 3, K 3, yo, Kb 1, yo, K 3 — rep from *, end P 3.
Row 4: * K 3, P 4, Kb 1, P 4 — rep from *, end K 3.
Row 5: * P 3, K 2, K 2 tog, yo, Kb 1, yo, SKP, K 2 — rep from *, end P 3.
Row 6: Same as Row 4.
Row 7: * P 3, K 1, K 2 tog, yo, K 1, Kb 1, K 1, yo, SKP, K 1 — rep from *, end P 3.
Row 8: Same as Row 4.
Row 9: * P 3, K 2 tog, yo, K 5 and pull 4 over 1 R (as in Tuft Stitch), yo, SKP — rep from *, end P 3.
Row 10: * K 3, P 2, Kb 1, P 2 — rep from *, end K 3.
    Starting with Row 1, rep these 10 rows.

Same uses as #165, but this stitch is a little more elaborate. It may be quite firmly blocked if you wish the pattern to stand out.

#168 TWINBERRY STRIPE—*Multiple of 10 sts plus 6.*

Row 1: P 5, * K 6, P 4 — rep from *, end P 5.
Row 2: K 1, * yo, K 2 tog b, K 2 tog, yo, P 2, (KPK)x2, P 2 — rep from *, end yo, K 2 tog b, K 2 tog, yo, K 1.
Rows 3, 5, and 7: P 5, * K 2, P 6, K 2, P 4 — rep from *, end P 5.
Rows 4 and 6: K 1, * yo, K 2 tog b, K 2 tog, yo, P 2, K 6, P 2 — rep from *, end yo, K 2 tog b, K 2 tog, yo, K 1.
Row 8: K 1, * yo, K 2 tog b, K 2 tog, yo, P 2, K 3 tog b, K 3 tog, P 2 — rep from *, end yo, K 2 tog b, K 2 tog, yo, K 1.
Row 9: Same as Row 1.
Row 10: K 1, * yo, K 2 tog b, K 2 tog, yo, P 6 — rep from *, end yo, K 2 tog b, K 2 tog, yo, K 1.
    Starting with Row 1, rep these 10 rows.

#166

#167

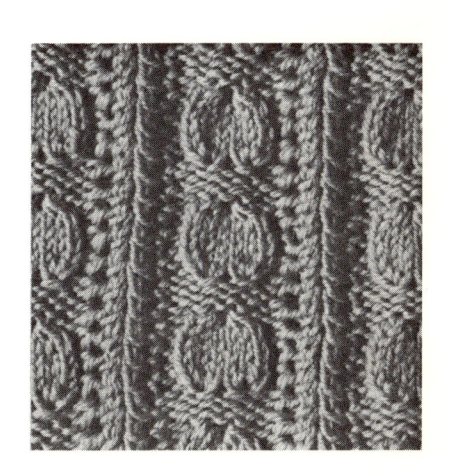

#168

#169

This is an excellent stitch for all the same uses as in #162 and #165. It is best in smooth or crepe yarns, but nubby yarns may be used. It may be firmly blocked or left unblocked entirely, depending upon its use.

#169 BABY FERN STITCH—*Multiple of 12 sts plus 1.*

All Odd-Numbered Rows: Purl all sts.
Row 2: K 1, P 1, * K 2 tog, K 2, yo, K 1, yo, K 2, SKP, P 1, K 1, P 1 — rep from *, end P 1, K 1.
Row 4: K 1, P 1, * K 2 tog, K 1, yo, K 3, yo, K 1, SKP, P 1, K 1, P 1 — rep from *, end P 1, K 1.
Row 6: K 1, P 1, * K 2 tog, yo, K 5, yo, SKP, P 1, K 1, P 1 — rep from *, end P 1, K 1.
    Starting with Row 1, rep these 6 rows.
Same uses as #162 and #165. This is an interesting stitch, very easy to make.

#170

#170 ARROWHEAD STITCH—*Multiple of 9 sts plus 1.*

Row 1: K 3, * K 2 tog, 00, SKP, K 5 — rep from *, end K 3.
Row 2: K 1, P 3, * KP, P 3, K 1, P 3 — rep from *, end K 1.
Row 3: K 2, * K 2 tog, yo, K 2, yo, SKP, K 3 — rep from *, end K 2.
Row 4: * K 1, P 8 — rep from *, end K 1.
Row 5: K 1, * K 2 tog, yo, K 4, yo, SKP, K 1 — rep from *, end same.
Row 6: Same as Row 4.
Row 7: K 2 tog, * 00, K 3 tog, 00, K 3 tog b, 00, SK2togP — rep from *, end 00, SKP.
Row 8: K 1, * KP, K 1 — rep from *, end same.
    Starting with Row 1, rep these 8 rows.
This all-over lace pattern may be used in many ways: for baby sacques, bed jackets, dressy cardigans, shawls, stoles, light-weight crib or carriage covers, strips for afghans — for almost any garment or article where a small lace pattern is indicated. It is a very good trimming or contrast stitch, particularly so in linen or cotton yarns, using the normal knitting and purling method.

#171

#171 GRAPEVINE STITCH—*Multiple of 8 sts plus 2.*

Row 1: K 1, * yo, Kb 1, yo, SKP, K 5 — rep from *, end K 6.
Row 2: P 5, * P 2 tog b, P 7 — rep from *, end P 4.
Row 3: K 1, * yo, Kb 1, yo, K 2, SKP, K 3 — rep from *, end K 4.
Row 4: P 3, * P 2 tog b, P 7 — rep from *, end P 6.
Row 5: K 1, * Kb 1, yo, K 4, SKP, K 1, yo — rep from *, end K 1, yo, K 1.
Row 6: P 2, * P 2 tog b, P 7 — rep from *, end same.
Row 7: K 6, * K 2 tog, yo, Kb 1, yo, K 5 — rep from *, end yo, Kb 1, yo, K 1.
Row 8: P 4, * P 2 tog, P 7 — rep from *, end P 5.
Row 9: K 4, * K 2 tog, K 2, yo, Kb 1, yo, K 3 — rep from *, end yo, Kb 1, yo, K 1.

216

Row 10: P 6, * P 2 tog, P 7—rep from *, end P 3.
Row 11: K 1, * yo, K 1, K 2 tog, K 4, yo, Kb 1—rep from *, end yo, Kb 1, K 1.
Row 12: * P 7, P 2 tog—rep from *, end P 2 tog, P 2.
    Starting with Row 1, rep these 12 rows.
Same uses as #170.

#172 **CROSS-OVER LEAF LACE**—*Multiple of 8 sts. (Warning: all rows do not carry the same multiple!)*

All Odd-Numbered Rows: Purl all sts.
Row 2: K 3, K 2 tog, * K 1, yo, K 1, SKP, K 2, K 2 tog—rep from *, end K 1, yo, K 2.
Row 4: K 2, K 2 tog, * K 1, (yo, K 1)x2, SKP, K 2 tog—rep from *, end K 1, yo, K 3.
Row 6: K 4, * yo, K 3, yo, K 1, SKP, K 1—rep from *, end yo, K 4.
Row 8: K 6, K 2 tog, * K 1, yo, K 1, SKP, K 2, K 2 tog—rep from *, end SKP, K 5.
Row 10: K 5, K 2 tog, * K 1, (yo, K 1)x2, SKP, K 2 tog—rep from *, end SKP, K 4.
Row 12: K 4, K 2 tog, * K 1, yo, K 3, yo, K 1, SKP—rep from *, end K 3.
    Starting with Row 1, rep these 12 rows.
This stitch offers the same uses as #170. It is a closer stitch and a little more conservative. It makes a good-looking jacket for a two-piece dress or suit.

#173 **BABY FAN**—*Multiple of 11 sts.*

Row 1: K 2 tog twice, * (yo, K 1)x3, yo, K 2 tog 4 times—rep from *, end (yo, K 1)x3, yo, K 2 tog twice.
Row 2: Purl all sts.
Row 3: Knit all sts.
Row 4: Purl all sts.
    Starting with Row 1, rep these 4 rows.
This tiny version of the well-known Feather-and-Fan Stitch is easily made and may be used the same as #170. Try just two repeats as an edging for baby undergarments or wherever a narrow lace edging is indicated. The stitch forms a scallop at the cast-on edge. No blocking is required.

#174 **OPEN DIAMOND STITCH LACE**—*Multiple of 10 sts plus 1.*

All Even-Numbered Rows: Purl all sts.
Row 1: K 4, * yo, SK2togP, yo, K 3, yo, SKP, K 2—rep from *, end yo, SK2togP, yo, K 4.
Row 3: K 2, K 2 tog, * yo, K 3, yo, SKP, K 3, K 2 tog—rep from *, end yo, K 3, yo, SKP, K 2.
Row 5: K 1, K 2 tog, * yo, K 5, yo, SKP, K 1, K 2 tog—rep from *, end yo, K 5, yo, SKP, K 1.
Row 7: K 2 tog, * yo, K 3, yo, SKP, K 2, yo, SK2togP—rep from *, end yo, K 3, yo, SKP, K 2, yo, SKP.

#172

#173

#174

Row 9: K 2, * yo, SKP, K 3, K 2 tog, yo, K 3 – rep from *, end yo, SKP, K 3, K 2 tog, yo, K 2.
Row 11: K 3, * yo, SKP, K 1, K 2 tog, yo, K 5 – rep from *, end yo, SKP, K 1, K 2 tog, yo, K 3.
Starting with Row 1, rep these 12 rows.

This stitch is used in the same ways as #170, although, like #172, it is a little more conservative.

#175 DIAMOND AND KNOT STITCH — Multiple of 14 sts plus 1.

Note: For Knot Stitch, see page 85.
All Odd-Numbered Rows: Purl all sts.
Row 2: K 6, * yo, SK2togP, yo, K 5, Knot, K 5 – rep from *, end yo, SK2togP, yo, K 6.
Row 4: K 4, * K 2 tog, yo, K 3, yo, SKP, K 7 – rep from *, end yo, SKP, K 4.
Row 6: K 3, * K 2 tog, yo, K 5, yo, SKP, K 5 – rep from *, end yo, SKP, K 3.
Row 8: K 2, * K 2 tog, yo, K 7, yo, SKP, K 3 – rep from *, end yo, SKP, K 2.
Row 10: K 1, * K 2 tog, yo, K 9, yo, SKP, K 1 – rep from *, end same.
Row 12: K 2 tog, * yo, K 5, Knot, K 5, yo, SK2togP – rep from *, end yo, SKP.
Row 14: K 2, * yo, SKP, K 7, K 2 tog, yo, K 3 – rep from *, end yo, K 2.
Row 16: K 3, * yo, SKP, K 5, K 2 tog, yo, K 5 – rep from *, end yo, K 3.
Row 18: K 4, * yo, SKP, K 3, K 2 tog, yo, K 7 – rep from *, end yo, K 4.
Row 20: K 5, * yo, SKP, K 1, K 2 tog, yo, K 9 – rep from *, end yo, K 5.
Starting with Row 1, rep these 20 rows.

Same uses as #170, but this stitch is a bit on the more tailored side, despite the Knot (which may be omitted). It makes a lovely trimming or contrast stitch, especially when a very fine two-ply yarn is used.

#176 LACE LEAF — Multiple of 10 sts plus 1.

All Odd-Numbered Rows: Purl all sts.
Row 2: K 1, * yo, K 3, SK2togP, K 3, yo, K 1 – rep from *, end same.
Row 4: K 2, * yo, K 2, SK2togP, K 2, yo, K 3 – rep from *, end yo, K 2.
Row 6: K 2 tog, * (yo, K 1)x2, SK2togP, (K 1, yo)x2, SK2togP – rep from *, end (K 1, yo)x2, SKP.
Starting with Row 1, rep these 6 rows.

Same uses as #170. Panels for evening gowns or dressy daytime garments can be made with smooth part-rayon novelty yarn. For linen thread, use the normal knitting method.

#177 FAN WITH RIBBING — Multiple of 13 sts plus 2.

Row 1: * P 2, (K 1, yo)x10, K 1 – rep from *, end P 2.
Row 2: * K 2, P 2 tog, P 17, P 2 tog b – rep from *, end K 2.
Row 3: * P 2, SKP, K 15, K 2 tog – rep from *, end P 2.
Row 4: * K 2, P 2 tog, P 13, P 2 tog b – rep from *, end K 2.
Row 5: * P 2, SKP, K 11, K 2 tog – rep from *, end P 2.

218

Row 6: * K 2, P 2 tog, P 9, P 2 tog b—rep from *, end K 2.
   Starting with Row 1, rep these 6 rows.
   Same uses as #170. However, this stitch is more conservative, more tailored.

#178 CABLE AND FAN—*Multiple of 24 sts plus 15.*

Set-Up Row—*Do Not Repeat:* * K 2, P 11, K 2, P 9—rep from *, end K 2.
Row 1: * P 2, (K 1, yo)x10, K 1, P 2, cable 3 and 3 front, K 3—rep from *, end P 2.
Row 2: * K 2, P 2 tog, P 17, P 2 tog b, K 2, P 9—rep from *, end K 2.
Row 3: * P 2, SKP, K 15, K 2 tog, P 2, K 9—rep from *, end P 2.
Row 4: * K 2, P 2 tog, P 13, P 2 tog b, K 2, P 9—rep from *, end K 2.
Row 5: * P 2, SKP, K 11, K 2 tog, P 2, K 9—rep from *, end P 2.
Row 6: * K 2, P 2 tog, P 9, P 2 tog b, K 2, P 9—rep from *, end K 2.
Row 7: * P 2, (K 1, yo)x10, K 1, P 2, K 3, cable 3 and 3 back—rep from *, end P 2.
Row 8: Same as Row 2.
Row 9: Same as Row 3.
Row 10: Same as Row 4.
Row 11: Same as Row 5.
Row 12: Same as Row 6.
   Starting with Row 1, rep these 12 rows.
   Same uses as #170.

#178

#179 SIMPLE LACE DIAMOND—*Multiple of 6 sts plus 1.*

All Even-Numbered Rows: Purl all sts.
Row 1: K 1, * yo, SKP, K 1, K 2 tog, yo, K 1—rep from *, end same.
Row 3: K 2, * yo, SK2togP, yo, K 3—rep from *, end yo, K 2.
Row 5: K 1, K 2 tog, * yo, K 1, yo, SKP, K 1, K 2 tog—rep from *, end yo, SKP, K 1.
Row 7: K 2 tog, * yo, K 3, yo, SK2togP—rep from *, end yo, SKP.
   Starting with Row 1, rep these 8 rows.
   Same uses as #170. This stitch is very easy to make.

#179

LACE STITCHES

#180 BABY LEAF LACE—*Multiple of 8 sts plus 1.*

All Odd-Numbered Rows: Purl all sts.
Row 2: K 1, * yo, K 2, SK2togP, K 2, yo, K 1—rep from *, end same.
Row 4: K 2, * yo, K 1, SK2togP, K 1, yo, K 3—rep from *, end yo, K 2.
Row 6: K 3, * yo, SK2togP, yo, K 5—rep from *, end yo, K 3.
Row 8: K 2 tog, K 2, * yo, K 1, yo, K 2, SK2togP, K 2—rep from *, end yo, K 2, SKP.
Row 10: K 2 tog, K 1, * yo, K 3, yo, K 1, SK2togP, K 1—rep from *, end yo, K 1, SKP.

#180

219

Row 12: K 2 tog, * yo, K 5, yo, SK2togP — rep from *, end yo, SKP.
   Starting with Row 1, rep these 12 rows.
Same uses as #170. This stitch may be fully blocked.

#181 **DIAMOND LEAF LACE** — *Multiple of 10 sts plus 1.*

All Odd-Numbered Rows: Purl all sts.
Row 2: K 3, * K 2 tog, yo, K 1, yo, SKP, K 5 — rep from *, end SKP, K 3.
Row 4: K 2, * K 2 tog, (K 1, yo)x2, K 1, SKP, K 3 — rep from *, end SKP, K 2.
Row 6: K 1, * K 2 tog, K 2, yo, K 1, yo, K 2, SKP, K 1 — rep from *, end same.
Row 8: K 2 tog, * K 3, yo, K 1, yo, K 3, SK2togP — rep from *, end yo, K 3, SKP.
Row 10: K 1, * yo, SKP, K 5, K 2 tog, yo, K 1 — rep from *, end same.
Row 12: K 1, * yo, K 1, SKP, K 3, K 2 tog, K 1, yo, K 1 — rep from *, end same.
Row 14: K 1, * yo, K 2, SKP, K 1, K 2 tog, K 2, yo, K 1 — rep from *, end same.
Row 16: K 1, * yo, K 3, SK2togP, K 3, yo, K 1 — rep from *, end same.
   Starting with Row 1, rep these 16 rows.
Same uses as #170. This pattern should be fully blocked.

#182 **LARGE LEAF PATTERN** — *Multiple of 14 sts plus 3.*

All Even-Numbered Rows: Purl all sts.
Row 1: K 2 tog, K 1, * yo, K 11, yo, SK2togP — rep from *, end yo, K 1, SKP.
Row 3: K 3, * yo, K 4, SK2togP, K 4, yo, K 3 — rep from *, end same.
Row 5: K 4, * yo, K 3, SK2togP, K 3, yo, K 5 — rep from *, end K 4.
Row 7: K 5, * yo, K 2, SK2togP, K 2, yo, K 7 — rep from *, end K 5.
Row 9: K 6, * yo, K 1, SK2togP, K 1, yo, K 9 — rep from *, end K 6.
Row 11: K 7, * yo, SK2togP, yo, K 11 — rep from *, end yo, K 7.
Row 13: K 2 tog, K 5, * yo, K 1, yo, K 2 tog, yo, K 4, SK2togP, K 4 — rep from *, end yo, K 5, SKP.
Row 15: K 2 tog, K 4, * yo, K 1, (yo, K 2 tog)x2, yo, K 3, SK2togP, K 3 — rep from *, end yo, K 4, SKP.
Row 17: K 2 tog, K 3, * yo, K 1, (yo, K 2 tog)x3, yo, K 2, SK2togP, K 2 — rep from *, end yo, K 3, SKP.
Row 19: K 2 tog, K 2, * yo, K 1, (yo, K 2 tog)x4, yo, K 1, SK2togP, K 1 — rep from *, end yo, K 2, SKP.
   Starting with Row 1, rep these 20 rows.
Same uses as #170. This stitch should be fully blocked.

#183 **POINTED LEAF** — *Multiple of 12 sts plus 2.*

Row 1: * P 2, yo, K 1, yo, P 2, K 2, K 2 tog, K 3 — rep from *, end P 2.
Row 2: * K 2, P 6, K 2, P 3 — rep from *, end K 2.

220

Row 3: * P 2, (K 1, yo)x2, K 1, P 2, K 2, K 2 tog, K 2 — rep from *, end P 2.
Row 4: * K 2, P 5 — rep from *, end K 2.
Row 5: * P 2, K 2, yo, K 1, yo, K 2, P 2, K 2, K 2 tog, K 1 — rep from *, end P 2.
Row 6: * K 2, P 4, K 2, P 7 — rep from *, end K 2.
Row 7: * P 2, K 3, yo, K 1, yo, K 3, P 2, K 2, K 2 tog — rep from *, end P 2.
Row 8: * K 2, P 3, K 2, P 9 — rep from *, end K 2.
Row 9: * P 2, K 2, K 2 tog, K 5, P 2, K 1, K 2 tog — rep from *, end P 2.
Row 10: * K 2, P 2, K 2, P 8 — rep from *, end K 2.
Row 11: * P 2, K 2, K 2 tog, K 4, P 2, K 2 tog — rep from *, end P 2.
Row 12: * K 2, P 1, K 2, P 7 — rep from *, end K 2.
Row 13: * P 2, K 2, K 2 tog, K 3, P 2, yo, K 1, yo — rep from *, end P 2.
Row 14: * K 2, P 3, K 2, P 6 — rep from *, end K 2.
Row 15: * P 2, K 2, K 2 tog, K 2, P 2, (K 1, yo)x2, K 1 — rep from *, end P 2.
Row 16: * K 2, P 5 — rep from *, end K 2.
Row 17: * P 2, K 2, K 2 tog, K 1, P 2, K 2, yo, K 1, yo, K 2 — rep from *, end P 2.
Row 18: * K 2, P 7, K 2, P 4 — rep from *, end K 2.
Row 19: * P 2, K 2, K 2 tog, P 2, K 3, yo, K 1, yo, K 3 — rep from *, end P 2.
Row 20: * K 2, P 9, K 2, P 3 — rep from *, end K 2.
Row 21: * P 2, K 1, K 2 tog, P 2, K 2, K 2 tog, K 5 — rep from *, end P 2.
Row 22: * K 2, P 8, K 2, P 2 — rep from *, end K 2.
Row 23: * P 2, K 2 tog, P 2, K 2, K 2 tog, K 4 — rep from *, end P 2.
Row 24: * K 2, P 7, K 2, P 1 — rep from *, end K 2.
  Starting with Row 1, rep these 24 rows.
Same uses as #170. This is a more elastic stitch and should be blocked to show the pattern more fully. Block firmly before taking the gauge.

#183

#184 LEAF AND TWIG — *Multiple of 12 sts plus 1.*

All Odd-Numbered Rows: Purl all sts.
Row 2: K 3, * yo, SKP, K 4 — rep from *, end yo, SKP, K 2.
Row 4: K 3, * yo, SKP, K 2, K 2 tog, yo, K 1, yo, SKP, K 3 — rep from *, end yo, SKP, K 1.
Row 6: K 3, * yo, SKP, K 1, K 2 tog, yo, K 1, (yo, SKP)x2, K 2 — rep from *, end yo, SKP, K 2.
Row 8: K 1, K 2 tog, * yo, K 1, yo, SKP, K 3, yo, SKP, K 2, K 2 tog — rep from *, end yo, SKP, K 2.
Row 10: K 2 tog, * yo, K 1, (yo, SKP)x2, K 2, yo, SKP, K 1, K 2 tog — rep from *, end yo, SKP, K 2.
   Starting with Row 1, rep these 10 rows.
This is an appropriate stitch for dressy cardigans or as a jacket for a dressy suit. Same uses as #170.

#184

221

#185

#185 LACE WINGS—*Multiple of 18 sts plus 1.*

However, to begin, cast on a multiple of 16 sts plus 1 and work the first 4 rows as follows:

Row 1: * K 1, P 15—rep from *, end K 1.
Row 2: * P 1, K 6, yo, SK2togP, yo, K 6—rep from *, end P 1.
Row 3: Same as Row 1.
Row 4: * P 1, K 2 tog, K 4, (yo, K 1)x3, yo, K 4, SKP—rep from *, end P 1.

Row 5: * K 1, P 17—rep from *, end K 1.
Row 6: * P 1, K 2 tog, K 3, yo, K 2 tog, yo, K 3, yo, SKP, yo, K 3, SKP—rep from *, end P 1.
Row 7 and All Odd-Numbered Rows from this point on: Same as Row 5.
Row 8: * P 1, K 2 tog, (K 2, yo)x2, K 1, SK2togP, K 1, (yo, K 2)x2, SKP—rep from *, end P 1.
Row 10: * P 1, K 2 tog, K 1, yo, K 3, yo, K 1, SK2togP, K 1, yo, K 3, yo, K 1, SKP—rep from *, end P 1.
Row 12: * P 1, K 2 tog, yo, K 4, yo, K 1, SK2togP, K 1, yo, K 4, yo, SKP—rep from *, end P 1.
Row 14: * P 1, K 2 tog, K 4, yo, K 1, yo, SK2togP, yo, K 1, yo, K 4, SKP—rep from *, end P 1.

Starting with Row 5, rep from Row 5 through Row 14 throughout.
Same uses as #170. Choose this pattern with discretion. It is a little on the large side.

#186 POPCORN—*Multiple of 4 sts plus 2.*

Row 1: Knit all sts (Wrong Side).
Row 2: K 1, * PKP in next st, K 3 tog—rep from *, end K 1.
Row 3: Knit all sts.
Row 4: K 1, * K 3 tog, PKP—rep from *, end K 1.

Starting with Row 1, rep these 4 rows.
This light but snugly warm stitch is fine for bed jackets. As it is such a close stitch, it may be combined with other lace stitches and may even be classed as a lace fabric stitch.

#186

#187 BELL PATTERN—*Multiple of 5 sts.*

Row 1: P 2, * Kb 1, P 2, yo, P 2—rep from *, end Kb 1, P 2.
Row 2: K 2, * Pb 1, K 2, PKPKPKP, K 2—rep from *, end Pb 1, K 2.
Row 3: P 2, * Kb 1, P 2, K 5, K 2 tog, P 2—rep from *, end Kb 1, P 2.
Row 4: K 2, * Kb 1, K 2, P 2 tog, P 4, K 2—rep from *, end Pb 1, K 2.
Row 5: P 2, * Kb 1, P 2, K 3, K 2 tog, P 2—rep from *, end Kb 1, P 2.
Row 6: K 2, * Pb 1, K 2, P 2 tog, P 2, K 2—rep from *, end Pb 1, K 2.
Row 7: P 2, * Kb 1, P 2, K 1, K 2 tog, P 2—rep from *, end Kb 1, P 2.
Row 8: K 2, * Pb 1, K 2, P 3 tog, K 1—rep from *, end Pb 1, K 2.
Row 9: P 2, * Kb 1, P 4—rep from *, end Kb 1, P 2.
Row 10: K 2, * Pb 1, K 4—rep from *, end Pb 1, K 2.

Starting with Row 1, rep these 10 rows.

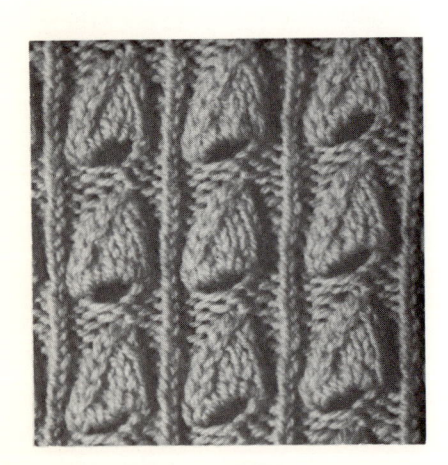

#187

#188 BELL STITCH PATTERN—*Multiple of 13 sts plus 3.*

Note: For any article or garment, this stitch must be based on a multiple of 3 sts, after Row 14 has been completed. When casting on, in Row 15, use Cast-On Method II—page 56—and Purl into the *fronts* of the sts on the next row.

Row 1: P 3, * K 10, P 3—rep from *, end same.

Row 2: K 3, * P 10, K 3—rep from *, end same.
Row 3: P 3, * SKP, K 6, K 2 tog, P 3—rep from *, end same.
Row 4: K 3, * P 8, K 3—rep from *, end same.
Row 5: P 3, * SKP, K 4, K 2 tog, P 3—rep from *, end same.
Row 6: K 3, * P 6, K 3—rep from *, end same.
Row 7: P 3, * SKP, K 2, K 2 tog, P 3—rep from *, end same.
Row 8: K 3, * P 4, K 3—rep from *, end same.
Row 9: P 3, * SKP, K 2 tog, P 3—rep from *, end same.
Row 10: K 3, * P 2, K 3—rep from *, end same.
Row 11: P 3, * K 2 tog, P 3—rep from *, end same.
Row 12: K 3, * P 1, K 3—rep from *, end same.
Row 13: * P 2, P 2 tog—rep from *, end P 3.
Row 14: Knit all sts.
Row 15: P 3, * cast on 10 sts, P 3—rep from *, end same.
  Starting with Row 2, rep from Row 2 through Row 15.

Use this pattern only for very elaborate, filmy articles or garments, bed jackets in particular. With just the first 14 rows used, it makes a particularly good ruffle edging.

#189-A BLUEBELLS I—*Multiple of 6 sts plus 2.*

Cast on and Purl one row to start—Right Side of work.
Row 1: K every stitch with 3 throws.
Row 2: P each st, letting all extra loops drop.
Row 3: K 1, * P 5 tog, KPKPK into the st below the next st and the one on the needle above it, working into both sts as one—rep from *, end K 1.
Row 4: Purl all sts.
Row 5: K 1, * KPKPK as above, P 5 tog—rep from *, end K 1.
Row 6: Purl all sts.
  Starting with Row 1, rep these 6 rows.

#189-B BLUEBELLS II—*Multiple of 6 sts plus 2.*

Cast on and Purl one row.
Row 1: K every st with 3 throws.
Row 2: P each st, letting all extra loops drop.
Row 3: K 1, * P 5 tog, KPKPK into st below the next st and the one on the needle above it, working into both sts as one—rep from *, end K 1.
Row 4: Purl all sts.
Row 5: Same as Row 1.
Row 6: Same as Row 2.

#188

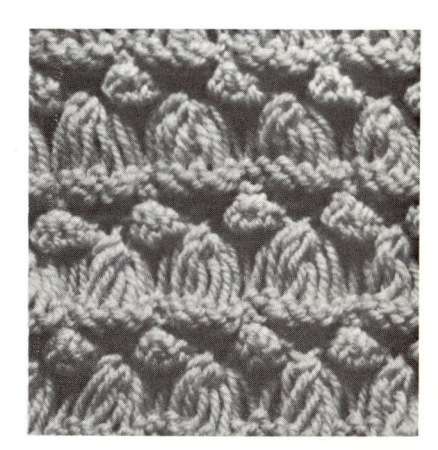

#189-A

#189-B

#190

Row 7: K 1, * KPKPK as above, P 5 tog—rep from *, end K 1.
Row 8: Purl all sts.
   Starting with Row 1, rep these 8 rows.
   Same uses as #188. For a tiny ruffle, use just one repeat of either pattern—Bluebells I or Bluebells II.

#190 **EYELET CROWN** (*Known as Crown of Glory or Cat's Paw in the Shetland Islands*)—Multiple of 14 sts plus 5.

Row 1: Purl all sts (Wrong Side).
Row 2: K 3, * SKP, K 9, K 2 tog, K 1—rep from *, end K 3.
Row 3: P 3, * P 2 tog, P 7, P 2 tog b, P 1—rep from *, end P 3.
Row 4: K 3, * SKP, K 2, OO, K 3, K 2 tog, K 1—rep from *, end K 3.
Row 5: P 3, * P 2 tog, P 2, KPKPK, P 1, P 2 tog b, P 1—rep from *, end P 3.
Row 6: K 3, * SKP, K 6, K 2 tog, K 1—rep from *, end K 3.
Row 7: P 3, * P 2 tog, P 7—rep from *, end P 9.
Row 8: K 3, * K 1, (yo, K 1)x6, K 1—rep from *, end K 3.
Row 9 and 11: Purl all sts.
Row 10 and 12: Knit all sts.
   Starting with Row 1, rep these 12 rows.
   This stitch is best used with very fine, light-weight yarns for shawls, stoles, or scarves.

#191 **LACE DROP STITCH PATTERN**—Multiple of 8 sts plus 2.

Row 1: P 4, * cross L (knitted), P 6—rep from *, end P 4.
Row 2: K 4, * P 2, K 6—rep from *, end K 4.
Row 3: P 4, * K 1, yo, K 1, P 6—rep from *, end P 4.
Rows 4, 6, 8, 10, and 12: K 4, * P 3, K 6—rep from *, end P 3, K 4.
Rows 5, 7, 9, and 11: P 4, * K 3, P 6—rep from *, end K 3. P 4.
Row 13: P 4, * sl 1 from LH needle, drop next st and return the sl st to LH needle, cross L, P 6—rep from *, end P 4.
Row 14: K 4, * P 1, M 1 (knit), P 1, K 6—rep from *, end K 4.
Row 15: P 3, * cross R, P 1, cross L, P 4—rep from *, end P 3.
Row 16: K 3, * P 1, K 3, P 1, K 4—rep from *, end K 3.
Row 17: P 2, * cross R, P 3, cross L, P 2—rep from *, end P 2.
Row 18: K 2, * P 1, K 1, K 2 tog, yo, K 2, P 1, K 2—rep from *, end same.
Row 19: P 1, * cross R, P 5, cross L—rep from *, end P 1.
Row 20: K 1, P 1, * K 1, (K 2 tog, yo)x2, K 2, P 2—rep from *, end P 1, K 1.
Row 21: * cross R, P 7—rep from *, end cross L.
Row 22: Same as Row 20.
Row 23: P 1, * cross L, P 5, cross R—rep from *, end P 1.
Row 24: Same as Row 18.
Row 25: P 2, * cross L, P 3, cross R, P 2—rep from *, end same.
Row 26: Same as Row 16.
Row 27: P 3, * cross L, P 1, cross R, P 4—rep from *, end P 3.
Row 28: K 4, * P 2 tog, P 1, K 6—rep from *, end K 4.

#191

Row 29: P 4, * cross L, P 6 — rep from *, end P 4.
Row 30: K 4, * P 2, K 6 — rep from *, end K 4.
Row 31: P 4, * K 1, yo, K 1, P 6 — rep from *, end P 4.
Rows 32, 34, 36, 38, and 40: Same as Row 4.
Rows 33, 35, 37, and 39: Same as Row 5.
Row 41: Same as Row 13, crossing R instead of L.
Row 42: K 4, * P 2, K 6 — rep from *, end K 4.
  Starting with Row 1, rep these 42 rows.
 This pattern may be used for exactly the same things as #170. It is, however, best as a trimming, using just one repeat of the pattern stitch. All types of smooth yarns, and particularly novelty ones, are right for this stitch.

#192 SUNBURST — *Multiple of 14 sts plus 1.*

Row 1: K 1, * yo, (K 1, P 2)x4, K 1, yo, K 1 — rep from *, end same.
Row 2: P 3, * (K 2, P 1)x3, K 2, P 5 — rep from *, end P 3.
Row 3: K 2, * yo, (K 1, P 2)x4, K 1, yo, K 3 — rep from *, end yo, K 2.
Row 4: P 4, * (K 2, P 1)x3, K 2, P 7 — rep from *, end P 4.
Row 5: K 3, * yo, (K 1, P 2)x4, K 1, yo, K 5 — rep from *, end yo, K 3.
Row 6: P 5, * (K 2, P 1)x3, K 2, P 9 — rep from *, end P 5.
Row 7: K 4, * yo, (K 1, P 2)x4, K 1, yo, K 7 — rep from *, end yo, K 4.
Row 8: P 6, * (K 2, P 1)x3, K 2, P 11 — rep from *, end P 6.
Row 9: K 5, * yo, (K 1, P 2)x4, K 1, yo, K 9 — rep from *, end yo, K 5.
Row 10: P 7, * (K 2, P 1)x3, K 2, P 13 — rep from *, end P 7.
Row 11: K 5, * (SK2togP)x5, K 9 — rep from *, end K 5.
Row 12: Purl all sts.
  Starting with Row 1, rep these 12 rows.
Same uses as #170 and #175.

#192

#193 LEAF LACE — *Multiple of 14 sts plus 1.*

Row 1: * K 1, yo, K 5, yo, SK2togP, yo, K 5, yo — rep from *, end K 1.
Row 2: Purl all sts.
Row 3: * K 1, yo, K 1, K 2 tog, P 1, SKP, K 1, yo, P 1, yo, K 1, K 2 tog, P 1, SKP, K 1, yo — rep from *, end K 1.
Row 4: P 4, * (K 1, P 3)x2, K 1, P 7 — rep from *, end P 4.
Row 5: * K 1, yo, K 1, K 2 tog, P 1, SKP, K 1, P 1, K 1, K 2 tog, P 1, SKP, K 1, yo — rep from *, end K 1.
Row 6: P 4, * (K 1, P 2)x2, K 1, P 7 — rep from *, end P 4.
Row 7: * (K 1, yo)x2, K 2 tog, P 1, SKP, P 1, K 2 tog, P 1, SKP, yo, K 1, yo — rep from *, end K 1.
Row 8: P 5, * (K 1, P 1)x2, K 1, P 9 — rep from *, end P 5.
Row 9: * K 1, yo, K 3, yo, K 3 tog b, P 1, K 3 tog, yo, K 3, yo — rep from *, end K 1.
Row 10: Purl all sts.
  Starting with Row 1, rep these 10 rows.
Same uses as #170 and #175.

#193

225

#194 **FERN PATTERN**—*Multiple of 27 sts plus 1.*

All Odd-Numbered Rows: P 13, * K 2, P 25 — rep from *, end K 2, P 13.
Row 2: K 1, * K 3 tog b, K 8, yo, K 1, yo, P 2, yo, K 1, yo, K 8, K 3 tog, K 1 — rep from *, end same.
Row 4: K 1, * K 3 tog b, K 7, (yo, K 1)x2, P 2, (K 1, yo)x2, K 7, K 3 tog, K 1 — rep from *, end same.
Row 6: K 1, * K 3 tog b, K 6, yo, K 1, yo, K 2, P 2, K 2, yo, K 1, yo, K 6, K 3 tog, K 1 — rep from *, end same.
Row 8: K 1, * K 3 tog b, K 5, yo, K 1, yo, K 3, P 2, K 3, yo, K 1, yo, K 5, K 3 tog, K 1 — rep from *, end same.
Row 10: K 1, * K 3 tog b, K 4, yo, K 1, yo, K 4, P 2, K 4, yo, K 1, yo, K 4, K 3 tog, K 1 — rep from *, end same.
Starting with Row 1, rep these 10 rows.

Same uses as #170. This is a large pattern and a wide one, so its use must be carefully considered. It forms a very deep scallop at the cast-on edge and should be fully blocked.

#195 **LADY SLIPPER**—*Multiple of 20 sts plus 4.*

Note: In the following pattern, the *0 and D* means to yarn-over and drop the yarn-over of the previous row.
Set-Up Row—*(Do Not Repeat):* K 2, P to the last 2 sts, K 2.
Row 1: K 2, * yo, SKP, K 8, yo, K 8, K 2 tog — rep from *, end yo, K 2.
Row 2: K 2, * 0 and D, P 2 tog, P 7, yo, P and K into the yo, yo, P 7, P 2 tog b — rep from *, end 0 and D, K 2.

Row 3: K 2, * 0 and D, SKP, K 6, yo, K 4, yo, K 6, K 2 tog — rep from *, end 0 and D, K 2.
Row 4: K 2, * 0 and D, P 2 tog, P 5, yo, P 6, yo, P 5, P 2 tog b — rep from *, end 0 and D, K 2.
Row 5: K 2, * 0 and D, SKP, K 4, yo, K 8, yo, K 4, K 2 tog — rep from *, end 0 and D, K 2.
Row 6: K 2, * 0 and D, P 2 tog, P 3, yo, P 10, yo, P 3, P 2 tog b — rep from *, end 0 and D, K 2.
Row 7: K 2, * 0 and D, SKP, K 2, yo, K 12, yo, K 2, K 2 tog — rep from *, end 0 and D, K 2.
Row 8: K 2, * 0 and D, P 2 tog, P 1, yo, P 14, yo, P 1, P 2 tog b — rep from *, end 0 and D, K 2.
Row 9: K 2, * 0 and D, SKP, K 8, yo, K 8, K 2 tog — rep from *, end 0 and D, K 2.
Row 10: K 2, P 1, yo, * P 7, P 2 tog b, 0 and D, P 2 tog, P 7, yo, P and K the yo, yo — rep from *, end P 7, yo, P 1, K 2.
Row 11: K 4, yo, * K 6, K 2 tog, 0 and D, SKP, K 6, yo, K 4, yo — rep from *, end yo, K 4.
Row 12: K 2, P 3, yo, * P 5, P 2 tog b, 0 and D, P 2 tog, P 5, yo, P 6 — rep from *, end yo, P 3, K 2.
Row 13: K 6, yo, * K 4, K 2 tog, 0 and D, SKP, K 4, yo, K 8, yo — rep from *, end yo, K 6.

Row 14: K 2, P 5, yo, * P 3, P 2 tog b, 0 and D, P 2 tog, P 3, yo, P 10, yo—rep from *, end yo, P 5, K 2.
Row 15: K 8, yo, * K 2, K 2 tog, 0 and D, SKP, K 2, yo, K 12, yo—rep from *, end yo, K 8.
Row 16: K 2, P 7, yo, * P 1, P 2 tog b, 0 and D, P 2 tog, P 1, yo, P 14, yo—rep from *, end yo, P 7, K 2.
Row 17: K 10, * K 2 tog, 0 and D, SKP, K 8, yo, K 8—rep from *, end SKP, K 10.
Row 18: K 2, yo, * P 2 tog, P 7, yo, P and K the yo, yo, P 7, P 2 tog b, 0 and D—rep from *, end yo, K 2.

    Starting with *Row 3*, rep from Row 3 through Row 18 throughout. Both sides of this stitch are striking. It forms a scallop at the bottom edge and is excellent for shawls, stoles, bed jackets, and as strips for afghans. It also makes a beautiful bedspread pattern.

#196 PINEAPPLE LACE STITCH—*Multiple of 12 sts plus 3.*

Row 1: K 1, * P 1, SKP, K 3, yo, K 1, yo, K 3, K 2 tog—rep from *, end P 1, K 1.
Row 2: K 2, * P 11, K 1—rep from *, end K 2.
Rows 3, 6, and 7: Same as Row 1.
Rows 4, 5, and 8: Same as Row 2.
Row 9: K 1, * P 1, yo, K 3, K 2 tog, P 1, SKP, K 3, yo—rep from *, end yo, P 1, K 1.
Row 10: K 2, * P 5, K 1—rep from *, end K 2.
Row 11: K 1, P 2, * yo, K 2, SKP, P 1, K 2 tog, K 2, yo, P 3—rep from *, end yo, P 2, K 1.
Row 12: K 3, * P 4, K 1, P 4, K 3—rep from *, end same.
Row 13: K 1, P 3, * yo, K 1, SKP, P 1, K 2 tog, K 1, yo, P 5—rep from *, end P 3, K 1.
Row 14: K 4, * P 3, K 1, P 3, K 5—rep from *, end K 4.
Row 15: K 1, P 4, * yo, SKP, P 1, K 2 tog, yo, P 7—rep from *, end yo, P 4, K 1.
Row 16: K 5, * P 2, K 1, P 2, K 7—rep from *, end K 5.
Rows 17, 19, 21, and 23: K 2, yo, K 3, * K 2 tog, P 1, SKP, K 3, yo, K 1, yo, K 3—rep from *, end yo, K 2.
Rows 18, 20, 22, and 24: K 1, P 6, * K 1, P 11—rep from *, end P 6, K 1.
Row 25: K 1, * P 1, K 2 tog, K 3, yo, P 1, yo, K 3, SKP—rep from *, end P 1, K 1.
Row 26: K 2, * P 5, K 1—rep from *, end K 2.
Row 27: K 1, * P 1, K 2 tog, K 2, yo, P 3, yo, K 2, SKP—rep from *, end P 1, K 1.
Row 28: K 2, * P 4, K 3, P 4, K 1—rep from *, end K 2.
Row 29: K 1, * P 1, K 2 tog, K 1, yo, P 5, yo, K 1, SKP—rep from *, end P 1, K 1.
Row 30: K 2, * P 3, K 5, P 3, K 1—rep from *, end K 2.
Row 31: K 1, * P 1, K 2 tog, yo, P 7, yo, SKP—rep from *, end P 1, K 1.
Row 32: K 2, * P 2, K 7, P 2, K 1—rep from *, end K 2.

    Starting with Row 1, rep these 32 rows.
Same uses as #170. This pattern should be fully blocked.

#196

#197 OPEN LEAF or PINEAPPLE—*Multiple of 19 sts plus 2.*

All Odd-Numbered Rows: Purl all sts.
Row 2: K 1, * SKP, K 3, (yo, SKP)x2, yo, K 1, yo, (K 2 tog, yo)x2, K 3, K 2 tog—rep from *, end K 1.
Rows 4, 6, and 8: Same as Row 2.
Row 10: K 1, * SKP, K 2, (yo, K 2 tog)x2, yo, K 3, yo, (SKP, yo)x2, K 2, K 2 tog—rep from *, end K 1.
Row 12: K 1, * SKP, K 1, (yo, K 2 tog)x2, yo, K 5, yo, (SKP, yo)x2, K 1, K 2 tog—rep from *, end K 1.
Row 14: K 1, * SKP, (yo, K 2 tog)x2, yo, K 7, (yo, SKP)x2, yo, K 2 tog—rep from *, end K 1.
Row 16: K 2, * (yo, K 2 tog)x2, yo, K 3, K 2 tog, K 4, (yo, SKP)x3—rep from *, end (yo, SKP)x2, K 2.
Row 18: K 2, * (yo, K 2 tog)x2, yo, K 3, K 2 tog, SKP, K 3, (yo, SKP)x2, yo, K 1—rep from *, end same.
Rows 20, 22, and 24: Same as Row 18.
Row 26: K 3, * (yo, SKP)x2, yo, K 2, K 2 tog, SKP, K 2, (yo, K 2 tog)x2, yo, K 3—rep from *, end yo, K 2.
Row 28: K 4, * (yo, SKP)x2, yo, K 1, K 2 tog, SKP, K 1, (yo, K 2 tog)x2, yo, K 5—rep from *, end yo, K 3.
Row 30: K 5, * (yo, SKP)x2, yo, K 2 tog, SKP, (yo, K 2 tog)x2, yo, K 7—rep from *, end yo, K 4.
Row 32: K 1, SKP, K 3, * (yo, SKP)x3, (yo, K 2 tog)x2, yo, K 3, K 2 tog, K 4—rep from *, end yo, K 5.
    Starting with Row 1, rep these 32 rows.

This stitch offers the same uses as #170. It is classed among the large patterns and, even though quite lacy and open, it is a conservative pattern. It does not require much blocking.

#197

#198 ECCENTRIC ZIGZAG—*Multiple of 10 sts plus 2.*

Row 1: K 1, * yo, K 8, K 2 tog—rep from *, end K 1.
Row 2: P 1, * P 2 tog, P 7, yo, P 1—rep from *, end yo, P 2.
Row 3: K 3, * yo, K 6, K 2 tog, K 2—rep from *, end K 2 tog, K 1.
Row 4: P 1, * P 2 tog, P 5, yo, P 3—rep from *, end yo, P 4.
Row 5: K 5, * yo, K 4, K 2 tog, K 4—rep from *, end K 2 tog, K 1.
Row 6: P 1, * P 2 tog, P 3, yo, P 5—rep from *, end yo, P 6.
Row 7: K 7, * yo, K 2, K 2 tog, K 6—rep from *, end K 2 tog, K 1.
Row 8: P 1, * P 2 tog, P 1, yo, P 7—rep from *, end yo, P 8.
Row 9: K 9, * yo, K 2 tog, K 8—rep from *, end yo, K 2 tog, K 1.
Row 10: P 1, * yo, P 8, P 2 tog b—rep from *, end P 1.
Row 11: K 1, * SKP, K 7, yo, K 1—rep from *, end yo, K 2.
Row 12: P 3, * yo, P 6, P 2 tog b, P 2—rep from *, end P 1.
Row 13: K 1, * SKP, K 5, yo, K 3—rep from *, end yo, K 4.
Row 14: P 5, * yo, P 4, P 2 tog b, P 4—rep from *, end P 1.
Row 15: K 1, * SKP, K 3, yo, K 5—rep from *, end yo, K 6.
Row 16: P 7, * yo, P 2, P 2 tog b, P 6—rep from *, end P 1.
Row 17: K 1, * SKP, K 1, yo, K 7—rep from *, end yo, K 8.

#198

228

Row 18: P 9, * yo, P 2 tog b, P 8 — rep from *, end P 1.
   Starting with Row 1, rep these 18 rows.
   Same uses as #170 and #195. This stitch should be fully blocked.

#199 DOUBLE LEAF AND FAGOT—*Multiple of 34 sts plus 4.*

Rows 1, 5, and 9: K 5, * K 2 tog, K 4, yo, P 2, (K 2, yo, SKP)x3, P 2, yo, K 4, SKP, K 6 — rep from *, end K 5.
Rows 2, 6, and 10: P 4, * P 2 tog b, P 4, yo, P 1, K 2, (P 2, yo, P 2 tog)x3, K 2, P 1, yo, P 4, P 2 tog, P 4 — rep from *, end same.
Rows 3, 7, and 11: K 3, * K 2 tog, K 4, yo, K 2, P 2, (K 2, yo, SKP)x3, P 2, K 2, yo, K 4, SKP, K 2 — rep from *, end K 3.
Rows 4, 8, and 12: P 2, * P 2 tog b, P 4, yo, P 3, K 2, (P 2, yo, P 2 tog)x3, K 2, P 3, yo, P 4, P 2 tog — rep from *, end P 2.
Rows 13, 17, and 21: K 2, * yo, SKP, K 2, yo, SKP, P 2, yo, K 4, SKP, K 6, K 2 tog, K 4, yo, P 2, K 2, yo, SKP, K 2 — rep from *, end K 4.
Rows 14, 18, and 22: P 2, * yo, P 2 tog, P 2, yo, P 2 tog, K 2, P 1, yo, P 4, P 2 tog, P 4, P 2 tog b, P 4, yo, P 1, K 2, P 2, yo, P 2 tog, P 2 — rep from *, end P 4.
Rows 15, 19, and 23: K 2, * yo, SKP, K 2, yo, SKP, P 2, K 2, yo, K 4, SKP, K 2, K 2 tog, K 4, yo, K 2, P 2, K 2, yo, SKP, K 2 — rep from *, end K 4.
Rows 16, 20, and 24: P 2, * yo, P 2 tog, P 2, yo, P 2 tog, K 2, P 3, yo, P 4, P 2 tog, P 2 tog b, P 4, yo, P 3, K 2, P 2, yo, P 2 tog, P 2 — rep from *, end P 4.
   Starting with Row 1, rep these 24 rows.

This elaborate all-over pattern should be selected with caution. In the first place, none but the finest two-ply or very fine novelty yarns should be used, as it is a heavy stitch in itself and loses its distinction when too heavy a yarn is used, or even when too much of the pattern is used. This pattern is good when used as a trim or contrast. It may be fully blocked or left entirely unblocked, according to the yarn used and the article made.

#199

#200 LEAF SCALLOP—*Multiple of 24 sts plus 3.*

Row 1: * P 3, yo, K 4, K 2 tog, K 3, P 3, K 3, SKP, K 4, yo — rep from *, end P 3.
Row 2: * K 3, P 1, yo, P 4, P 2 tog b, P 2, K 3, P 2, P 2 tog, P 4, yo, P 1 — rep from *, end K 3.
Row 3: * P 3, K 2, yo, K 4, K 2 tog, K 1, P 3, K 1, SKP, K 4, yo, K 2 — rep from *, end P 3.
Row 4: * K 3, P 3, yo, P 4, P 2 tog b, K 3, P 2 tog, P 4, yo, P 3 — rep from *, end K 3.
   Starting with Row 1, rep these 4 rows.

This stitch requires careful planning. It forms a deep scallop at the cast-on edge, and may be used in the same ways as #170. To show the pattern more fully, it should be quite firmly blocked, but may, however (in only the finest yarns), be left entirely unblocked. Just one repeat, plus Rows 1 and 2 again, makes a very nice scalloped edging.

#200

INDEX

Abbreviations, knitting, 45-53; British, 47; French, 47-50; German, 50-51; Spanish, 52; Swedish, 52-53; United States, 46-47
Acorn Pattern, 158
Alpaca, 33
Alternate Ribbing and Cable, 205
Alternating Broken Check, 145
Aluminum needles, 16-17, 18, 19
Aluminum crochet hooks, 23
Angora, 34
Aran Islands, 41, 101, 168
Argyle knitting, 93-95, 99
Armhole measurement, 117
Arm-length measurement, 117
Arrowhead Stitch, 216
Assembling and finishing, 119-30; dry blocking, 123-25; front borders for cardigans, 120-122; linings, 127-30; sweaters, 119-22, 123; tailored finishing, 126-127; wet blocking, 125-26; zippers, inserting, 122-23
"Average" knitting measurements, 116

Baby Cross-Braid Stripe, 165
Baby Cross-Cable Ribbing, 170
Baby Cross-Stitch Stripe, 164
Baby Fan, 217
Baby Fern Stitch, 216
Baby Leaf Lace, 219-20
Baby Variegated Ribbing, 156

Baby yarns, 37, 38, 40
Baby Zigzag Cable, 166-67
Basic knitting procedures, 54-114
Basket Weave, 147-48
Basket Weave (Combined Rib and Welt), 174-75
Basket-Weave Cable, 208-209
Basting, 126-27
Bell Pattern, 222
Bell Stitch Pattern, 223
Binding off, 64-67; crocheted, 65; lace, 66-67; pattern stitch, 65-66; plain, 64; ribbing, 65; two pieces together, 66
Blocking, 123-26
Blocking screen, making a, 125-26
Blouses, linings for, 128
Bluebells I, 223
Bluebells II, 223-24
Bobbins, 26
Bone crochet hooks, 22
Bone knitting needles, 17
Bound-off seams, sweaters, 120
Bowknot Stitch I, 86, 194
Bowknot Stitch II, 194
Braided Stitch, 181
Bridal Veil Stitch, 201
Brioche Stitch, 146
British knitting abbreviations and terms, 47
Broken Check, 144

Broken Chevron, 173
Broken Ribbing I, 145-46
Broken Ribbing II, 146
Broken Ribbing III, 146
Broken Ribbing IV, 148
Broken Ribbing V, 171
Bubble Stitch, 87
Bulky yarns, 40-41
Bust measurement (women), 117
Butterfly Lace Stitch, 204-205
Butterfly Stitch, 86, 194
Buttonholes, crocheted, 112-13; knitted, 127
Buying yarns, 43

Cable and Fan, 219
Cable Bowknot, 193
Cable Braid, 82
Cable stitch holders, 26
Cable Stitches, 211-19; Arrowhead Stitch, 216; Baby Fan, 217; Baby Fern Stitch, 216; Cable and Fan, 219; Cross-Over Leaf Lace, 217; Crossed Cable and Fagot, 214; Diamond and Knot Stitch, 218; Fan with Ribbing, 218-19; Fancy Horizontal Stripe, 212; Feather and Fan, 217; Grapevine Stitch, 216-17; Herringbone Lace Pattern, 214; Lace Leaf, 218; Lace Rosebud and Leaf, 215; Lattice Stitch I, 211-12; Lattice Stitch II, 212; Open Cross-Lattice Stitch, 213; Open Diamond Stitch Lace, 217-18; Pointed Lace Pattern, 213; Simple Lace Diamond, 219; Twinberry Stripe, 215-16; Woven Cable, 215; Zigzag and Fagot, 213-14
Cardigans, front borders for, 120-22; linings for, 129. *See also* Sweaters
Carding, 36
Case to hold small items, 27
Cashmere, 32-33
Casting on methods, 55-59
Cat's Paw, 224
Chain stitch (crochet), 111, 113-14
Chest measurement (men and children), 117
Chevron Ribbon Stitch, 106
Chevron Seed Stitch, 172

Chevron (combined), 143-44
Children's measurements, 116
Choosing yarns, 37-41
Choosing your pattern, 131-37
Circular needles, 19-22, 29; choosing, 20-22
Clover and Diamond, 198
Coats, linings for, 127-28
Cockleshells, 162-63
Colored pencils, 27
Colors (yarn), 36
Combined cross and plain knitting, 63, 137
Combing, 36
Crocheted finishes, 111-14; chain stitch, 111; double crochet, 113; single crochet, 112-13; slip stitch, 111
Crochet hooks, 22-24; for giant or jiffy knitting, 23-24; materials and sizes for, 22-23
Crocheted bind-off, 65
Crocheted borders, 122
Cross-Braid Ribbing, 169
Cross knit, 63
Cross-Over Leaf Lace, 217
Cross-over stitches, 79-84; cables, 79-80; multiple, 80-84
Cross purl, 63
Cross-Stitch Block, 187
Cross-Stitch Diamond Fabric, 189
Cross-Stitch Fabric I, 192
Cross-Stitch Fabric II, 192
Cross-Stitch Fabric III, 192
Cross-Stitch Pattern, 105
Cross-Stitch Ribbing, 165
Cross-Weave Fabric, 185
Crossed Cable and Fagot, 214
Crossed Ribbing I, 163-64
Crossed Ribbing II, 165
Crossing on an uneven number of stitches, 84
Crossing on three stitches, 84
Crown of Glory, 224

Dacron, 41
Darning needle, 96
Decorative Ribbing, 164
Decreasing, 67-71; knit, 68-70; purl, 70-71

Detergents, 31
Diagonal Cross Fabric—Left, 179
Diagonal Cross Fabric—Right, 179
Diagonal Lace Stripe I, 161
Diagonal Lace Stripe II, 161-62
Diagonal Ribbing or Chevron (Left Slant), 143
Diagonal Ribbing or Chevron (Right Slant), 143
Diagonal Seed Stitch I, 171
Diagonal Seed Stitch II, 171
Diamond and Knot Stitch, 218
Diamond Cross, 189-90
Diamond in a Diamond, 204
Diamond Leaf Lace, 220
Diamond Ribbing Pattern, 160-61
Dolman sleeve, 128
Double Cable, 82-83
Double crochet, 113
Double English Knitting, 181
Double Leaf and Fagot, 229
Double-pointed needles, 18, 29
Double Seed, Moss, or Rice Stitch, 176
Double slip decrease, knit, 70; purled, 71
Double throw, 63-64
Drafting, 36
Dresses, yarns for, 38-39
Drop Stitch Pattern, 155
Dry blocking, 123-25; skirts, 124-25; sweaters, 123-24
Duplicate stitching, 96-99
Dye-lots, 43
Dyes, 42-43
Dylanized yarns, 38

Ear of Corn, 157-58
Eccentric Zigzag, 228
Embossed Leaf Pattern, 196-97
Embroidery, 96
Emery board, 28
"English" method knitting, 59-60
Equipment, 15-30; care of, 29; choosing needles, 15; crochet hooks, 22-23; extras, 24-29; for giant or jiffy knitting, 23-24; needle types and sizes, 18-23
Eyelet Crown, 224
Eyelet Diamond, 159-60
Eyelet Fabric, 156-57

Fabric Block, 183-84
Fabric Stitch, 177
Fabric Stitches, 170-98; Basket Weave (Combined Rib and Welt), 174-75; Bowknot Stitch I, 194; Bowknot Stitch II, 194; Braided Stitch, 181; Broken Chevron, 173; Broken Ribbing V, 171; Butterfly Stitch, 194; Cable Bowknot, 193; Chevron Seed Sitch, 172; Cross-Stitch Block, 187; Cross-Stitch Diamond Fabric, 189; Cross-Stitch Fabric I, 192; Cross-Stitch Fabric II, 192; Cross-Stitch Fabric III, 192; Cross-Weave Fabric, 185; Diagonal Cross Fabric—Left, 179; Diagonal Cross Fabric—Right, 179; Diagonal Seed Stitch I, 171; Diagonal Seed Stitch II, 171; Diamond Cross, 189-90; Double English Knitting, 181; Double Seed, Moss, or Rice Stitch, 176; Embossed Leaf Pattern, 196-97; Fabric Block, 183-84; Fabric Stitch, 177; Flat Diamond I, 174; Flat Diamond II, 184-85; Gathered Ribbing, 187; Heavy Woven Bias Fabric, 184; Herringbone Cross Fabric, 179; Herringbone Stripe, 178; Knotted Trellis Stitch, 191; Lazy Daisy, 195; Leaf Fabric, 195-96; Mock Cable Fabric, 179; Modified Schiaparelli, 180; Modified Seed Stitch, 176; Oblique Knot Stitch, 197-98; Open Chevron, 172; Overlay Stitch, 192; Palm Leaf *Knit* Fabric, 188; Palm Leaf *Purl* Fabric, 188-89; Ribbing with Diagonal Slip Stitches, 186; Schiaparelli Cross Left, 180; Schiaparelli Cross Right, 180; Seed and Stockinette Diamond, 175-76; Seed Stitch Blocks, 173; Shirred Stockinette Stitch, 170; Slip Check, 186; Slip Cross Fabric, 193-94; Slip Diagonal Fabric I, 176; Slip Diagonal Fabric II, 177; Slip Fabric Stitch, 182; Smocked Honeycomb, 190-91; Staggered Check, 183; Staggered Slip Check, 185; Stockinette Stitch, 170; Stockinette Stitch Wave, 186; Striped Fabric Stitch, 178-79; Traveling Diamond and Ribbing, 190; Triangles, 174; Tufted Rosette, 197;

Vertical Herringbone, 177; Waffle Fabric Stitch, 181; Waffle Stitch, 187-88; Waved Welt, 173; Woven Fabric Stitch I, 182; Woven Fabric Stitch II, 183; Zigzag Stockinette Fabric, 178
Fagot and Cable, 210-11
Fagot and Cable Stripe, 158
Fair Isle knitting, 93-95, 98
Fan with Ribbing, 218-19
Fancy Cable, 206
Fancy Horizontal Stripe, 212
Fancy Ribbing Stitch, 169
Feather and Fan Stitch, 217
Felting, 31, 42
Fern Pattern, 226
Fingering yarns, 38-39
Finishing. See Assembling and finishing
Flat Cable Fabric, 206-207
Flat Diamond I, 174
Flat Diamond II, 184-85
Flat Diamond, Outlined, 151
Fleece, quality of, 34-36
Forming patterns, 62-64
French knitting abbreviations and terms, 47-50
"Fuse-cut" ribbon, 42

Garter Stitch, 64, 91, 141
Garter stitch grafting, 91
Garter Stitch Worked on the Bias, 141-42
Gathered Fabric Stitch, 153
Gathered Ribbing, 187
Gauge cards, 28
Gauge counters, 25
Gauge, determining, 99-102, 131-33, 135-137
German knitting abbreviations and terms, 50-51
"German" or "Continental" method, knitting, 60-61
Germantown yarns, 40, 98
Giant knitting, crochet hooks for, 23-24; needles, 23
 yarns for, 37, 38
 90-92; garter stitch, 91; horizontal, 91; sweater, 120; from two vertical, 92
 stitch, 216-17

Graph paper, 27-28

Hair yarns, 32-34; alpaca, 33; angora, 34; cashmere, 32-33; mohair, 32; vicuña, 33-34
"Heather" mixtures, 39
Heavy Cable and Garter Stitch, 209-10
Heavy-weight yarns, 40
Heavy Woven Bias Fabric, 184
Hems, knitted, 89-90, 127
Herringbone Cross Fabric, 179
Herringbone Lace Pattern, 109, 214
Herringbone Ribbing, 168
Herringbone Stripe, 178
Hip measurement, 118
"Homespun" yarns, 40
Horizontal grafting, 91
Horizontal Leaf, 152
Horizontal Ribbing or Welting, 142
Horseshoe Cable Stripe, 207

Icelandic yarns, 41
Increasing, 71-78; knit, 71-75; purl, 75-78; miscellaneous, 78
Infant wear, yarns for, 37, 38
Infant's measurements, 116
Invisible increase, knit, 75; purl, 77
Italian stitch, 63

Jackets, linings for, 128; yarns for, 40
Jiffy knitting, crochet hooks for, 23-24; needles, 23
Joining seams. See Assembling and finishing
Jumper needles, 20

Kitchener Stitch, 90-91
Knit and purl the same stitch, 74
Knit decreases, 68-70; knit three together, 69; knit two together, 68; left-cross double decrease, 69-70; right cross double decrease, 69; slip, knit, and pass 68
Knit increases, 71-75; invisible, 75; lifted, 74; plain, 73; plain yarn over, 71-72; reverse yarn-over, 72-73
Knit three together, 69
Knit two together, 68
Knitted articles, care of, 31

Knitted hems, 89-90
Knitted ribbing, 120-22; horizontal, 121-122; vertical, 120-21
Knitting a loop from below, 64
Knitting abbreviations. *See* Abbreviations, knitting
Knitting and purling methods, 59-64
Knitting bags, 28-29
Knitting counters, 24
Knitting methods. *See* Procedures, basic knitting
Knitting stitch patterns. *See* Pattern stitches, selection and use
Knitting terms. *See* Terms, knitting
Knitting yarns, 31-44; alpaca, 33; angora, 34; bulky, 40; buying, 43; cashmere, 32; choosing, 37-41; dacron 41, hair, 32-34; laundering, of man-made fibers, 41, 42; manufacture of worsted and woolen, 34-37; mohair, 32; nylon, 41; orlon, 41; pricing of, 42-43; rayon, 41; vicuña, 33; weights of, 37-41; wool, 31, 34-41
Knot Stitch, 85
Knot Stitch Fabric, 155
Knotted Trellis Stitch, 191

Lace Drop Stitch Pattern, 224-25
Lace Leaf, 218
Lace pattern, bind-off, 66-67
Lace Rosebud and Leaf, 215
Lace Stitches, 219-29; Baby Leaf Lace, 219-20; Bell Pattern, 222; Bell Stitch Pattern, 223; Bluebells I, 223; Bluebells II, 223-24; Cat's Paw, 224; Crown of Glory, 224; Diamond Leaf Lace, 220; Diamond Leaf and Fagot, 229; Eccentric Zigzag, 228; Eyelet Crown, 224; Fern Pattern, 226; Lace Drop Stitch Pattern, 224-25; Lace Wings, 222; Lady Slipper, 226-27; Large Leaf Pattern, 220; Leaf and Twig, 221; Leaf Lace, 225; Leaf Scallop, 229; Open Leaf or Pineapple, 228; Pineapple Lace Stitch, 227; Pointed Leaf, 220-21; Popcorn, 222; Sunburst, 225
Lace Triangles, 159
Lace Wings, 222
Lady Slipper, 226-27

Large and Small Diamonds, 151-52
Large Leaf Pattern, 220
Lattice Stitch I, 211-12
Lattice Stitch II, 212
Laundering agents, 31
Laundering of man-made fiber yarns, 41-42
Lazy Daisy, 195
Leaf and Twig, 221
Leaf Fabric, 195-96
Leaf Lace, 109, 225
Leaf Ribbing, 166
Leaf Scallop, 229
Leaf Stitch, 87
Left-cross double decrease, 69-70
Left-handed knitting, 61-62
Lifted increase, knit, 74; purl, 77
Linings, for cardigan borders, 129; for skirts, 129
Linings and lining materials, 127-30
Lozenge, 150

Machine-washables, 31, 41
Man-made fibers. *See* Synthetic fibers
Manufacture of yarns, 34-36
Materials, lining, 129-30
Matting, 31
Measurements, 115-18; "average" knitting, 116; how to take, 117; how to use, 117-118
Medium weight yarns, 38-39
Men's measurements, 116
Metallic yarns, 39
Mittens, yarns for, 39
Mock Cable Fabric, 179
Modified Ribbing, 149
Modified Schiaparelli, 180
Modified Seed Stitch, 176
Mohair yarn, 32, 41
Multicolor knitting, 26, 93-95
Multiple stitch cross-overs, 80-84; cable cross, 80-81
Multiple stitches, 85

Nail file, 28
Neck to shoulder measurements, 117
Neck to waist in back measurement, 117-118

Needles, knitting, 15-22; aluminum, 16-17, 18; bone, 17; care of, 29; choosing, 15-22; circular, 19-22, 29; double-pointed, 18, 29; for giant or jiffy knitting, 23; jumper, 20; nickel-plated, 16; plastic, 17, 18, 19, 29; single-pointed, 18, 29; for special uses, 18-22; steel, 16, 18, 19, 29; straight, 18; tubes for storing, 29; types and sizes of, 18-22; wood, 17, 18, 19

Nonallergenic yarns, 41

Non-reversible Stitches, 198-205; Bridal Veil Stitch, 201; Butterfly Lace Stitch, 204-205; Clover and Diamond, 198; Diamond in a Diamond, 204; Open Stripe, 202; Piqué Stitch, 203; Purl Fabric Stitch, 203; Rambler Rose, 199-200; Simple Lace Stitch, 204; Simple Lace Pattern, 202-203; Small Diamond Dot, 201; Tear Drop, 202; Tiny Eyelet Ribbing, 202; Tiny Leaf Fabric, 203; Tiny Tower, 200-201; Triplet Ribbing, 201-202; Winding Vine and Stripe, 200

Notebooks, 27

Novelty yarns, 41

Nylon yarn, 26, 34, 36, 41

Oblique Knot Stitch, 197-98

Open Blocks, 161

Open Chevron, 172

Open Cross-Lattice Stitch, 213

Open Diamond Stitch Lace, 217-18

Open Drop-Stitch Cable, 208

Open-Laced Cross-Stitch, 147

Open Leaf or Pineapple, 228

Open Seed-Stitch Blocks, 147

Open Stripe, 202

Open Wave Lace, 157

Orlon yarn, 36, 41

Overlay Stitch, 192

Palm Leaf *Knit* Fabric, 188

Palm Leaf *Purl* Fabric, 188-89

Pattern stitch bind-off, 66-67

Pattern stitches, 131-229; cable, 211-19; fabric, 170-98; lace, 219-29; list of, 138-40; non-reversible, 198-205; reversible, 141-59; ribbing, 159-70; selection and use of, 131-37; "small," 205-11

Pick up one stitch, 78

Picking up stitches, 88-89, 96

Pineapple Lace Stitch, 227

Piqué Stitch (non-reversible), 203

Piqué Stitch (ribbing), 166

Plain bind-off, 64

Plain increase, knit, 73; purl, 77

Plain yarn-over, knit 71-72; purl, 76

Plaited Cable, 207

Plaited Stockinette stitch, 63

Plastic crochet hooks, 23

Plastic knitting needles, 17, 18, 19, 29

Point protectors, 25

Pointed Lace Pattern, 213

Pointed Leaf, 220-21

Pompadour yarns, 36, 38

Popcorn Stitch, 87, 109-10, 222

Pricing of yarns, 42-43

Procedures, basic knitting, 54-114; binding off, 64-67; casting on, 55-59; crocheted finishes, 111-14; cross-over stitches, 79-84; decreasing, 67-71; determining gauge, 99-102; duplicate stitching, 96-99; grafting, 90-92; increasing, 71-78; knitted hems, 89-90; knitting and purling methods, 59-64; left-handed knitting, 61-62; more-than-one-color knitting, 93-95; picking up stitches, 88-89, 96; purling methods, 60-64; ribbon knitting, 102-10; slipped stitches, 87; turning and shaping, 92-93; uneven knitting, 62

Professional blocking, 125

Pullover (Mock) Cable, 211

Purl decreases, 70-71

Purl Fabric Stitch, 203

Purl increases, 75-78; invisible, 77; lifted, 77; plain, 77, plain yarn over, 76; reverse yarn over, 76; yarn over, 76-77

Purl three together, 71

Purl two together, 70-71

Purling methods. *See* Knitting and purling methods

Quaker Stitch, 142

Rambler Rose, 199-200

236

Rayon, 36, 41
Reverse yarn-over, 72-73, 76
Reversible Stitches I, 141-50; Alternating Broken Check, 145; Basket Weave, 147-148; Brioche Stitch, 146; Broken Check, 144-45; Broken Ribbing I, 145-46; Broken Ribbing II, 146; Broken Ribbing III, 146; Broken Ribbing IV, 148; Chevron (combined), 143-44; Diagonal Ribbing or Chevron (Left Slant), 143; Diagonal Ribbing or Chevron (Right Slant), 143; Garter Stitch, 141; Garter Stitch Worked on the Bias, 141-142; Horizontal Ribbing or Welting, 142; Lozenge, 150; Modified Ribbing, 149; Open-Laced Cross-Stitch, 147; Open Seed-Stitch Blocks, 147; Quaker Stitch, 142; Ribbing and Garter, 145; Ribbing and Welt, 144; Seed, Moss, or Rice Stitch, 142; Small Check, 144; Tall Diamond II, 150; Tall Diamond, Outlined I, 149-50; Uneven Basket Weave, 148; Wide Chevron, 149
Reversible Stitches II, 150-59; Acorn Pattern, 158; Baby Variegated Ribbing, 156; Drop Stitch Pattern, 155; Ear of Corn, 157-58; Eyelet Fabric, 156-57; Fagot and Cable Stripe, 158; Flat Diamond, Outlined, 151; Gathered Fabric Stitch, 153; Horizontal Leaf, 152; Knot Stitch Fabric, 155; Lace Triangles, 159; Large and Small Diamonds, 151-52; Open Wave Lace, 157; Shirred Ribbing, 156; Small Cross-Stitch Pattern, 153; Striped Fagoting, 157; Tall Diamond in Relief III, 150-51; Vertical Chevron, 151; Waved Ribbing, 154-55
Rib Cable, making a, 81
Ribbing and Garter, 145
Ribbing and Welt, 144
Ribbing bind-off, 65
Ribbing Stitches, 159-70; Baby Cross-Braid Stripe, 165; Baby Cross-Cable Ribbing, 170; Baby Cross-Stitch Stripe, 164; Baby Zigzag Cable, 166-67; Cockleshells, 162-63; Cross-Braid Ribbing, 169; Cross-Stitch Ribbing, 165; Crossed Ribbing I, 163-64; Crossed Ribbing II, 165; Decorative Ribbing, 164; Diagonal Lace Stripe I, 161; Diagonal Lace Stripe II, 161-62; Diamond Ribbing Pattern, 160-61; Eyelet Diamond, 159-60; Fancy Ribbing Stitch, 169; Herringbone Ribbing, 168; Leaf Ribbing, 166; Open Blocks, 161; Piqué Stitch, 166; Ribbing with Tight Braid, 165; Slipped Ribbing, 164; Spider Web Lace, 163; Split Cable and Stripe, 167-168; Stocking Heel Stitch, 164; Teardrop Ribbing, 169; Zigzag Ribbing, 162
Ribbing with Diagonal Slip Stitches, 186
Ribbing with Tight Braid, 165
Ribbon knitting, 41-42, 102-10
Ribbon Stitch 1, 104
Ribbon Stitch 2, 104
Ribbon Stitch 3, 104
Ribbon Stitch 4 (Cross-Stitch Pattern), 105
Ribbon Stitch 5, 105
Ribbon Stitch 6, 106
Ribbon Stitch 7 (Chevron Stitch), 106
Ribbon Stitch 8, 107
Ribbon Stitch 9, 107
Ribbon Stitch 10 (Seed Stitch), 108
Ribbon Stitch 11 (Wave Lace), 108
Ribbon Stitch 12 (Leaf Lace), 109
Ribbon Stitch 13 (Herringbone Lace), 109
Ribbon Stitch 14 (Popcorn Stitch), 109-10
Right and left cross-over, 83
Right-cross double decrease, 69
Ring markers, 25
Rosebud, 86
Rulers, 26

Saxony yarns, 35, 38
Scandinavian knitting, 93-95
Scarves, yarns for, 38
Schiaparelli, Cross Left, 180
Schiaparelli, Cross Right, 180
Scissors, 26
Seams, 119-20
Seed and Stockinette Diamond, 175-76
Seed, Moss, or Rice Stitch, 142
Seed Stitch, 108
Seed Stitch Blocks, 173

Setting up. *See* Casting on
Sewing needles, 26
Shaping. *See* Turning and shaping
Shawls, yarns for, 37, 38
Shetland yarns, 37, 40
Shirred Ribbing, 156
Shirred Stockinette Stitch, 170
Shoulder pads, 129-30
Shoulder to shoulder in back measurement, 117
Shoulder to waist in front measurement, 117
Shrinkage, 31, 35, 42
Side seams, 120
Silk organdy ribbon, 108
Simple Lace Diamond, 219
Simple Lace Pattern, 202-203
Simple Lace Stitch, 204
Single crochet, 112-13, 119
Single-pointed needles, 18, 29
Sizes. *See* Measurements
Skirts, dry blocking, 124-25; finishing, 113-14; length measurements, 117, 118; lining, 129
Sleeves, length measurement, 117; linings, 128
Slip Check, 186
Slip Cross Fabric, 193-94
Slip Diagonal Fabric I, 176
Slip Diagonal Fabric II, 177
Slip Fabric Stitch, 182
Slip, knit, and pass, 68-69
Slip, knit two together, and pass, 70
Slip-stitch (crochet), 111, 119, 126
Slipped Ribbing, 164
Slipped stitches, 87
Small Check, 144
Small Cross-Stitch Pattern, 153
Small Diamond Dot, 201
"Small" Stitches, 205-11; Alternate Ribbing and Cable, 205; Basket-Weave Cable, 208-209; Fagot and Cable, 210-211; Fancy Cable, 206; Flat Cable Fabric, 206-207; Heavy Cable and Garter Stitch, 209-10; Horseshoe Cable Stripe, 207; Open Drop-Stitch Cable, 208; Plaited Cable, 207; Pullover (Mock) Cable, 211; Smocked Ribbing, 211; Spreading Cable, 207; Staggered Horseshoe Cable, 208; Stockinette Cable Fabric, 209; Tiny Twisted Ribbing, 206; Traveling Cross Cable, 205

Smocked Honeycomb, 190-91
Smocked Ribbing, 211
Smocking Stitch, 85
Socks, yarns for, 37, 38, 39
Spanish knitting abbreviations and terms, 52
Specialty yarns, 32-34, 39
Spider Web Lace, 163
Split Cable and Stripe, 167-68
Sports-weight yarns, 39-40
Spreading Cable, 207
Squares, 27
Staggered Check, 183
Staggered Horseshoe Cable, 208
Staggered Slip Check, 185
Steaming, 126-27
Steel crochet hooks, 22, 29
Steel knitting needles, 16, 18, 19, 29
Stitch gauge, 131-36
Stitch holders, 24
Stitches, suitability of, 131-37
Stockinette Cable Fabric, 209
Stockinette Stitch, 63, 96, 98, 100-101, 170
Stockinette Stitch Wave, 186
Stocking Heel Stitch, 164
Stoles, yarns for, 38
Straight needles, 18
Striped Fagoting, 157
Striped Fabric Stitch, 178-79
Suits, yarns for, 40
Sunburst, 225
Super-weight yarns, 40-41
Swatches, 27, 99-102, 131-32
Sweaters, dry blocking, 123-24; finishing, 119-22; yarns for, 37-41
Swedish knitting abbreviations and terms, 52-53
Swiss darning, 96
Synthetic fibers, 34, 41-42

Tailored finishing, 126-27
Taking a large number of stitches together, 71
Tall Diamond II, 150

Tall Diamond in Relief III, 150-51
Tall Diamond, Outlined I, 149-50
Tape measures, 25, 100
Tapestry needles, 26, 96
Tear Drop, 202
Teardrop Ribbing, 169
Terms, knitting, 45-53; British, 47; French, 47-50; German, 50-51; Spanish, 52; Swedish, 52-53; United States, 46-47
Thread laces, 66-67
Tie Stitch, 85
Tiny Eyelet Ribbing, 202
Tiny Leaf Fabric, 203
Tiny Tower, 200-201
Tiny Twisted Ribbing, 206
Tracing outlines, 28
Traveling Cross Cable, 205
Traveling Diamond and Ribbing, 190
Triangles, 174
Triplet Ribbing, 201-202
Tuft Stitch, 85
Tufted Rosette, 197
Turning and shaping, 92-93
Twinberry Stripe, 215-16
Twist Stitch, 63
Tubes for storing needles, 29

Underarm to waist measurement, 117
Uneven Basket Weave, 148
Uneven knitting, 62
United States knitting abbreviations and terms, 46-47

Vertical Chevron, 151
Vertical grafting, 92
Vertical Herringbone, 177
Very light-weight yarns, 37-38
Vicuña, 33-34

Waffle Fabric Stitch, 181
Waffle Stitch, 187-88
Wave Lace Pattern, 108
Waved Ribbing, 154-55
Waved Welt, 173
Weights of yarn, 37-41
Wet blocking, 125-26
Wide Chevron, 149
Winding on, 36
Winding Vine and Strip, 200
Women's measurements, 116
Wood crochet hooks, 23
Wood knitting needles, 17, 18, 19
Wool yarns, 31, 126; making, 34-37
Woven Cable, 215
Woven Fabric Stitch I, 182
Woven Fabric Stitch II, 183

Yarn bobbins, 26
Yarn-making, 34-37
Yarn-overs, knit, 71-73; purl, 76-77
Yarns. *See* Knitting Yarns

Zigzag and Fagot, 213-14
Zigzag Ribbing, 162
Zigzag Stockinette Fabric, 178
Zippers, inserting, 122-23